THE SINGAPORE AND MELAKA STRAITS

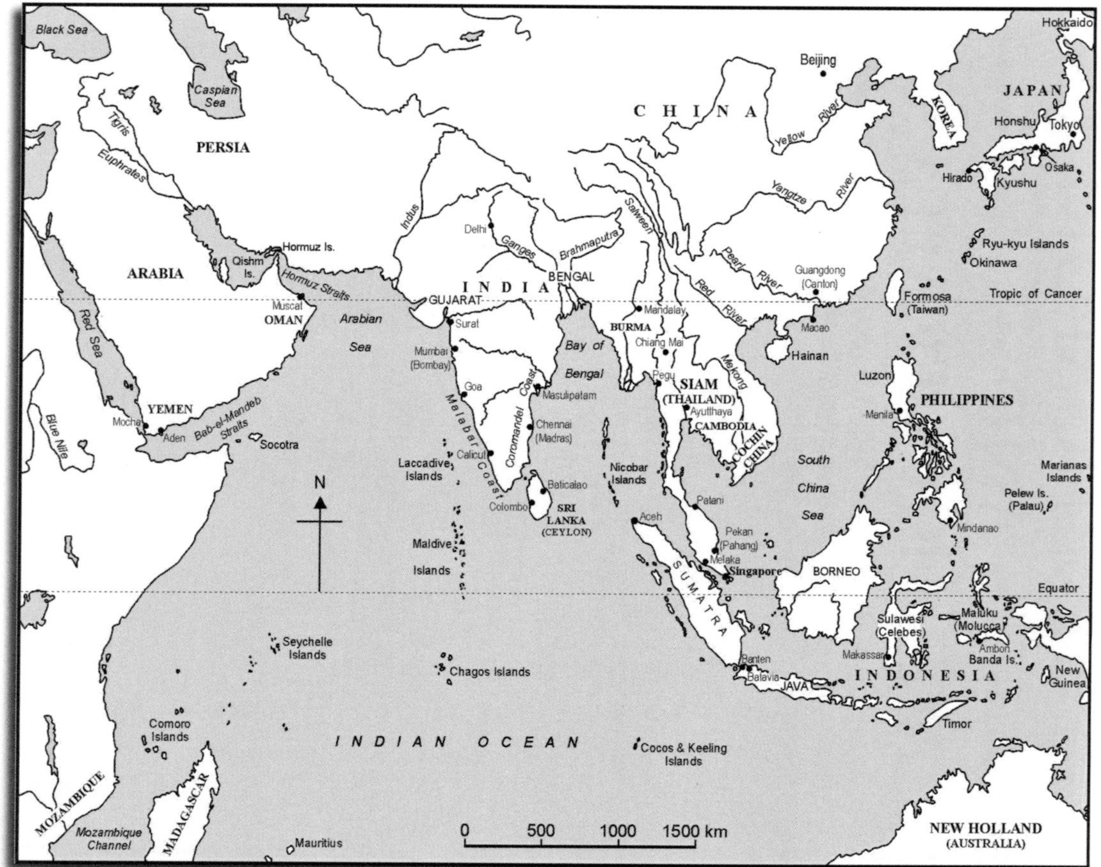

Map of South, Southeast and East Asia.

THE SINGAPORE AND MELAKA STRAITS

Violence, Security and Diplomacy in the 17th Century

Peter Borschberg

NUS PRESS
SINGAPORE

Published with support from the Nicholas Tarling Fund.

© NUS Press
National University of Singapore
AS3-01-02, 3 Arts Link
Singapore 117569

Fax : (65) 6774-0652
E-mail : nusbooks@nus.edu.sg
Website : http://www.nus.edu.sg/nuspress

ISBN 978-9971-69-464-7 (Paper)

First edition 2010
Reprint 2015

National Library Board Singapore Cataloguing in Publication Data

Borschberg, Peter.
The Singapore and Melaka Straits: violence, security and diplomacy in the 17th century / Peter Borschberg. – Singapore: NUS Press, c2010.
p. cm.
Includes bibliographical references and index.
ISBN-13: 978-9971-69-464-7 (pbk.)

1. Geopolitics – Singapore Strait – History – 17th century. 2. Geopolitics – Malacca, Strait of – History – 17th century. 3. Singapore Strait – History, Naval – 17th century. 4. Malacca, Strait of – History, Naval – 17th century. I. Title.

GC801
911.16472 – dc22 OCN318953272

Cover:
Front: Partial view of a printed hand painted map *Insulae Indiae Orientalis* (The Islands of the East Indies) by Jucodus Hondius, 1606. (Collection Peter Borschberg Sr.)
Back: Partial view of a hand coloured map of Asia by António Sanches, 1641 (Koninklijke Bibliotheek, The Hague, 129 A 25 fols. 16verso-17recto)

Typeset by: International Typesetters Pte Ltd
Printed by: Mainland Press Pte Ltd

Contents

List of Illustrations

List of Abbreviations

AA J. de Coutre, *Andanzas asiáticas*, ed. E. Stols, B. Teensma and J. Verbeckmoes (Madrid: História, 1991).

BKI Bijdragen van het Koninklijk Instituut voor Land-, Taal-, en Volkenkunde

BOC P. van Dam, *Beschryvinge van de Oostindische Compagnie,* ed. F. W. Stapel, 8 vols. (The Hague: Martinus Nijhoff, 1931).

BV I. Commelin, *Begin ende Voortgang vande Vereenigde Neerlandsche Geoctroyeerde Oost-Indische Compagnie*, 4 vols. (Amsterdam: no publisher, 1646).

CB H.T. Colenbrander and W. Ph. Coolhaas, eds., *Jan Pieterszoon Coen: Bescheiden Omtrent zijn Bedrijf in Indië*, 9 vols. (The Hague: Martinus Nijhoff, 1919–54).

DJP H. Grotius, *De Jure Praedae Commentarius: Commentary on the Law of Prize and Booty*, ed. Martine J. van Ittersum (Indianapolis: Liberty Fund, 2006).

DRB H.T. Colenbrander, ed., *Dagh-Register gehouden int Casteel Batavia vant passerende daer ter plates als over geheel Nederlandts-Indie* (The Hague: Martinus Nijhoff, 1898–1935).

DUP *Documentação Ultramarina Portuguesa*, 2 vols. (Lisbon: Centro de Estudos Históricos Ultramarinos, 1960–2).

GM *Generale Missiven van Gouverneurs-Generaal en Raden an Heeren XVII der Verenigde Oostindische Compagnie*, W. Ph.

Coolhaas, ed., Rijks- Geschiedkundige Publicatiën, Grote Serie (The Hague: Martinus Nijhoff and Instituut voor Geschiedenis, 1960–2001).

JO J.K.J. de Jonge, *Opkomst van het Nederlandsch Gezag in Oost-Indië. Verzameling van Onuitgegeven Stukken uit het Oud-Coloniaal Archief*, 16 vols. (The Hague: Martinus Nijhoff, 1866–1909).

JSBRAS Journal of the Straits Branch of the Royal Asiatic Society

JMBRAS Journal of the Malaysian Branch of the Royal Asiatic Society

JSEAH Journal of Southeast Asian History

JSEAS Journal of Southeast Asian Studies

LM R.A. de Bulhão Pato and A. de Silva Rego, ed., *Documentos Remettidos da Índia ou Livros das Monções*, 10 vols. (Lisbon: Typographia da Academia Real das Sciencias and Academia das Sciencias de Lisboa, 1880–1978).

NJS E. Netscher, *Nederlanders in Djohor en Siak* (Batavia: Bruining & Wijt, 1870).

PI E.H. Blair and J.A. Robertson, ed., *The Philippine Islands, 1493–1898*, 55 vols. (Cleveland: A.H. Clark Co., 1903–9).

PMC Armando Cortesão and Avelino Teixeira de Mota, *Portugaliae Monumenta Cartographica*, 6 vols. (Lisbon: no publisher, 1960). A second, smaller and qualitatively inferior, edition of this work was printed in Lisbon by Imprensa Nacional — Casa de Moeda, 1987. That also features a supplementary volume 7 not printed in the first edition of 1960.

SO Tomé Pires, *Suma Oriental*, ed. and trans. Armando Cortesão, 2 vols. (London: Hakluyt Society, 1944).

TB P.A. Tiele and J.E. Heeres, *Bouwstoffen voor de Geschiedenis der Nederlanders in den Maleischen Archipel*, 3 vols. (The Hague: Martinus Nijhoff, 1886–95).

VOC Vereenigde Oost-Indische Compagnie, United East India Company; commonly known as the Dutch East India Company.

Acknowledgements

This book incorporates research conducted over a period of almost a decade. Institutional support and funding have been indispensable over the years. The author wishes to thank especially the Department of History of the National University of Singapore; the Department of Asian Studies at the Ludwig-Maximilians-Universität in Munich, Germany; the Netherlands Institute for Advanced Studies of the Royal Netherlands Academy of Social Sciences, in Wassenaar, the Netherlands; the Fundação Oriente, Lisbon, Portugal; and the Folger Library, in Washington, D.C.

The present author has been studying ideas pertaining to "big concepts" such as sovereignty, security, diplomacy, trade and cartography in the region around the Singapore and Melaka Straits for approximately one decade. Individual sets of ideas were developed in a series of articles which have been published in recognised international journals under the auspices of Association Archipel, the Fundação Oriente, the Journal of Southeast Asian Studies, the Journal of the Siam Society, the Revista de Cultura (Macao), NUS Museums and the Zeitschrift der Deutschen Morgenländischen Gesellschaft. The current study brings the individual strands together into a single, expanded study.

The author wishes to express his utmost appreciation for the access, understanding, forthcoming cooperation and scholarly assistance he has received over the years from various libraries and museums around the world: Amsterdam University Library, the Netherlands; Archivo Nacional/Torre do Tombo, Lisbon, Portugal; Bayerische Staatsbibliothek, Munich, Germany; Biblioteca de la Academia das Ciências de Lisboa, Portugal; Biblioteca da Marinha, Lisbon; Biblioteca Nacional do Brasil, Rio de Janeiro, Brazil; Biblioteca Nacional de Portugal, Lisbon; Biblioteca Nacional, Madrid,

Spain; Bibiothèque Royale de Belgique, Brussels; Bibliotheca Thysiana, Leiden, the Netherlands; the British Library, London, United Kingdom; Staatsbibliothek Berlin (Preussischer Kulturbesitz), Germany; Cambridge University Library, United Kingdom; Casa de Bragança, Vila Viçosa, Portugal; Bibliothek der Ernst-Moritz-Arndt Universität, Greifswald, Germany; Harvard University Map Collection, Cambridge, United States; Herzog-August-Bibliothek, Wolfenbüttel, Germany; Huntington Library, San Marino, United States; Koninklijke Bibliotheek, The Hague, Netherlands; Library of Congress, Washington, D.C.; Collectie Bodel Nijenhuis, Leiden University Library, the Netherlands; Collectie Dr. W.A. Engelbrecht, Maritiem Museum Prins Hendrik, Rotterdam, the Netherlands; Nationaal Archief (formerly Algemeen Rijksarchief); Rijksbureau voor Kunsthistorische Documentatie (RKD), the Hague, Netherlands; the Vatican Library; and last but certainly not least, the Central Library of the National University of Singapore. Special thanks are due to Nicholas Tarling, who supported this publication with a generous grant from the Nicholas Tarling Fund.

This book could have not been written without the input, feedback and stimulation from numerous friends and colleagues. I would particularly like to thank Leonard Blussé, Derek Heng, Martine van Ittersum, Paul Kratoska, Kwa Chong Guan, Anton van der Lem, Anthony C. Milner, Ng Chin Keong, Roderich Ptak, Merle Ricklefs, as well as Peter Borschberg Sr., Pierre-Emmanuel Jacob, Jerry Lee Kah Seng, Bruce Lockhart, Mohamed Effendy bin Abdul Hamid, Gilles Massot, Roopanjali Roy, and Tim Yap Fuan.

Introduction

The Straits of Singapore and the nearby Strait of Melaka mark a crucial point of strategic interest in Southeast Asia. Regional and long-distance maritime trading networks converge in these maritime arteries, which link ports in Europe, the Mediterranean, eastern Africa, the Arabian Peninsula and the Indian subcontinent with key centres of trade in Thailand, Indochina, insular Southeast Asia, China, Korea and Japan. This is not just a modern truism. Drawing on familiar and unfamiliar source materials of both Asian and European origin, this book argues that the Straits of Singapore and Melaka have for centuries stood at the forefront of geo-strategic concerns. Before the dawn of the 17th century, it had become clear to the officials of the Portuguese crown as much as to the directors of the Netherlands' United East India Company, better known by its historic initials VOC (*Verenigde Oost-Indische Compagnie*), that whoever controlled the waters off modern Singapore and the two Karimun Islands gained a firm grip on regional as well as long-distance intra-Asian trade. If tightened by regular naval patrols or by imposing blockades on key regional ports, this maritime stranglehold could be used to intimidate regional princes, enhance the prowess of early European colonial powers or, with reference to inter-European rivalry, serve as a nodal point at which to sever communications and trade between the far-flung ports of the Portuguese *Estado da Índia*.[1]

The Straits of Singapore and Melaka have long served as principal maritime arteries of commerce with consequences of geopolitical and geostrategic significance. Strategic interest in the region — seen either within the narrower confines of the historic powers surrounding the Straits, or even from the perspective of Europe's princely courts and East India Company boardrooms — only makes sense against the backdrop of trade, trading networks and the perceived need to facilitate, guarantee or protect the flow of commerce. But strategic interest cannot be separated from trade and commerce. To better grasp the evolution of strategic perceptions and security policies, it is important to understand the scope and nature of regional geography as well as the political powers around the Straits.

This book is about the geo-strategic and geopolitical interests of the European powers around Sumatra and the Malay Peninsula during the late 16th and early 17th centuries. An understanding of this period entails an appreciation of the topographical sciences of the age, the style of diplomacy undertaken, the cooptation of local commercial and political elites, as well as the contemporary knowledge, physical control and protection of existing maritime trading routes. This book addresses a number of "big issues" — issues that are of concern in the 21st century and have proven to be of enduring historical value. These big issues involve trade and commerce, security, sovereignty, military hegemony and diplomatic engagement — all of which require a deeper understanding of the region and of the shifting powers that surrounded the Singapore and Melaka Straits.

Readers will quickly appreciate that this volume is not an imperial history of the sort written during the 19th and early 20th centuries. While drawing heavily on surviving European colonial documents, the author does not intend to argue in favour of European dominance in terms of trade, political power, military prowess or even cultural values.

While acknowledging the inherent limitations and challenges to the modern historian, the author hopes to let the primary documents speak for themselves. A distinctive feature of this book is the insistence that not only indigenous sources, but also non-English-language European source materials of the period are of an uneven quality, nature and intention; they also differ considerably in levels of formality. The *Dagh-Register Batavia* (Dairy of the Castle at Batavia) and correspondence between VOC's factors consist in part of chatter and gossip that modern readers often find difficult to contextualise. Still, source materials such as the *Dagh-Register* also often contain useful nuggets of information on how traders, factors and visitors thought about a given situation or development at any point in time. In other words, these materials often have their finger on the pulse of emerging developments and act as a barometer of developing crises. It goes almost without saying that these materials were written by clerks of different backgrounds and varying levels of experience in the Indies. Correspondingly, they are laced with a spectrum of personal prejudices and agendas. These informal, or at least "less formal", sources contrast sharply with the formal reports and instructions filed by higher-ranking officers, either of the *Estado da Índia* or from within the VOC administration in Asia as well as the Netherlands. Often these "more formal" source materials, such as the *Generale Missiven* or "Annual Reports from Asia", stake out a bigger picture for the VOC directors and politicians in Europe. As their hallmark, the *Generale Missiven* provide a helicopter view of developments around Asia, explain tricky problems in greater detail, and spell out options with their likely long-term consequences. While extremely useful, reports such as the *Generale Missiven* sometimes skew or exaggerate adverse developments in order to explain away low profit margins or justify high capital expenses. Formal reports filed by both the Dutch and — especially — the Portuguese often assume positions along the lines of "everything is under control", "the situation is completely out of control", or "do whatever you can", in the hope that superiors in Goa, Lisbon, Madrid or Amsterdam would readily concur and rush supplies, manpower and money to their forts and factories around Asia.

The source materials offer a refreshing spectrum of views of both formal and less formal nature. The plurality of opinion is especially true during the first two decades of the 17th century, before the VOC centralised its Asian commerce and administration in Batavia. At this time Luso-Spanish cooperation in the East Indies could still arouse hopes at the courts of Lisbon and Madrid that the Dutch menace could be dealt with either by power broking with Asian allies or simply by the force of arms. On the Portuguese side, the documents express a deep understanding of regional dynamics of power and of trading arrangements, both of which were vital to ensure the long-term survival of the *Estado da Índia*. Far from painting a picture of heavy-handed Lusitanian diplomacy, early modern gunboat politics or religious bigotry, the situation on the ground demanded that the Portuguese recognise and acknowledge their vulnerabilities. Their survival demanded carefully balanced diplomatic relations with neighbouring

Printed map of Asia by Henricus à Langren, 1600. The insert on the bottom right depicts the altar of a (Chinese) deity and a bird's eye view of Banten (Amsterdam University Library, OK 127).

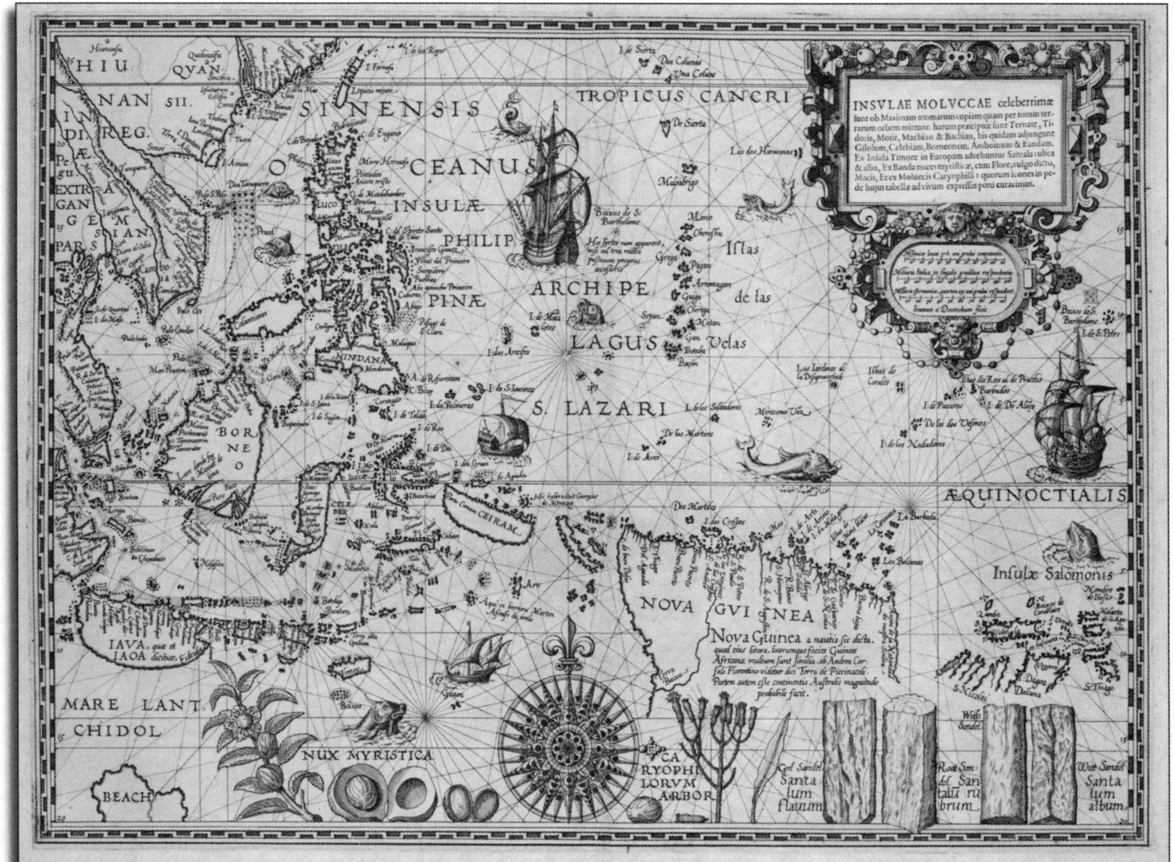

Map of the East Indies titled *Insulae Moluccae* (The Maluku Islands) by Pieter Plancius (Platvoet) of 1592 featuring most of insular and mainland southeast Asia, New Guinea and the Solomon Islands. At the bottom of the page are depictions (from left to right) of nutmeg, cloves and different types of sandalwood. (Amsterdam University Library, OK 131)

powers, and religious zeal often had to be sacrificed in order to develop more fruitful relations within the wider sphere of Hindu, Buddhist or Muslim cultural environments. In short, early Portuguese colonial practices often reveal acquiescence, accommodation, compliance and societal insertion. This practice is a far cry from the way the Portuguese portrayed themselves as a colonial power for consumption in the European home market, or even from the rabid anti-Lusitanian rhetoric that pervades period documents of the VOC.

At the dawn of the 17th century, the Portuguese had accumulated a century's worth of experience in Asia, which they jealously guarded with secrecy and heavy censorship. The first Dutch ships arrived only in 1595–6, around the time when Jan Huygen van Linschoten published his *Reysgeschrift* (Travel Account) and *Itinerario* (Itinerary). The early Dutch arrivals faced a steep learning curve striking up trade and alliances across Asia, and this willingness to amass information and retain an open mind — evident from documents of the early 17th century — proves particularly rewarding to readers today. The Dutch were willing to learn about markets and societies, to acknowledge Asian princes as sovereign equals, and to accept Asian peoples as partners in commerce and war. VOC-generated documents from the first two decades of the 17th century espouse a spectrum of opinions, views and possibilities that reflect the willingness of the Dutch to learn as much as possible about the peoples they were engaging with commercially, culturally and sometimes also in war.

As with any individual or organisation facing a steep learning curve, the Dutch faced not only setbacks but also inevitable dilemmas. With an eye cast on the region around the Straits of Singapore and Melaka, the Dutch soon found themselves part of a four-way relationship that involved Johor, Aceh and the *Estado da Índia*, a relationship that was not static but constantly evolving. VOC manuscripts and, to a far lesser extent, formal Portuguese materials of the *Estado da Índia* record and reflect an evolving relationship on two different planes and feature completely different dynamics of interaction: At one level there are the European colonial powers interacting with one another employing established European rules of diplomacy, trade and military engagement; and on the other, there are the European powers interacting with neighbouring Asian princes and peoples. In the latter aspect, the Dutch had far less experience than the Portuguese; and the VOC's deference to European practices in commerce, law and warfare frequently proved problematic. In the period under review, the Dutch only imperfectly understood how the monarchs of Southeast Asia interacted with one another, and in the first decades of the 17th century they only imperfectly comprehended the origins, nature and dynamics of the Patani-Johor-Aceh rivalry.

In the first half of the 17th century, relations between Johor and Aceh and their ever-shifting relations with the Portuguese posed one of the greatest challenges to the VOC in its efforts to dominate the Singapore and Melaka Straits. The image best illustrating the complex challenges faced by the Dutch is that of VOC servants groping in the dark. The early European colonial powers clearly recognised that they could remain and trade in the territories around the Straits simply because they were tolerated, and often also because they served a specific, useful function to Johor, Aceh and other powers as allies-in-arms and, more frequently, as trading partners. At the opening of the 17th century, the Dutch were the proverbial new kids on the block in what was clearly a rough neighbourhood to begin with. As is evidenced in this book, there was wheeling and dealing, broken promises, shifting alliances, and almost inevitably some diplomatic "bloody noses". All were party to some rough, or at least questionable, behaviour.

Historical accounts of Singapore, and indeed the region immediately surrounding the Straits, touching on the period before 1819 are sparse compared to studies on other countries of the present-day ASEAN family, notably, Indonesia, Thailand and Vietnam. Among the extant publications and dissertations, a majority were published during the colonial period more than half a century ago, or they were published in languages such as Dutch, French, German and Portuguese, which prevents them from being readily accessible to many contemporary readers in the Southeast Asian region.

One may gain the impression that the early modern history of the Straits is sandwiched between the pre-colonial period of Srivijaya, Temasek, the Melaka Sultanate and the rise of Johor on the one hand, and the eclipse of VOC dominance at the close of the 18th century on the other. According to the Singapore-based archaeologist John Miksic, the consequence specifically for Singapore is unambiguous: "The period of Singapore's history between the Portuguese attack of 1613 and the British arrival in 1819 is nearly completely blank."[2] With regard to the pre-colonial period, there are a number of outstanding studies, for example, Pierre-Yves Manguin, Edward McKinnon, Miksic and Derek Heng that resort extensively to archaeological materials in support of their conclusions.[3] Historical studies, especially on Srivijaya, have been undertaken notably by Oliver Wolters as well as the German academic Hermann Kulke.[4] The examination of Chinese sources dating from the Song and Ming periods has been undertaken by Wang Gungwu, Roderich Ptak and Geoff Wade, among others.[5] These sources include information on the Ming fleets of Admiral Zheng He, as well as on the diplomatic, military and commercial repercussions of these Chinese voyages. The recent compilation of Wade published by the Malaysian Branch of the Royal Asiatic Society, in Kuala Lumpur, reprints a useful array of shorter studies touching on the Chinese presence in Southeast Asia in the 15th century, with Zheng He strategically placed at the forefront of scholarly attention.[6] Taking a much broader perspective, Ptak's recently published German-language work *Die Maritime Seidenstrasse* (The Silk Route of the Sea) synthesises in a very accessible volume most of the research on the pre-colonial and early colonial trade of the late medieval and early modern period.[7] Inspired by Fernand Braudel, Ptak argues for the existence of a *Mediterranée Asiatique* (Asian Mediterranean) that interlocked the regions around the Indian Ocean and the South China Sea into a comprehensive regime of material and cultural exchange aided by, amongst other factors, the annual monsoon winds.[8] He critically questions whether the significance of Melaka as a trading emporium has been overstated, but treats the Straits of Singapore and Melaka as geo-strategic points of trade.

With reference to the period of transition from the Melaka Sultanate to the arrival of the Portuguese in the Straits, one can point to the many scholarly studies published by Luís Filipe R. Thomaz on the 16th-century Portuguese colonial presence in Melaka and around Southeast Asia at large.[9] Thomaz and the "Lisbon School", as it is sometimes called, have also spawned important studies on Burma, Aceh, Melaka, Johor and the Malukus, all of which have been consulted in writing or reviewing the chapters of the present book.[10] Other studies concerning the region around the Straits in the 16th century include the important surveys of M.-A.P. Meilink-Roelofsz and Anthony Reid, as well as the miscellaneous contributions on regional waters and polities by Peter Borschberg, Malcolm Dunn, Muhammad Yusof, Anthony Milner, Edward McKinnon and Tengku Luckman Sinar, Sanjay Subrahmanyam, Manuel Teixeira and Christopher Wake.[11]

Active scholarly interest in the history of the Straits region is mirrored by a focus on the volatile period toward the close of the 18th century, which sees political and dynastic disturbances within Johor, the apparent resuscitation of Melaka as a trading entrepôt, and the demise of VOC hegemony in the Straits as well as across much of insular Southeast Asia.

One can point in this context to the published studies of Barbara Andaya, Nordin Hussin, Dianne Lewis, Meyer Timmerman Thijssen and Radin Fernando with specific reference to Melaka and surrounding territories, as well as to Reinout Vos in relation to developments in Riau, and Timothy Barnard for Siak in the 18th century.[12]

The half century between c. 1590 and 1640 has remained surprisingly under-researched. While occasionally useful, the older contributions by E. Netscher and Richard Winstedt are hopelessly outdated, reflecting a condescending colonial mindset that is no longer viable or acceptable in present-day historical circles.[13] The now classic exposé of Leonard Andaya, *The Kingdom of Johor*, was published more than 30 years ago, and in any case it gives only cursory attention to the region before the fall of Portuguese Melaka to the Dutch in January 1641.[14] Arun das Gupta's doctoral thesis completed at Cornell University in 1962 remains a useful survey that focuses on Aceh and its relations with the English, Dutch and Portuguese in the early 17th century.[15] In a similar vein, the more recent Portuguese-language study of Paulo Pinto, *Portugueses e malaios*, casts principal focus on the late 16th century. It touches only scantily on events and developments of the early 17th century, and it offers a synopsis of unfolding historical developments chiefly limited to Portuguese-language sources.

This leaves readers with a number of works that touch on the region between about 1590 and 1641 but do not have the Straits as their specific focus or concern. In this context, one should point to several contributions by the French academics Denys Lombard and Manguin, as well as the published doctoral dissertations of Ernst van Veen and Martine van Ittersum.[16] Lombard's work on Iskandar Muda of Aceh is important for appreciating the backdrop of Acehnese imperial expansion across Sumatra and the Malay Peninsula during the first decades of the 17th century, as well as their relations with neighbouring powers, including the Portuguese.[17] Among the publications of Manguin, one encounters his valuable study of Portuguese navigation and trade along the coast of Vietnam, the critical edition of Bishop Dom João Ribeiro Gaio's rutter for northeast Sumatra and the Malay Peninsula (which he co-published with Jorge Alves), as well as a number of smaller studies on regional polities of Sumatra and Portuguese Melaka.[18]

The abovementioned studies are supplemented by van Veen's *Decay or Defeat*, which focuses on the mixed fortunes of the Portuguese *Estado da Índia* during the late 16th and early 17th centuries. This study helps understand the actions of Portuguese Melaka within the broader context of developments across the *Estado* between approximately 1580 and 1645.

Bhawan Ruangslip's recently published doctoral dissertation, completed as part of the Toward a New Age of Partnership Programme (TANAP) at Leiden University, focuses chiefly on Siam and the Ayutthaya court's relations with the early European colonial powers. Ruangslip offers valuable insights on Siamese diplomacy towards the European powers, as well as important Siamese vassal states such as Patani during the reign of King Prasat Thong in the third decade of the 17th century.[19] Van Ittersum, by contrast, focuses on the very early phase of Dutch commercial and colonial activity in the waters of Southeast Asia. She questions why the famous Dutch humanist and jurisconsult Hugo Grotius wrote his *De Jure Praedae Commentarius* (Commentary on the Law of Prize and Booty) between 1604 and 1609.[20] Central to the composition of this work were the developments immediately preceding the capture of the Portuguese carrack *Santa Catarina* in the Straits of Singapore in February 1603, and the wider repercussions that this incident was to have in Asia and, especially, in Europe. The present volume stresses the *Santa Catarina* incident insofar as it meaningfully and verifiably influenced security plans for the Singapore and Melaka Straits. The arrival of the Dutch in the Straits and Southeast Asia at large, the structural and financial constraints faced by the *Estado da Índia*, as well as the expansionist, imperial drive of Aceh redefined the balance of power in the region, drew attention to realigned political interests, alliances, and reprioritised security needs for the Straits.[21]

This books aims to explore a range of early modern European charts, maps and publications to illustrate Europe's evolving visualisation of the Singapore and Melaka Straits across a period of approximately 100 years between the mid-16th and mid-17th centuries. Many, if not most, of these sources are "new" in that they have never been adduced in other academic works, or in this book are being studied from a different vantage point. Attention is centred on the elasticity of toponyms, such as *Singapura*, as they are employed in early colonial documents and publications; the various maritime routes that linked the Straits of Melaka with the South China Sea; and the latter's evolution on European hydrographic charts, maps and globes. One special feature of early modern European cartographical depictions of the region around the Straits of Singapore and Melaka will be discussed at length, namely, the imagined maritime channel that European cartographers believed crossed the Malay Peninsula, linking the coastal port towns of Muar in the west and Pekan (Pahang) in the east.

These explorations into the history of cartography are brought together in Chapter 1, "Landscapes, Seascapes and Imagination at the Southern Tip of the Malay Peninsula", on the grounds that discussion about security and strategic location makes little sense unless placed within the context of how such spaces were historically understood, depicted and illustrated.

After staking out the topographical and cartographical context of European security plans, the book explores how, in the early 17th century, the Dutch projected their war of liberation with the united crown of Spain and Portugal into the Asian theatre at large. The projection of the war into the region around the Singapore and Melaka Straits is perhaps best exemplified by the seizure of the Portuguese carrack *Santa Catarina* off the coast of Singapore on 25 February 1603. What began as a single incident of freebooting quickly evolved into a more comprehensive policy aimed at weakening the Portuguese presence in Asia by routinely plundering commercial vessels. Emphasis is placed on the *Santa Catarina* incident not only because it was the first major act of despoliation by the Dutch in the waters of the Singapore Straits, but also because subsequent developments triggered a realignment of allegiances and shifted the balance of power around the Malay Peninsula and Sumatra. Heightened violence between the Dutch, the Portuguese and their respective allies in the region placed Johor in the spotlight. Improved Luso-Johor relations probably triggered direct military intervention by Aceh, as a result of which Johor and later also Pahang became client states in a rapidly expanding Acehnese empire. These developments straddling the decade between the arrival of the Dutch in Singapore waters in late 1602 and the Acehnese invasion of 1613 stand at the centre of Chapter 2, "Security in the Straits: The European Struggle for Naval Hegemony".

The European powers responded to the serious disruptions in mercantile shipping and the new balance of power by drawing up and discussing a range of plans to secure the waters around the southern tip of the Malay Peninsula. Leading officers of the *Estado da Índia* as well as officials of the Portuguese crown in Europe discussed several options, including the construction of forts around key locations along the Straits and the Johor River estuary. The finances of the *Estado da Índia* could hardly be stretched to meet the full security needs of commercial vessels across the region. As a result, the Portuguese opted for what was arguably a cost-effective option — deploying escort fleets at strategic locations in and around the Straits. Naval security was positioned at the eastern entrance of the Singapore Strait around the Hook of Berbukit during the period of the northeast monsoon (October–February), when richly laden carracks from Japan, China, Cochinchina, Siam and Makassar would make their journey to Melaka and Goa. During the period of the southwest monsoon (April–August), the security fleets would be stationed around Cape Rachado to anticipate the arrival of ships from the western Indian Ocean and ports around the Bay of Bengal.

The construction of forts, however, always remained a point of discussion and debate, not just for the Portuguese but especially for the Dutch and surprisingly also the Spanish. Two such fort projects for the Singapore Straits will be discussed in greater detail: Dutch plans to construct a fortress on the northeastern coast of Karimun Besar and Jaques de Coutre's proposal to build two fortifications around Singapore. The *Santa Catarina* incident, the ensuing shift in the balance of power around the Straits, and the changing security concerns of the nascent European colonial powers are explored in Chapter 3, "Naval Security and Forts for the Straits, c. 1584–1630".

It is worth underscoring that both the Portuguese and the Dutch were painfully aware of their limitations in terms of funds, military reach (which at this time was limited chiefly to naval forces) and manpower. Both realised that without forging alliances of war or less formal agreements for cooperation and mutual assistance with regional polities, the colonial enterprise would be doomed. In the long term, diplomacy always proved far more effective than the force of arms. The Portuguese learned the delicate art of Asian diplomacy soon after seizing control of Melaka in 1511.[22] But as their Dutch counterparts would also come to understand, Asian allies were equally keen to capitalise on any advantage to enhance their position of power and prestige and, not surprisingly, were not always keen on abiding by the letter or spirit of agreements.

Recognising their vulnerability to the projection of Dutch power in the Southeast Asian region and beyond, the Spanish and the Portuguese pooled naval forces to cleanse Southeast Asian waters of Dutch "rebels, pirates and freebooters". The logistics and funds required for the joint naval action were nothing short of monumental, an effort literally encompassing the globe, involving governments in Europe, the Portuguese viceroy in Goa, the Spanish viceroy of New Spain (Mexico), and the Spanish governor of the Philippines. As developments would show, poor timing, inadequate preparation, coordination bottlenecks and Acehnese intervention brought the armada of Spanish-Philippine governor Juan de Silva to anchor in the waters off Singapore island. The Luso-Spanish naval force failed to unite as planned, and the episode ended in an unmitigated fiasco, with the destruction of all Portuguese warships and the death of Governor de Silva at Melaka. The Luso-Spanish naval cooperation that brought one of the largest Spanish armadas of its day to anchor off Singapore and the annihilation of the Portuguese warships will be discussed in Chapter 4, "Luso-Spanish Naval Intervention, 1615–6".

At the open of the 17th century, the Dutch regarded Melaka as a jewel in the crown of the Portuguese *Estado da Índia*. After plucking the island of Ambon in 1605, the Dutch launched several attempts to wrest Melaka from Iberian control, with the naval siege of Admiral Cornelis Matelieff de Jonge in 1606 among the best documented. As history would show, however, Melaka could not be easily taken from the Portuguese, and by the time the Dutch finally succeeded in January 1641, they were confronted with a very different constellation of power around the region of the Straits than in 1606. Acehnese expansion during the second and third decades of the 17th century was certainly an important factor, but so were developments in Siam, in Patani and on the Malay Peninsula. Johor had oscillated between supporting the Dutch and supporting the Portuguese, depending on which faction at the court in Batu Sawar held the upper hand. But the VOC, too, had evolved into a different creature.

In 1606 the company was weighing its options for a permanent base in Asia. For reasons linked to history and trade, Melaka was an obvious choice, and so, incidentally, was Johor. But the decision to move to Batavia was made by Governor-General Jan Pieterszoon Coen by the early 1620s. By then, belief in Melaka's commercial primacy had faded, and the VOC's resources and attention focused on consolidating power along the north coast of Java. Still, the Straits remained an acknowledged maritime artery in the geo-strategic deliberations of the VOC. Chapter 5, "VOC Blockades in the Singapore and Melaka Straits: Diplomacy, Trade and Survival, 1633–41", examines the intermittent Dutch blockade of Melaka over a period of eight years. Of special interest are the tactics employed by the Dutch blockaders, the strategies devised by the Portuguese of Melaka to evade the blockade, and, also important, how each relied on their regional allies and information networks to outwit the other. What becomes clear is that the fall of Melaka to the Dutch in January 1641 was due not so much to force of arms as to famine, disease and, inevitably, diplomacy.

The appendices feature discussions, transcripts and translations of important documents to critically engage the reader with the main text. Appendix 1 takes up the theme that is at least implicit in every one of the preceding chapters — the difficulties faced by contemporary researchers in reading or evaluating sources from the early modern period. Focus is placed in this instance on Melaka, the transition to Portuguese rule, and the reliability of Portuguese-language sources, such as Tomé Pires' *Suma Oriental* (c. 1515–7). Appendix 2 provides a transcript and translation of a Portuguese letter written by Dom Paulo Lima de Pereira to King Philip II of Spain in 1587 giving his personal account of the destruction of Johor Lama. Appendix 3 contains the original Dutch text provided by Jan Huyghen van Linschoten for navigating the Old Strait of Singapore. Appendix 4 transcribes the French text and translates into English the opening paragraphs from book 11, chapter 24, of André Thevet's *Cosmographie Universelle* (1575), titled "Of the Island of *Cingaporla*, near Malaca, and a Few Islands in the Direction of China". Appendix 5 transcribes from the original Spanish and translates into English the memorial of the Flemish diamond merchant Jaques de Coutre dating from the 1620s in which he advises the king of Spain to construct forts on present-day Sentosa, on Singapore island and at the Muar River estuary. Appendices 6–9 comprise a series of minor excerpts from quoted works in their original Portuguese, Dutch and Spanish. This includes in appendix 6 part of a letter by Affonso de Albuquerque to King Manuel I of Portugal, written in Portuguese, reporting the assistance of a Javanese pilot in the acquisition of topographical knowledge of Southeast Asia. Appendix 7 forms part of a log-entry by Joris van Spilbergen in which he describes the cargo and appraised value of the carrack *Sta. Catarina* seized by Jakob van Heemskerk off Singapore on 25 February 1603. Appendix 8 is an account by Pedro Teixeira, written in Spanish and published in 1610, describing the twists, turns and dangers in the maritime route along the west coast of Singapore island and the Old Strait of Singapore. Appendix 9, finally, represents an excerpt in Dutch from the *Dagh-Register Batavia* dating from the early 1630s and describes how a patrolling VOC squadron chased after a Portuguese merchant vessel. This chase was accomplished with the assistance of a local Malay or *orang laut* father-and-son team. But once the squadron began to close in, the Portuguese captain set his ship and cargo ablaze in order to prevent their seizure by the Dutch.

In completing the present study, the author has relied on a spectrum of published and unpublished documents, letters, reports, briefs, diaries, directors' resolutions, minutes of VOC board meetings, logbooks as well as scores of printed and manuscript charts. These different types of sources feature a wide range of European languages, including Dutch,

German, Italian, French, Portuguese, Spanish, Latin and English. Asian sources include the Malay-language *Sejarah Melayu* (Malay Annals), other Hikayats such as the *Hikayat Raja-Raja Pasai* (Story of the Kings of Pasai),[23] the *Hikayat Patani* (The Story of Patani),[24] Nuruddin al-Raniri's, *Bustan as-Salatin* (The Garden of Kings),[25] as well as select Chinese source materials in translation.[26] For related Arabic-language materials the author has consulted the French translations of Gabriel Ferrand, G.R. Tibbets' critical English translation of Ahmad bin Majid al-Najdi and his cross-references to Ibn Majid,[27] and the German translation by Bittner and Tomaschek of Sidi Çelebi's geographic chapters of the *Muhît*.[28] But Arabic materials ultimately proved of limited value to the present study, as Tibbetts so succinctly concludes in his article "The Malay Peninsula as Known to the Arab Geographers":

> The very limited knowledge that the Arabs possessed of Malaya was, I think, entirely due to the route they followed. The texts ... show that the majority of places known to them were on the west coast and, moreover, only in the northern part of that coast, from Pegu to Kedah, or perhaps as far as Klang.[29]

So much for the early Arab navigators. With reference to toponyms and orthography, the early modern sources in Western languages employ seriously corrupted place names and titles. For example, the rulers of Johor and Aceh are usually called "kings" and the ruler of "Borneo" (Brunei) is sometimes attributed the title of "emperor" in late 16th and early 17th century European materials and manuscripts. The early 17th century mind evidently found it appropriate to understand or "translate" Malay terms such as *negeri* as "kingdom" and *raja* as "king". Patani is dubbed a "vassal" of Siam, which reflects a European understanding of feudal relationships that has little bearing on the intricate relationships of power and authority prevailing in Southeast Asia at the time. It is important not to jump to unwarranted conclusions about how familiar a given author may have been with the specific cultural or political contexts that he is describing. In keeping with the intent to let the documents speak for themselves, the author has retained period nomenclature and concepts as far as possible. Portuguese and sometimes also Dutch documents employ phoneticised renditions of Malay, Javanese, Thai or Chinese names. As these can prove extremely confusing to the reader, orthography has been adopted to the modern spelling — for example, Pahang for Pam, Pão or Pahão; Tioman for Timon, Timão or Tiomão; and Johor for Jor, Ior, Ioor or Jhor.

Published and unpublished charts proved invaluable for gaining a deeper understanding of early modern texts. Toponyms could be employed in a very elastic manner, and it is therefore not always clear to the contemporary reader. Take, for example, the name Singapura and its many, sometimes hardly recognisable, orthographical variants. What does this name refer to? A town? An island? The straits? A promontory? A kingdom? A broader geographic space? Cartographic materials greatly helped unlock the ambiguity or even multiplicity of possible meanings, the multiplicity and elasticity of which is incidentally not unique to European source materials, but is also evident from Malay sources such as the *Sejarah Melayu*.[30] Many of the individual maps and charts consulted are one of a kind, of unique historical value, or accessible only in private collections in Europe, the Americas and Asia. The author believes that his extensive use of manuscript charts and maps in conjunction with published and unpublished document materials greatly deepens knowledge of pre-Raffles Singapore and also offers new material and perceptions on the wider historical and geo-political significance of Sumatra and the Malay Peninsula. There is obvious significance here in providing historical depth to the study of present-day geo-strategic relations in Southeast Asia. The strategic centrality of the Straits of Singapore and Melaka four centuries ago, and the way Europeans and local rulers responded to this may even be relevant to developing priorities and policies today.

CHAPTER 1

Landscapes, Seascapes and Imagination at the Southern Tip of the Malay Peninsula

Monsoons, Emporia and the Straits of Singapore

The emporium of modern Singapore is located in a relatively narrow geographical zone. It spans from Southern Thailand in the north to the Strait of Sunda in the south, with two major maritime trading zones and monsoonal weather systems intersecting and overlapping. To the west there is the trading zone of the greater Bay of Bengal, and in the east the mainland and island ports of the South China Sea. Historically, this zone has been home to several prominent historical trading cities — from Srivijaya in the Middle Ages to Melaka on the Malay Peninsula, the northern Sumatran ports, Georgetown on the island of Penang since the late 1700s, and Singapore after the early 1800s. Long before the age of European colonialism, this region emerged as one of the historically most significant maritime meeting points in Asia, if not the world. The wealth generated by trade and commerce within and through this zone was almost legendary. By the late 1400s and early 1500s, merchants and traders from Western Europe had entered the stage. The societies that grew out of this interaction of goods, peoples and ideas were open and cosmopolitan in

Full map of Asia by António Sanches, 1641 (Koninklijke Bibliotheek, The Hague, 129 A 25 fols. 16verso-17recto)

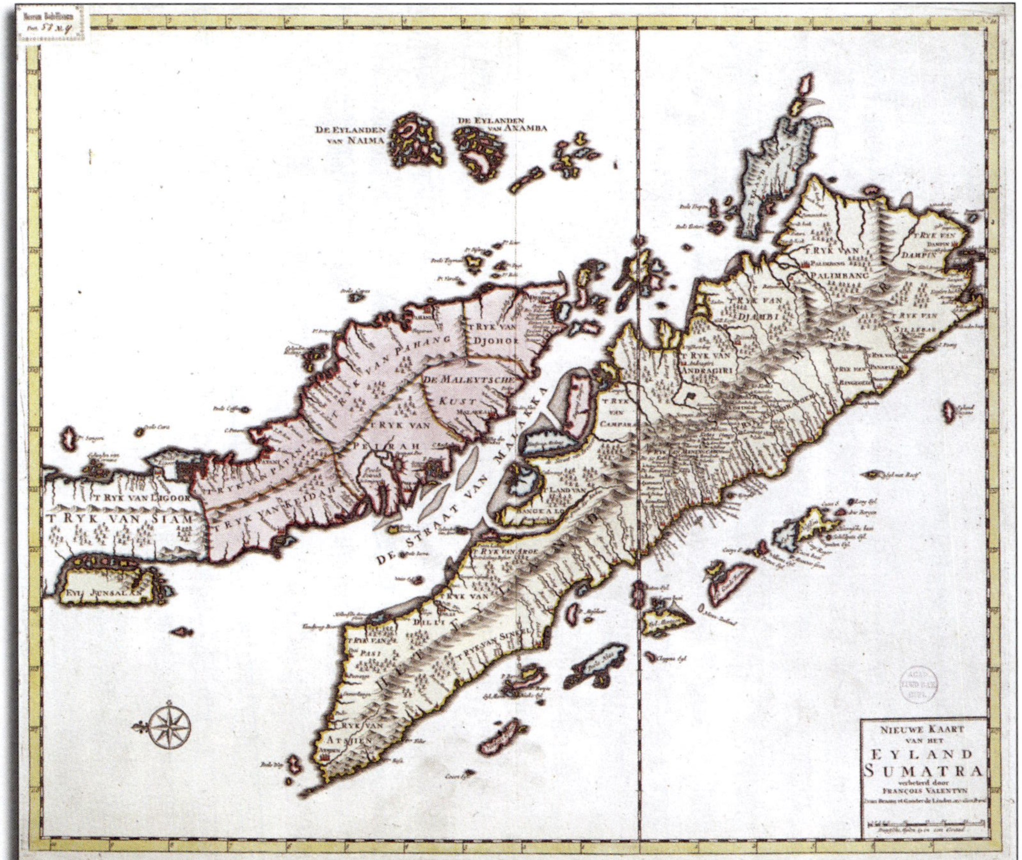

Printed, hand-coloured map from the early 18th century depicting Sumatra and the Malay Peninsula (University of Leiden, map collection, 58 n. 4)

nature, providing a base or home — seasonal, transitional or permanent — to peoples from across Asia and beyond. Modern Singapore represents, in this sense, a comparatively recent addition to a long list of commercial emporia within this region.[1]

In the process of attracting trade and cultural interaction to its shores, this zone also became one of the most politically contested. One need only consult the annals of the Malay principalities of Sumatra and the Peninsula to appreciate how fragile the balance of power remained and how many different agents and factions contended for power and supremacy. As there were many centres of trade competing against one another, strategic location in this zone usually implied — and indeed still does — the ability to successfully attract commerce to one's shores.

By the time the first European colonial powers arrived in the Straits, the polity of Singapura had already been eclipsed by its rival Melaka, located along the western coast of the Malay Peninsula in the north.[2] Little about this period of commercial transition was known to the early European chroniclers. The famed early 16th-century Portuguese apothecary Tomé Pires has nothing to say about the reasons behind the decline of medieval Singapura. This contrasts sharply with information that can be gleaned from the work of the Portuguese chronicler João de Barros and implicitly the anonymous Dutch pamphlet *Held-dadige Scheeps-togt* (Heroic Maritime Expedition) printed in the early 18th century. According to Barros as well as the aforementioned anonymous Dutch pamphlet, there were both human and natural factors to explain the decline. The human factor is Parameswara, the founder of Melaka, who murdered his host Sangesinga at Singapura before moving on to settle down at Muar with his band of 2,000 thieves and hoodlums.[3] The source of this claim is most probably of Malay or Javanese origin. The second principal cause was weather conditions, and this natural factor assumes centre stage in explaining medieval Singapura's decline. Reportedly, the city was not as well-situated as Melaka to efficiently exploit the shifting monsoon winds that mark the different trading seasons.[4] It is this locational disadvantage that supports Barros' etymological deconstruction of the name Singapura. He claims it translates into Portuguese as *falsa demora*, which means "a place where you land but subsequently discover that it is not what you were looking for". Singapura, it would appear, was not the ideal place for merchants to anticipate the seasonal change of the monsoon winds.[5]

With reference to early modern European cartography and nomenclature, this claim raises a number of important issues that are addressed in the present chapter, namely: What is meant by the name Singapura and its many, sometimes hardly recognisable, orthographical variants?[6] What do the early European charts, maps and texts say? Exploring these questions in detail will lead to a greater understanding of how strategic the location of the Singapore and Melaka Straits — or, for that matter, the whole southern portion of the Malay Peninsula — had become by the 16th and early 17th centuries. This will not only provide important insights into interpreting early modern texts but, significantly, also grant important insights into European ideas about the region as a strategic nodal spot within the broader framework of (long-distance) intra-Asian trade.

Where Exactly is Singapura According to Early Colonial Texts?

While geographic terms and places in present times are narrowly defined, the reader of early modern European and many Asian sources will undoubtedly note that topographical names were employed quite loosely. The observation applies equally to Singapura and all the variants of this name that cartographers or travellers between 1500 and 1800 used to designate one or all of five things: the southern regions of the Malay Peninsula, the cape or southern extremity of the Asian continent, the many straits, the main island of the modern Republic of Singapore, or the town of Singapura.[7]

On the earliest maps dating from the colonial period, especially the 16th century, the town of Singapura is never placed on what could recognisably be present-day Singapore island; rather, it refers to a settlement or fortified city on the Asian mainland, south of the Muar River. Several renowned cartographers feature Singapura thus, including Gerhard Mercator, Giacomo Gastaldi and Abraham Ortelius.[8] The Portuguese generally speak of Singapura in terms of a cape (*cabo*), point or promontory (*ponta, punta*), strait (*estreito*) and settlement (*povoação*), but in the 17th century it was chiefly spoken of as a maritime strait.[9] Importantly, the Portuguese chronicler Barros also mentions an ancient city named *Cingapura* in the context of recounting Parameswara's founding of Melaka.[10]

Where are the Singapore Straits?

At first glance, this question may appear to be basic and simple: Where are the Singapore Straits? But historically, the answer has been nothing short of problematic. The name "Straits of Singapore" and its many variants was applied to a number of maritime routes linking the South China Sea in the east and the Strait of Melaka in the west and north. A relic of this in our everyday language is that one tends to speak of the "Straits" of Singapore, implying not a singular, but a plurality of maritime passages that connect the Strait of Melaka with the South China Sea. Interested researchers will soon discover that the name Strait of Singapore or *Estrecho de Singapura* is also used to designate the southern reaches of the Melaka Strait, a practice that has survived into the present. The consensus in English-speaking circles is that "Straits of Singapore" refers collectively to the maritime passages located between the main island of Singapore and as far east as Pedra Branca and to the south along the northern coast of Bulan, Batam and Bintan islands.

Before describing briefly the different passages that were historically navigated and are collectively known as the "Straits of Singapore", it is useful to raise yet another basic but important question: What do cartographers of the region historically depict to the south of the Singapore Straits?

Charts and maps of the region dating from 1500 to 1700 — even those drawn up by authorities with extensive first-hand knowledge and familiarity with the region — reveal that navigators and cartographers were not sure of the topographical features located to the south of the Singapore Straits. Manoel Godinho de Erédia's maps featured in the *Declaraçam de Malaca* (Description of Melaka), owned by the Bibliothèque Royale in Brussels, Belgium, are far from state-of-the-art for its own day and depict the equator running through the island of Bintan rather than farther south through the island of Lingga.[11]

As late as the mid-1600s, the Riau Archipelago was depicted as a fantastic agglomeration of impenetrable islands (see p. 23), shown in its most explicit form by the *Atlas Miller* of 1519.[12] A classic description of this maze is found on a map that is virtually unknown to many contemporary experts on Singapore. It presently forms part of the Collectie Bodel Nijenhuis at Leiden University and represents the state of knowledge on the Straits and the Riau Archipelago from the period around 1610 to 1640 (see p. 24). This chart features the following entry in large script: "De zuidzijdt vande Straat Sincapura zijn alle gebrooken Eilanden" (The southern side of

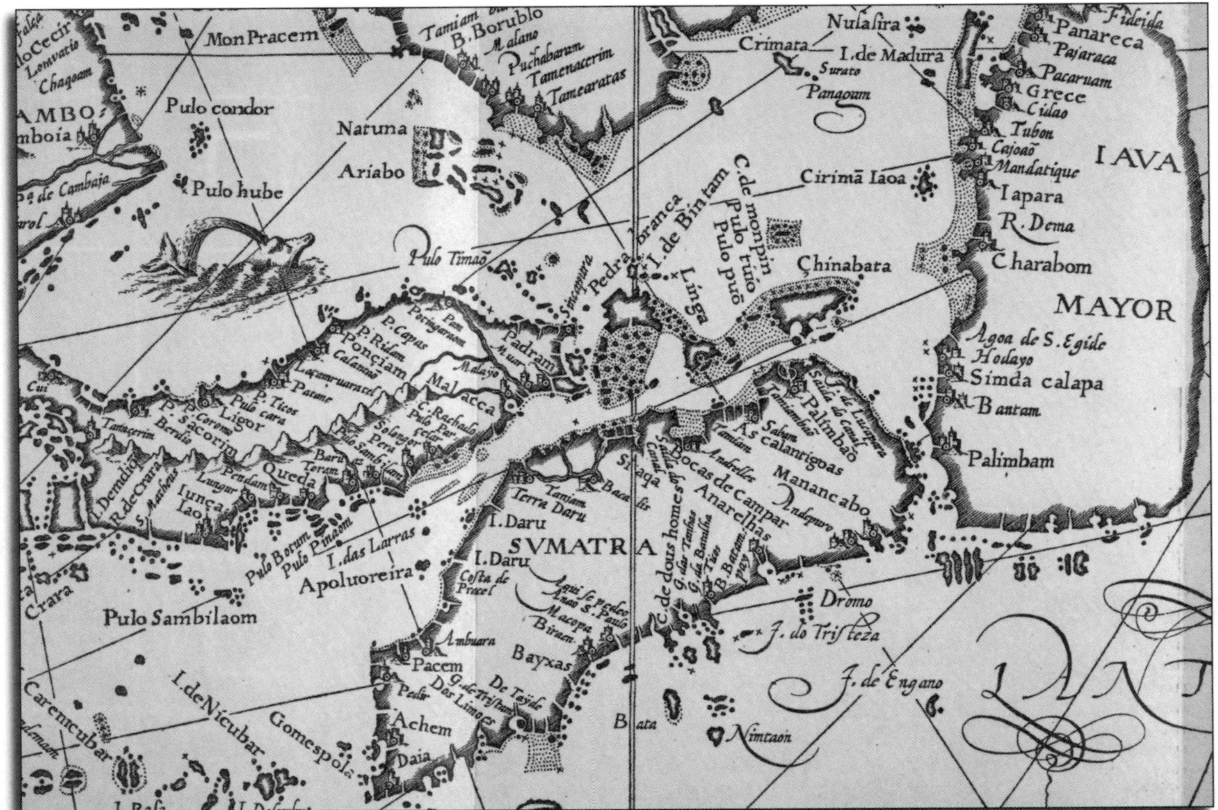

Partial view of a printed map by Cornelis Claesz dating from 1595. The Riau Archipelago is depicted as a fantastic agglomeration of islands surrounded by shallow or impenetrable waters. The Muar and Pahang Rivers form a connecting channel across the Malay Peninsula, while the name “Singapura” appears to refer to a town on the mainland. (Amsterdam University Library, OK 139)

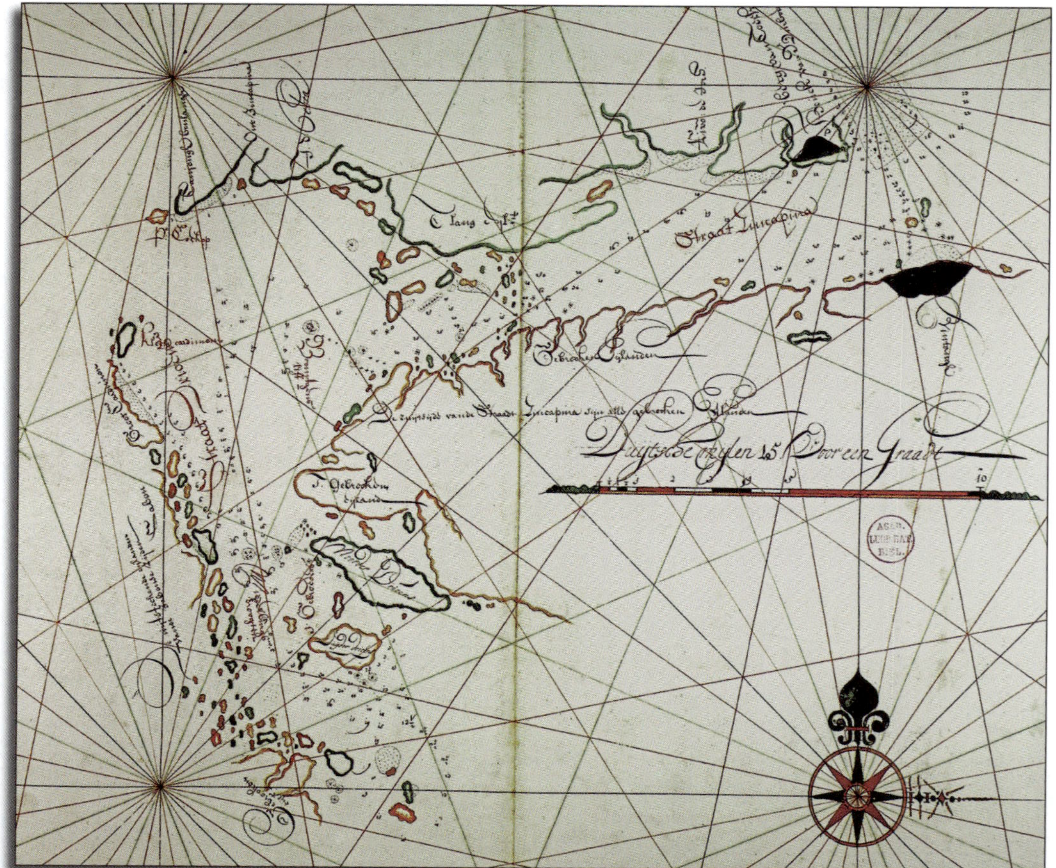

Hand coloured, drawn map of the Singapore Straits copied in the late 18th century, but probably based on an older unknown specimen dating from the 17th century. Singapore bears the name *'t Lang Eylant* that is Long Island or Pulau Panjang. Pulau Ubin is clearly visible in yellow, as are Johor Hill (Berbukit) and Gunung Bintang marked as visible features in black ink. To the south, across what is now Bulan and Batam islands, the entry reads "De zuidzijdt vande Straat Sincapura zijn alle gebrooken Eilanden" that is "On the southern side of the Singapore Straits are all broken islands". This means there are many islands that do not form a single land mass. (Leiden University Library, Collectie Bodel Nijenhuis, 006-15-021)

the Singapore Straits are all broken [or fragmented] islands) (see p. 24).[13] Similar statements are repeated across the same chart. It would appear that the geography of the islands to the south of the Singapore Straits — especially present-day Batam and Bulan — remained sparsely known and therefore improperly charted well into the 18th century. On the famous map of the southern Malay Peninsula penned by the royal French cartographer Jacques Nicolas Bellin (1755), there are two entries to this effect: "Il y a ici un grand nombre de petites isles dont la situation n'est pas connue" [Here are a large number of small islands of which the situation is not known], and the explanatory entry "Toutes les îles paroissent faire une grande terre" (All these islands appear to form a large landmass).[14]

European knowledge of the Riau Archipelago's topography and geomorphology deepened in the period around 1630 to 1650. There appear several pertinent reasons for this. The first relates to a series of crippling naval blockades imposed by the VOC on ports of the *Estado da Índia* that reached an apex in the 1630s, about a decade before the fall of Melaka to the Dutch (1641). As will be shown in greater detail below, the blockades forced Lusitanian traders to search for alternative routes as a result of which they could evade seizure of ship and cargo by Dutch squadrons. This is discussed in greater detail in the final chapter of this book. The VOC's economic stranglehold on Portuguese Melaka drove the city's merchants into closer cooperation with Malay and *orang laut* chieftains. These closer ties resulted in 1631 in the opening up of a new maritime passage that cut right across the Riau Archipelago and brought Portuguese merchant ships around the southern shores of Batam, Galang, Rempang and Bintan islands. This new southern route soon found entry in charts as the *Derrota de Conceição de Nossa Senhora* (Route of the Conception of Our Lady).

How Many Straits of Singapore?

Before Sir Thomas Stamford Raffles founded his emporium on Singapore island in 1819, a captain sailing between the Strait of Melaka and the South China Sea still had several choices. He could opt for one of the Singapore Straits, the route around Batam, Galang and Bintan, as well as a passage that led him even farther southwards around Singkep and Lingga. Which one he would select for his onward passage depended on a number of factors: the direction, strength and reliability of the winds; the tides;

and, of course, socio-political conditions. Certain passages were prone to attacks by pirates and potential harassment by Malay princes, their subjects or naval squadrons of the European colonial powers.

By far the shortest (but not necessarily most convenient) passage from the Strait of Melaka to the South China Sea led through the Singapore Straits. There were a total of four basic routes to choose from, but before 1580 only one of these was viable or known to European (and evidently even most Asian) sailors or pilots. When Raffles founded the modern emporium, only three of the original four were still remembered, and these only in historically garbled form. The four routes were: the Old Strait of Singapore, known as the *Canal de Varela* in Portuguese and Spanish sources;[15] the New Strait of Singapore, which also became known as the Canal de Santa Barbara; the Tebrau Strait, also known as the Strait of Johor; and finally the Phillip's Channel, known before the 1800s as the Governor's Strait, Estrecho de Gobernador, Estreito de Governador, Détroit du Gouverneur or, far less frequently, the Strait of John de Silva.

The first passage, the *Canal de Varela* or Old Strait, was plied by Asian mercantile ships long before the arrival of the European colonists in the 1500s. Its ancient use in the long-distance intra-Asian trade is supposedly confirmed by Chinese sources, where its western entrance is thought to have known as the Longya-men or Dragon Teeth Gate.[16] This statement leads us to two new problems: Where were the Old and New Straits of Singapore?

Where Exactly was the Old Strait of Singapore?

Some maritime historians in the 1800s and well into more recent times identified the Old Strait with the present-day Tebrau Strait, which hugs the northern shores of Singapore island and now forms the border between the city republic and the Malaysian state of Johor. Their insights have probably been based on a series of naval charts and written logs that date chiefly from the 1700s and early 1800s. Indeed, there is ample cartographical evidence from Dutch, French and even English sources that confirms this view. Unfortunately, this finding is not accurate. After W.D. Barnes in 1911, Carl Alexander Gibson-Hill published two seminal studies on the history of the Singapore Straits in which he adduces a broad range of documentary evidence to prove that the Old Strait did not run along the northern shores of Singapore island, as opined by many an authority, including the celebrated James Horsburgh, but rather between what is now

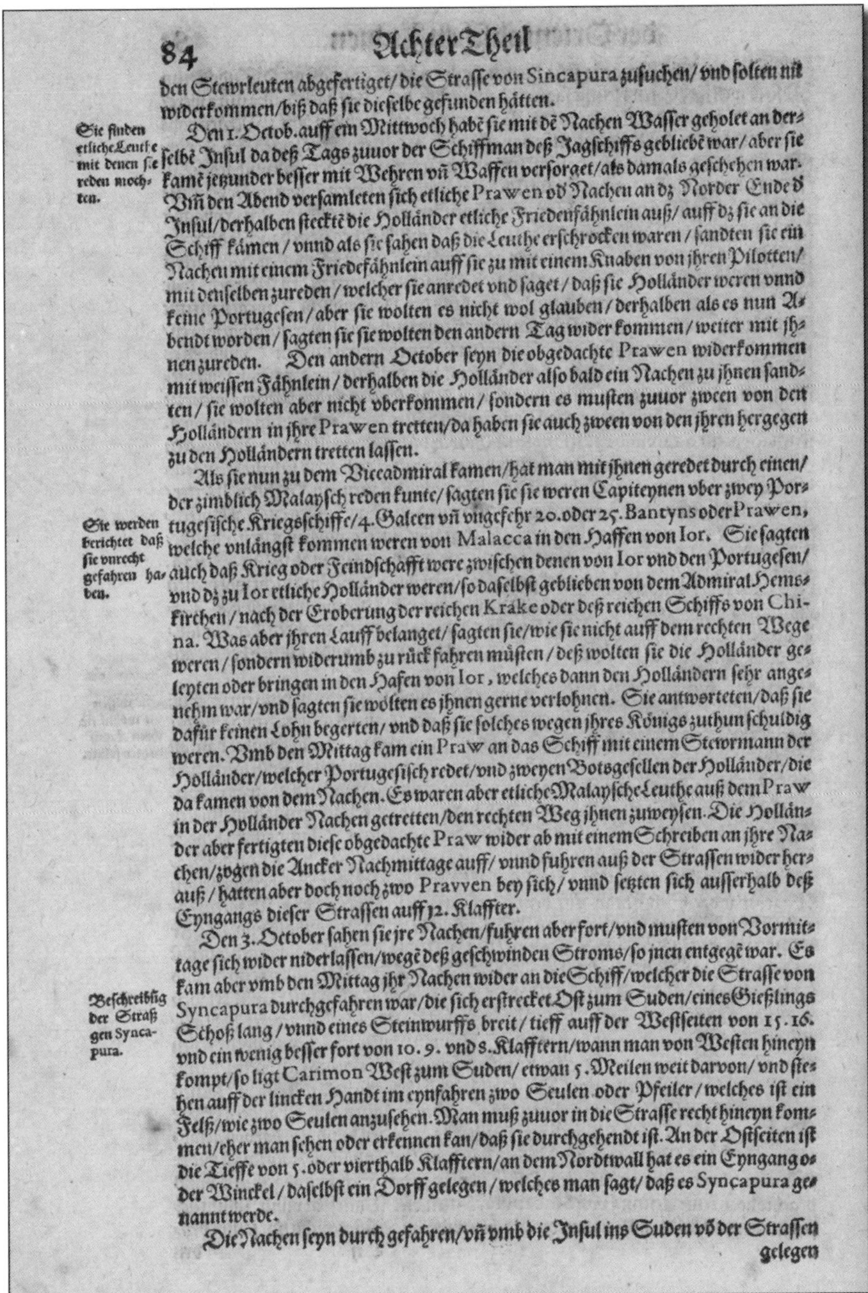
84 Achter Theil

den Stewrleuten abgefertiget/ die Strasse von Sincapura zusuchen/ vnd solten nit widerkommen/biß daß sie dieselbe gefunden hätten.

Sie finden etliche Leuthe mit denen sie reden mochten.

Den 1. Octob. auff ein Mittwoch habē sie mit dē Nachen Wasser geholet an derselbē Insul da deß Tags zuuor der Schiffman deß Jagschiffs gebliebē war/ aber sie kamē jetzunder besser mit Wehren vñ Waffen versorget/als damals geschehen war. Vñ den Abend versamleten sich etliche Prawen od' Nachen an dz Norder Ende d' Insul/derhalben steckte die Holländer etliche Friedenfähnlein auß/ auff dz sie an die Schiff kämen / vnnd als sie sahen daß die Leuthe erschrocken waren / sandten sie ein Nachen mit einem Friedefähnlein auff sie zu mit einem Knaben von jhren Pilotten/ mit denselben zureden / welcher sie anredet vnd saget / daß sie Holländer weren vnnd keine Portugesen / aber sie wolten es nicht wol glauben / derhalben als es nun Abendt worden / sagten sie sie wolten den andern Tag wider kommen / weiter mit jhnen zureden. Den andern October seyn die obgedachte Prawen widerkommen mit weissen Fähnlein / derhalben die Holländer also bald ein Nachen zu jhnen sandten / sie wolten aber nicht vberkommen / sondern es musten zuuor zween von den Holländern in jhre Prawen tretten/da haben sie auch zween von den jhren hergegen zu den Holländern tretten lassen.

Sie werden berichtet daß sie vnrecht gefahren haben.

Als sie nun zu dem Viceadmiral kamen/hat man mit jhnen geredet durch einen/ der zimblich Malaysch reden kunte/ sagten sie sie weren Capiteynen vber zwey Portugesische Kriegsschiffe/4. Galeen vñ vngefehr 20. oder 25. Bantyns oder Prawen, welche vnlängst kommen weren von Malacca in den Haffen von Ior. Sie sagten auch daß Krieg oder Feindschafft were zwischen denen von Ior vnd den Portugesen/ vnd dz zu Ior etliche Holländer weren/so daselbst geblieben von dem Admiral Hemskirchen / nach der Eroberung der reichen Krake oder deß reichen Schiffs von China. Was aber jhren Lauff belanget/ sagten sie/wie sie nicht auff dem rechten Wege weren / sondern widerumb zu rück fahren müsten / deß wolten sie die Holländer geleyten oder bringen in den Hafen von Ior , welches dann den Holländern sehr angenehm war/vnd sagten sie wölten es jhnen gerne verlohnen. Sie antworteten/daß sie dafür keinen Lohn begerten/ vnd daß sie solches wegen jhres Königs zuthun schuldig weren. Vmb den Mittag kam ein Praw an das Schiff mit einem Stewrmann der Holländer/welcher Portugesisch redet/vnd zweyen Botsgesellen der Holländer/die da kamen von dem Nachen. Es waren aber etliche Malaysche Leuthe auß dem Praw in der Holländer Nachen getretten/den rechten Weg jhnen zuweysen. Die Holländer aber fertigten diese obgedachte Praw wider ab mit einem Schreiben an jhre Nachen/zogen die Ancker Nachmittage auff/ vnnd fuhren auß der Strassen wider herauß / hatten aber doch noch zwo Pravven bey sich/ vnnd setzten sich ausserhalb deß Eyngangs dieser Strassen auff 32. Klaffter.

Beschreibūg der Straß gen Syncapura.

Den 3. October sahen sie jre Nachen/fuhren aber fort/vnd musten von Vormittage sich wider niderlassen/wegē deß geschwinden Stroms/so jnen entgegē war. Es kam aber vmb den Mittag jhr Nachen wider an die Schiff/welcher die Strasse von Syncapura durchgefahren war/die sich erstrecket Ost zum Suden/eines Gießlings Schoß lang / vnnd eines Steinwurffs breit / tieff auff der Westseiten von 15. 16. vnd ein wenig besser fort von 10. 9. vnd 8. Klafftern/wann man von Westen hineyn kompt/so ligt Carimon West zum Suden/ etwan 5. Meilen weit darvon/ vnd stehen auff der lincken Handt im eynfahren zwo Seulen oder Pfeiler / welches ist ein Felß/wie zwo Seulen anzusehen. Man muß zuuor in die Strasse recht hineyn kommen/eher man sehen oder erkennen kan/daß sie durchgehendt ist. An der Ostseiten ist die Tieffe von 5. oder vierthalb Klafftern/an dem Nordtwall hat es ein Eyngang oder Winckel / daselbst ein Dorff gelegen / welches man sagt/ daß es Syncapura genannt werde.

Die Nachen seyn durch gefahren/vñ vmb die Insul ins Suden vō der Strassen gelegen

Page 84 of the *Achter Theil der Orientalischen Indien* describing in German how the ships of Jakob Pietersz van Enkhuysen were searching for the western entrance to the Old Strait of Singapore. The passage through the Old Strait is featured at the bottom of the page. (Amsterdam University Library, OTM OF 82-5-7)

Drawing by Jackson (1823) of the Singapore "Varella" which was known to mariners by a variety of names, including Lot's Wife, Sail Rock, Batu Berlayer, Batu Blair, and possibly Long-ya-men. Once located in present-day Labrador Park this rock formation marked the Western entrance to the Old Strait of Singapore. It was Singapore island's most recognized feature. (© The British Library Board, WD 2972)

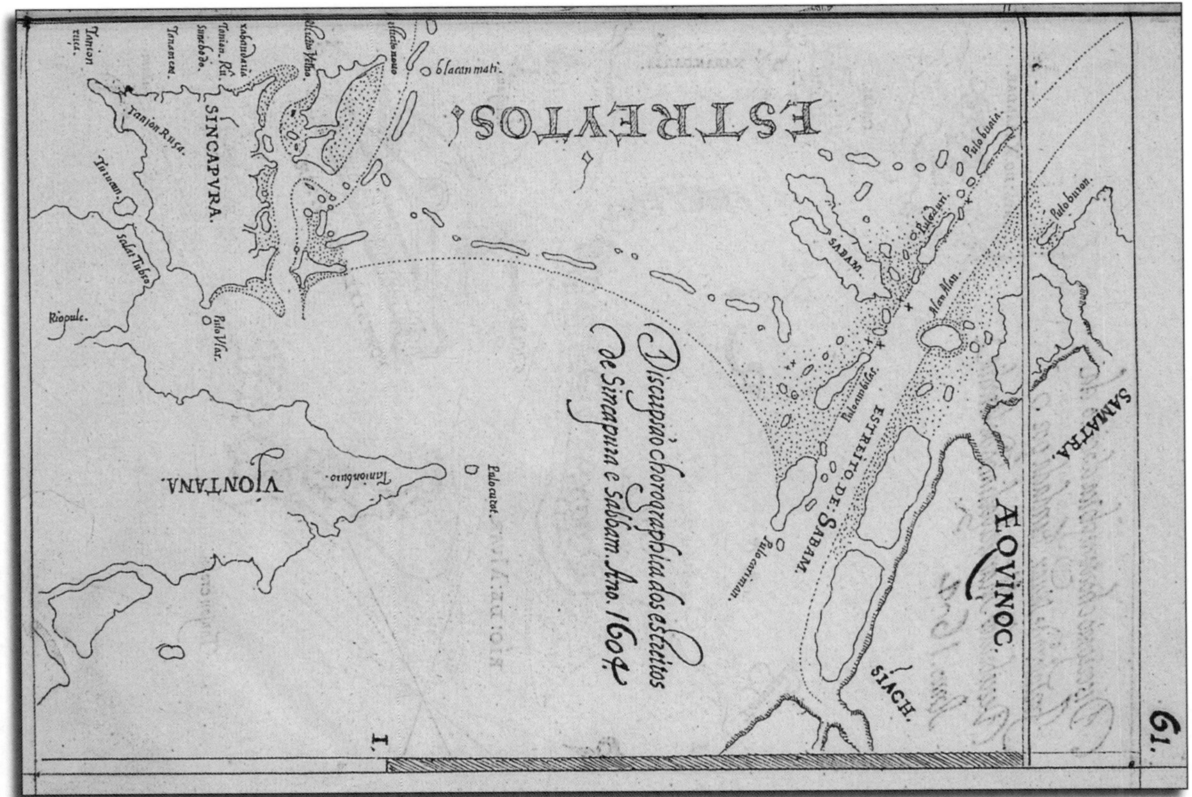

A map by Manoel Godinho de Erédia dated 1604 and featured in his manuscript *Declaraçam de Malaca* (c.1613) featuring the Straits of Singapore and Sabam (Kundur), as well as Singapore Island and part of the Malay Peninsula in southerly perspective. The New and the Old Straits of Singapore are clearly marked, as are some other features and names relating to Singapore Island, such as the "xabandaría" (shahbandar's compound). (Bibliothèque Royale de Belgique, Brussels, Ms. 7264).

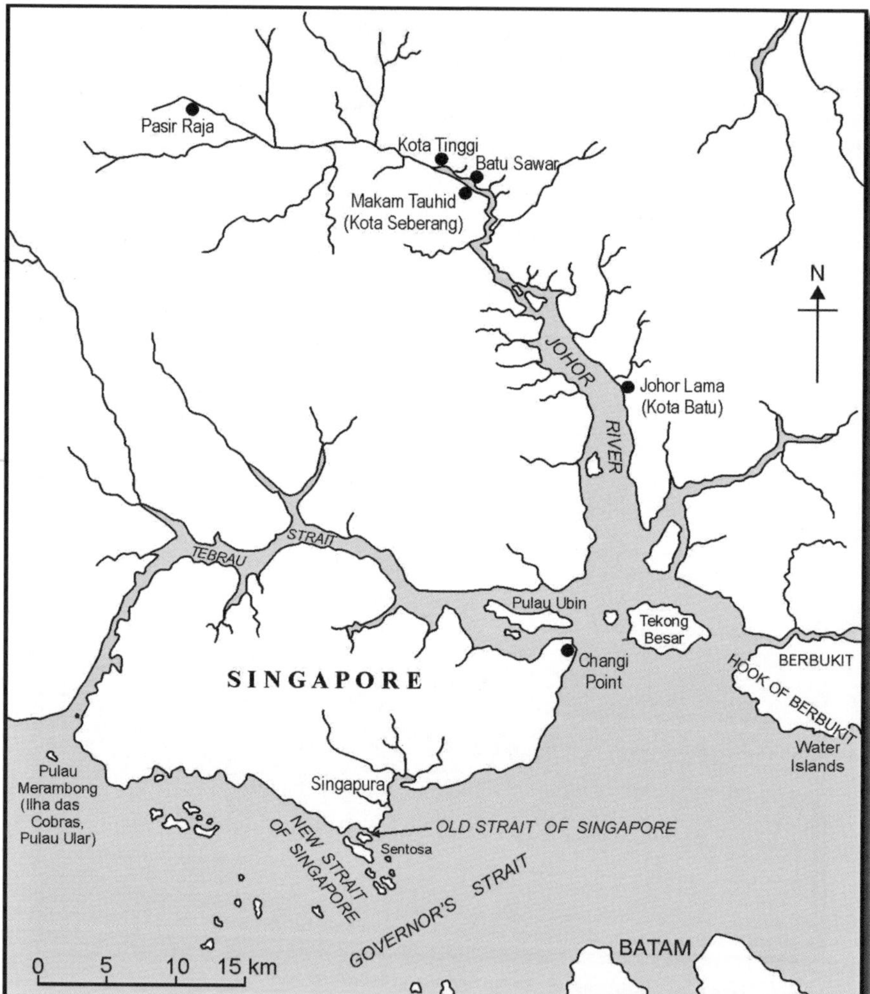

Map of the different Singapore Straits, Singapore island, the Johor River, and its historic upstream towns.

Sentosa and Telok Blangah.[17] What Col. William Farquhar identified as a natural and protected point of anchorage — which was later developed into Keppel Harbour — was treated in earlier centuries by Chinese, Portuguese and Dutch mariners as a maritime channel, passage or strait. The western entrance of the Old Strait was marked by a pillar-shaped rock formation in what is now Labrador Park. This feature is known throughout history by a variety of names: the Dragon Teeth Gate in anglicised Chinese; Batu Berlayar (or its corruption Batu Blair) in Malay; the Varella or Varela in Portuguese, Spanish and Italian; as well as Lot's Wife, Rock Bluff or Sail Rock in English.

On one of the maps contained in his *Declaraçam de Malaca*, which bears the date 1604, Erédia marks the entrances to two passages and names them the "Entrance to the Old" and "Entrance to the New" Strait of Singapore.[18] Portuguese ships of the late 16th and early 17th centuries plied one of these two straits, which took different routes around the present-day island of Sentosa.

According to Jan Huyghen van Linschoten's *Itinerario*, published towards the close of the 16th century,[19] ships arriving from Melaka took a sharp turn portside off the northeastern coast of Karimun Kecil, plied the shallow waters in an easterly direction towards the Sembilan Islands (now Jurong Island), then entered the channel (Sembilan Straits, Jurong Fairway) between this cluster of islets and the main island of Singapore.[20] After skirting Singapore's western shores along Pasir Panjang (sometimes called "lange strand" or "long beach" in Dutch travel literature), ships would arrive at the aforementioned pillar-shaped rock formation.[21] Near Lot's Wife and the northwestern tip of Sentosa, the Old and the New Straits forked and ran their separate courses. While the Old Strait followed the northeastern coast of modern Sentosa, the New Strait skirted the southwestern coast until crossing through the Buran Channel.[22] The New and Old Straits merged again off the southeastern tip of present-day Sentosa (around Sentosa Cove), and ships continued their onward journey to the South China Sea along the eastern shores of Singapore island and the southeastern tip of Johor.

While the Old Strait was already known to Chinese mariners long before the arrival of the Portuguese around 1511, the New Strait was reportedly "discovered" in the 1580s. It opened up as a result of heightened political tensions between Portuguese Melaka and Johor.[23] The Portuguese chronicler João de Barros explains the "discovery"[24] of the New Strait in the following words:[25]

> … And seeing that the Strait [the Old Strait of Singapore or Varella channel] was completely impeded by the junks which had been sunk there, he [the Portuguese captain Dom Manoel de Almeida] ordered bantins to investigate the islands and to see if they could find another channel through which might pass the vessels he was expecting from China and the Moluccas. … [A]nd passing to the south of that island, they found another channel which had not been used. Entering it, they went on, slowly sounding and noting it and found 7, 8 and 9 fathoms there, it being no longer than a camelete shot and at its largest 100 fathoms wide, while at the entrance and in the middle it was not more than 14 fathoms wide. They decided that the vessels would very easily pass through it, and gave it the name the Channel of Santa Barbara.[26]

The overwhelming majority of sources touching on the Old and New Straits of Singapore emphasise how treacherous they are, and warn not only of the strong currents resulting from tidal changes, but also of the many unseen dangers lurking beneath the water. These dangers appear to the eye only at a low spring tide. A set of navigational instructions of Portuguese origin, printed as an appendix to J.C.M. Warnsinck's modern Dutch-language edition of Linschoten's *Reysgeschrift*, features the classic instructions and caveats for plying the waters of western Singapore and the Old Strait. In English, the full set of instructions is available only in a garbled early modern rendition that cannot be considered a translation proper. The following furnishes the reader with a full modern English translation, with the 16th-century Dutch text featured in appendix 3:[27]

> The mouth, or entrance, of this Strait lies between two high hills about one stone's throw in breadth, and extends towards the east with the length of about one shot of a 12-pounder. The channel of this strait measures at the time of the lowest tide about 4.5 *vadem* [7.6 metres] in depth.[28] Next to the entrance, at the foot of the mountain on the northern side, is a stone cliff which in its appearance resembles a pillar. This is generally named by all nations who sail this passage the Varella of the Chinese; and from the southern side, which is a bit inward from the entrance of the strait, the [channel] forms an inlet. In the middle of this inlet there is a submerged cliff that has a bank running off it towards the middle of the channel. A bit farther ahead, on the same side, [about] the length of a pipe shot, there is an opening that runs into the sea and extends over to the other side, [thus] creating an island. This opening is full of shallow waters, and [it] can only be used by small foists. In the middle of the bay where this stands, there is a rock or stone plate, submerged under two *vadem* [about 3.4 metres] of water. This stone

ITINERARIO,
Voyage ofte Schipvaert / van Jan Huygen van Linschoten naer Oost ofte Portugaels Indien inhoudende een corte beschryvinghe der selver Landen ende Zee-custen/ met aenwysinge van alle de voornaemde principale Havens/ Revieren/ hoecken ende plaetsen/ tot noch toe vande Portugesen ontdecht ende bekent: Waer by ghevoecht zijn / niet alleen die Conterfeytsels vande habyten/ drachten ende wesen/ so vande Portugesen aldaer residerende/ als vande ingeboornen Indianen/ ende huere Tempels/ Afgoden/ Huysinge/ met die voornaemste Boomen/ Vruchten/ kruyden/ Speceryen/ ende diergelijcke materialen/ als ooc die manieren des selfden Volckes/ so in hunnen Godts-diensten/ als in Politie en Huijs-houdinghe: maer ooc een corte verhalinge van de Coophandelingen/ hoe en waer die ghedreven en ghevonden worden/ met die ghedenckweerdichste geschiedenissen/ voorghevallen den tijt zijnder residentie aldaer.

Alles beschreven ende by een vergadert, door den selfden, seer nut, oorbaer, ende oock vermakelijcken voor alle curieuse ende Liefhebbers van vreemdigheden.

t'AMSTELREDAM.
By Cornelis Claesz. op't VVater, in't Schrijf-boeck, by de oude Brugghe.
Anno CIↃ. IↃ. XCVI.

Hand coloured title page from J.H. van Linschoten's first edition of the *Itinerario,* 1596. (Koninklijke Bibliotheek, The Hague, 1702 B 4)

Hand coloured printed portrait of Jan Huyghen van Linschoten featured in the first edition of his *Itinerario* of 1596. (Koninklijke Bibliotheek, The Hague, 1702 B 4).

plate extends as far into the bay as the land extends into the water, and somewhat more, reaching into the middle of the channel. After passing this inlet, the land forms a promontory or a point [featuring] a steep, broken-off hill, where the channel [also] ends. After sailing around this, one reaches a red hill, where one finds deep and clean ground; and when one has passed this, the land then extends farther in a southeasterly direction.

On the shore to the north of this strait — to wit, from the beginning to the end — there are three inlets, of which the first two are small and the third large. The third inlet is situated to the right, opposite the [aforementioned] promontory or point [with] the red hill, where the strait ends. This third inlet features a stone bank, which is exposed with a spring tide at low water, and [it] extends from the one point to the other. One has to be careful not to run into it. All of this is located on the northern side, the bank being outside the bay, across the entire channel from one point to the other, clean and nice.

Towards the exit of the strait, after having passed this [bay], there are two reefs, the first situated directly opposite the exit of the strait, one shot of a *lepel*[29] to the east. This [first reef] extends from the land on the north [side] and extends towards the south. The other [reef] is situated [on] the south [side], about one shot of a 12-pounder[30] away from the shore; from the strait, [it extends out] towards the east. Together, the two pass through each other like a cross. Between the two reefs there is the channel, and the two reefs can be seen exposed at the low water of a spring tide. This channel that runs between the two [reefs] barely measures 4 *vadem* [6.8 metres] in depth; the ground within the channel is muddy, and outside the channel it is sandy. I wanted to explain this all in detail for the service and convenience of those who henceforth desire to pass through [the strait], for older descriptions of the route, or navigational [instructions] prepared for it, are very short and not easily understood by those who have never [before] passed through. For this reason many ships have run aground, or scraped the hull and experienced great danger, indeed, even lost [both ship and cargo].

A far shorter account that also touches on the dangers, twists and turns of the west coast and Old Straits derives from the travel account of the early 17th-century traveller Pedro Teixeira. The relevant passage from the original Spanish text edition translates as follows:[31]

And coasting the continent, and passing by the rivers therein named Muar and Polé,[32] we came to the Strait of Sincapurá, between that and the isles[33] which form the other of Sabam [that is Kundur].[34] This is

> of the figure of a [numeral] 5, and for half a league so narrow that the ships, bound either for India or China, cannot tack therein. Therefore they anchor at either entrance, awaiting a good tide, with which, and a boat sent ahead to help the helm, to pass the strait. It happens often that they must wait for three, four or five days; for so long, more or less, the tide runs ever one way, a thing surely worth wonder.[35]

Teixeira's illustrative comparison of the maritime route to the shape of the Arabic numeral "5" greatly assists the reader in appreciating the sharp twists and turns that the passage entailed, as well as the sandbanks, shoals and reefs that had to be avoided in this treacherous navigational obstacle course.

Teixeira is naturally not alone in attesting to the narrowness of this vital maritime passage. His contemporary, the Florentine merchant-adventurer Francesco Carletti, claims that tree branches brushed against the mast and sails as his Portuguese carrack passed through the Old Strait en route to Melaka and Goa at the eve of the 17th century.[36] Similar statements are encountered in the writings of Giovanni Botero, Barreto de Resende, Fernão Lopes de Castanheda and António Bocarro as well as Spanish-language materials of the Flemish diamond merchant Jaques de Coutre.[37] The latter claims that the islands between the Karimuns and around the Straits of Singapore were heavily grown in by large, sprawling trees.[38] Ships passing through the Old Strait, as de Coutre and other sources underscore, had to be especially careful, not least on account of the strong currents.[39] But the branches of sprawling trees that could rip sails to shreds or break off masts were only part of the danger. Running aground was common, even with veteran and highly experienced pilots aboard. Carletti, again, laments that his Portuguese carrack ran aground while traversing the Old Strait, but he sighs with evident relief that, fortunately, none of his merchandise on board was damaged.[40]

In the late 16th century and the first decade of the 17th, present-day Sentosa was positioned between two key maritime shipping lanes. This strategic location of the island finds mention in the writings of the Fleming de Coutre. In one of the memorials written for and addressed to the king of Spain and Portugal,[41] he intimates that the islet is eminently suited for a fort or citadel.[42] From this particular location, he further observes, one can ideally monitor and control the flow of maritime traffic through the Old and New Straits and, if need be, as de Coutre highlights elsewhere, the Old Strait is sufficiently narrow that one can block it off by spanning a chain across.[43]

The Governor's Strait

The main fairway of the modern Singapore Straits finds entry on early modern maps and hydrographic charts as the Governor's Strait, Estreito do Gobernador, Estrecho de Gobernador, Straat Gouverneur, Détroit du Gouverneur and, far more infrequently, as the Strait of John de Silva.[44] Its first recorded use by Europeans is credited to the armada of the Spanish-Philippine Governor Juan de Silva in early 1616. The arrival of the Spanish armada in the Singapore Straits will be discussed in greater detail in Chapter 4. On this occasion, de Silva's flagship *La Salvadora* ran aground, and judging from Spanish, Portuguese as well as Dutch source material, the "discovery" of the Governor's Strait may very well have been a fortuitous accident.[45]

Whatever the case may have been, ships arriving from the west found the entrance to the Governor's Strait by spotting a "round islet with trees growing on it".[46] This islet, which is most probably Round Island found on early 19th century maps, is featured on 17th and 18th century hydrographic charts as a key navigational landmark. One Dutch map calls it *Boompjes Eiland* (Little Trees Island), while the 1795 manuscript chart of Andreas Everardus van Braam van Houckgeest preserved at Leiden University calls it *Zaandplaat met de Boomen* (Sand bank with the trees) (see p. 37).[47] When approaching this islet from the north, ships turned portside and plied a course east-southeast. A chain of sandbanks and rocks is clearly depicted as reaching down to the northern coast of Bulan, indicating to captains that they needed to be careful not to veer too far starboard.

The second principal navigational landmark of the Governor's Strait is represented by a rock formation off the northern coast of Bulan. Van Braam van Houckgeest explains that it "protrudes only at low tide" (*by laag water alleen bloot*). The submerged rocks mark the southernmost point of the Governor's Strait. Between this location and Rabbit and Coney, ships altered their course from east-southeast to east-northeast, passing Buffalo Rock (*Buffel Rots* on Dutch maps) to the right and an elongated shoal or sandbank (in the area where Pulau Semkau and Pulau Sakeng are located), the *Eiland St. Jan* (St. John's Island) as well as the *Twee Gebroeders* (Two Brothers, Sister Islands) to the left.

From this location, ships could further plot one of two basic courses in their onward journey to the South China Sea. One route hugged the southeastern shores of the Malay Peninsula and continued along the peninsular coast to Romania Point (*Ponta da Romania*).[48] The second option brought maritime traffic along the northern coast of Batam, passing

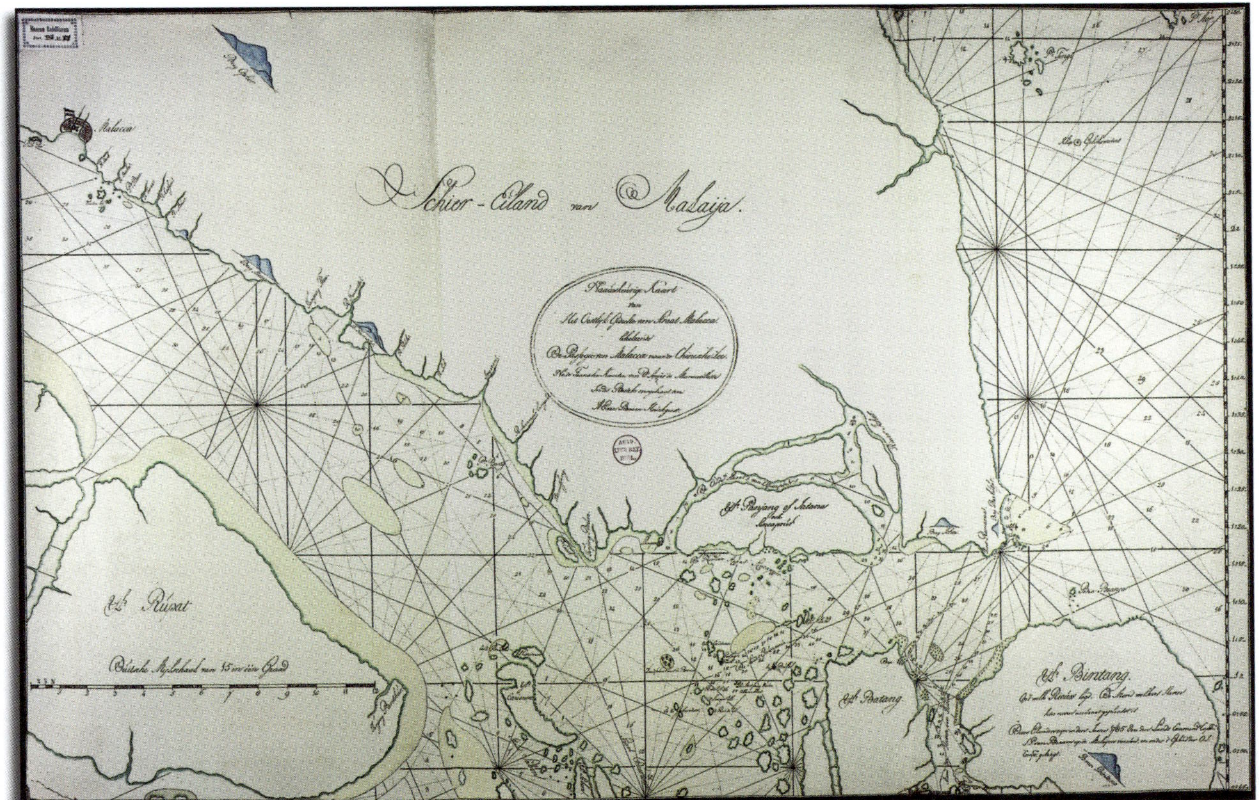

Hand drawn and coloured map of the Southern portion of the Malay Peninsula with the Melaka and Singapore Straits by A.E. van Braam van Houckgeest, c. 1790 (Leiden University Library, Collectie Bodel Nijenhuis, 006-14-015).

what are marked on charts as *klippen boven water* (rocks [protruding] above water), the two landmark Nongsa Islets, the entrance to the Riau Strait, and the northern coast of Bintan, all at starboard. Most charts mark the waters between Pedra Branca and northern Bintan as a danger zone, and captains are exhorted on hydrographic charts as well as in written navigational instructions to sail past the great white rock at their starboard. Van Linschoten offers the classic warning to passing mariners. This can be found in Chapter 20, titled "The Navigation and Correct Courses from Malaca to Macao in China":[49]

> From these small islands [being the two small islands off present-day Nongsa Point at the northeastern tip of Batam] approximately two [Dutch] sea miles [about 15 kilometers] in a south-southeasterly direction is situated Pedra Branca (which means the "White Rock"), which is an islet featuring white protruding rocks and boulders. Located nearby there are also other sharp rocks and boulders that are situated to the side of the island of Bintan. … Around Pedra Branca and close by the water measures six *vadem* deep [or about 11.3 meters] on clean ground. But you also have to watch out for the protruding rocks and boulders that are situated close by.[50] … You should hold course for Pedra Branca (or the "White Rock"). … And should you not make it past the reefs, you will then be forced to sail through the channel that runs between Pedra Branca and the Island [of Bintan].

The Tebrau or Johor Strait

In addition to the passages running to the south of Singapore island, there is also the Tebrau Strait (sometimes corrupted as Salatburo, Salat Tubro or Salleta de Brew), which skirts the northern coastline.[51] One deeply entrenched school of thought, which finds one of its chief English-language advocates in James Horsburgh, holds that this northerly route was known in Portuguese and early Dutch colonial times as the Old Strait of Singapore.[52] A number of late 17th- and predominantly 18th-century sources appear to lend support to this view, including specifically maps and hydrographic charts. Source material not consulted by either Barnes or Gibson-Hill includes Portuguese charts published in Cortesão and Teixeira de Mota's *Portugaliae Monumenta Cartographica*; naval charts of VOC origin in the Collectie Bodel Nijenhuis in the Leiden University Library; the Dr. W.A. Engelbrecht Collection now owned by the Maritiem Museum Prins Hendrik in Rotterdam; the map collection at the University of Amsterdam;

the National Archives in The Hague; key public and private collections in the United States; as well as all collections that after World War II became virtually inaccessible behind the Iron Curtain, including, importantly, the collection held by the Staatsbibliothek Berlin (Preussischer Kulturbesitz).

In his seminal study published in 1954 and expanded in 1956, Gibson-Hill authoritatively and conclusively dismisses the entrenched association of the present-day Tebrau Strait with the Old Strait of Singapore as an error of history.[53] Still, the view that the Old Strait ran along the northern coast of Singapore island finds its adherents in more recent times.[54]

If the Tebrau Strait is not, as was falsely assumed for centuries, the Old Strait of Singapore, could the confusion still bear indication of its significance in early modern times? What evidence might be adduced to explain its use by European — specifically Portuguese — shipping in the early modern period?

In his learned article published in the Dutch-language *Bijdragen tot de Taal-, Land en Volkenkunde van Nederlandsch-Indië*, Gerrit Pietersz Rouffaer readily acknowledges that the Tebrau Strait was familiar to Asian sailors since ancient times,[55] but he expresses serious doubts over whether its waters were ever plied by Portuguese craft even during the late 16th century.[56] Nevertheless, Rouffaer produces evidence to suggest that Portuguese craft began to ply the Tebrau Strait around or shortly after 1603.[57]

Dutch sources not listed or consulted by Rouffaer can also be adduced to corroborate this view. Additional evidence derives from the journal of the *Griffioen*, a cutter belonging to the expedition of Pieter Willemszoon Verhoeff that arrived in Johor waters in early 1609. Records and logs pertaining to the expedition were published by the van Linschoten Society (*van Linschoten Vereeniging*) in a critical edition prepared by van Opstall in the 1970s. It transpires from these as well as other unpublished sources that the Portuguese responded in anger and frustration to the budding Johor-Dutch alliance by imposing blockades on the Johor River.[58] In order to keep an eye open for suspicious movements of the Portuguese armada, Verhoeff ordered two ships to hold guard in the Johor River estuary, one of them being the cutter *Griffioen*. Its crew positioned the ship roughly at 1 degree, 24 seconds northern latitude, which would place it in the Johor River approximately at the latitude of present-day Pulau Ubin.[59] This location on the van Braam van Houckgeest chart (see p. 37) features as a point of safe anchorage, undoubtedly marking the eastern entrance to the Tebrau

Strait. From this point of anchorage, importantly, the crew of the *Griffioen* could monitor the movements of vessels and also foil any surprise attack that the Melaka-based Portuguese naval squadron, or even pirates, might launch on them or the settlements along the navigable reaches of the Johor River.[60]

While prominently featured since the late 17th century as the Old Strait of Singapore, the Tebrau Strait is clearly less prominent on earlier maps — if it is even charted. Erédia, who is widely believed to have possessed first-hand experience of the region, marks the Strait as a maritime channel proper. Evidence suggests, however, that the Dutch had only minimal knowledge of the Tebrau or Johor Strait. De Bry's sketch of Singapura and adjacent waters marks both entrances to the Tebrau Strait as river estuaries,[61] with present-day Pulau Ubin clearly recognisable in the east (see p. 80). Similar observations can be made for charts of Dutch provenance. In a map belonging to the Collectie Bodel Nijenhuis in the Leiden University Library (see p. 24) Singapore island is marked as *'t Lange Eiland* (the Long Island),[62] but the Tebrau Strait is not featured at all. It is tempting to conclude from this evidence that the northern route around Singapore island may or may not have been known to the early European mariners, but it was almost certainly not regularly used.

Which Maritime Route was the Most Important Around 1620–50?

As skippers could choose from several main routes across the archipelago at the middle of the 17th century, it is both useful and informative to ask a few basic questions about their significance and viability.

First, if one were to rank the relative significance of the various routes through the Straits of Singapore and across the Riau Archipelago as well as the Malay Peninsula towards the middle of the 17th century, which should be deemed the most important? Also, on the basis of extant material that includes non-English European sources, is it possible to rank these various maritime passages by their respective significance to early modern European — and long-distance Asian — mercantile shipping?

What this historical account has sought to clarify is that while early Asian navigators of the Song or early Ming period had far fewer options to rely on — such as for example the Old Strait of Singapore, the route around Bintan, Lingga and Singkep, or the overland Pahang-Muar riverine route — the period that followed the fall of Melaka to the Portuguese sees not a reduction, but a proliferation of charted routes across the Riau Archipelago. The discovery, or at least more frequent use, of these new maritime passages was less the outcome of curiosity or adventure than the result of necessity and survival tactics, as will be demonstrated in Chapter 5. The New Strait of Singapore was "discovered" as a result of a Johorean blockade of the Old Strait; the *Canal* or *Derrota de Conceição de Nossa Senhora* (the Channel or Route of the Conception of Our Lady) was "discovered" by the Portuguese as a way of evading a Dutch blockade of principal maritime arteries.[63] According to the sources consulted, the "discovery" of the Governor's Strait in 1616 was simply good fortune.

The relative significance that these routes bore to one another can be partially reconstructed by reference to security concerns of the nascent colonial powers. Portuguese and Spanish plans for a fort on Sentosa were evidently designed to control, or at least monitor, the flow of maritime traffic through the New and the Old Straits of Singapore. De Coutre's suggestion, found in one of his epistolary reports to the king of Portugal and Spain, to build a fort along the east coast of Singapore island was designed to monitor activity in and out of the Johor River estuary and perhaps also the Tebrau Strait. One suspects that nothing became of such infrastructure projects because political and economic attention after 1615 began to shift southwards. In the wakc of Acehnese attacks in 1613 and 1615, the Johor monarch transferred his residence and court from Batu Sawar — in the upper reaches of the Johor River — to the island of Bintan (1615) and later to Lingga (1618). Additional aspects relating to the Acehnese attacks on Johor will be discussed in Chapter 2.

The southward shift of Johor's political and economic life is mirrored by the transfer of permanent Asian operations of the VOC to Batavia in the early 1620s. It was to have important consequences for the flow of maritime traffic in the Indonesian Archipelago as a whole. The VOC's monopoly over trade elevated Batavia to a core trading node, as a result of which maritime routes running north-south, such as the Strait of Sabam and probably also the Riau Strait, were upgraded in their commercial significance within the freshly emerging networks of maritime trade and interaction. By contrast, east-west routes such as the Straits of Singapore and the *Derrota de Conceição de Nossa Senhora* lost out to commercial reorientation. The priority of north-south over east-west maritime trading routes would last until the collapse of the VOC in the late 18th century and the rise of British trade between India and the Far East that followed in the early 19th century.

Hand drawn and coloured map of the Singapore and Melaka Straits, the Malay Peninsula, Eastern Sumatra and the Riau Archipelago by Andé Pereira dos Reis, c.1654. This map is of special interest, because it features names on the island of Singapore, reveals the "discovery" of the *Derrota de Conceição de Nossa Senhora* by Pedro Bertollo in 1633, and plots various maritime passages through the Straits and across the Riau Archipelago. It also features the twin peaks on the island of Lingga. (Maritiem Museum Prins Hendrik, Rotterdam, Collectie Dr. W. E. Engelbrecht, WAE-900-10a)

The southward shift of maritime traffic and economic activity after 1616, particularly after the collapse of Portuguese rule in Melaka after 1641, is also evidenced by the errors found on late 17th-century hydrographic charts. On many of these, the Tebrau Strait is confused with the Old Strait of Singapore. It is possible, if not likely, that the two passages were confused because they were no longer plied by European mariners. This explanation makes perfect sense. One need only recall the sailing instructions of van Linschoten or eyewitness accounts such as Carletti's to appreciate how dangerous the passage through the Old Strait of Singapore really was.

The Puzzle of Shifting Seascapes and Geomorphological Change

The reader may still feel nagged by more questions: If a maritime passage such as the Governor's Strait existed before 1616, why was it not plied by Malay sea-gypsies or *orang laut*, who also sometimes acted as paid pilots and guides to passing Asian and European ships?[64] Why would any captain — Asian or European — sail into the narrow and dangerous Old Strait of Singapore running between Sentosa and Telok Blangah if there was a viable alternative? Was the Governor's Strait there all along, just waiting to be "discovered", or was it indeed not a viable passage before 1616? Could a changing geomorphology or seascape be the reason?

Admittedly, historians, geographers and archaeologists had already raised these important issues in earlier decades. One of the most thought-provoking contributions was published by Victor Obdeijn in the journal of the Royal Netherlands Geographic Society in 1942. Obdeijn's geomorphology thesis represents one particular aspect in his extensive and scholarly enquiries into the rise of the Melaka Sultanate and the factors facilitating its ascent to the status of an international maritime entrepôt. Heavily influenced by ideas and concepts borrowed from Ptolemaic geography as understood in Europe during the age of Renaissance and Humanism, the Dutch scholar contends that the Straits of Singapore are the outcome of tectonically "recent" developments (up to the 14th century), and that the rise of Melaka as an entrepôt is simultaneously linked to the opening up of these important new straits.[65]

Since the publication of this study more than six decades ago, geomorphology theses with or without express reference to Obdeijn have found a mixed response among more contemporary scholars. In his critical introduction to a collection of memorials and documents by Jaques de Coutre titled *Como Remediar o Estado da Índia*? (How to Remedy the Estado da Índia?), the Dutch academic Benjamin Teensma points to a map fragment of Gerrit de Haan (1760) to argue that Pulau Ubin used to be considerably larger.[66] Its reduced size must, therefore, be the result of shifting geomorphology.[67]

A further instance derives from the critical edition of VOC Admiral Verhoeff's voyage to the East Indies. Its editor, van Opstall, explains one particular incident in terms of the changing geomorphology of the Straits. In January 1609 the admiral arrived with his ships and men in the Johor River estuary. His officers were navigating with the assistance of charts that appear to have been seized from a Portuguese vessel attacked and plundered some weeks earlier in the Strait of Melaka. Admiral Verhoeff's officers noted with open astonishment that they sailed without difficulty across areas that were specifically marked as shallow or impassable.[68]

In the course of the present chapter, it has become clear — and the maps of Erédia can be taken as a case in point — that whilst the charting of the Peninsula, and even the Johor River estuary, was quite accurate, the topography of the Riau Archipelago before the middle of the 17th century and even thereafter remained very uncertain. This situation lasted well into the 18th century, as is evidenced, for example, by the 1755 map of the Malay Peninsula and the Singapore and Melaka Straits by the royal French cartographer Jacques Nicolas Bellin.[69] As a rule, hydrographic charts mark the waters along the southern reaches of the Singapore Straits as a confusing and impassable maze of islands and waterways that may very well have appeared and disappeared with the tide. Waters marked impassable on a Portuguese map and mentioned in Verhoeff's log almost certainly represent such uncertain and uncharted waters, and it is thus most unlikely that their disappearance was due to sudden geomorphologic changes as van Opstall surmised.

Emphasis is placed here on the word "unlikely", for it is known that riverine silting, mangrove growth, tidal deposits and erosion, as well as alterations in the growth of coral reefs can significantly affect any given seascape. Research conducted by the historian and archaeologist Miksic concludes that silting and mangrove growth have contributed little to altering the coastline of the Malay Peninsula, which leaves tidal silting and erosion as possible scenarios to explain significant geomorphologic change.[70] More likely, however, the existence of many islands and islets around Singapore, and the frequent reports of abundant marine life in the

Straits, point towards shifting coral reefs as the likely factor underlying meaningful changes in the Singapore seascape. The presence of extensive coral reefs may very well have earlier blocked the waters for maritime passage by large ships. Silting, erosion and especially the growth or contraction of reefs could serve to explain why the Governor's Strait was not used, or could not be used, before 1616. Indeed, as the episode of Vice-Admiral Pietersz van Enkhuysen evidences in Chapter 2, the Governor's Strait was then perhaps unknown, even to local inhabitants.

Cingaporla in 1575: Imagined Cities, Spaces and Waterways

Attention shall now be shifted from the Singapore Straits to the present-day island of Singapore and the region roughly covering the modern Malaysian state of Johor. In order to better appreciate the evolution of strategic thinking, security arrangements and commercial policies by the early European colonial governments and East India Companies, it is important to examine in greater detail a unique feature of late 16th- and early 17th-century European cartography.[71]

The point of departure for the present discussion is a claim made by the French royal geographer André Thevet in his *Cosmographie Universelle* (1575), in the chapter titled "Cingaporla and the Islands Beyond".[72] In this, Thevet refers to "the port of Cingaporla [is] called *Muare,* a city built on the shore".[73] Whilst the former clearly represents a corruption of the name Singapura, how is it possible that Muar was Singapura's principal port?[74]

Most contemporary scholars would shrug off this statement as yet another error of early modern cartographic science and a hopeless expression of confused geographic nomenclature. Muar is, of course, situated in the present-day Malaysian state of Johor up the western coast of the Malay Peninsula from the present-day city republic of Singapore. It is tempting to conclude that Thevet just did not know what he was talking about and that the sources at his fingertips simply rendered garbled topographic information. This section argues why such a line of reasoning would be too simplistic and why a revisitation of such historic materials is thus warranted.

Thevet, a Franciscan monk from France working at the end of his career for the French crown, is not simply rendering muddled information. Thanks to his patronage from the king, Thevet was in a position to reproduce state-of-the-art knowledge of the region's geography, as far as it could have been known. The year of publication pre-dates Linschoten's historically very influential *Reysgeschrift* and *Itinerario* by approximately two decades.[75] As a result of Portuguese policies of secrecy, information on the marketplaces, peoples, produce, geography and hydrography of the region — even of the well-frequented areas around the Singapore and Melaka Straits — was sparse and hardly accessible.[76] What little was known in Western Europe derived chiefly from rutters, or early Portuguese navigational expeditions to the East Indies, rare third-party (sometimes non-European) sources and, of course, from paid informants or materials collated surreptitiously for the kings, princes and merchants across Europe.

A concrete example of how early cartographic information was interchanged and acquired by the early colonial powers is found in a letter by Affonso de Albuquerque dated 1 May 1512,[77] in which he informs King Manuel I of Portugal that he is sending him a "piece of a chart that" was taken from ...[78]

> ... [a] large chart of a Javanese pilot, containing the Cape of Good Hope, Portugal and the land of Brazil, the Red Sea, and Sea of Persia, the Clove Islands, the navigation of the Chinese and the Gores,[79] with their rhumbs and direct routes followed by the ships, and the hinterland, and how the kingdoms border on each other. It seems to me, Sire, that this was the best thing I have ever seen, and that Your Highness would be very pleased to see it; it had the names in Javanese writing, but I had with me a Javanese who could read and write. I send this piece to Your Highness, which Francisco Rodrigues traced from the other,[80] in which your Highness can see where the Chinese and Gores (Taiwanese) come from, and the course your ships must take to the Clove Islands, and where the gold mines lie, and the islands of Java and Banda, of nutmeg and mace, and the land of the King of Siam, and also the end of the navigation of the Chinese, the direction it takes, and how they do not navigate farther. The main chart was lost in *Frol de la Mar*.[81] With the [Javanese] pilot and Pero de Alpoim I discussed the meaning of this chart, in order that they could explain it to Your Highness; you can take this piece of chart as a very accurate and ascertained thing, because it is the very navigation by which they come and go. The archipelago of the islands called *Celate* (Selat),[82] which lie between Java and Melaka, is missing.[83]

The enduring debate over the name Singapura, its etymology, and its many orthographical variants shall be left aside here.[84] As is evidenced,

Thevet claimed that the most important port of Cingaporla was Muar.[85] In the first volume of his *Cosmographie Universelle*, we find this not as a loose, stray utterance, but in the context of a whole chapter dedicated to discussing "The Island of Cingaporla, near Malacca, and of a Few Islands in the Direction of China, etc."[86] The Franciscan geographer explores a range of aspects: the topography and size of the island, its history and political dependence on Siam, and even a 12-foot "giant ferocious fish" living in the waters around Cingaporla.[87]

There are three facets of Thevet's chapter that merit further elaboration in this immediate context. The first concerns his rudimentary awareness of Cingaporla's historic connections with the kingdom of Siam and its position within the regional spice trade:

> The Governor of *Cingaporla* had not only the king of Siam (Sian) as his overlord, but also a *Paraà,* that is a secretary, and a *Concussaà* who was the treasurer, levying taxes and tolls for the king as well as his lord. The island abounds with pepper.[88]

The second — and, for the purpose of this discussion, highly interesting — geographic outline concerns the island of Cingaporla. Thevet notes:

> This island is large, over thirty *lieues* in circumference, beautiful and rich, except near the centre where it is hilly: for which reason the valleys are an abundant source of water for the emerging brooks and small streams.[89]

What the Frenchman had in mind was certainly not today's Singapore island, but the whole southern tip of the Malay Peninsula![90] This conclusion is evidenced when examining the following excerpt from Thevet's chapter:[91]

> To describe the location of *Cingaporla,* and how it is separated from Melaka, and what distance there is between the two, let us look at how Sicily is distant from the country of Calabria, what points and promontories there are, and then we see that the space and distance there is between Sicily and Calabria is quite comparable to the one between Malaca and Cingaporla. ... If we believe the ancients who say that Sicily was formerly connected to Calabria and that it became separated through an earthquake, then we could make a similar statement also for this island and the Kingdom of Malaca, seeing that the two are separated from each other by a small maritime channel that is only two or three *lieues* wide. But I strongly advise you not to enter this channel. And those who leave the port of Cingaporla called *Muare,* a city built on the shore, should enter the open sea, leaving the channel to their

> right,[92] taking the Melaka route which makes the voyage somewhat longer, just like the Strait of Calais is avoided in our sea for fear of the tempests and thunderstorms, and it is preferable to go on the high sea in order to reach a harbour in England....

In this excerpt, which illustrates the third important point in Thevet's chapter — the Pahang-Muar Channel — the Franciscan certainly describes a far larger Cingaporla than one is familiar with today. Thevet's Cingaporla is separated from the mainland by a channel that is two or three *lieues* wide, and Muar is the main port on the island created by this strait or channel. Interestingly, the map of Asia that was inserted at the beginning of Thevet's section on Asia does not match the verbal descriptions contained in the text and this is why it is important to resort to other specimens.[93] To gain a fuller appreciation of what Thevet is describing, it is necessary to examine four widely available depictions of the Malay Peninsula to which Thevet almost certainly could have had access: the 1541 globe of Mercator,[94] the father of the so-called Mercator projection still widely used in cartography today; volume 1 of Giovanni Battista Ramusio's *Navigazioni e Viaggi*, printed in Venice in 1554 (see p. 51);[95] Gastaldi's *Planisphere, Terza parte dell'Asia*, dating from 1561; as well as the 1570 *Theatrum Orbis Terrarum* (atlas) of the Flemish cartographer Abraham Ortelius.[96]

Mercator was consistent in showing a narrow but continuous trans-peninsular waterway on his maps, even if, at a first glance, this hardly appears to be the case. On the 1541 globe the channel reaches from Paam (Pahang, also variously spelt Pam, Pahão or Pão on other maps of the Malay Peninsula) all the way to Melaka, which is, of course, a port city. This is somewhat obscured on the Harvard University specimen by the brown terrestrial colouring that "bleeds" into the adjacent sea.[97] On the 1569 chart the channel is interrupted by the toponym Mubar (Muar), but from the 1598 map of Asia it is clear that Mercator never abandoned the transpeninsular waterway that he first drew in 1541.

Ortelius is equally consistent in showing a wide channel on his 1564 world map, the large 1567 Asia wall map[98] and the 1570 Asia map that was included in the *Theatrum Orbis Terrarum*. The *Theatrum Orbis Terrarum* also contains a chart titled *India Orientalis*, which is based on Mercator's design. On the Asia map, the waterway is interrupted by the letters of two toponyms, Malaca and Mubar (Muar).

Ortelius (1570) places a town by the name of Cingatola (yet another corruption of Singapura) on the western coast of the Malay Peninsula, close to the Muar River estuary. This, however, is most likely an engraving error. The inscription "Cingatola" belongs to an unnamed city farther south, as correctly shown on Ortelius' earlier maps of 1564 and 1567 and on Gastaldi's *Terza parte dell'Asia* of 1561.

If Thevet had consulted the printed maps of Ramusio (1554), Gastaldi (1561) and Ortelius (1570), together with some contemporary manuscript charts, his assertion that the channel was approximately six kilometres wide was no exaggeration but simply a repetition of what was then commonly accepted in Europe. It also becomes clear why the land south of the Pahang-Muar Channel was perceived as an "island". The large island formed by this channel is certainly Thevet's Cingaporla. The French geographer shares company with many 16th-century cartographers in specifically naming the southern portion of the Malay Peninsula Cincapola, Cincapula, Cingatola or some other seriously corrupted variant of Singapura.[99] By contrast, maps dating from the early 16th century, such as the one penned by Giovanni Vespucci (1524), a nephew of the (in)famous explorer Amerigo Vespucci, refer to the southern reaches of the Peninsula as "Punta de Melaca", that is, Melaka Point; Francesco Ghisolfi (1550) calls it "c. Malaca" (Cape Malaca); and Lopo Homem (1540) calls it "C: de cima" (*Cabo de Cima*, Cape of China).[100] In the monumental *Décadas da Ásia*, João de Barros mentions the "Cabo", and "Ponta de Cingapura" (Cape Singapura, Singapura Point). The Portuguese chronicler is also aware of a city by the same name which he places at the tip of the Peninsula.[101]

At this juncture, it is useful to dwell on two points of special interest: the greater island of Singapura, as well as the Pahang-Muar Channel.

In early modern European sources, which invariably include maps and charts of the region before approximately 1800, nomenclature was applied in an elastic manner. It is not always certain what a particular term or expression illustrates. The name Singapura can be taken as a classic illustration of this problem: What does the term mean in any given context? The port and the city? Today's main island of Singapore? One of the four straits? A cape or promontory? The whole southern portion of the Malay Peninsula, which corresponds roughly the present-day Malaysian state of Johor? In early modern European sources, documents, charts and maps, Singapura and all its orthographical variants can refer to any of these.[102] The sources are not always clear what they refer to, and this lack of clarity adds to the difficulty in evaluating many early modern materials.

It is also worth highlighting here that in Europe, today's Singapore island was known by a variety of names before the modern settlement was founded in 1819. Materials from the VOC, such as the *Dagh-Register*

Batavia, ships' logs, official correspondence and hydrographic charts prepared by the company, generally refer to the island as by its Malay name Pulau Panjang (Long Island)[103] or by its Dutch equivalent, 't Lange Eylant.[104] These toponyms survived well into the late 18th century, as can be easily evidenced from maps of Dutch, Flemish, and French origin. As late as 1803, the British Captain Milner knew this island only as Pulo Panjang.[105] It is only after the period of the Dutch-Riau Wars (1780s) that the name *Sinkapoor* is featured regularly on charts and maps. A classic example is offered by the previously mentioned hydrographic chart of van Braam van Houckgeest owned by Leiden University (see p. 37).[106] Here the island features in the entry "Pulau Panjang, Iatana, ook Sinkapoor" (Long Island, Land's End, also Singapore).[107] The second name listed on this map — Iatana — represents a corruption of the Malay *Ujong Tanah*, meaning "Land's End", a name that is encountered among other sources in the *Hikayat Raja-Raja Pasai* as well as many European reports, texts, chronicles and maps dating from the 16th and 17th centuries.[108] Among the classic Portuguese testimonies are the two treatises of the Eurasian engineer and adventurer Manoel Godinho de Erédia.[109] A careful study of his *Informação da Aurea Chersoneso* (Report on the Golden Chersonese, 1595–1600) and *Declaraçam de Malaca* (1613–4) clearly reveals not only the elasticity with which toponyms were employed, but also how problematic geographic nomenclature of the early modern period proves to be.[110] In both treatises, Erédia names the whole southern portion of the Peninsula Singapura, Viontana or sometimes also Maleucolone.[111] This nomenclature, incidentally, contrasts with the earlier testimony of the Portuguese apothecary and diplomat Tomé Pires, who, writing at the beginning of the 16th century, applied the name "Singapura" strictly to a small kingdom with little territory as well as to the region immediately around the Singapore Straits, but not to the present-day island.[112]

To the best of the author's knowledge, the island is named Singapura only in seven instances: on two maps by Manoel Godinho de Erédia,[113] André Pereira dos Reis around 1654 (see p. 42), Thomas Bowrey in 1670 (see p. 178), Eberard Dupré in 1700, Gerard van Keulen in 1753, and the aforementioned van Braam van Houckgeest (see p. 37). The latter, in turn, based his chart on the French cartographer Jean-Baptiste Denis d'Après de Mannevillette.[114] In the case of van Braam van Houckgeest, however, the name Sinkapoor is featured only in third place, after Long Island (Pulau Panjang) and Land's End (Iatana being a corruption of Ujong Tanah), an observation that certainly needs to be driven home.[115]

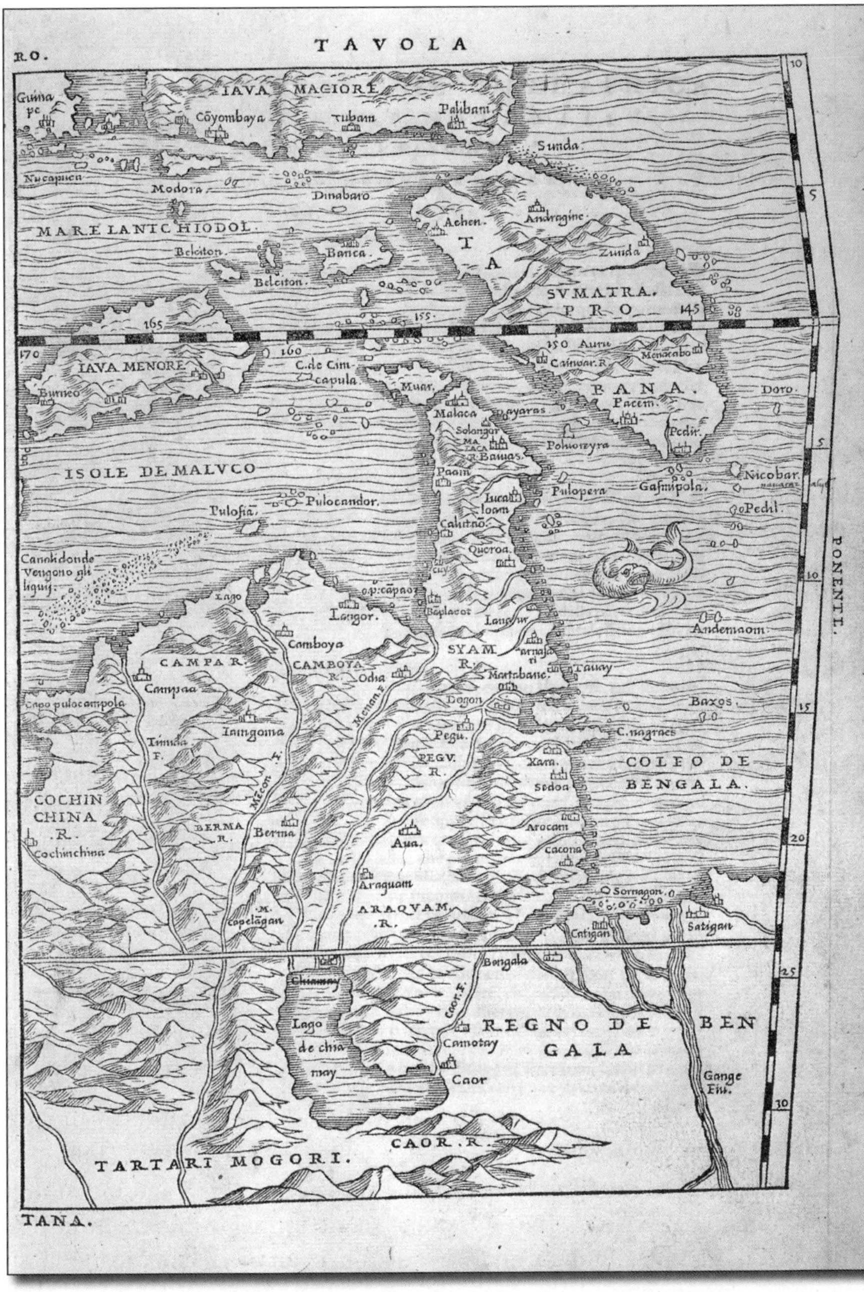

Printed map of the Malay Peninsula and mainland Southeast Asia in southern orientation. A channel running between Muar and Pahang separates the southern portion of the Peninsula from the mainland. From Giovanni Battista Ramusio, *Delle navigationi et viaggi in molti luoghi* (Of the Navigations and Voyages to Many Places) vol. I, Venice, 1554. (Leiden University Library, 368 A 13)

Locating the town or city of Singapura is a problem of a completely different nature. In view of the elasticity of the name Singapura, and the fact that the island was not widely known or recognised by that name until the late 18th or even the dawn of the 19th century, one should not be surprised that the town or settlement of Singapura moves about the region.[116] Sometimes the town bears a different name altogether. The Fleming Jaques de Coutre who briefly mentions the settlement in his description of a voyage to Pahang in 1594, refers to the settlement as *Shahbandaria* (that is the shahbandar's compound, the town with the shahbandar's compound).[117] For the sake of brevity, the two most common locations shall be highlighted.

The first and predominant one is on the left bank of the Johor River. The settlement of Cingapola was placed there in 1541 by no less an authority than Mercator. The error was repeated for decades, well into the first half of the 17th century. The second location can be found on the peninsular mainland about halfway along the Johor or Tebrau Strait. A classic example can be found in François Valentijn's *Oud en Nieuw Oost-Indiën* (Old and New East India), printed in 1724 (see p. 19).[118]

What about the site of the contemporary metropolis? There are three important testimonies extant: first, the entries on charts penned by both Erédia (1604) and André Pereira dos Reis (c. 1654) feature a *xabandaría,* or shahbandar's compound, on the island (see p. 42). The second derives from the travel log of Jakob Pietersz van Enkhuysen, who sailed under the command of Admiral Wijbrand van Warwijk to the East Indies in 1601.[119] He crossed through the Old Strait of Singapore (between present-day Sentosa and Telok Blangah) in October 1603 and also mentioned a settlement named Singapura (see also p. 27).[120]

The Pahang-Muar "Channel"

From the south side of the greater island of Cingapola, attention shall now be shifted to its supposed northern end, which, according to Thevet, is bordered by a channel reminiscent of the Strait of Messina and measuring two or three *lieues* wide. Two questions merit further exploration in this context: First, by whom, how and when is this strait or channel featured on European cartography of the 16th and early 17th centuries? And second, when did the "channel" appear and disappear? What evidence is at hand from early modern source materials that the channel may have influenced European understanding of the region and, implicitly, also colonial policy?

It is difficult to reliably ascertain who the creator of this fictitious maritime channel was. Older Ptolemaic manuscripts found in Naples, Paris, London and, most significantly, the Vatican Library[121] feature several rivers on the *Aurea Chersonesus* (Golden Chersonese or the Malay Peninsula), but there is no waterway that runs clear across the Peninsula. The "creator" of this fictitious "channel" appears to have been Nicolaus Germanus, who created a manuscript of Ptolemy's *Geographia* for Duke Borso d'Este in 1466 and which in turn influenced most of the editions printed thereafter, especially those of Rome (1478), Ulm (Holle, 1482) and Strassburg (Schott, 1513).

Whatever the case might have been, there was probably more than one such important riverine network used by Asian traders. Paul Wheatley recognised the significance of the Pahang-Muar riverine network for the 16th century, primarily in the production or panning for gold dust in parts of the Malay Peninsula,[122] but surviving documentary evidence suggests that the commercial significance at the close of the 16th and the opening of the 17th centuries extended beyond the supply of gold. Following the takeover of Melaka by the Portuguese in 1511, more is learnt about the dynamics and flow of trade in the region as well as the political conditions that facilitate or impede it. The Portuguese were well-aware of this transpeninsular route and may have occasionally used it when the *saletes* (sea gypsies, *orang laut*) with the support of the deposed sultan of Melaka rendered maritime navigation through the Singapore and Melaka Straits a very risky venture.[123]

Erédia reportedly explored the course of the two rivers and identified the drag or portage place (*panarícan*, *penarikan*), a short stretch that separates the Muar River and the nearest navigable tributary of the Pahang River.[124] This exploration took place at the turn of the 17th century, and Erédia penned at least four maps that show the branches of the Muar and Pahang Rivers together with the *panarícan*. But Erédia's sketches, together with his verbal testimony of the riverine passage, were not widely known to his contemporaries. They were published only in the 19th century.

What is evident from Erédia's *Declaraçam de Malaca* and some of the earliest documents prepared by servants of the VOC is that the Portuguese themselves began to use the riverine network more frequently. This was most certainly not a short cut, but rather a route for evading what after 1603 became an annual invasion of Dutch East Indiamen scouring the waters of the Singapore Straits and the open seas as far as Tioman.[125] The remaining four chapters of this book will highlight several

Hand coloured printed map of Asia from c. 1548 based on Claudius Ptolemy by the German humanist and cartographer Sebastian Münster. (Private collection Peter Borschberg)

Drawn, hand coloured map by Manoel Godinho de Erédia dated 1602 depicting Melaka and the surrounding region "controlled" or "claimed" by the Portuguese around the city. Striking are the riverine networks, the depiction of the overland trails, the "penarícan", as well as the geneology of the kings of Melaka from 1411. (Biblioteca Nacional do Brasil, Rio de Janeiro, CAM. 001,007 fl. 502b cartografia).

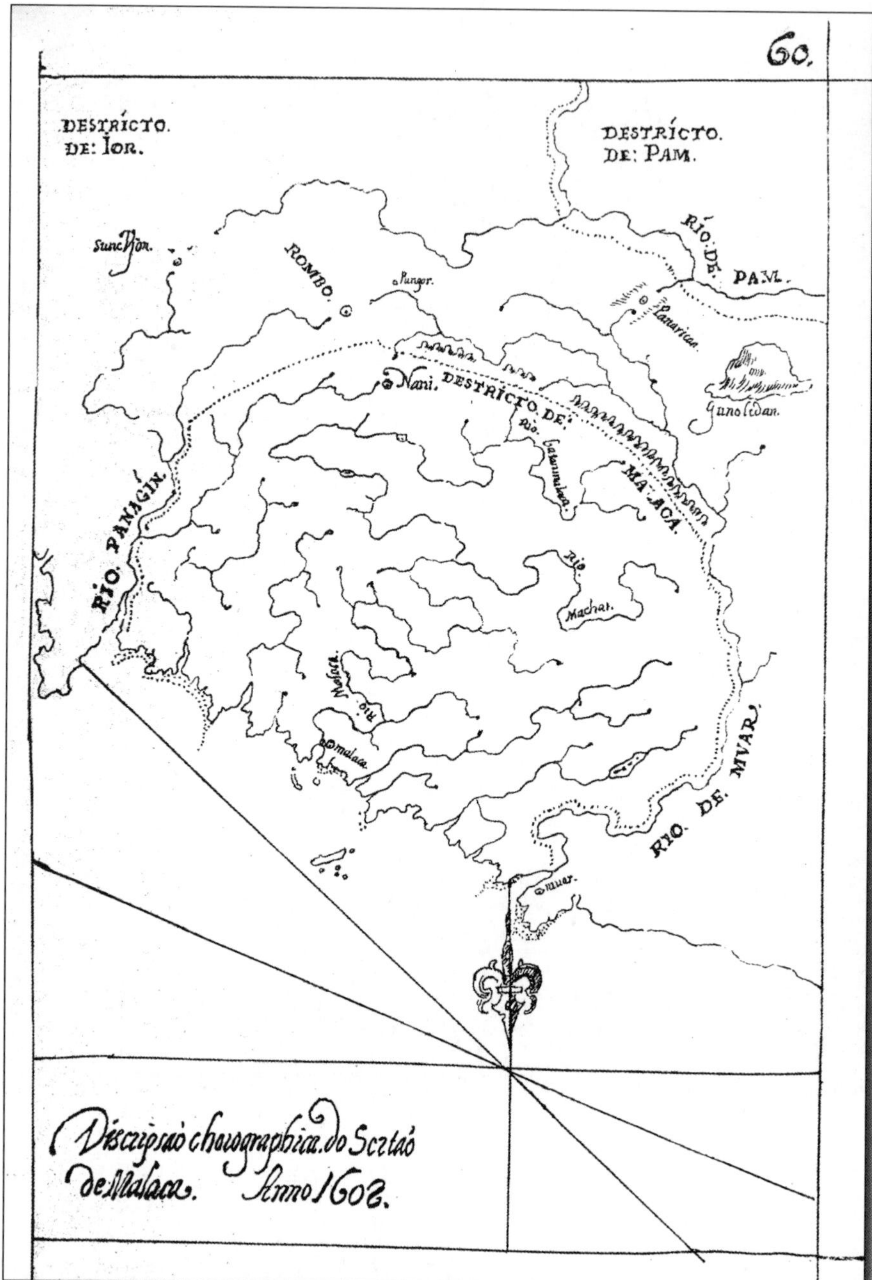

Map of the area controlled by the Portuguese around Melaka in 1608. From Manoel Godinho de Erédia, *Malaca l'Inde Méridionale et le Cathay,* 1882, Chart 60.

concrete historical episodes to illustrate this point. Informants working for the Portuguese were stationed in Tioman (a much-frequented provisioning station and watering hole for all sorts of ships of all nationalities) to warn Lusitanian captains and pilots of Dutch freebooters.[126] Dutch sources explain how Portuguese-flagged vessels were re-routed to the port of Pahang and unloaded there, and goods were transported along the rivers and the *panarícan* across the Peninsula to Muar.

Dutch policies of plundering and despoiling their Lusitanian enemy in the region of the Straits, especially after the *Santa Catarina* incident in 1603 (discussed in Chapter 2), evidently led to an upgrading of the Pahang-Muar riverine network. This had two immediate consequences: first, the Portuguese officials in Melaka were keen on cultivating relations with Pahang and encouraging "political independence" from Johor-Riau; and second, they were keen to extend the "border" of Portuguese Melaka to the other bank of the river in Muar. The situation was indeed messy, but it was perhaps not unusual in the Malay world of that period, with Pahang acknowledging both Johor and Patani as "overlord" and at the same time cultivating good political and commercial relations with Portuguese Melaka. The cordial relations of Pahang with the Portuguese appear to have lasted until the Acehnese attacks on Pahang in 1617–8, after which the situation on the ground becomes murky.

Erédia was a man on the spot. He explored the *panarícan* in 1602 and accompanied the captain-major of Melaka, Admiral André Furtado de Mendonça, on a military campaign in 1604.[127] Erédia supposedly also founded the Portuguese fort in Muar, but serious questions remain as to whether the triangular-shaped fort, featured in his *Declaraçam de Malaca* (Description of Melaka) remained anything more than just a plan on paper. The question arises significantly because Jaques de Coutre's memorial to Philip III of Spain (who also ruled as Philip II of Portugal) believed to date from the 1620s recommends the construction of a fort at the Muar River estuary, a clear independent and first-hand testimony that Erédia's fort was never completed.[128] If one is to take Erédia's charts seriously, then one can reconstruct on the basis of his cartographic materials that during this period the Portuguese extended their control from the near right bank of the Muar River across to the left,[129] thus acquiring control over the whole river estuary. This extension of control took place against the backdrop of heightened Dutch freebooting activities in the Straits of Singapore and Melaka as well as an enhanced viability of the Pahang-Muar riverine network. The VOC dispatched reports to Europe explaining

Portuguese efforts to skilfully evade their naval blockades and freebooting activities. (Further details on the blockades follow in Chapter 5.) On the ground the geographic situation was clear to the European adventurers and traders, but it took years — and in some instances decades — for the geographic information to be visualised in maps and charts.

Afterthoughts

Based on the evidence presented so far, it appears that the origins of this supposed channel or strait can only be tenuously retraced to the printed editions of Ptolemy. It grew into a full-fledged sea-level channel "as wide as the Strait of Messina" (to cite Thevet's now familiar analogy) during the 1530s. It was popularised by Mercator and Ortelius, but it gradually disappeared as the 17th century progressed. Right up to the conquest of Melaka by the Dutch in January 1641 (see Chapter 5), this waterway continued to appear on Portuguese maps;[130] and on Dutch, French and British charts it can be found as late as the 1660s. By the 1680s, the Dutch diplomat and adventurer Johan Nieuhof observed that although the Pahang River was "wide", it could not be accessed with galleys except during the rainy season.[131] It is of course within the realm of possibility that the river estuary had silted up.

Before the imagined channel would vanish entirely, it was relocated along what appear to be different riverine networks. The maps of Hondius and Blaeu, dating from the 1630s, have the channel run from Pahang to Johor, but this route would not have offered relief from a possible blockade along the strategic northern coast of the Karimun Islands, where several important sea lanes from India, Burma, eastern Sumatra, Indochina, China, Japan, Borneo, Makassar, Java, Timor and the Malukus converge.

As has been noted, Thevet advanced the curious claim that Muar was the most important port of Cingaporla. He was not thinking of the island that hosts the present-day city republic of Singapore, but a large portion of the lower regions of the Malay Peninsula, supposedly severed from the Asian continent to the south by a six-kilometre-wide channel between Pahang and Muar. There is, of course, no such natural channel that could offer a serious alternative to the Singapore Straits. Erédia supposedly explored the interior of the Peninsula and charted rivers of the Malay Peninsula, their tributaries, and the *panarícan*. He was there — or at least so one is told — and he was a man on the spot, quite unlike Mercator, Ortelius or indeed the French geographer Thevet.

Maybe Thevet was wrong about the channel or strait cutting across the Malay Peninsula between Muar and Pahang. But he was evidently correct about Muar being in a wider geographic space known as Cingaporla, at least according to prevailing European toponyms of the late 16th and early 17th centuries![132] This is not quite the end of the present deliberations. The following excerpt from John Leyden's translation of the *Sejarah Melayu* or Malay Annals bears strong echoes of Thevet's understanding of a "greater Singapura":[133] "The country of Singhapura is of great extent, and frequented by merchants unnumerable from every quarter, and its ports are very populous." Perhaps it was not just the European understanding of Singapura that ultimately requires closer scrutiny!

In Chapter 2, attention will turn from questions pertaining to topographic nomenclature, cartographical representation and European understanding of geopolitical space to developments around the Straits of Singapore and Melaka. At the centre of attention stands the arrival of Dutch vessels in the region of the Straits and the strategies they pursued to despoil Portuguese intra-Asian commercial shipping. The exposé will include some of the early reactions of the *Estado da Índia* and how the Lusitanian authorities sought to respond to budding relations between the VOC and Johor. A new balance of power began to emerge at the southern tip of the Malay Peninsula after 1603. These developments were shaped not least by perceptions of geopolitical considerations addressed in this chapter. By the second decade of the 17th century, the nascent European colonial powers, especially the Portuguese and the Dutch, seriously reappraised naval hegemony and maritime security for the region.

CHAPTER 2

Security in the Straits: The European Struggle for Naval Hegemony

Setting the Stage

Whilst it is true that the Singapore and Melaka Straits represent historically long-established arteries of long-distance intra-Asian trade, knowledge of the region is plagued by the elasticity of toponyms and the tenuous knowledge of the lands and waters that lay beyond the well-frequented Straits. Understanding the evolving geographic knowledge in Europe from the early 16th century through to the middle of the 17th not only helps the contemporary student of history understand the broader ramifications of policy decisions made in the courtly settings of Europe, Goa and, later, Batavia, but also highlights the blind spots that agents on the ground could exploit to their benefit.

The arrival of northern European competitors from the Netherlands, England, and later France and Denmark,[1] intensified the defensive posture of Portuguese Melaka, and indeed of the whole of the *Estado da Índia*. In October 1602, the English Admiral James Lancaster seized in a freebooting operation a Portuguese carrack en route from São Thomé on the southeastern coast of India (or the Coromandel Coast) to Melaka.[2] The operation was supported by his Dutch counterpart Joris van Spilbergen.[3] Lancaster seized the vessel with a letter of marque issued by the High Admiralty in England,[4] that legitimised all hostile naval operations of this kind as a seizure of booty in war, no matter where it might take place on the Seven Seas.

The joint operation in the Strait of Melaka in many ways symbolically heralded two future developments that would plague the Portuguese *Estado da Índia* in the region for much of the 17th century. First, the escalation of maritime violence globally,[5] and especially in the waters of the Straits, and second, the dynamics of Anglo-Dutch cooperation. The latter is perhaps best evidenced in the negotiations during the second decade of the 17th century for a merger of the English and Dutch East India Companies.[6] As history would have it, the merger never took place, but was supplanted by a cooperation agreement between the two rivalling companies that was strained right from the start and at least symbolically ended at the latest with the so-called "Massacre of Amboina" (Ambon) in March, 1623.[7] Due to their peace with the Spanish Empire in 1604, the English soon became unwilling, or at least very reluctant, participants in the Dutch Republic's war concluded in Southeast Asia, the Americas and beyond. Anglo-Dutch rivalry in the waters around the Straits intensified, a rivalry that Aceh sought to actively exploit to its own benefit.[8] After 1623 the English gradually withdrew (or, should one better say, were effectively eliminated by the Dutch) from Southeast Asian trade and concentrated their efforts in West Asia and the Indian subcontinent until the close of the 18th century.[9]

Unlike the English, the Dutch sustained their attacks on and plundering of Portuguese and also Spanish mercantile shipping on a world-wide scale.[10] The classic cases at the dawn of the 17th century include the *Santa Catarina* incident off Johor and Singapore, and the *Santo António* incident at Patani that will be discussed in greater detail below. These incidents amongst others forced the officers of Portuguese Asia to rethink their security arrangements and develop forward strategies for the region, and especially rethink their positions in the Straits.

In order to better appreciate the factors that led to a serious shift in Portugal's security at the southern tip of the Malay Peninsula, it is important to first provide a synopsis of the arrangements that had been put in place before the dawn of the 17th century.

After the second half of the 16th century, specifically the 1570s and 1580s, the *Estado da Índia* became increasingly concerned about the security of its vessels from Japan, China, Makassar and the Spice Islands. Portuguese Melaka witnessed the rise of the Johor-Riau Kingdom, which traced its cultural and political roots to the fallen Melaka Sultanate. In the first half of the 16th century, following the seizure of Melaka by the Portuguese, the spiritual, cultural, political and economic centre gravitated down the western coast of the Malay Peninsula — to Muar, to the island of Bintan, and then to the banks of the Johor River at Johor Lama and other towns upstream. Security in the Singapore Straits thus became a vital issue for the *Estado da Índia*, leading it to weaken Johor by attacking Bintan in 1525 and again in the 1530s. Tensions with the rising Sumatran power Aceh and unstable relations with Johor led to the sacking and destruction of the fortress Kota Batu in 1587.[11] Luso-Johor relations thus proceeded on a track of almost extreme oscillation, ranging from close commercial relations to armed confrontation on land and at sea.

In order to protect shipping inbound from East Asia and parts of the Southeast Asian archipelago, several proposals were drafted and evaluated by leading officers (and clerics) of the *Estado da Índia*. Viewed from a broader perspective, the region around the Straits of Singapore and Melaka represented far more than just a zone of vacillating and often uncertain politico-economic relations. It represented, in the eyes of Portuguese officials, a crucial confluence of the various arteries of long-distance intra-Asian trade, linking the Bay of Bengal in the west with the Java Sea in the south and the South China Sea to the east. Lusitanian officials grew increasingly wary — especially after the arrival of the Dutch in the late 1500s — that it might be possible for a militarily strong enemy to gain control of the Straits. By closely patrolling regional waterways, the enemy could effectively sever the lines of communication and supply among the geographically far-flung ports of the *Estado da Índia*. This, in turn, could seriously hamper commercial activity in Portuguese colonial settlements such as Macao, Hirado and the Malukus, as well as disrupt the dispatch of military and financial support from Goa. Indeed, so it came to pass in the first half of the 17th century.

As is evident from official documentation, two basic security arrangements for the Straits were seriously contemplated: first, the construction of forts at crucial nodal points; and second, the positioning of naval craft at points of strategic concern. It is hardly surprising that *Estado da Índia* officials opted for security or escort fleets. Unlike the fixed structures of land-based forts, the security fleets were mobile and could be (re)deployed at various points of strategic interest at different times of year, depending on the monsoon winds and seasonal trading patterns. Apart from being more flexible, the escort fleet was also far more cost-effective. Manning and maintaining a series of fixed fortified structures represented a costly proposition that the *Estado da Índia* could ill afford, especially in an uncertain political and trading environment.

Security in the region of the Straits of Singapore and Melaka was organised along the following lines: From October to March, the Portuguese escort fleet would be placed at the eastern entrance of the Singapore Straits to anticipate the arrival of ships from Macao and Japan; in April it could be stationed at the northern reaches of the Melaka Strait, specifically, off Cape Rachado and farther north towards the Bay of Bengal.

It should be mentioned in this context that the Portuguese tailored the composition of their escort fleets to their operating environment and to the tactics of their Malay and *orang laut* adversaries. Prior to the arrival of the Dutch in the waters of the Melaka and Singapore Straits, Portuguese Melaka found itself engaged chiefly with vessels of the Malay princes and the *orang laut*, or sea gypsies. For this reason, the security or escort fleet was composed of numerous smaller vessels, such as banteens, galleys and prahus, which were suitable for entering shallow waters along the coast and harassing settlements along the shore, or for chasing the enemy up estuaries, rivers and narrow maritime channels.

The arrival of the Dutch in the waters of the Singapore and Melaka Straits radically changed the security environment of the *Estado da Índia*. The escort fleets, comprising many small vessels, were suitable for responding to the hit-and-run tactics of the *orang laut* and the Malay princes, but they were quite unsuited for engaging the European enemy skilled in the latest naval tactics and equipped with an array of naval artillery. As the Flemish historian John G. Everaert observed, the Portuguese armadas stationed in the Straits featured "too few genuine warships". The smaller Portuguese sailing craft, galleys and locally constructed prahus were no match for the well-armed Dutch fleets.[12] For this reason, a small VOC squadron — such as that of Vice-Admiral Jakob Pietersz van Enkhuysen — could successfully engage in battle an armada of some 40 vessels that was holding position around the Johor River estuary.

In face of the new security challenge posed by the arrival of the Dutch, Portuguese Melaka devised three strategies in the hope of vanquishing, or at the very least containing, its enemy. First, it launched a diplomatic offensive on the Johor court, pitting top officers against one another and engineering a deal with the Johor monarch that would bring peace with the *Estado da Índia* and sought to sever of Johor's commercial and diplomatic ties with the VOC. With the benefit of hindsight, it was this diplomatic offensive on the Johor court that was not only to transform Luso-Johor relations, but indeed induce a political and economic realignment of regional powers on the Malay Peninsula and the great island of Sumatra with noteworthy long-term consequences for the region. Second, plans were revived and actively discussed to construct land-based fortified structures at key points along the Straits. And finally, the *Estado da Índia* was to join forces with Spain within the context of the Union of the Two Crowns, with the objective of ousting the Dutch from Asian maritime space once and for all.

Dutch Assessment of Security in the Straits, c. 1602–3

Before discussing the different strategies adopted by the *Estado da Índia* to reassert security in the Straits and rein in the Johor monarch, a few comments need to be made about the Dutch assessment of the security situation in the region and the Dutch war in Asia against the Iberian powers at large.

At the end of the 16th century, Dutch traders, initially under the flags of regional overseas trading firms (*voorcompagniën*)[13] and subsequently under the banner of the VOC, arrived in the waters of insular and mainland Southeast Asia in search of trading opportunities. Their Portuguese competitors regarded this penetration into their region as a clear infringement on their exclusive rights of trade, which they historically asserted and defended in word and deed.[14] The arrival of the Dutch marked the beginning of fierce competition for markets, political influence and military supremacy that would characterise and give shape to the history of the region in the final years of the 16th century and the opening decades of the 17th.

The heightened Luso-Dutch tensions during this period expressed itself in various forms. The Portuguese flexed their military muscle, and more often than not, they backed their show of might with hard-nosed diplomacy.

In the first two decades of the 17th century, the VOC sought to gain a foothold and consolidate its role in the region. As is known from the histories of Europe, the Dutch fought a long and protracted "war of liberation" from Spanish "tyranny", a process known as the Dutch Revolt. After Portugal was "conquered" in 1580 by King Philip II of Spain, who thereafter also ruled as Philip I of Portugal, the Dutch war against Spain was extended to cover Portugal as well. With the inception of Dutch voyages to the East Indies, Hispano-Dutch and Luso-Dutch hostilities were projected beyond Europe, including Southeast Asia, a region that — according to the Treaties of Tordesillas (1494) and Zaragoza (1529) — broadly fell within the Portuguese sphere of interest.[15]

The conflict that spilled over from Europe to Asia reflected two key strategies. The first was to inflict as much damage as possible to Portuguese and Spanish assets, both on land and at sea. The VOC was formed in 1602 by bringing together six regional trading firms on to a common account. The purpose of this "amalgamation" was in the opinion of one English negotiator of the early 17th century to achieve a "compacted power to make war against the Portugals".[16] The Spanish in Manila and around the Pacific were of course part of the picture as well.

The shift in policy leading to heightened attacks on Spanish and Portuguese shipping outside the European scenario occurred at the turn of the 17th century. According to the Dutch maritime historian Johan Elias, the States General (Federal Assembly) of the Dutch Republic began to dispatch fleets with the aim of despoiling the Iberian enemy in the Americas, Africa and Asia around 1599. Elias opines that the shift in policy can be explained by the dismal state of finances of the republic's Admiralty Boards. For each prize taken to the home port, the local Admiralty Board received a certain portion of the booty, customarily 20 per cent, known in Dutch as *gerechtigheid van het land* (literally: the justice of the land). Prize and booty became an important source of income for the Admiralty Boards, and according to Elias, the States General reported such revenue under "balance of payments".[17] A similar observation is made by Nils Steensgaard in his now classic work *The Asian Trade Revolution of the Seventeenth Century*:[18]

> There can be no doubt, however, that the merger of the East India Companies in 1602 immediately resulted in a change of policy as regards aims and means. Whereas the admirals of the voorcompagniën were instructed to avoid armed conflict, van der Hagen's instructions of 1603, the first to be drawn up by the Heren XVII, has been characterized

> as "definitely offensive and militant". Both this fleet and the following one under Matelieff de Jonge were instructed to undertake a military cruise before seeking a return cargo for the ships.[19] We do not know the details connected with this alteration in policy, but there is no doubt that those circles that, in the establishment of the United Company, had seen the creation of an instrument of power for use in the fight against Spain-Portugal immediately took the initiative.[20]

With the benefit of hindsight, so it came to pass. The VOC launched offensives on key Iberian positions around the Indian Ocean basin and in East Asia, including the Malukus, Manila, Macao and Melaka, scoring initial successes chiefly in the first-mentioned region. At sea the Dutch attacked Portuguese merchant ships bound from Hirado and Macao to Melaka and Goa, and also Spanish galleons en route between Manila and the Mexican port of Acapulco. According to the Dutch maritime and naval historian Victor Enthoven, about 200 craft of various sizes and values were seized in Asia in the first two decades of the 17th century.[21] As will become clear below, some of the prizes taken were spectacular by any measure.

The second aspect of Dutch policy was to contain the spread of Portuguese and Spanish influence. This was achieved by courting independent kings and princes in the region, and offering them "protection" and assistance against possible encroachment by the Iberian powers, in return for special — and usually exclusive — trading rights.[22] For this reason, VOC admirals concluded a web of treaties with several Asian sovereigns during the first decades of the 17th century,[23] but the Dutch were fully aware that not all sovereigns in the region required their "assistance".[24] Such treaties were usually concluded with kings and princes of smaller or weaker polities, and it was fully recognised even in Europe that the great kings of Asia — including the emperor of China and, of course, the king of Siam — were well-positioned to hold their own.[25] At the dawn of the 17th century, therefore, European trade and influence in Southeast Asia ran along two distinct tracks.

As previously mentioned, one aspect of Dutch strategy in the early 17th century was to win over and form alliances with kings and rulers in strategic locations throughout Southeast Asia. One of the best-known alliances was forged in 1603 between the king of Johor and Jakob van Heemskerk.[26] In the early phase of the VOC's corporate life, freebooting arose and remained a lucrative activity for the Dutch. The Straits of Singapore and the Johor River estuary quickly emerged as preferred spots to prey on Portuguese merchant ships.

The Lusitanian counterparts from Lisbon to Goa, Melaka and Macao were most certainly not complacent about their mounting losses. After Furtado de Mendonça assumed authority as captain-major of Melaka, punitive expeditions were dispatched in the South China Sea's monsoon season of 1603–4 and again in 1604–5, because Johor established and maintained friendly relations with Dutch traders. Simultaneously, the Portuguese armada stationed in the Johor River estuary anticipated the arrival of their merchant vessels inbound from Japan, China and Makassar, and lent them naval escort through the treacherous waters of the Singapore Straits to Melaka.[27]

In the first years of the 17th century it became a key objective of the VOC to penetrate new markets in the East, contain the commercial and strategic expansion of the Iberian powers in Asia, and establish a rendezvous location for home-bound vessels as well as a permanent residence for the governor-general.[28]

The Dutch merchants were in favour of unimpeded market access and free trade in the East Indies. Their cause was chiefly directed against the rights of exclusive trade asserted by the two Iberian powers, Spain and Portugal. Africa, Asia and the New World, as well as the navigable sea lanes leading to them, were claimed by the two nascent colonial powers as their exclusive trading preserve. They asserted their trade monopoly on legal grounds that included, notably, "the right of first discovery" (*terra nullius*), transfer of imperial authority and papal donation.[29] It would be erroneous to equate Dutch claims to "free trade" with contemporary arguments on the same issue.[30] A noteworthy portion of early Dutch trading activity was, in fact, little more than outright robbery committed under (the pretext of) the law of war. Thus, it is hardly a surprise that the victims of Dutch "commercial" aggression, notably merchants operating under Spanish and Portuguese flags, branded these northern European traders as "pirates".

The present chapter now turns to examine the developments in and around the Straits of Singapore and Melaka that considerably influenced the *Estado da Índia*'s assessment of its military, diplomatic and economic position in the region. In the following sections, attention will be placed on three well-documented episodes occurring between 1602 and 1608 that impacted thinking on the ground and sent political ripples from Southeast Asia to the corridors of power in Goa, Lisbon and Amsterdam. The first is the "*Santa Catarina* incident" of February 1603. The second is the blockade of the Johor River estuary and the Luso-Dutch naval engagement in late September and early October 1603. This also saw the escalation of freebooting activities in and around the Straits of Singapore between 1604 and 1608, climaxing with the third well-documented episode — the seizure of the Portuguese carrack *Santo António* in 1605.

What is the "*Santa Catarina* Incident"?

The "*Santa Catarina* incident" emerged as one of the milestones in 17th century colonial expansion and the history of international law. The Portuguese-flagged 1,400-ton carrack *Santa Catarina* was outbound from Macao en route to Melaka and Goa when it was attacked and seized by the Dutch Admiral Jakob van Heemskerk off Singapore on 25 February 1603.[31] According to extant reports, the ship carried on board 700 *soldados* (soldiers) and scores of merchants, women and probably children. The loss of this ship and cargo dealt a serious blow to the merchant community of Macao. Brought back to the Netherlands as bounty of war, the carrack's merchandise yielded at a public auction the staggering sum of about 3.5 million florins (guilders). At the time, this was equivalent to one half the paid-in capital of the VOC, and more than double the paid-in capital of its English counterpart, the Honourable East India Company (EIC), based in London and founded in 1600.[32]

The *Santa Catarina* incident, as it is called in several recent publications,[33] is of special interest not only to historians of Southeast Asia, but also to researchers concerned with the history of political thought and the genesis of modern international relations theories. This is because its wider repercussions encompassed far more than the seizure of a Portuguese-flagged carrack as a prize of war. It emerged as an event with truly international and broad-based implications, acting, as some scholars contend, as a cornerstone of events that were to unfold within the first two decades of the 17th century. The seizure of the *Santa Catarina* marks the first widely publicised incident in which the Dutch, under either the VOC or any of its legal predecessors, seized a Portuguese merchant vessel in the waters around the Singapore Straits, the Karimuns, Pedra Branca and the waters south of Tioman island. As history would clearly demonstrate, this region, near the southern tip of the Malay Peninsula (called *Cabo de Cincapura* or *Viontana* on many Portuguese maps of the 16th and 17th centuries), emerged as one of the preferred locations of the Dutch for

Printed portrait of Jakob van Heemskerk from the 1647 edition of Emanuel van Meteren's *Commentariën ofte Memoriën van den Nederlantsen Staet, Handel, Oorloghen ende Gheschiedenissen van onsen Tyden* (Commentaries or Memoirs concerning the Dutch State, Trade and War, and the History of our Times) (Koninklijke Bibliotheek, The Hague, 1790 A 122)

Printed portrait of the young lawyer and humanist Hugo Grotius (Huig de Groot) around 1613. (Rijksbureau voor Kunsthistorische Dokumentatie, The Hague)

preying on inbound Lusitanian vessels from Macao, Japan, Cochinchina, Makassar and Borneo.

The *Santa Catarina* incident and other acts of aggression committed against Portuguese-flagged mercantile shipping raised the awareness of the VOC directors and the regents of the Dutch Republic as to how profitable the policy of freebooting and despoiling the enemy could be; it also raised their awareness of the *Estado da Índia*'s geographically conditioned vulnerabilities.[34] The Strait of Singapore had long been perceived in Macao, Melaka and Goa as one of the weaker links — if not the weakest — in the intricate networks of trade spanned by the far-flung possessions and dependencies of the *Estado da Índia*.[35] But the arrival of the northern European competitors in the waters of insular Southeast Asia, coupled with the *Santa Catarina* incident, placed considerable pressure on the viceroy to step up security in the Straits. Should he fail in this, the *Estado da Índia* would not only be placed on the defensive, but would be severed in two if the Dutch successfully secured the Singapore Straits and imposed a stranglehold on Portuguese traffic, trade and revenue from its Far Eastern operations. Lusitanian officials were painfully aware not only that it was necessary to formulate a new policy for the Singapore Straits, but also that the period of relative peace and tranquillity enjoyed since the destruction of Johor Lama in 1587 had drawn to a definitive close.[36] The destruction of Johor's fortress and royal residence was undertaken to thwart further consolidation of political and economic power on the Malay Peninsula and adjacent islands in competition to Portuguese Melaka.

This awareness that the Straits of Singapore represented a potential Achilles heel in the *Estado da Índia*'s maritime security provides the immediate historical context not only for the carrack's seizure, but also for its legal defence by Hugo Grotius, the Dutch jurisconsult frequently upheld in early 20th-century literature as the "father of modern international law". As a young man of 22, Grotius wrote an apology legitimising van Heemskerk's recourse to violence. This defence gave Grotius the opportunity to familiarise himself with pertinent legal issues surrounding trade, war, peace, the taking of plunder from the enemy, and access to ports and emporia around the globe, and to explore key dimensions of international alliances and treaty making.[37]

Casting an eye on events on the ground, the present chapter provides an account of the *Santa Catarina* incident taking into consideration important research findings of van Ittersum.[38]

Both Dutch- as well as Portuguese-language materials suggest that the incident can be placed within the broader context of Luso-Dutch rivalry in the Malay world. It shall be shown in this context that the seizure of the *Santa Catarina* acted as an important trigger for several decisions taken by the *Estado da Índia* and also by the newly formed VOC. Security for inbound shipping from China, Japan, Makassar and Timor became paramount for the Portuguese. Apart from beefing up forts and fleets, they developed a forward policy for Southeast Asia that combined effective diplomacy and military muscle. What also becomes very transparent in the course of the present account is how important the Macao merchants really were to the *Estado da Índia*. Their networks of trade spanned deep into Southeast Asia, and despite suffering a number of severe setbacks as a result of VOC freebooting activities, they managed to recuperate with amazing agility and perseverance.

The *Santa Catarina* Incident, 25 February 1603

The unexpectedly poor business prospects and dearth of cargo that van Heemskerk encountered after his arrival in Asia in 1602, together with his discovery that 17 Dutch sailors had been executed at the hands of the Lusitanian authorities in Macao,[39] made the admiral hostile towards the *Estado da Índia*.[40] He was deeply suspicious that Portuguese officers had agitated with several Southeast Asian princes to close Dutch factories, confiscate their goods, and bring these northern European interlopers to "justice". More significantly, perhaps, his efforts to source for cargo proved futile. In Patani, on the Gulf of Siam, an earlier visit by Admiral Jakob van Neck had depleted the port's ready supply of pepper.[41]

With the intention of heading for the Banda Islands, van Heemskerk set sail from Patani on 16 November 1602.[42] He set his immediate course for Tioman, a provisioning island and navigational landmark off the eastern board of the Malay Peninsula.[43] This was at the beginning of the South China Sea's monsoon season, and it is during this period that Portuguese carracks outbound from Macao and Japan would skirt the coast of modern Vietnam, cross the Gulf of Siam between Pulau Condor and Tioman, and then continue their voyage through the Singapore Straits and on to Melaka. The location had been earlier recommended to van Heemskerk in Patani by Raja Hijau, the ruling queen of Patani.[44]

Anchored off the coast of Tioman, van Heemskerk convened his ship's *breede raad* (officers' council) and with the unanimous consent of his officers, on 4 December 1602 he resolved to attack the Portuguese China mercantile fleet.[45] Time was now working against the Dutch admiral and his men.

The wait off Tioman lasted longer than originally anticipated.[46] While the Dutch were waiting, they received an emissary who had been despatched by Raja Bongsu of Johor. In a letter dated 27 August 1603 addressed to the directors of the United Amsterdam Company (one of the *voorcompagniën* that was amalgamated into the VOC), van Heemskerk recalls the arrival of the Johorean emissary and the suggestion made by the Johorean royals:[47]

> Meanwhile the young King of Johor [that is Raja Bongsu] had been informed about our intention to intercept the Macao carrack — some proa [prahu] had spotted our ships near Tiuman [Tioman]. In spite of the adverse monsoon winds, he immediately dispatched one of his noblemen in a proa [prahu] or foist, who delivered the King's letter and offered me a golden dagger [kris] on his behalf. The King wrote that he had received my letters and presents sent from Jortan, along with my communications from Patani. He also acknowledged the great honours done to his brother, the Prince of Siak,[48] when the latter paid a visit to our ships at Patani. He was disappointed that we had not called at his harbors yet, contrary to the intentions expressed in our letters, but put the blame on our pilot. He was pleased at the news that we were lying in wait for the Macao carrack near the island of Tiuman [Tioman], and wished we had already captured it. Yet he argued that his river was the best place to await it, as all carracks must pass through the Strait of Singapore. Even if they should try to pass the Strait by night, which was impossible, they could never do so without being observed from the river. He added that open war had broken out between him and Malacca three months earlier due to some recent nuisance caused by the Portuguese, along with the many old and new injuries which the Portuguese had daily inflicted upon him and his subjects, regarding them as little more than dogs. When the Portuguese in Malacca became aware of our correspondence, they had positively ordered him not to befriend the Dutch, saying the Dutch were all thieves, intent on conquering his kingdom under the pretext of friendship. If he contravened their orders, he would be considered an enemy. In reply, the King had denied ever hearing anything bad about the Dutch, who traded in the friendliest manner with the inhabitants of every place they visited. He had furthermore told the Portuguese not to meddle in the affairs of his kingdom, prescribing with whom he could or could not engage in trade. As a result, three Portuguese

> warships — one whereof was first captured and then released by the English — and four or five foists had been stationed near Johore Head [that is the Hook of Berbukit], where they awaited the aforesaid ships from Macao in order to convoy them to Malacca. They had inflicted as much damage as they could and prevented others from navigating freely upon his river. The King assured me that I would not encounter just the Macao carracks, but vessels from every corner of the earth if I went there.

Van Heemskerk took the advice from the Johor monarch as "food for thought" and after carefully considering the possibility that this invitation in the end might just represent a Portuguese plot to kill the Dutch, he eventually heeded the advice.[49] After hearing news that Macao carracks had been sighted, van Heemskerk arrived at the Johor River estuary, to the east of Singapore island, on 24 February 1603. But here he was informed that one carrack had already passed through the treacherous Singapore Strait (almost certainly the *estreito velho* or Old Strait) just five days earlier. As luck would have it, the following morning (February 25) van Heemskerk and his men spotted the *Santa Catarina* at anchor.[50]

> At the crack of dawn on February 25, we saw with our own eyes that waking up early, keeping a close watch, and running fast availed us nothing without the blessing of the Almighty, He heard our prayers while we were asleep in order that we might not pride ourselves on our own accomplishments. Right in front of us was the second Macao carrack, a brand-new ship of 800 last [approximately 1,400 tons]. After we had carefully prepared ourselves, we hauled anchor at approximately 8 A.M. and approached the carrack, which set sail as well. All day long we pounded the carrack with both our ships, though we tried to aim for the mainsails, lest we destroy our booty by means of our own cannonades.

The *Sta. Catarina,* which, according to extant testimonies, did not find itself in the protective company of other ships, was taken under fire in an exchange that lasted from morning until dusk. The two Dutch ships, the *Witte Leeuw* (White Lion) and *Alkmaar*, shot through the mainsails of the carrack in a well-chosen strategy to immobilise the vessel and thus also sparing the carrack's cargo from suffering excessive damage. Portuguese documents explain that the soldiers aboard the *Santa Catarina* experienced serious difficulties in returning fire, not least because of all the commotion and confusion aboard the packed vessel involving one hundred women,[51] possibly children, merchants and other non-military personnel.[52] The early 17th-century Dutch historian Emanuel van Meteren further blamed the

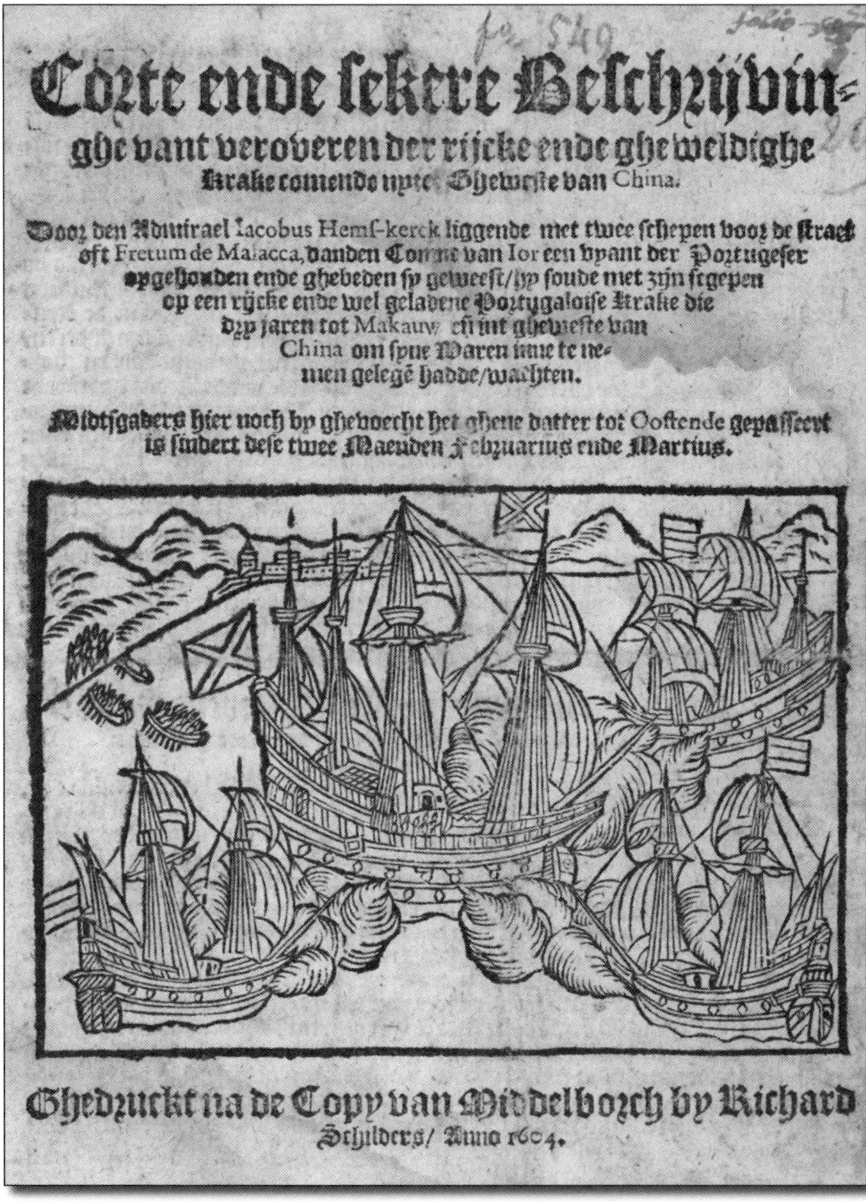
Corte ende sekere Beschrijvinghe vant veroveren der rijcke ende gheweldighe krake comende uyte Ghewerste van China.

Door den Admirael Iacobus Hems-kerck liggende met twee schepen voor de stract oft Fretum de Malacca, vanden Coninc van Ior een vyant der Portugeser opgehouden ende ghebeden sy geweest/ hy soude met zijn schepen op een rijcke ende wel geladene Portugaloise krake die drij jaren tot Makauw een int ghewerste van China om syne Waren inne te nemen gelegē hadde/ wachten.

Midtsgaders hier noch by ghevoecht het ghene datter tot Oostende gepasseert is sindert dese twee Maenden Februarius ende Martius.

Ghedruckt na de Copy van Middelborch by Richard Schilders/ Anno 1604.

Dutch pamphlet titled *Corte ende sekere Beschrijvinghe* (Short and Accurate Description) printed in Middelburg in 1604 announcing the attack on and capture of the *Sta. Catarina* in February 1603. The image depicts the three vessels of Jakob van Heemskerk attacking the Portuguese carrack, while troops and some oared vessels of the Johor ruler arrive at the scene of action. The landscape and the city in the background are pure imagination (Amsterdam University Library, OTM Pfl. K 26)

problems faced by the Portuguese on the crude weaponry carried on board the carrack, as well as the superior design of the Dutch ships, which were more manoeuvrable and presented a much less conspicuous profile as they lay lower in the water.[53]

Dutch materials emphasise how throughout the course of hostilities, a member of the royal family was present on board van Heemskerk's flagship, the *Witte Leeuw*. Theodore de Bry's *Indiae Orientalis Pars Octava* (Part Eight of the Voyages to the East Indies, 1607) as well as François Valentijn in his *Oud en Nieuw Oost-Indiën* (Old and New East India) identify specifically the presence of Raja Bongsu aboard the *Witte Leeuw*; but a petition by the admiral to the Dutch States General as well as Grotius claimed that the occasion was graced by none other than the Johor monarch Ala'ud'din Ri'ayat Shah III, in the company of Johorean *orang kaya*.[54] Their presence was later used by Grotius in his legal defence of the seizure to argue that the *Santa Catarina* was despoiled under the direct auspices and with the express consent of the Johor monarch.

By the time evening fell, the carrack had suffered extensive damage by shots and fire, and it was leaking dangerously. Incapable of manoeuvring, the ship was drifting towards rocky shores. Given the strong tides in the Straits of Singapore, as well as the shoals and reefs that once dotted its waters, it is likely that the *Santa Catarina* was helplessly adrift off the eastern coast of Singapore island. There was a real threat that if action were not taken promptly, the ship and cargo would be lost to the sea. The Portuguese captain of the carrack, Sebastião Serrão, and the *soldados*, now counting 70 casualties,[55] surrendered. It was agreed by negotiation that the ship and cargo would be forfeited in return for the sparing of all lives and the granting of unimpeded passage to Melaka for the surviving crew, soldiers and passengers. Meanwhile, the load of the carrack was lightened; the most valuable portion of the ship's cargo was brought to safety by transferring most of the porcelain, sugar, silks and precious woods, such as *pao d'aquila* (eaglewood), to two Dutch ships.[56]

The Immediate Aftermath, March 1603–January 1604

Extant documents from the Portuguese side reveal that van Heemskerk did indeed live up to his end of the agreement and that he brought all the surviving members to Melaka. Anchored near one of the islands off the coast of the Portuguese-held fort, identified in one source as the *Ilha Grande* (presumably present-day Pulau Besar, or possibly also Pulau Jawa, where ships would normally lie at anchor), van Heemskerk kept Captain Serrão and a Catholic priest, Fray António, as hostages on board and exchanged a series of letters with the Lusitanian authorities on shore. In a letter drafted on 9 March 1603 by Paulo Mendes de Vasconcelos and co-signed by members of Melaka's city council, the officials were evidently following protocol when they thanked the Dutch admiral for keeping good faith in a language atypically plain and unusually unpretentious for its age.[57] No sooner had the magistrates rendered their thanks, they intimated to van Heemskerk that he was extremely fortunate to have encountered this richly laden carrack from China, and that it had fallen into their enemy hands through the "unfathomable will of God".[58]

That very day in March, Melaka's Captain-Major Fernão de Albuquerque, a man of great ancestry who himself would serve as Portuguese viceroy in Goa, wrote a letter to van Heemskerk, extending his gratitude and dwelling particularly on the point as to why the Dutch admiral had had good fortune on his side when he attacked and seized the *Santa Catarina*.[59] Fortune was truly on van Heemskerk's side, for he was lucky not to have encountered any other ships of the Portuguese armada. Albuquerque then voiced a warning regret:[60] "I am sorry for one thing, however: that your Honour did not encounter my ship, so that you could have seen the difference in armaments and defensive capacity."

It would appear that Albuquerque was also well informed about some of the factors that were directly responsible for triggering the attack, specifically the fate of those 17 Dutch mates of van Neck's fleet who were executed by drowning in Macao.[61] He expressed his regret over the incident, especially the grounds upon which the atrocity had been committed. Albuquerque underscored that the person responsible had been apprehended. It is at this juncture that the captain-major proceeded to request a favour of van Heemskerk that in some ways does not befit the tone of the letter and the occasion. He asked van Heemskerk to intervene with Johor's King Ala'ud'din and also with Raja Bongsu to negotiate the release of hostages (taken from an inbound junk from Macao) held in Johorean captivity, and to secure their safe passage to Melaka.[62] On the basis of a second letter from Albuquerque to the Dutch admiral, dated 26 March 1603, it would appear that the said "Christian" hostages taken by the Johoreans "under the pretext of peace" were still not free.[63] Albuquerque reminded van Heemskerk that he was making no demands for "restitution of the junk" and its cargo, only for the "Portuguese and the Christian" hostages. To pave the way further for negotiations with the Johor royals,

Albuquerque declared that he would entrust van Heemskerk with two envoys, whom he named as Filipe Lobo and Pero Mascarenhas.[64]

Certainly the most moving communication reproduced by de Bry is a letter dated 24 March 1603 penned by the captain of the *Santa Catarina*, Sebastião Serrão.[65] The letter evidences the captain's personal plight and tragedy. Serrão expresses his profound regret that the only means at his disposal to thank van Heemskerk for sparing his life and keeping faith is mere words, for Serrão has lost everything. "I am among strangers here, with poverty as my bedfellow" the broken captain laments.[66] Relieved of his cargo, in which he undoubtedly invested a major portion of his personal fortune, Serrão was left with nothing but the clothes he was and still is wearing. He humbly beseeches van Heemskerk:[67]

> What I am currently wearing is so torn and spoiled from the hail of gunfire from Your Honor's ship that it can no longer be used as a garment. For this reason I entreat Your Honor to do me a good turn and send me a piece of velvet for a new set of clothes. If Your Honor grants my request, I would consider it a great kindness and gladly receive your alms.

Van Heemskerk proceeded to Banten, where his ships and the captured carrack were sighted. It must have left a deep impression on the admiral's fellow Dutchmen, for on 20 June 1603 Joris van Spilbergen made the following entry in his logbook:[68]

> On the twentieth of the said month Admiral Sr. Jacob Heemskerk arrived with his ship named the *White Lion* at Banten Roads, together with Jan Pauwelssz, his Vice-Admiral on the ship named *Alkmaar*. They brought with them a large new carrack that had arrived from Macao, in China, and wanted to proceed to Melaka. The said men waited around Johor, and after a long wait God delivered this ship into their hands. Even though the Portuguese defended her valiantly for some time, they were forced to surrender the ship, cargo, and persons. The said carrack carried as ballast, copper, spelter, alum, some aloes wood and *radix Chinae*.[69] It also carried raw and fine silk, some gold specie and many other precious things so that it[70] was appraised together with the plunder at more than seven million guilders.[71]

Melaka's Retaliation

With the seizure of the *Santa Catarina*, one of the richest cargos to leave China in many years, the merchant community of Macao is estimated by

Charles Boxer to have suffered losses of one *conto de oro* or one million cruzados.[72] These were heavy losses that would take time to recoup, and involved a sum of money that most certainly could not be ignored. Security in the Straits of Singapore and Melaka had long been an issue — and a costly one — for the *Estado da Índia*. Much of the region surrounding these two navigational lanes were controlled by Johor, a kingdom seen by many in the Malay world as the rightful and moral successor of the fallen Melaka Sultanate. Given Johor's moral and historical status as well as its geographic proximity to Melaka, it is hardly surprising that Luso-Johor relations were volatile and even in the best of times seriously strained. In the aftermath of the *Santa Catarina* incident, it was clearly recognised that Dutch presence in, and friendship with, Johor was not only undesirable, but indeed a serious strategic and commercial threat to be stifled in its infancy.[73]

The Portuguese were determined to take strong action, not only against the Dutch "rebels", "intruders" and "pirates", but also against Malay polities that traded with, and lent active support to the Dutch. What began as a single incident off the coast of Johor established itself with a pattern of predictable and alarming regularity, much to the detriment of the Portuguese *Estado da Índia*. Since the Dutch launched many of their attacks in the region between Tioman and the Straits of Melaka, securing the sea lanes linking trade between Portuguese India, Melaka, Macao and the Malukus became paramount. Portuguese punitive expeditions, such as the ones dispatched in 1603 and again in January 1604, were intended to back diplomatic efforts with the force of arms and persuade the king of Johor to expel the Dutch from the waters around the Straits of Singapore and the Johor River estuary. Neither King Ala'ud'din nor Raja Bongsu was intimidated by the Portuguese, and they both continued to cultivate commercial and political relations with the Dutch traders. After van Heemskerk's visit to Johor in 1603, the Dutch maintained a resident agent by the name of Jakob Buys (or Buysen) in Johor's royal residence of Batu Sawar.[74] Particularly after the incident surrounding the seizure of the *Santa Catarina*, the Portuguese dispatched naval squadrons to the Johor River estuary to anticipate the arrival of their China mercantile fleet and give the ships armed escort to Melaka. In practice, however, the Dutch — or, in one instance, a party described as the English — engaged the Portuguese armada in battle, drove them out of the Johor River estuary, and lifted the crippling blockade on the riverine settlements. The latter included the capital of Batu Sawar as well as the reconstructed fortress Kota Batu (Johor Lama).[75]

De Bry's Schematic Sketch of a Luso-Dutch Naval Confrontation off Singapore, October 1603: Text and Context

The maps and steel cuts of the three German cartographers Johann Theodor, Johann Dietrich and Johann Israel de Bry have long been cherished among scholars of history and armchair travellers. In volume VIII of their celebrated collection of voyages to the East and West Indies, one finds in appendix XII, under "Icones seu gennuinae et expressae delineationes omnium memorabilium" (Images or True and Exact Descriptions of All Memorable Things and Events)[76] — the map of a Dutch-Portuguese naval battle that took place in the Johor River estuary off the eastern coast of Singapore. The printers also added a small commentary on the course of the battle, which is written in German and broadly corresponds to the more substantial account of the conflict compiled by M. Gotthard Arthus, a native of Danzig and a teacher (later *conrector* or co-principal) at Frankfurt am Main's Latin College.[77]

Like many of the other early accounts of Dutch activities in the East Indies, the story found its way into the first important historical account published by Isaac Commelin the title of which translates into English as the *Beginning and Continuation of the United Netherlands East India Company*.[78] Full and partial renditions into French and English are extant.[79] Commelin's compilation of early eyewitness accounts and historically relevant material also reproduces a number of the prints that can be retrieved in the travel-related works of Theodor de Bry and his sons.

With specific reference to the map found in appendix XII, the accompanying text reconstructs the sequence of armed engagements that took place in the Johor River estuary and the Singapore Straits between three ships under the command of Dutch Vice-Admiral Jakob Pietersz van Enkhuysen and the Portuguese armada of Estêvão Teixeira de Macedo between 6 and 11 October 1603.[80] This virtually unknown chapter in the history of early modern Johor is of considerable significance for understanding both the origins, as well as the course of, Johor-Dutch relations in the first two decades of the 17th century.[81]

Teixeira de Macedo, a seasoned officer and previously captain of the Portuguese fort at Ambon, *Nossa Senhora da Anunciada* (Our Lady of the Annunciation)[82] dispatched his armada to the Singapore Straits to impose a blockade of the Johor River as well as to protect inbound vessels of the

Printed schematic depiction of the battle between the three ships of Vice-Admiral Jakob Pietersz van Enkhuysen and the Portuguese armada in the Johor River (Rio Batusabar), off Pedra Branca, and along the north shore of Batam. The legend featured in the box in the centre left-hand side is written in German. Johor's fleet is anchored near a shoal running off the eastern coast of Singapore. The east and western entrance to the Tebrau or Johor Strait are marked as river estuaries, with the eastern portion of Pulau Ubin clearly visible. The legend must be read against the text of M. Gotthard Arthus. From De Bry, *Icones Seu Gennuinae et Expressae Delinationes omnium Memorabilium, quae in hac octava Indiae Orientalis parte annotata sunt*, 1607, image XIII. (Bibliotheca Thysiana, Leiden, THYS 874)

Folgen etliche Figuren vnd Conterfeytungen/ ſo zum theil in das vorige Achte Theil/ als nemlich die Stadt Amacao, vnd die Schlacht in dem Fluß Batuſabar geſchehen/ zum theil in dieſen Appendicem gehörig/ ſampt kurtzer Erklärung eines jeden Kupfferſtücks.

Alles in Kupffer geſtochen vnd an Tag geben

Durch

Johan Dieterich vnd Johan Iſrael de Bry gebrüder.

Title page of the image appendix to the *Achter Theil der Orientalischen Indien* which features "artists impressions" of key moments from the text. It also contains the schematic map of the naval battle between Pietersz van Enkhuysen and the Portuguese armada off the coast of Singapore. (Amsterdam University Library, OTM OF 82-5-7)

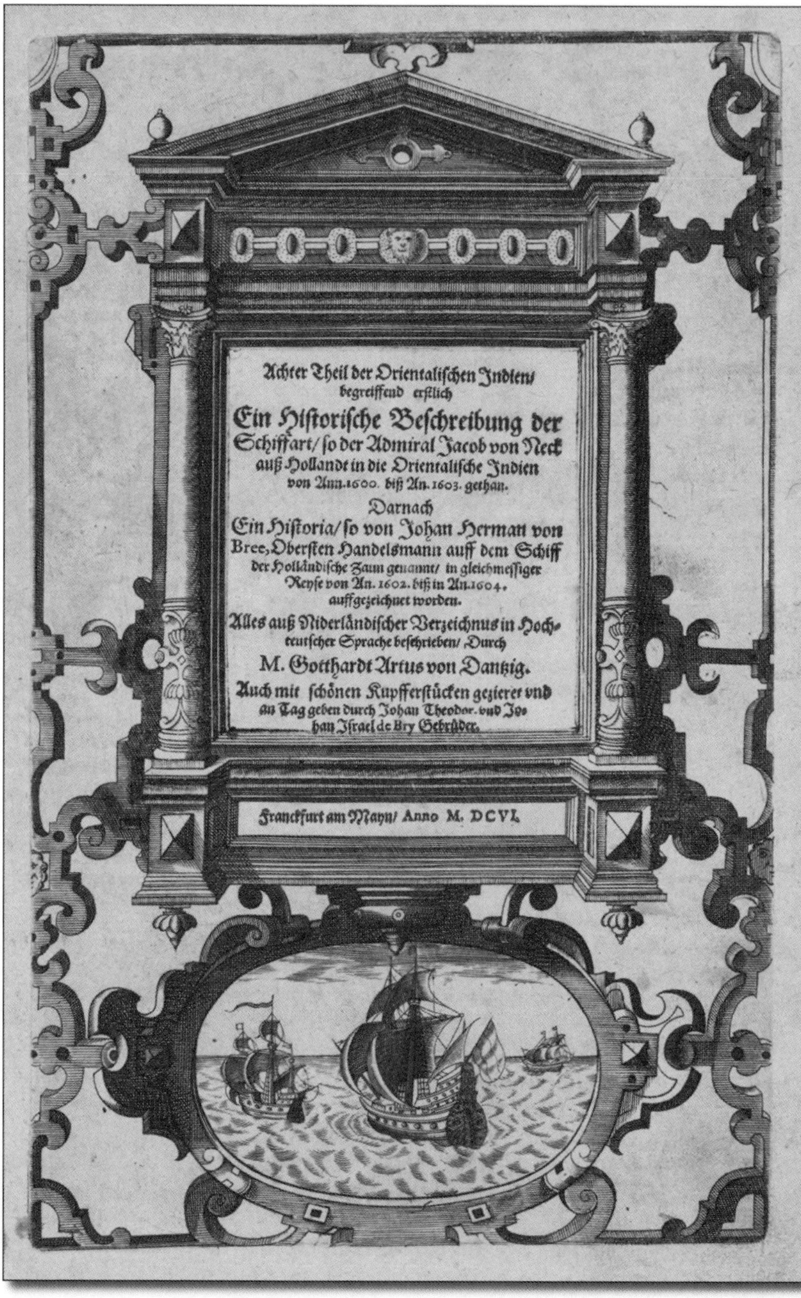
Achter Theil der Orientalischen Indien/
begreiffend erstlich
Ein Historische Beschreibung der
Schiffart/ so der Admiral Jacob von Neck
auß Hollandt in die Orientalische Indien
von Ann.1600. biß An.1603. gethan.
Darnach
Ein Historia/ so von Johan Herman von
Bree, Obersten Handelsmann auff dem Schiff
der Holländische Zaun genannt/ in gleichmessiger
Reyse von An. 1602. biß in An.1604.
auffgezeichnet worden.
Alles auß Niderländischer Verzeichnus in Hoch-
teutscher Sprache beschrieben/ Durch
M. Gotthardt Artus von Dantzig.
Auch mit schönen Kupfferstücken gezieret und
an Tag geben durch Johan Theodor. und Jo-
han Israel de Bry Gebrüder.
Franckfurt am Mayn/ Anno M. DCVI.

Title page of the 1606 German text edition which contains among others the account of Jakob Pietersz van Enkhuysen's voyage to the East Indies, and his engagement with the Portuguese armada off Singapore in October 1603. The German translation was prepared by M. Gotthard Arthus (Artus) from the Dutch original. (Amsterdam University Library, OTM OF 82-5-7)

Portuguese China fleet. According to the testimony of David van Lochum dated 10 October 1604, the armada consisted of vessels that had recently returned from battling the Dutch for supremacy in the Malukus.[83] It also transpires from Lochum's testimony that Johor Lama (*Oudt Ior* on de Bry's map) had briefly come under the direct control of the Portuguese.

The incident surrounding the seizure of the *Santa Catarina* certainly raised eyebrows in Europe and fired the imagination of traders over the riches to be earned (or, in this case, robbed from the enemy) in the East Indies. Not surprisingly, embarrassed Portuguese officials from Goa to Macao resolved that such an incident should not be repeated. The king of Portugal himself expressly instructed his viceroy in Goa, in a letter dated 27 December 1604, to dispatch an armada to the region. The ships were to be divided into squadrons and to patrol the waters around the Straits of Singapore, Melaka, Sabam, and Sunda in order to protect shipping to and from Portuguese Melaka.[84]

On their arrival in the East Indies, Warwijk's fleet separated and proceeded to call at different destinations in India, China and insular Southeast Asia. While van Warwijk set course for Patani, the three ships under Vice-Admiral Sebald de Weert (also Sibold de Waert) headed for Ceylon and Aceh.[85] After casting anchor off the coast of Baticalao, de Weert travelled by elephant to Kandy, where he was courteously received by its ruler, Vimala Dharma Suriya I.[86] The maharaja sought the assistance of the Dutch in expelling the Portuguese from their strongholds in Colombo, Cruz and Galle. De Weert promised to sail to Aceh and return with more ships.[87] He kept his word, returning in April 1603 from the north Sumatran city in the company of seven ships, three sloops and an embassy comprising two Acehnese delegates. The Dutch managed to seize four Portuguese vessels off the coast of Ceylon, but when the ruler of Kandy suspected that the Dutch were planning to capture and kill him, he had de Weert and 47 members of his Dutch crew murdered in cold blood on 1 June 1603.[88] Three days later, on 4 June, van Enkhuysen[89] was elected by his peers to the position of vice-admiral to replace the assassinated de Weert.[90] The new vice-admiral's ships set sail for Aceh. On 24 August 1603, van Enkhuysen and the three vessels *Zierikzee*, *Hollandsche Tuin* (Dutch Garden) and *Papagaaiken* (Little Parrot) set sail for Patani in the hope of procuring a cargo of pepper.[91] In the Straits of Melaka, the vice-admiral intercepted several vessels and exacted information about markets, cargo, trade routes and topography from their crews.[92]

The assassination of Sebald de Weert in Ceylon. The "Emperor" of Kandy is depicted wearing his crown, and Dutch ships are anchored off the coast. From De Bry, *Icones seu Gennuinae et Espressae Delineationes Omnium Memorabilium* (Images or Authentic and Accurate Depiction of all Memorable Events), Frankfurt am Main, 1607, image IX. (Bibliotheca Thysiana, Leiden, THYS 874)

Searching for the Old Strait of Singapore, September 1603

In the final days of September 1603, the three craft of Pietersz van Enkhuysen approached the Karimun Islands.[93] In these waters they encountered strong adverse currents and unpredictable winds. Although the Dutch ships carried two Malay pilots on board, it does not appear that they were sufficiently familiar with the geomorphology of the Singapore Straits. The region presented itself to the Dutch crew and Malay pilots as a maze of islets, reefs and sandbanks that lay around shallow waters or surfaced at low tide. De Bry's map gives some indication of this and even provides the depth of water measured in key areas by the Dutch crew.[94] The disoriented officers thus resolved, on 27 September, to man two sloops[95] and set out to find the passage through the Strait of Singapore to the South China Sea. The search continued for several days around small islands and through narrow maritime channels, but the Strait of Singapore remained elusive to the vice-admiral's men.[96]

On 30 September, seven mates went on land to find fresh water and gather firewood. Unaware of any danger, the unarmed men were ambushed by angry locals[97] who apparently mistook the Dutch sailors for Portuguese soldiers. When their mates heard the commotion on land, they quickly dispatched a sloop to shore, finding one of the sailors dead and three men seriously wounded. The attackers meanwhile took flight in four prahus that had been left at the other side of the islet.[98]

As evening fell the following day, the Dutch mates spotted a number of prahus assembling near the fateful island. Signalling to the locals that they should come closer, the Dutch displayed a white flag. Still, the local warriors or fishermen were afraid and kept a cautious distance. Noting this, the Dutch launched a sloop, carrying on board one of their Malay pilots, a white flag and the important message that the ships were Dutch and not Portuguese. Sensing that this might be a trick, the local men used the imminent sunset to return to shore and pledged to return at dawn.

The following morning the prahus regrouped as promised. As a precaution, each party exchanged two members of its crew. On board the *Zierikzee*, two of the locals explained that there was now great hostility between Johor and Portugal. Van Enkhuysen also learned that two large ships, together with four galleys and 20–25 banteens, were holding guard in the Johor River estuary.[99] After van Heemskerk's infamous capture of the *Santa Catarina*, the Portuguese officials in Melaka were on their toes and determined to lend armed protection to their merchant fleet through the dangerous and treacherous waters of the Straits.[100]

Extant sources reveal that Teixeira de Macedo's armada was intended to fulfil a dual function. First, it imposed a blockade in punishment for Johorean cooperation with the Dutch, specifically for their active support to van Heemskerk during the *Santa Catarina* incident. As long as the Portuguese vessels were holding guard in the Johor River, they were able to disrupt direct trade between the sea and Johor's riverine towns, including the royal capital at Batu Sawar, which is said to have been located about six Dutch sea-miles (about 44 kilometres) upstream.[101] Second, the Portuguese armada was instructed to await the arrival of the Portuguese merchant ships from Hirado, Macao and Makassar and grant them armed protection for their onward journey to Melaka.[102] The Dutch vice-admiral also learned on this occasion that before returning to Europe, van Heemskerk deployed members of his crew as agents, including Jakob Buys, who now headed the new VOC factory at Batu Sawar.[103] Van Enkhuysen hesitated no longer. He asked the locals to show his craft the passage through the Strait, promising a reward for their services. The locals replied that they were not seeking reward or remuneration but, rather, that they had come to assist their Dutch friends on the instructions of their monarch. The vice-admiral issued orders to weigh anchor, and with his Johorean guides on board he proceeded to the western entrance of the Old Strait of Singapore.[104] The local guides instructed the Dutch to "go back" because they were "not near the Strait".[105] It appears that the Dutch ships had proceeded too far south and had dropped anchor near the northern coast of Bulan or Batam, indicated on de Bry's map as *Valsch Sinca Pora* (False [Strait of] Singapore). Their further course cannot be reconstructed with certainty, but they did eventually arrive at a location that clearly fits the description of the old Dragon Teeth Gate.[106]

The Old Strait of Singapore is described (with some exaggeration, no doubt) as "a stone's throw" wide and "a cannon shot long".[107] Entering from the northwest, the crew spotted on the left-hand side two columns or pillars.[108] Nearby they sighted a "fine bay" — which is almost certainly the present-day Telok Blangah area — as well as a settlement known by the name *Singapura*, the exact location of which, unfortunately, cannot be ascertained from the Dutch source.[109] In the afternoon a southwesterly breeze helped the ships steer clear of dangerous cliffs along the shores of Sentosa. Once the ships cleared the Straits, they plied a north-northeasterly course, skirting the eastern shores of Singapore island.

Preparing for Battle

The following day, 4 October 1603, the three Dutch ships made their way towards "Patana", described as the principal "port of Johor".[110] This is almost certainly the islet in the Johor River known as Pulau Patani, which is located about five kilometres upstream from Johor Lama.[111] Several prahus are reported to have gathered around the Dutch ships. One of them carried a Johorean official who is described as the "governor of Bintan".[112] A second prahu bore messages from the king and Jakob Buys.[113] These documents explain the reasons for the Portuguese blockade, and that the armada of Teixeira de Macedo was waiting for inbound vessels from Japan, China and Makassar. Van Enkhuysen swiftly responded to these written messages with pledges to attack the Portuguese and engage them in battle. He also asked the Johor monarch and Buys to come aboard his vessel as soon as possible in order that further negotiations could proceed in person. The Dutch crew then spotted several Portuguese craft holding guard in the Johor River estuary. Under cover of night, the Dutch dispatched a few sloops and prahus for reconnaissance, but the Portuguese immediately took flight when they suspected enemy vessels approaching.

At dawn on 5 October 1603, a southerly breeze carried the Dutch ships farther upstream. After passing two unidentified islands on their right-hand side, they were suddenly surrounded by several prahus that appeared from all directions. The prahus apparently belonged to small traders and peddlers who sought to break through the Portuguese blockade under the armed protection of the Dutch ships, and reach the upstream towns that had been cut off from commerce and supplies. The Portuguese naval force was now only about 1.5 Dutch sea-miles, or nine kilometres, farther upstream. The Dutch dropped anchor, waiting for the currents of the incoming tide to help them move to the upper reaches of the Johor River.

At about three o'clock in the afternoon, a couple of foists and boats came to get a better glimpse of the newcomers, but they quickly turned around and headed back after realising that they were dealing with enemy ships. That night, under cover of darkness, the *Zierikzee* and *Hollandsche Tuin* weighed anchor and quietly moved their position farther upstream. The *Zierikzee* reportedly ran aground, but thanks to the swift response of its mates, the ship was soon afloat and ready for battle.

A Portuguese *renegado* (defector) by the name of "Codsa de Delsab",[114] working in the services of the Johor monarch, arrived with a letter written in Malay and accompanied by a Dutch translation prepared by Jakob Buys. In his message, the monarch beseeched the vice-admiral to do all in his power to help relieve Johor of the blockade and to drive the Portuguese from the river. From a private note of Buys that accompanied the official letter, it transpires that the king publicly welcomed the vice-admiral's earlier pledge of support. This message, Buys explained, evoked much rejoicing among the people of Batu Sawar and raised hopes that the Portuguese blockade may soon be lifted with Dutch help.[115]

The Naval Battles in the Johor River Estuary of October 1603

At dawn the Dutch ships were only two cannon shots' distance from the Portuguese armada. Slowly, they glided towards the eastern shores of the Johor River towards the enemy. The Dutch crew said their prayers and then engaged Teixeira de Macedo with the first cannon blast. The Portuguese returned fire with their smaller artillery. The battle lasted for most hours of daylight. Just before dusk, at five o'clock, the Portuguese flagship broke through the Dutch vessels and headed for the sandbank or shoal on which the *Zierikzee* had earlier run aground.[116] Many Portuguese *soldados* are thought to have lost their lives in this tactical move, but with the benefit of hindsight, it saved the flagship and the remaining vessels of the armada from suffering more extensive damage. On the Dutch side, the vice-admiral counted on his flagship three casualties and several men who had been wounded or crushed. François Valentijn, in his monumental *Oud en Nieuw Oost-Indiën*, claims that "[t]he only losses suffered in that fight were five or six men killed, and a few men wounded on both [Dutch] vessels".[117]

Throughout the hours of daylight, Raja Bongsu,[118] Jakob Buys and many *orang kaya* in their company held watch in prahus of Johor's royal fleet on the western shoreline of the Johor River. When the Portuguese flagship broke through the Dutch vessels, the Johoreans made their way across the water towards the victorious crew. Raja Bongsu presented van Enkhuysen with a beautiful kris and thanked him for his contribution in lifting the crippling blockade. The Johoreans also brought fruit and arak on board and celebrated with the Dutch mates their victory over the Portuguese.[119] The following morning, 8 October 1603, the Dutch crew discovered that the Portuguese ships, at high tide and under cover of darkness, had made their way across the aforementioned sandbank or shoal and taken flight down the Johor River. As the tide had already reversed by dawn, it was not possible to raise anchor and chase after them.

Meanwhile, the king of Johor moved with the remaining part of his fleet, consisting of four or five "magnificent" galleys and about 40 prahus, into the Johor River etuary.[120] He was determined to chase the remainder of the Portuguese armada out of his waters. De Bry's map places them near a finger-shaped shoal off the eastern coast of Singapore that is now reclaimed land in the vicinity of Tanah Merah and the new Changi Naval Base. The Johor monarch was reportedly present aboard the largest galleys. Raja Bongsu and the Prince of Siak were each aboard their own personal craft. During the morning hours they encountered strong currents, with the tide against them. By afternoon, however, the tide had begun to reverse, and the proud Johorean fleet glided upstream. They spotted the enemy, anchored in the river at a distance of about two Dutch sea-miles, or approximately 15 kilometres. Later they were joined by the Dutch ships. The king and the vice-admiral resolved to attack the following morning.

At dawn on 10 October 1603, Raja Bongsu, together with many *orang kaya* and the Dutch agent Jakob Buys, transferred onto the *Zierikzee*, from where they could better monitor the battle.[121] A westerly breeze carried them towards the enemy, whose remaining craft were quickly gathering in formation towards the eastern side of the river. The vice-admiral resolved to attack the flagship. The crew again said their prayers and manoeuvred themselves to the side of the Portuguese flagship. The exchange of fire began sometime between nine and ten o'clock in the morning and lasted a full seven hours. The Dutch crew fired at the sails of the Portuguese flagship in a tactical move to immobilise it. Pietersz van Enkhuysen and his Johorean guests observed how the Portuguese soldiers were abandoning ship, transferring personnel from the larger craft into their smaller galleys and prahus. The armada headed for the open sea, making its way towards Pedra Branca,[122] at the eastern entrance of the Singapore Straits. As evening fell, the remains of the Portuguese armada assembled off the northeastern coast of Batam.

Raja Bongsu, who supervised the entire naval operation aboard the *Zierikzee*, transferred back to his personal galley at sundown. He left Buys behind, with express instructions to keep a close eye on all developments and to brief him the next morning.

At dawn the following day, 11 October, the Dutch crew spotted the Portuguese armada anchored off the northeastern coast of Batam at a distance of about one Dutch sea-mile, or seven kilometres. The Portuguese, too, were alert and had already spotted the Dutch ships heading towards them. Dreading a third round of attacks, the Portuguese quickly hoisted their sails and took off. Seeing this, van Enkhuysen dispatched a sloop with a message for the king, Raja Bongsu and the Johorean fleet that the Portuguese were now definitely taking flight.[123] The sea battle was won! With the Portuguese defeated and on the run, the king was now reportedly in a position to bring the settlement at Johor Lama back under his control.[124]

Closer Ties between the VOC and Johor

The vice-admiral moved his three ships into the safer waters of the Johor River, where the crew could rest for a few days from the exertions of combat. One rainy day, the whole fleet of Johor, together with the king, his two brothers and many *orang kaya* came towards the Dutch vessels. The vice-admiral and Buys boarded the royal galley, inside which they found the king seated on a carpet. Raja Bongsu joined them soon after.

The king thanked the vice-admiral for keeping faith and for lending armed assistance. Since he had little wealth, the king wondered aloud how he would be able to repay his Dutch friends. Offers had been made earlier, on 9 October to be precise, to procure pepper from Kampar and Indragiri and unspecified "other places", presumably all on Sumatra.[125] Even a man referred to as the "Governor of Kampar" (who reportedly had a very good command of the Portuguese language) was in the company of the Johor monarch at the time and informed the vice-admiral as to whether there would be sufficient pepper in stock.[126] This was evidently not the case. The king then explained that there was not sufficient pepper available at the present time, but in the event that the Dutch friends could return in four or five months' time, or better still, remain in Johor waters, there would be abundant supplies at hand.[127] Van Enkhuysen replied that the ships and crew had already been in the region for quite some time, and they would need to find cargo soon so that they may set out on their voyage home. The Dutch party extended an invitation to the king to visit them aboard the *Zierikzee* for a farewell. This invitation was accepted. Raja Bongsu then took his leave, and the Dutch party escorted him back to his galley.

Shortly thereafter, the king, Raja Bongsu, the Prince of Siak and several *orang kaya* arrived on board the *Zierikzee* and entered the vice-admiral's cabin.[128] Dressed in fine silk, the king seated himself with a pillow on a "table-shaped" *singgasana*. Next to him, on a "small bench", the Prince of Siak took a seat, and Raja Bongsu used a "Spanish chair".[129]

Raja Bongsu heading in his oared galley to the flag ship of Jakob Pietersz van Enkhuysen after the defeat of the Portuguese armada off the coast of Singapore. An artist's impression of the town Singapura is provided in the top right-hand portion of the image. From De Bry, *Icones seu Gennuinae et Espressae Delineationes Omnium Memorabilium* (Images or Authentic and Accurate Depiction of all Memorable Events), Frankfurt am Main, 1607, image VII. (Bibliotheca Thysiana, Leiden, THYS 874)

The *orang kaya* seated themselves on mats. The king showered his Dutch friends with words of praise and thanked the vice-admiral for delivering Johor from the Portuguese blockade. Van Enkhuysen presented the Johor monarch with a silver-hilted Japanese sword and Raja Bongsu with a musket.[130] The subsequent round of discussions appears to have focused largely on opportunities that had opened up with the lifting of the riverine blockade. Now that the waters had been cleared of enemy craft, pepper could be brought in from Sumatra and trade could flourish once more. The Johorean guests bid their hosts farewell. After bringing on fresh water and waiting for the wind to pick up, Pietersz van Enkhuysen weighed anchor on 14 October and set sail for Patani, where he arrived on 4 November 1603.[131] The cutter *Papagaaiken* was dispatched to Banten, where the crew delivered news of their victorious engagement with the Portuguese.[132] Yet the words of the young lawyer and jurisconsult Hugo Grotius — who defended Dutch aggression in the East Indies — doubtless reflect an over-optimistic and greatly exaggerated view of Dutch achievements in the region: "… the conquest of an entire fleet; the liberation of Johore, and the release of a very friendly king from a state of siege."[133]

Escalation of Luso-Dutch Violence around the Malay Peninsula, 1604–5

Van Heemskerk's seizure of the *Santa Catarina* off the east coast of Singapore and his primordial defence alliance with Johor heralded an escalation of violence in the waters of the Singapore Straits and the Johor River estuary. The armed showdown between Vice-Admiral van Enkhuysen and the Portuguese Captain Teixeira de Macedo marked only the second — but nevertheless important — chapter in this unfolding story.

The Portuguese officials of the *Estado da Índia* were growing painfully aware that the Dutch competitors were not only seeking to wrest the spice-producing Malukus from their control, but they were engaging in acts that seriously disrupted vital trading routes linking Japan and China with the Malay Peninsula, India, Arabia and east Africa. The arrival of van Enkhuysen surely gave cause for serious concern, as the Portuguese China mercantile fleet would now be exposed to the violent actions of Dutch "thieves, liars and pirates". It is, therefore, scarcely a surprise that the Portuguese armada — or whatever parts of it might have remained seaworthy — reappeared just days after the Dutch vice-admiral set sail for Patani. Significantly also, Fernão de Albuquerque's new successor at Melaka, André Furtado de Mendonça, an officer seasoned in combat, assumed his office just shortly before hostilities erupted with van Enkhuysen on 1 September 1603. He used this change of political leadership to launch a diplomatic offensive at the Johor court that some years later resulted in a peace treaty. Furtado de Mendonça was willing to hold out an olive branch to the king, provided that he sever his good ties with the Dutch, expel the factors from Batu Sawar, and confiscate their property. On the express advice of Raja Bongsu, however, the king replied on 8 February 1604 that he would rather lose his entire kingdom than give in to such preposterous demands.[134] This surely ruffled Furtado's ego. It is evidenced by a number of studies that during this period — the early months of 1604 — the Portuguese attacked targets along the banks of the Johor River. They failed to capture the capital, Batu Sawar, but they succeeded in reoccupying Johor Lama.

The seizure of the *Santo António* in 1605 took place against the backdrop of heightened tension between the Dutch, Johoreans and Portuguese over security in the Singapore Straits, the Johor River estuary, as well as the waters off Pedra Branca up to Tioman. These issues have already been discussed in depth in the preceding sections. It remains a hitherto largely neglected chapter that marks an important turning point in regional politics, diplomacy and trade. The "*Santo António* incident" reveals much about the political complexity and fragility of political relations, the balance of power on the Malay Peninsula, in Siam, as well as the flow and nature of intra-Asian trade in the early 17th century.

With special regard to issues surrounding regional politics and diplomacy, the *Santo António* incident also marks an important shift in Patani's relations with the Portuguese and paved the ground for improved relations with the Dutch. By turning its back on Lusitanian traders and the comparatively peaceful, if sometimes strained, relations with Portuguese Melaka, Patani hoped to reposition itself commercially, especially since the Dutch (unlike the Portuguese) had at the time no direct access point in the trade with China.[135] Doubtless, the moves of both Patani as well as the VOC were carefully monitored by regional competitors, including the Johoreans (who were allies in arms with the Dutch after 1603 and with whom Patani had a dynastic quarrel at the time),[136] Pahang and the Siamese court in Ayutthaya. As is known, King Ekathosarot would soon dispatch Siam's first ever diplomatic mission to the West, namely, to Prince Maurice of Orange, the Stadholder of Holland and Zealand.[137] This move was viewed with considerable alarm by Philip III/II, the king of Spain and Portugal,[138] but some years later the Siamese court actively sought to steer relations with the *Estado da Índia* on an improved diplomatic footing.[139]

Despoiling the Lusitanian Enemy: Plunder, Commerce and Diplomacy

The seizure of the *Santo António* took place in the immediate context of escalating violence in the waters around Singapore and, indeed, around much of the southern tip of the Malay Peninsula.

In early May 1604, three ships belonging to the fleet of Admiral Wijbrand van Warwijk, the *Hollandia*, *Vlissingen* and *Sphaera Mundi*, arrived in Johor waters. After a formal exchange of diplomatic gifts[140] and niceties as well as ascertaining trade opportunities in the region, van Warwijk set sail for Patani and China on 20 May 1604. He returned with the monsoon winds that December without having been able to conduct trade in China.[141] In early January 1605, Warwijk's ships dropped anchor off the coast of Tioman, where they lay in wait to prey on richly laden carracks from Japan, Macao and Makassar.

Warwijk's return to the waters around the Malay Peninsula marked in a symbolic way the beginning of Furtado de Mendonça's *annus horribilis* in his position as captain-major of Melaka. The year 1605 saw the Portuguese *Estado da Índia* in insular and peninsular Southeast Asia stretched to its limits, financially as well as militarily. The Dutch were stepping up their attacks on Portuguese fortifications in the Malukus, and in February 1605 the fort *Nossa Senhora da Anunciada* on the island of Ambon was lost to the northern European intruders.[142] The serious problems experienced in the Malukus may help explain why the first squadron — initially smaller than in the previous trading season — arrived later than usual in the waters of the Johor River estuary. The Portuguese naval presence did not deter van Warwijk from stepping up Dutch freebooting activities in the waters around the southern tip of the Malay Peninsula and the Riau Archipelago. On 14 January 1605, the *Vlissingen*, belonging to Warwijk's fleet, succeeded in capturing a Portuguese vessel off Pedra Branca that was inbound from Cochinchina (presently Vietnam).[143] The cargo seized by the crew of the *Vlissingen* included rice, textiles, angelwood (174.5 *picul*), Chinese camphor (two barrels of unspecified weight),[144] benzoin (33.5 *picul*) and six pieces of artillery.[145] Further prizes followed. In the Straits of Singapore, Warwijk's men also

Landing of the Dutch fleet of Admiral Jakob van Neck at Patani in 1602. From De Bry, *Icones seu Gennuinae et Espressae Delineationes Omnium Memorabilium* (Images or Authentic and Accurate Depiction of all Memorable Events), Frankfurt am Main, 1607, image IX. (Bibliotheca Thysiana, Leiden, THYS 874)

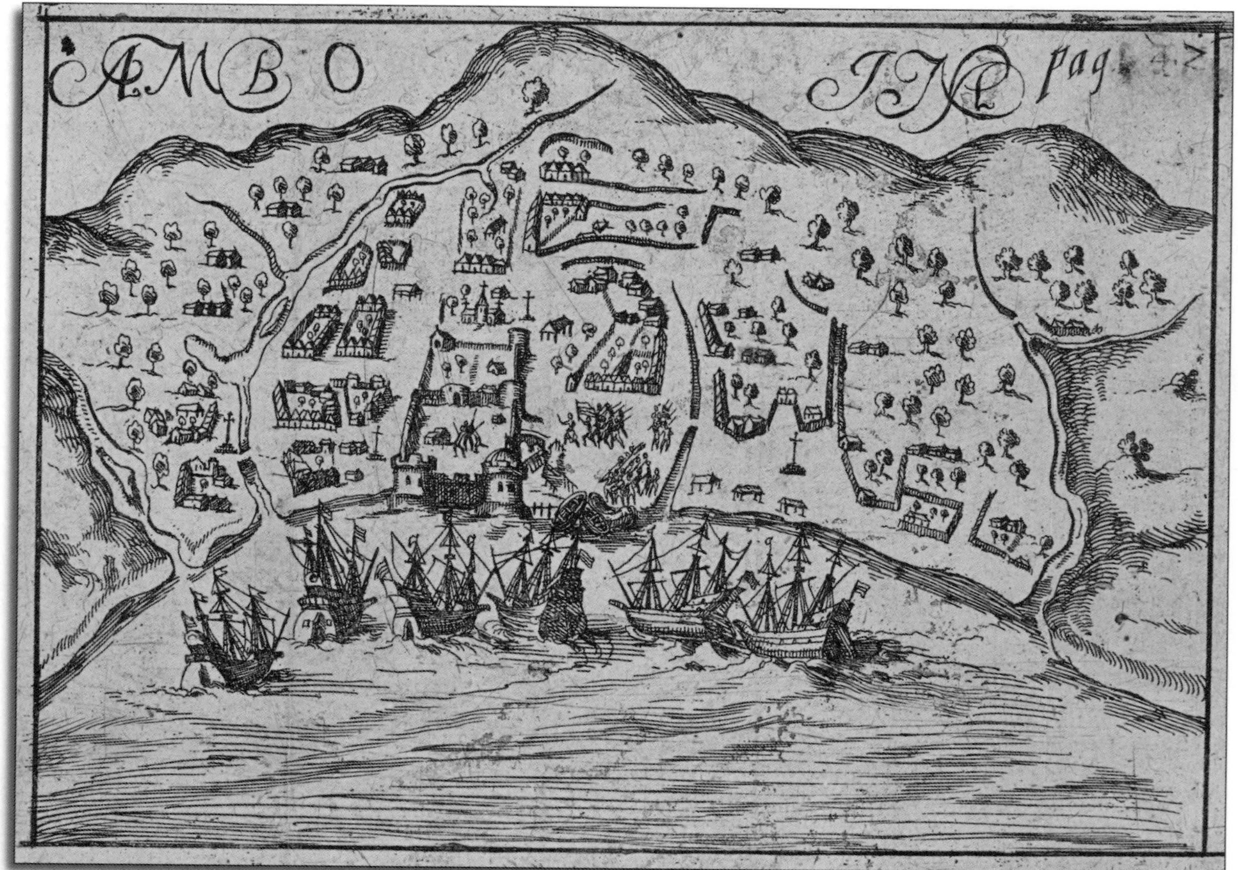

The Dutch fleet arrives off Ambon in 1605 from Isaac Genius and Levinus Hulsius, *Neundte Schiffart* (Ninth Voyage to the East Indies), 1612 (Koninklijke Bibliotheek, The Hague, 2112 C 4).

took one of Furtado de Mendonça's junks that was loaded with provisions for Melaka. Some weeks later, in June 1605, the Dutch also seized a smaller craft arriving from the island of Solor that was carrying a precious cargo of white sandalwood and sea-turtle shell.[146]

Anticipating Dutch attacks in the Johor River estuary, the Portuguese authorities in Melaka mustered all available naval support around the region and in late February dispatched an armada through the Singapore Straits under the personal command of Furtado de Mendonça. This consisted of 7 galleons, 30 banteens, 20 foists and 10 Javanese *champans* (sampans).[147] The seasoned Lusitanian admiral's presence was more than just proverbial sabre rattling and early modern gunboat diplomacy. As in the previous year, the Portuguese undertook an extended military campaign against Johor and laid siege to Batu Sawar.[148] This royal residence and capital city was also known as "New Johor".[149] Documentary evidence suggests that Furtado de Mendonça was very confident of his imminent victory over Johor and issued written threats to the king. The admiral boasted that should this military enterprise fail, he and the residents of Melaka would gladly pay tribute to the king of Johor. This was a clear act of hubris committed in the heat of confrontation. While one cannot possibly claim that the great admiral actually lost the military campaign, he certainly did not succeed in his enterprise either. After wasting much precious gunpowder and ammunition and suffering many casualties, the Portuguese abandoned their siege of Batu Sawar. The Johor capital was well-provisioned and protected by thick wooden palisades.[150] Furtado de Mendonça not only lost time, men and opportunities, he also lost a good deal of credibility, and he certainly never gave a single pardao in tribute. While the Portuguese armada was busy pursuing their futile siege in the upper reaches of the Johor River, Warwijk's ships scoured the waters in the open sea around Tioman and Pedra Branca, hoping to spot and attack easy Portuguese merchant prey.

The Seizure of the *Santo António* at Patani, 1605

In January 1605 a carrack by the name of *Santo António* set sail from Macao for Melaka and Goa. It was undertaking the voyage together with a second vessel, belonging to João Caiado de Gambôa, that had departed the port of Hirado in November 1604 and was reportedly "richly laden" with silver from Japan.[151] This silver was in payment for the substantial cargo of silks sold in Japan that year, and this not only brought in "very fat profits" for the principal trading season in 1604, it also wiped out much of the debt left behind from the earlier loss of the *Santa Catarina* to van Heemskerk.[152] For their voyage through the dangerous and pirate-infested waters of the South China Sea, as well as the Singapore and Melaka Straits, the two merchant vessels were under armed escort of a galleon.[153]

According to extant reports of both Portuguese and Dutch origin, the merchant fleet experienced stormy weather, in the course of which the *Santo António* lost its helm off Pedra Branca near the eastern entrance to the Straits of Singapore.[154] Given that the ship was damaged and difficult to manoeuvre, and most certainly could not pass through the treacherous Singapore Straits, it sailed on 17 February 1605 into the port of Patani, in the Gulf of Siam.[155] The other vessels of the merchant fleet, including Caiado de Gambôa's silver ship from Japan and a royal Portuguese galleon, continued their onward journey to Melaka, where they arrived safely. But the *Santo António* was left behind in Patani for repairs.[156]

At the turn of the 17th century, Patani was ruled by Raja Hijau.[157] The port represented an important node in the regional trading networks that linked Siam, Pegu, Borneo, the Malay Peninsula and China.[158] Patani was also on nominally peaceful terms with the *Estado da Índia*. For this reason, the *Santo António*'s call at the port and payment of fees should not have given rise to any exceptional concerns for the security of the ship and its cargo, estimated in official Portuguese reports at around 80,000 cruzados at cost.[159] The bulk of this, appraised at 50,000 cruzados, was earmarked for transhipment to the final destination Goa.[160]

The crew of the *Santo António* were almost certainly aware that the Dutch maintained a factory in Patani, and also that their trading ships had earlier visited the port. But the political climate, normally favourably disposed towards the Portuguese merchants, was rapidly changing before their very eyes.

Claes Simons Meelbael had taken over from his predecessor van der Leck as head of the VOC factory in Patani. The Dutch factor reportedly placed considerable pressure on Raja Hijau of Patani and her councillors (the *menteri* or *mantri*) to consent to their seizure of the Portuguese carrack *Santo António* and its cargo.[161] With the benefit of hindsight, one can say that this diplomatic move paid off. The queen yielded to Dutch agitation and ultimately agreed to divide up the booty.[162]

On 25 March 1605, Admiral van Warwijk was still stationed with his fleet off the coast of Tioman, hoping to waylay Portuguese vessels inbound from China and Makassar. On this day he received news that Raja Hijau had consented to the Dutch seizure of a vessel anchored in her port on the Patani River. Van Warwijk did not hesitate a moment longer. He gave instructions to set course for Patani, where he arrived the following day, 26 March. His ship moved close to the ill-fated *Santo António* and dropped anchor.

The crew of the Portuguese carrack were evidently aware of their impending fate, and they pledged to defend ship and cargo to the last drop of blood. That very same evening, the *Santo António*'s mates were ferried ashore,[163] leaving the carrack and its cargo in Dutch hands. The ship was taken, unceremoniously, without one casualty or a single shot fired![164]

One should perhaps more accurately state "remaining cargo", for reports have it that the most valuable part of the *Santo António*'s load had been earlier transferred to shore and brought via the land path across the Isthmus of Kra via Kedah to Melaka and other unidentified places on the Malay Peninsula. The portion of the *Santo António*'s cargo that escaped Dutch seizure included 700 to 800 *picul* of raw silk, about 200 bales of silk and some three *bahar* in gold.[165] It is scarcely a surprise — and one Dutch source bitterly complains about this — that the value of the cargo seized from the *Santo António* was significantly less than it would have been had the ship been captured on open sea.

Nevertheless, what remained in the hull still made this rather effortless catch financially worthwhile. The Dutch prize consisted of the following items:[166] 2,000 *picul* of white powdered sugar, baskets of sugar candy, 4,500 *picul* of *tintinago* or spelter, 223 *fardels* (bundles, packs) of Chinese camphor, 18 lead boxes of musk cods,[167] 11 chests of vermilion,[168] 22 chests containing Chinese fans, 209 *fardels* of raw silk, 75 *fardels* of "bad yellow raw silk", 6,000 pieces of coloured sundry porcelain, and ten casks of both coarse and fine porcelain. Other items in the cargo that are not listed in detail included *radix Chinae*, taffettas, damask,[169] gold thread, wooden boxes or chests, benzoin and a range of other objects manufactured in China.[170]

At Patani, van Warwijk further organised the purchase of 430 *picul* of raw silk for a total value of about 49,500 ryals-of-eight and another 3,000 ryals-of-eight worth of *gewrochte zijde,* a form of raw silk.[171] It is believed that the goods bought here in Patani originally stemmed from the cargo of the *Santo António*, and possibly had been impounded by the authorities in the city of Patani, or sold by the Portuguese to raise money for repairs on the ailing vessel.

Diplomatic and Commercial Repercussions of the *Santo António* Incident

A series of primary sources, including the autobiography of Jaques de Coutre, written in Spanish, reveal how relations between Patani and the Portuguese had been strained since the assassination of António de Saldanha, a *casado* of Melaka, at Patani and the establishment of a Dutch factory there in 1602.[172] The seizure of the *Santo António* marked the symbolic rupture of friendly, if occasionally strained, relations between Patani's monarch and the Portuguese. As a result of Dutch pressure — and, one might also add, greed — Patani had now turned its back on the Lusitanian merchants, and once the seizure was committed, fear began to permeate the Patani court and the circle of Dutch traders over possible retaliation from Furtado de Mendonça.[173]

Portuguese Melaka did retaliate. An anonymous report written in 1605 holds out the possibility that Furtado de Mendonça deploy part of his armada from Johor to Patani in order to save face. The author is (perhaps deliberately) unsure whether the carrack was still in the port of Patani and, therefore, salvageable.[174] The Melaka authorities detained and impounded a junk belonging to the Patani merchant "Radzia Caltana" (possibly a corruption of Raja Kelantan) and confiscated its cargo. Also, on 3 April 1605, "the Japanese" set fire to warehouses that destroyed a good portion of the silk stock, estimated by Heert Terpstra at 200 *picul*. The journal of van Warwijk's voyage printed by Commelin is not clear as to who these "Japanese" culprits really were.[175] Terpstra opines that they were mercenaries in the employ of the Portuguese. According to him, this act of revenge made things worse for the Portuguese since the mercenaries set fire not to the cargo seized by the Dutch, but to the silk supposedly impounded or confiscated by Raja Hijau.

Between the court officials at Patani and the Dutch, there was a good deal of wrangling and haggling over damages suffered by the Patanese and the indemnity that the Dutch had to pay. Eventually, van Warwijk and his men paid a fee of 12,000 ryals-of-eight together with gifts for various parties. They also reimbursed "Radzia Caltana" the sum of 2,640 ryals-of-eight for the loss of his junk and cargo. The Dutch, too, feared some form of retaliation for their hostile act, and they had carpenters work on the *Santo António* to make repairs and undertake alterations to the external appearance of the vessel.[176]

On the basis of Portuguese sources consulted, it is evident that the fear was mutual. Losses to Portuguese merchant shipping around the region during the early trading season of 1605 were the largest ever, and Furtado de Mendonça lamented that there was no end in sight to these intolerable conditions.[177] No doubt the Portuguese had their ears tuned to any suspicious developments in the region, and they would have heard from their sympathisers about Johorean plans to launch a joint attack with the Dutch on Melaka. With the benefit of hindsight, the officers of the *Estado da Índia* were right to surmise that an attack on Melaka was imminent. In 1606 Admiral Cornelis Matelieff de Jonge arrived with a fleet from Europe and launched several seaborne attacks on the Portuguese stronghold. Matelieff's attack is discussed further in Chapter 5.

Heightened vigilance was also extended to Melaka's trading interests around the region. Pinto reports in his book *Portugueses e malaios* that from early 1606 (the beginning of the next trading season with China after the *Santo António* incident), the Melakan officials stepped up the patrolling of waters around the peninsula to protect inbound vessels from Macao and Japan.[178] Heightened security efforts focused on freebooting hotspots, such as the Straits of Singapore and the sea between Pedra Branca and Tioman.

Despite these efforts at protecting inbound merchant shipping from China and Japan, business sentiment in Melaka had soured by the opening weeks of 1606. According to a letter of February 1606 cited by Pieter Anton Tiele,[179] "A Malay merchant from Palembang who made a voyage to Melaka" reported that there were only a "few or no soldiers" stationed in the city, but that "more than two hundred of them" were dispatched to the Johor River, no doubt anticipating the arrival of ships from Japan, China and Makassar. The same merchant also underscored that the *casados* of Melaka dared not risk going to sea, fearing the wrath of the freebooters, whom he identified as the *ingresen* (English).[180] Perhaps he confused them with the Dutch or simply could not keep the two apart. But the business mood was reportedly so depressed that foreign merchants were leaving town and the *casados* of Melaka were not engaging in trade but were trying to eke out a living from farming.[181]

Return to Europe and Sale of the *Santo António*'s Cargo

After several months in Patani, the *Santo António* was dispatched on 15 September 1605, under the command of Vice-admiral Cornelis Sebastiaanse, to the Johor River. He was to ascertain whether a cargo of pepper could be procured there.[182] Van Warwijk himself remained in Patani for a few more weeks, winding up business there, and appointing Ferdinand Miechels as the new head of the VOC factory at Patani. He set sail with the *Hollandia* and arrived on 12 November 1605 in Johor River estuary. At Batu Sawar, van Warwijk and Sebastiaanse entered into negotiations and agreements with the Johor monarch and also with the king's powerful half-brother, Raja Bongsu. The monarch exhorted the Dutch party to join him in an attack on Portuguese Melaka.[183] But van Warwijk and Sebastiaanse evidently felt that with their ships already laden with goods, the stakes were too high. To the disappointment of the Johor royals, the Dutch "traders" declined.

From Johor, van Warwijk proceeded on 12 December with the ship *Vlissingen* to Banten. Cornelis Bastianzoon with his ship the *Amsterdam*, as well as the *Santo António* followed a day or two later. All had reached their destination by 27 December 1605. After completing some business in Java, and inspecting the seaworthiness and comfort of the captured Portuguese carrack for the long voyage home, van Warwijk and his men weighed anchor on 6 January 1606, and set sail for Europe.[184]

The further course of events is reconstructed only with difficulty, but it transpires that the original cargo of the *Santo António* was distributed among several other vessels of van Warwijk's fleet and brought to Europe.

According to a letter from Banten's *opperkoopman* (chief merchant or factor) Jacques l'Hermite to the directors of the VOC in Amsterdam dated 28 January 1608, the *Santo António* began to take on water and the ship had to be abandoned. Its remaining cargo was brought onto an islet near the Bay of Antogil off the northeastern coast of Madagascar. Jan Fransz, the Dutch captain of the *Santo António*, returned to Banten with a cutter and arrived in west Java on 17 November 1607. Here he explored the possibility of sending a ship to Madagascar to load the salvaged cargo and complete its journey to Europe. Initially, VOC officials at Banten toyed with the idea of dispatching the *Grote Sonne*, which was at anchor taking on provisions, but the needs of the Dutch military positions in Ternate proved more pressing. On 3 December the *Grote Sonne* set sail for Gresik and Makassar, where it was to procure additional provisions of beans and rice before setting course for the Malukus.[185] As luck would have it, the 700-ton *Mauritius* arrived from the port of Patani shortly thereafter with only a little cargo in its hold.[186] The ship was quickly provisioned, and on 27 December 1607 it set sail on its homeward journey.

It is known that the *Mauritius* left the port of Antipera on 5 April 1608, but only days into its onward journey the ship began to experience serious problems.[187] On 28 April 1608 it dropped anchor in the Bay of Saint Augustine, on the southwestern coast of Madagascar. The crew unloaded the cargo and made substantial repairs to the ship. The *Mauritius* set sail again on 27 October 1608. It rounded the Cape of Good Hope on 1 February 1609 and visited the Congo River estuary on 19 March. Near Cabo Lope Gonsalves,[188] the *Mauritius* literally fell apart. The crew dispatched a sloop to the Gold Coast and purchased a vessel there that would be capable of transporting the salvaged cargo to the Netherlands. On 6 August 1609, the Amsterdam directors of the VOC expressed their grave concern to the *Landsadvocaat* (the Land's Advocate) and leading Dutch statesman Johan van Oldenbarnevelt that they had not yet heard anything about the *Mauritius*, which had sailed from Banten to Madagascar to salvage the cargo of the *Santo António*. Only weeks later, on 8 September 1609, some three and a half years after the seizure of the Portuguese carrack at Patani,[189] the remains of what was once the *Santo António*'s and later the *Mauritius*'s cargo finally arrived at Texel.

In a second epistolary report to van Oldenbarnevelt dated 11 September, the same directors vividly recount the harrowing experiences of the surviving crew and lament that so little of the cargo could be salvaged. The directors, no doubt hoping for sympathy and perhaps also a subsidy, wondered aloud whether the sales proceeds from the few salvaged goods would even cover the expenses and salary of the ship's mates.[190] But when looking at the broader picture, as will become evident below, their carping was surely unjustified.

Another portion of the *Santo António*'s cargo travelling with van Warwijk's fleet also ran into difficulty and had to be redistributed because one of the ships, the *Vlissingen*, sprung a leak and the *Hollandia* and *Dordrecht* were no longer seaworthy. Van Warwijk resolved to set course for the island of Mauritius, where the five-ship convoy arrived on 6 April 1606. Here the cargo, particularly the silks, was redistributed among the three vessels the *Amsterdam*, *Zeelandia* and *Vlissingen*. The *Zeelandia* received 150 *fardels* (bundles or bales) of silk weighing a total of 14,459 Amsterdam pounds, the *Amsterdam* received 200 *fardels* weighing 19,682 pounds, and the *Vlissingen* received 15 *fardels* weighing 1,344.5 pounds, all of this, as is reported, representing silk purchased from the queen of Patani. Also transferred to the *Vlissingen* was a chest comprising ten "lead containers" of musk cods weighing about 102 pounds. The provenance of this precious commodity can also be traced back to the ill-fated Portuguese carrack.[191]

Van Warwijk and his officers resolved to split the fleet. The *Amsterdam*, *Zeelandia* and *Vlissingen* would proceed on their homeward journey on 21 April 1606, while the cargo of the ailing *Hollandia* and *Dordrecht* would remain behind to be brought ashore and sheltered in facilities built for this purpose. These two latter ships were repaired and set sail on 4 November 1606. After a sojourn on the island of St. Helena in the South Atlantic, they arrived at the homeports in Zealand and Holland in June 1607.

Although the *Vlissingen* had been leaking, it managed to return in the company of the *Amsterdam* and *Zeelandia* to its homeport on the Isle of Walcheren in Zealand as early as 13 October 1606.[192] According to the excellent study of Enthoven,[193] the sale of this specific portion of the *Santo António*'s cargo yielded gross receipts of £2,050 Flemish or 12,300 guilders. After deducting £50 Flemish for expenses, £400 Flemish in tax was ceded to the local Admiralty Board, being the so-called *gerechtigheit van het land* (20 per cent), and £66 Flemish (or 1/30 of net proceeds) to the Stadholder, Prince Maurice of Orange.[194] The mates and officers of the *Vlissingen* received £61 Flemish. This sum represented 4 per cent of the net proceeds and was considerably less than the portion of 6.3 per cent customarily allocated to the crew of merchant vessels.[195] In addition to the £61 Flemish, the crew of the *Vlissingen* later received a lump sum of £250 Flemish to distribute among themselves. This sum was later subdivided into 92¼ *paeyen* (pay, parts or portions), equivalent to £2:14:2½ Flemish and distributed among the surviving crew of the *Vlissingen* according to their rank and function. Admiral van Warwijk received a sum equivalent to eight *paeyen*, or £21:13:4 Flemish; the skipper and *coopman* (merchant) each received 6 *paeyen*, or £16:4:15 Flemish; and the ship's boys, the lowest-ranking men on board, received the equivalent of ½ *paey*, or £1:7:¾ Flemish.[196]

In their letter to Oldenbarnevelt dated 11 September 1609, the Amsterdam directors were perhaps too narrowly focused on the shipwreck of the *Mauritius*. According to Pieter van Dam, the levy (*gerechtigheit van het land*) charged by the Admiralty Boards on goods seized in acts of freebooting amounted to 317,000 guilders from the cargo of the *Santo António* alone.[197] Given that the cargo's value at cost had been originally appraised at 80,000 cruzados, and that the "more valuable part" of the

The VOC's "East India House" in Amsterdam from J.I. Pontanus, *Rerum et Urbis Amstelodamensium Historia* (History of the City of Amsterdam), 1611 (Koninklijke Bibliotheek, The Hague, 136 B 20).

A procession of elephants with the Queen of Patani. From De Bry, *Icones seu Gennuinae et Espressae Delineationes Omnium Memorabilium* (Images or authentic and accurate depiction of all memorable events), Frankfurt am Main, 1607, image IV. (Bibliotheca Thysiana, Leiden, THYS 874)

goods had reportedly "escaped overland" to Melaka,[198] the theoretical gross profit margin was several hundred per cent.

It should be emphasised that the *Santo António*'s cargo was the second most valuable single prize taken by the Dutch from a Portuguese merchant ship at the time, exceeded only by the *Santa Catarina*. The proceeds from the *Santo António* were greater than from the cargo of the *São Jorge*,[199] a Portuguese vessel captured in the South Atlantic on its way from Goa to Lisbon in 1602.[200]

But this is not quite the end of the saga. The cargo from the other vessels seized by van Warwijk in 1605 and also by Dutch Admiral Steven van der Hagen brought additional revenues of 133,000 guilders to the Admiralty Boards.[201]

Despoiling the Portuguese enemy and their Asian allies proved to be a noteworthy source of income for the VOC in the early years of its corporate lifespan. Nevertheless it was not all about plundering the Iberian enemies. If one is to believe van Oldenbarnevelt's right-hand man, Hugo Grotius, the cost borne by the VOC for maintaining security in the East Indies became formidable — so formidable that profits were being seriously eroded, if not completely wiped out.[202] Perhaps Grotius was exaggerating the point, but there is little doubt that in the early years of its corporate monopoly, the VOC became a victim of its own success, as a war machine, as a diplomatic agent, and as a commercial success story at home and in the East Indies.

The *Estado da Índia*'s Diplomatic Offensive on Johor

From the boardrooms and the battlefronts of the VOC, attention shall now turn to an examination of the *Estado da Índia*'s early responses to the challenge posed by the northern European newcomers in the region around the Straits. On the basis of source material consulted, it is difficult to ascertain how divided the Johor court might have been around 1603, when the Dutch forged their first contacts with King Ala'ud'din and Raja Bongsu. Judging from both Portuguese as well as Dutch materials, it would appear that whilst the king and his half-brother and successor favoured the Dutch, Johor's *orang kaya* together with some leading officials of the Johor court, such as specifically the *laksamana* and the Prince of Siak were generally well-disposed towards the Portuguese, not least on account of the trading opportunities that their friendly relations might yield. The arrival of the Dutch and the establishment of a VOC factory in Batu

Sawar not only failed to alter this pattern of factionalism, but in fact appear to have even reinforced it. One can easily surmise why this was the case: competition from the Dutch company, prices offered, or better terms of exchange. The Johoreans appear to have maintained more active and extensive commercial links with Portuguese Melaka than even early Dutch sources would venture to concede. This serves to underscore that while goods and money continued to flow despite highly volatile relations between the *Estado da Índia* and Johor, engagement with the VOC was regarded in Johor as inherently political and strategic by nature, and only in a second instance as a commercial relationship. Trade relations between Batu Sawar and Portuguese Melaka were evidently deeper and far more developed than many of the Dutch documents openly admit.

VOC ships called regularly at Johor until 1608, but the long gaps between visits were cleverly exploited by the Portuguese to divide the Johor court with generous gifts, bribes, promises and as time progressed some sort of a provisional peace agreement.[203] The *orang kaya* — and especially also the Prince of Siak — are reported to have represented the core of the pro-Portuguese faction at the court.[204] By contrast, the king himself, as well as Raja Bongsu, supported the Dutch cause. Backing their diplomatic efforts at the court with military force, the Portuguese used their escort fleet to impose a blockade on riverine traffic. Consequently, riverbank settlements such as Batu Sawar and Johor Lama were cut off from vital supplies of rice, most of which had to be imported from as far away as Java, Siam or Pegu.

The outcome of Portugal's military and diplomatic offensive on Johor was a Luso-Johor peace agreement hammered out in October 1610; but as early as 1606, there had been rumours among VOC circles that the Johor monarch was also extending the olive branch to the Portuguese. Sensing that such an agreement might soon be in the offing, Admiral Verhoeff and his *breede raad* submitted a written proposal that the Dutch and the Johoreans work closer together, and that neither enter into negotiation with the common enemy (the Portuguese) without informing the other.[205] With the benefit of hindsight, one can claim that it was simply too late. The Dutch Republic signed a truce with Spain (and implicitly with Portugal through the Union of the Two Crowns) that very year. But the closer cooperation proposed by Verhoeff was taken rather badly by Raja Bongsu, as will be explained in greater detail below.

According to the testimony of Jacques Obelaer, the resident VOC factor in Batu Sawar at the time, Portuguese Ambassador João Lopes de

Morero arrived to finalise and sign the peace treaty with the Johor monarch. This was ratified by the king on 16 October 1610 and subsequently endorsed on 22 October by the captain-major of Melaka, Dom Francisco Henriques, in the presence of two Johorean ambassadors and the bishop of Melaka, Dom Frei Cristóvão de Sá e Lisboa.[206] According to Teixeira in his *Portuguese Missions in Malacca and Singapore*,[207] it was the king of Johor who personally ventured to Melaka to attend the signing ceremony. Whatever the case might have been, the treaty of October 1610 was not to be. Ratification of the peace was subsequently rejected by the Portuguese viceroy in Goa, Rui Lourenço de Távora, who reportedly objected to specific words or conditions of the treaty.[208] The inception of the document was evidently postponed until the objectionable clauses had been eliminated, but Teixeira fails to inform his readers whether these conditions were ever met. Unfortunately, neither the draft nor the final treaty is featured among the monumental collection of treaties published in the 19th century by Biker.[209] In a more recent study of the Portuguese treaty system, António Vasconcelos de Saldanha testifies that the document no longer survives.[210] It is not sufficiently clear from sources consulted whether the treaty of October 1610 was deferred and ultimately implemented, or whether peace between Johor and Portugal was the result of a second agreement struck at a later date, that is, after the 1613 Acehnese invasion of Johor. (This event will be discussed later in the present chapter.) One informed Dutch source reports that the Johor monarch was negotiating with the Portuguese in the closing weeks of 1614. Another observes that a peace was concluded in 1618, but opines that this was accepted by Johor only under duress.[211] Whatever the case may be, a peace agreement — or probably it would be more accurate to say several agreements of varied legal formality, validity and acceptability — were concluded in the second decade of the 17th century. Their existence was reportedly known across the archipelago. Commercial relations between Portuguese Melaka and Johor may have been strained at times, but they occasionally flourished. In 1622 these relations were evidently at an apex. Disturbed by the potential consequences of this flourishing relationship on the war effort, the VOC exhorted the Johor monarch, the company's contractual ally-in-arms, to refrain from trading with the enemy in Melaka and instead deepen commercial ties with the then recently founded Dutch Batavia.[212]

In a colorful testimony written by the resident Dutch factor, one learns that shortly after the ratification of the Luso-Johor peace agreement of 1610, Raja Bongsu paid an unusual nocturnal visit to the Dutch factory.[213]

He apologised profusely for the treaty, which, as it further transpires, was ratified only under considerable pressure. This stemmed not just from the Portuguese, but notably also from within the ranks of the Johor court itself. A Dutch report speaks of a possible popular uprising. Here again one encounters the name of the Prince of Siak, invariably the head of the pro-Lusitanian lobby at the Johor court who drew considerable support for his political machinations from the ranks of the *orang kaya,* the *bendahara* and *laksamana*. Yet a closer examination of the sources also reveals considerable pent-up frustration — leading almost to resignation — within the ranks of the pro-Dutch lobby. Whispers turned to outright accusations that the Dutch were not only avoiding Johor as a trading destination but, worse, were now increasingly calling at the arch-rival port of Patani and trading there. However, increasing trade with Johor's "enemy" was only the tip of the proverbial iceberg. Raja Bongsu was already infuriated because every VOC admiral sailing through Johor sought to fiddle with the terms and conditions of the Johor-Dutch treaty. In a royal letter of complaint dated 6 February 1609, Raja Bongsu made it very clear that he did not want to "change" the conditions of the treaties originally signed with Matelieff de Jonge in 1606.[214] The signing of the 1606 treaty will be discussed in greater detail in Chapter 5. Perhaps the depths of dissatisfaction are expressed in a letter by Raja Bongsu dated 8 December 1609 in which he unambiguously voices his dissatisfaction over the state of the Johor-Dutch alliance to Prince Maurice of Orange, the stadholder of Holland and Zealand, and whom Asian rulers regularly address as the "King of Holland" in their period correspondence. The following excerpt from this little-known letter speaks for itself.[215] Responding to an earlier dispatch of Prince Maurice, Raja Bongsu replied:

> Further, our brother [Prince Maurice] asks us in his letter to renew or amplify the existing treaty. Why should this be changed or renewed? It was our desire that our brother send us hither a person of respect and bestowed with plenipotentiary powers and authority so that a treaty may be concluded which cannot be broken and will last until the Day of Judgement. Twenty or 30 admirals have come here ...; now comes an admiral with whom we strike one good agreement, and then comes another and changes it. Like this, there shall be no end to making treaties.

But that was not the end of Raja Bongsu's lamentations. He was also peeved (the actual term employed in Dutch was *bedroeft*, which means "saddened") that the good prince in Europe had negotiated a truce with

Portugal (via the Dutch-Spanish Truce signed at Antwerp in April 1609);[216] and against the backdrop of the closer cooperation and collaboration proposed by Admiral Verhoeff, Raja Bongsu evidently felt left out in the cold as he had not been consulted or informed of the matter but presented with a fait accompli.[217] All this endless fiddling with the 1606 treaties — leaving the Johorean allies in the dark — and openly trading with arch-rivals Patani and Aceh amounted to a serious breach of good faith, and most important of all, this was certainly not the way sovereign "brothers" treated one another. In view of this profound dissatisfaction with the way the Dutch were treating their Johorean allies, the pressure at court in Batu Sawar and the prolonged (and repeated) Portuguese blockade of the Johor River, should it really come as a surprise that Raja Bongsu and the Dutch lobby lost out and caved in to the rival faction at the Johor court when peace with Portugal was signed in October 1610?

It was not known that the Portuguese viceroy would later reject individual clauses of the peace deal, and within only a few days of the treaty's public proclamation, the public mood began to change profoundly in Batu Sawar. The Dutch factor wrote with an eye to the empty cash till that the residents of Batu Sawar were strutting about clothed in the latest Indo-Portuguese fashion. While the cheap cotton attire brought by the Luso-Melakan traders was selling fast, the VOC's own staple of cloth, alas, was not.

As old foes began to make peace with one another, the balance of power began to shift among the polities around the Straits of Singapore and Melaka. The Luso-Johor treaty would doubtlessly lead to a resurgence of Portuguese maritime trade through the Singapore Straits from the South China Sea. After the Dutch assault on Melaka in 1606 (which will be discussed in greater detail in Chapter 5), trade in the famed city had slowed to a trickle for more than a year. The situation in Portuguese Melaka was reportedly so dire that merchants, fearful of going out to sea, sought to eke out a living from farming, while Dutch freebooters scoured the waters for easy Portuguese merchant prey.[218]

But there was another development in seemingly faraway Europe that would nurture a new constellation of power in the region. As mentioned, a 12-year truce between the Dutch Republic and the Spanish-Habsburg Empire had been negotiated since February 1608 and was ratified in April 1609, and this, by extension, also affected Dutch relations with the Portuguese. Secret amendments to the truce made in the presence of the English and French ambassadors, however, foresaw a continuation of the hostilities outside of the European scenario. Initial reports sent mixed, if not confusing, signals on the truce's immediate implications on trade and politics in Asia. VOC servants learned of the formal truce well before their Lusitanian and Spanish counterparts did, and news of the silencing of arms from the dreaded Dutch "pirates" and "rebels" was understandably met in Iberian circles with a good dose of scepticism, not least for fear that this could represent a Dutch trap or plot.

Aceh Attacks, 1613

If caution reigned among the rivaling Europeans, it was ambitious and opportunistic jostling that overcame some of the Asian allies. Raja Bongsu quite evidently felt shafted by the VOC. But it was not just Johor that began to reassess the dawn new Luso-Dutch and Hispano-Dutch relations, but also the resulting shift in the balance of power around the Straits. Aceh, too, sat up in attention, noting specifically that the other common enemies of its dreaded Lusitanian foe, Johor and the VOC, had already concluded separate peace treaties with Portuguese Melaka. It is hard to blame the Acehnese for sensing diplomatic isolation in their increasingly strained relations with the *Estado da Índia*, and perhaps even fearing that they were confronted by a (growing) bloc of potentially hostile — or at least indifferently opportunistic — neighbouring powers. Part of Aceh's response to the new constellation of power was to launch a massive assault on Johor.

Aceh's attack on Johor in 1613 represents an important event in the history of early modern Johor, including the island of Singapore, and has been discussed in some depth by Denys Lombard as well as Jorge Alves, Manuel Lobato and Paulo Pinto. The forces that triggered the assault are complex and directly connected to the long-standing rivalry between Aceh and Johor for cultural leadership in the Malay world, and Iskandar Muda of Aceh's aggressive territorial expansion on Sumatra as well as the Malay Peninsula. Evidence further indicates that the isolation or perceived "confrontational encirclement" of Aceh that resulted from the Luso-Dutch and Luso-Johor "peace" agreements were clearly recognisable factors behind the attack.[219]

On 4 May 1613 a substantial Acehnese force generously estimated at 20,000 to 40,000 men[220] and an armada estimated by Dutch Governor-General Pieter Both at 60 to 70 galleys[221] ran up the Johor River, attacking coastal settlements such as Johor Lama, Batu Sawar and, in all also

Printed portrait of Pieter Both, the first VOC Governor-General (Rijksbureau voor Kunsthistorische Dokumentatie, The Hague)

Printed portrait of VOC Governor-General Jan Pieterszoon Coen (Rijksbureau voor Kunsthistorische Dokumentatie, The Hague)

likelihood, the town of Singapura.[222] Dutch sources emanating from the besieged capital report of some confusion during the onslaught. The Acehnese demanded that the Dutch remain neutral during the conflict. The VOC servants retorted that they were bound by treaty to defend the Johor monarch, but they were initially unsure as to how exactly to behave towards the Acehnese, who were also allies of the VOC. The resident members of the Dutch factory set their premises ablaze to prevent their goods from falling into Acehnese hands.[223] Six members of the Dutch factory, together with 25 men from the ship *Hoop* anchored in the Johor River estuary, fought side by side with their Johorean allies.[224] Its forces hopelessly outnumbered, Batu Sawar fell on 6 June 1613. Raja Bongsu and leading *orang kaya*, together with 22 Europeans, were taken as prisoners to Aceh.[225] The whereabouts of King Ala'ud'din were unclear; one (evidently incorrect) story had it that he was taken to Aceh and killed there. In his letter to Thomas Aldridge at Surat dated 12 July 1613, the English factor Thomas Best claims that "the king and his brother" were brought to Aceh, but there may well have been a mix-up of identities, as at least three leading nobles, Raja Bongsu, the Prince of Siak and the ruler of Pahang, were all brought to Aceh.[226] Another story claims that King Ala'ud'din of Johor fled to the island of Lingga, where he passed away some months later in 1615.[227]

It is important in the context of the present study that Raja Bongsu was married off to a sister of the Acehnese monarch[228] and returned to Johor as the new king. One of the conditions imposed by the Acehnese on the new Johor ruler, who ascended the throne as Abdullah Hammayat Shah, was that he rescind the peace agreement with Portugal and launch an attack on Melaka together with the king of Aceh.[229] As one of the traditional leaders of the pro-Dutch faction of the court, and now a client or "vassal" of Aceh, Abdullah Hammayat Shah obliged. He even sought to entice the Dutch to join them in this offensive. Several reports dating from the second half of 1614 raised the prospect of the imminent attack of Aceh and Johor on Melaka, but the planned offensive was dropped for reasons that appear closely linked with the growing tension between the two regional powers. As already mentioned, information was at hand in VOC circles that the Johor monarch was treating with the Portuguese by the closing weeks of 1614 (under duress, so it is said), and by early March 1615 it was clear to Jan Pieterszoon Coen that nothing would become of this military enterprise.[230] Also, against the backdrop of rapidly deteriorating relations between Aceh and Johor, the Dutch declined requests to dispatch four or five warships to support the maritime attack on Portuguese Melaka.[231]

Afterthoughts

As the city of Batu Sawar was reconstructed, expanded and garrisoned with Acehnese help,[232] the new Johor ruler almost immediately set out to mend fences with the Dutch. In the early autumn of 1614, the VOC's Banten factory received what is described as a muddled message from the Johor monarch.[233] In this, Abdullah Hammayat Shah professed his sincere friendship to the Dutch company and now declared himself ready to discuss certain "urgent" but unspecified issues. In a dispatch to the VOC's board of directors, the Heren XVII, the company servants in Banten rightly surmised that the monarch, in the aftermath of the Acehnese onslaught and new unsettled constellation of power at home, was now willing to discuss the construction of a Dutch fort on Johorean soil.[234] This scheme will be discussed in greater detail in Chapter 3. On the Dutch side, concrete proposals were put on the table as early as 1606, that is, around the time the Dutch-Johor treaty was struck.[235] But Abdullah Shah's predecessor, Ala'ud'din, openly dreaded the implications that such a project might have on Johor's relations with regional powers such as the *Estado da Índia*, Aceh or Patani, as well as how it might adversely affect his own — some might argue notoriously unstable — support within the ranks of the Johor courtiers and the *orang kaya*. As could be expected, noteworthy opposition to such a Dutch project emanated also from Johor's *orang kaya*, who, before the Acehnese invasion of 1613, selfishly favoured improved relations with the *Estado da Índia*.

Thus, the Lusitanian officials in Melaka and Goa pursued a three-pronged approach in their dealings with Johor. The first was to step up diplomatic pressure on the court and draw Johor, and especially Batu Sawar, closer into the commercial orbit of Portuguese Melaka and its merchants. The objective of the diplomatic and commercial "offensive" was to split the court down the middle and to win over as many officials and *orang kaya* as possible. A divided court would further erode the position of the sultan and implicitly also weaken support at the Batu Sawar court for the VOC. The second strategy was to reassert naval hegemony over the Straits by constructing and maintaining fortresses in the region. This was not a new proposal, but in the wake of the Acehnese invasion it found fresh interest among officials from

Melaka to Goa and even Lisbon. Portuguese schemes for enhanced military presence in the Straits were mirrored by very similar proposals not only by subjects of the king of Spain, but also by the Dutch. Rumours doing the rounds in VOC circles even claimed that the English might have been planning a fortress for the Karimuns. The third strategy was to overcome the historic rivalry with Spain and to merge naval forces to oust the Dutch once and for all from the Straits — indeed, from Asia at large. The construction of fortifications around the Straits as well as the joint Luso-Spanish naval offensive against the VOC will provide the focus of the next two chapters.

CHAPTER 3

Naval Security and Forts for the Straits, c. 1584–1630

Portuguese Security Plans, c. 1584–1609

Plans for fortresses or citadels around the Straits of Melaka, Singapore and Kundur (Sabam) were conceived in direct response to developments that adversely affected the *Estado da Índia*'s security, particularly the security of its merchant shipping. Initial plans were designed to cope with changes in Portuguese relations with local overlords, particularly Aceh, Johor, Pahang and Jambi. Already before the Portuguese set out to destroy Johor Lama in 1587,[1] the fragile political conditions and the instability this brought to the flow of trade evoked an initial suggestion to build a fort around Aceh and also in the Straits of Singapore. One such proposal was devised in 1584.[2] At this time Johor and Aceh were on good terms, and their efforts against the Portuguese led to serious difficulties for Lusitanian trade with ports in Japan, China and around the Gulf of Siam. Rumour in Portuguese circles had it that the Johoreans and the Acehnese were planning to build a fortification of their own. If constructed, such a fort could have had serious repercussions on Portugal's long-distance trade with the Far East, the Malukus and Makassar. The Portuguese scholar

Manuel Lobato claims that he has not retrieved any credible evidence to substantiate these rumours. He contends that Johor was conceivably unwilling to consent to such a scheme, especially since this would have given the Acehnese a presence very close by, if not in Johorean territory as such.[3] Johor and Aceh had become bitter enemies by the turn of the century, and Lobato's deliberations certainly retain validity.

In Chapter XLVI of his *Roteiro das Cousas do Achem*, Dom João Ribeiro Gaio, bishop of Melaka, who may well have been aware of these rumours, floats the idea of constructing a *fortaleza*, or fort, in the Straits of Singapore[4] but fails to mention a specific location for this enterprise. He simply states that it would be of great benefit to navigation to, and commerce with, the regions in East Asia.[5] He suggests that the crown dispatch to the region 5,000 men who could then help open markets. Judging from his description of the current conditions, the capital and fortress at Johor Lama were still standing.[6]

About a decade later, Johor Lama was destroyed and the *fortaleza* in the Straits of Singapore was still not constructed. The project appears to have been now placed in the hands of the Portuguese viceroy in Goa, Dom Francisco da Gama, who was evidently of the opinion that such a fortification would prove ineffective. In a letter addressed to the king of Portugal and Spain, dating from about 1597, he expressed his clear preference for dispatching an armada to the region. The task of this fleet was to patrol the waters around the Straits.[7] With the hindsight of history, the implementation of the viceroy's recommendation was certainly the more cost-effective and flexible solution pursued by the Portuguese.

However, the Lusitanian authorities viewed Dutch and also English commercial penetration and freebooting in Southeast Asia with considerable alarm.[8] Local princes and overlords began to conclude treaties with parties hostile to the Portuguese cause, and entertained diplomatic relations with other European powers for the first time. For example, the archbishop of Goa lamented in a letter to King Philip III/II, dated 6 April 1603, that Johor had dispatched an ambassador to the Dutch Republic and separately established contacts with Queen Elizabeth I of England.[9]

The Portuguese proposed, at the instigation of Manuel Godinho de Erédia in 1604, to build a Portuguese fortress in the vicinity of Johor Lama or somewhere in the region of the Johor River estuary.[10] This would have enabled them to control the flow of trade on the river and to enhance the protection of their China fleets, which were periodically looted near the Straits of Singapore by local pirates and, increasingly since the "*Santa Catarina* incident" of 1603, also by Dutch "traders". As Gibson-Hill highlights in his important article "Johor Lama and Other Ancient Sites", nothing appears to have come of this project. He opines that the idea was probably "abandoned when it was appreciated that the fort would be very vulnerable, unless it was of considerable strength, and heavily garrisoned".[11] It can be assumed that the actual reasons transcended considerations grounded in strategic or military thinking and that funds were not readily forthcoming from Goa.[12]

It transpires from several letters preserved in the *Livros das Monções* (otherwise known as the Letters of the Monsoon) that the dual crown of Portugal and Spain remained seriously concerned about security in the Singapore Straits and particularly about Dutch plans to fortify the Straits. In a letter written in Madrid, dated 27 January 1607, King Philip III/II instructs his viceroy at Goa, Dom Martim Affonso de Castro, to urgently construct two forts, one in the Strait of Kundur (Sabam), the other near Singapore. This project was to "secure the navigation of my vassals".[13] These plans, however, did not materialise, not least because financial resources became seriously stretched during this period due to the upgrading of forts from Hormuz and Mozambique to Macao. In fact, archival material reveals that after the Dutch attack on Melaka in 1606, a good proportion of locally available funds were being diverted towards the building of a fort or security post on the *Ilha das Naus*, which is located off the coast of Melaka.[14]

Jaques de Coutre's Memorial Urging the Construction of Two Forts around Singapore

One of the most comprehensive plans emanated from the merchant-traveller Jaques de Coutre. His autobiography and other documents of historical interest contain several concrete — and, on one occasion, rather detailed — proposals to construct forts on present-day Sentosa and Singapore island.

In a memorial reproduced in full with English translation in appendix 5,[15] de Coutre attempts to convince King Philip of Spain and Portugal that the ailing commercial fortunes of the *Estado da Índia* could be reversed with the construction of fortresses or citadels to protect the Straits of Singapore and Melaka. The location for one fort is on the *Ysla de Arena* (presently Sentosa), which lies, as he sees it, "in the middle of the [two] Singapore Straits". This island is rocky and represents in its own sense a "natural" fortress, ideally suited to this project. All shipping must pass in view of this island, and the waters feature a current in the Old Strait (*estreito velho*) that is reminiscent of a flowing river. The *Ysla de Arena* has many large trees growing on it, and fresh water is available. The shore of the *estreito velho* or *estrecho viejo* is reported to be quite steep and rocky and therefore not suited for the landing of ships, but the opposite side, along the New Straits of Singapore, is much better suited for bantins and galleys to land and bring in supplies. All these conditions combine into an ideal place to construct a fort, and this could be accomplished, as the native of Bruges does not fail to point out, at relatively low cost.[16]

De Coutre also proposes the construction of a second fortification in the region of the Straits. This should ideally be built at the mouth of the Johor River, towards the easternmost point of the *Ysla de la Sabandaría Vieja*, that is present-day Singapore island. De Coutre estimates the island's length at more or less seven *legoas*, or about 21 kilometres, and points out that this second fortress would be situated at a distance of about three *legoas*, or around nine kilometres, from the first fort located on the *Ysla de Arena*. This relative proximity also implies, as de Coutre does not fail to underscore, that it would be possible for the planned fortifications to lend mutual assistance, either by land or by sea, and the two separate islands upon which they would be built were separated only by the New and the Old Strait of Singapore. This body of water, de Coutre testifies, resembles a river. The latter can be easily closed with a chain, if need be. In any case, the two fortresses should be backed up with a naval squadron of five or six well-armed "Manila galleys" that would be permanently stationed around the islands and patrol the waters there.

In hindsight, the most intriguing — one might say almost visionary — proposals advanced by de Coutre in this memorial concern the use of the port, which he claims is one of the "best in all India", and the founding of a city that would, in all likelihood, serve as an entrepôt. According to his recommendation, this city would evidently be situated on the *Ysla de la Sabandaría Vieja*, and de Coutre exhorted his monarch to acquire suzerainty over the island and the kingdom of Johor.[17]

The political conditions and events described in de Coutre's *Emformación* bear some indications as to when this undated piece was written. For example, de Coutre explains that the king of Johor fled to the island of Bintan[18] and that the Acehnese had stormed the capital city, Batu Sawar, some 12 *legoas* — about 36 kilometres — upstream and occupied it with 1,500 men.[19] Acehnese troops are also reported to have overrun and occupied Pahang (*Pam*), a polity whose fate was closely connected with Johor's in the late 16th to early 17th century.[20] The abovementioned points reflect the conditions after 1615 but the memorial itself probably dates from around the mid-1620s.[21]

These are, admittedly, not the only recommendations for the construction of forts that de Coutre advances in his writings. He also proposes the construction of strongholds for the Strait of Sabam and along the coast of Sumatra. Among the Fleming's various pieces, one finds the *Emformación para ... remediar el Estado en la Índia Oriental* (Information relating to … the improvement of the *Estado* in the East Indies), which is addressed to his sovereign.[22] This memorial appears to stem from the late 1620s. In this, de Coutre advances a series of concrete proposals for reversing the ill fortunes of Portuguese India, and specifically also the entrepôt of Melaka. One of the more striking plans de Coutre offers to the Iberian monarch in this context reads as follows:[23]

> Your Majesty should mandate that the lands of Melaka, which are very good and fertile, be populated with people that are called *Chincheos* [people from Zhangzhou, or just Fujianese in general],[24] just like the Spaniards have in Manila. These people are very agile, and are workers who cultivate the lands. … They are great fishermen and work in all professions: carpenters, stone masons, smiths and all other professions one requires to run a city.…

To the contemporary reader, these plans appear forward-looking and rather modern, heralding events that were to unfold at the tip of the Malay Peninsula — not under Portuguese or Spanish rule, but two centuries later, during British colonial times.

Dutch Security Arrangements for Johor, c. 1606–9

The officers of the *Estado da Índia* were not the only ones attempting to consolidate their hegemony in the region in the first and second decades of the 17th century. As has been explained previously, a chief objective of the VOC at the time was to contain the spread of Iberian influence in the region, sabotage the trading network of the Portuguese and Spanish as much as possible, and despoil the Iberian enemy whenever possible. There was also a plan, from an early stage, to wrest Melaka from Lusitanian control. As will be shown in greater detail in Chapter 5, two formal treaties were concluded to this effect between the Dutch party — signed by Admiral Matelieff de Jonge — and the Johor monarch

Ala'ud'din, who was acknowledged by Malay and European parties as a legitimate claimant to the throne of the fallen Melaka Sultanate.[25] Their treaty of May 1606 foresaw joint attacks on the Portuguese stronghold. In the event that the Dutch should succeed, they would be legitimately ceded the city with some surrounding territory, while the Johor monarch would establish authority over the peoples on parts of the peninsula that at that time fell under Lusitanian suzerainty. It can be assumed that the Dutch-Johorean alliance of 1606 represents a formalisation of existing arrangements that date to 1603, when Jakob van Heemskerk seized the carrack *Santa Catarina* with the active cooperation, and under the direct auspices of, the Johor monarch.[26] The Heemskerk expedition then brought to the Dutch Republic envoys of the Johor monarch, the chief delegate of whom was one Megat Mansur.[27] The Johorean nobleman was to bring a personal message from the monarch to Prince Maurice of Orange. Mansur passed away on the long voyage back to Europe. But other members of the Johor entourage made it to the Netherlands, including one Encik Kamar, who returned to Johor with the fleet of Matelieff de Jonge in 1606.[28] Encik Kamar appears to have played a role in facilitating negotiations between the Dutch and the Johoreans. There is evidence to suggest that a deal to jointly attack and "liberate" Melaka from Portuguese suzerainty originated with King Ala'ud'din Ri'ayat Shah III, or Raja Bongsu, and that his ambassador, Megat Mansur, may well have been dispatched to the Netherlands to propose this scheme.[29]

In view of the commercial and strategic significance of the Straits of Singapore and Melaka, particularly also the prospect of expelling the Portuguese and acquiring the entrepôt of Melaka, the VOC developed and maintained for some years a commercial and special political interest in Johor. Before settling definitively in Batavia in 1621, the VOC toyed with the idea of establishing the residence of the governor-general in Johor[30] or selecting a rendezvous point, where VOC ships could assemble before setting sail for Europe in convoy.[31] In any case, it was maintained that Johor was "a place where commerce and trade must be maintained at all costs".[32] During the first decade of the 17th century, Johor was seen by many as a key ally in Asia, and as an important agent in Dutch efforts to contain Iberian expansion. This view was shared not only by the officers of the VOC fleets, but also by key players and stockholders in Europe.

The Dutch-Johorean alliance proved difficult and also fateful for both parties. While Johor's relations with Portuguese Melaka vacillated considerably, especially after the second half of the 16th century, its open relations with the VOC meant that it had formally turned its back on the Portuguese. In fact, Victor Sprinckel, the VOC factor at Patani, wrote to his counterpart at Banten, Jacques l'Hermite, on 27 December 1608, lamenting that the company had dragged Johor into the Dutch war against the Iberian powers and that the peoples of Johor were now imploring the king to conclude a peace with Portugal.[33] The VOC, too, found itself pressured by its Johorean ally to declare war against its competitors and enemies. Repeated requests were made by the Johor monarch to "deal with" Aceh and Patani,[34] powers with whom the Dutch maintained formally peaceful relations at the time. Johorean demands, which were attached to the granting of privileges, occasionally placed the VOC and its servants in diplomatically fragile, if not compromising, positions.

As long as Melaka was not plucked from the Portuguese, the Dutch view of Johor was that this Malay kingdom was almost completely surrounded by hostile powers. Although the directors of the VOC frequently drafted plans and issued instructions to their outbound fleets, it often took several years before they had any knowledge of how these had been implemented and whether they had succeeded. Thus, on 13 October 1607, the Heren XVII of the VOC issued instructions to the outbound fleet of Admiral Verhoeff and his *breede raad* that ran through a series of hypothetical scenarios.[35] For example, the directors urge Verhoeff to conclude a treaty with the king of Johor, and if this has already been accomplished, to expand and build on it. The same treaty, the directors continue, should also be offered to Aceh and other neighbouring princes. This is to deprive the Portuguese of any opportunity in the future to forge alliances with their neighbours against VOC interests. In the event that Melaka should still be Portuguese, opportunities for conquest should be explored and, if feasible, executed. The instructions also contain a proposal to build a fort with the consent, advice and assistance of the king after the conclusion of an expanded treaty. The purpose of this fort, the directors continue in their instructions, is to provide security to the kingdom of Johor and specifically also the Straits of Singapore.[36] The directors finally remind Verhoeff how important the trade in spices and Chinese silks remains for the company, and admonish him to wind up any outstanding business, leave Melaka or Johor, and proceed to the Malukus as soon as possible.[37]

To the best of the author's knowledge, this is the first time the VOC directors issued concrete instructions to erect a fort in the region of the Singapore Straits. François Valentijn, however, whose voluminous *Oud en*

Nieuw Oost-Indiën remains a treasure trove for students of early modern history and Dutch colonial politics, errs when he claims that Admiral Cornelis Matelieff de Jonge personally supervised the early construction of a fortification project in 1606.[38] What the admiral supervised was not the construction of a fort in the upstream town Batu Sawar, but merely the reinforcement of the Dutch factory and its adjacent residences in Johor's capital city.[39] The task of suggesting the construction of a Dutch fort in Johor fell, in fact, to Verhoeff, who arrived in Johor in the first days of the year 1609 after previously ascertaining the viability of attacking Melaka. Verhoeff's fleet also succeeded in capturing several prizes, including two ships carrying a cargo of rice and cloves, and two vessels inbound from Macao, carrying cargos of silks, porcelain, pepper, *radix Chinae* and cash. One of the ships captured was the carrack *Nossa Senhora del Pare*.[40] It is fortunate that many documents and writings relating to the visit of Admiral Verhoeff in Johor have survived, including transcripts of his conversations and negotiations with the king. It is clear from these that Verhoeff followed to the letter his instructions regarding Melaka and Johor; it is also clear that the Dutch officers encountered some difficulties in selling the merits of their plan to the elite of the Johorean court, notably their allies Raja Bongsu and the king himself.

Verhoeff arrived in the Straits of Singapore on 5 January 1609 and proceeded with four sloops and several of his officers upstream to Batu Sawar.[41] Valentijn describes the capital city as quadrangular in shape, measuring 1,300 paces in circumference. It was fortified with palisades that were some 40 feet tall. The town was densely populated with many *atap* (thatched) houses within the palisades, but the houses belonging to the king and "courtiers" were constructed of wood. Most of the population lived outside of the walls. Together with a settlement on the opposite bank of the Johor River known as Kota Seberang, measuring some 400–500 paces in circumference, there were an estimated 3,000–4,000 men who were fit to defend the settlements.[42]

It was the month of Ramadan, the fasting month of the Muslims. Verhoeff's initial objective was to solicit the active support and participation of Johor in the assault on Melaka, and for this purpose he put forward several specific demands to the king.[43] This was in line with the Dutch-Johor treaty signed between Ala'ud'din Ri'ayat Shah III and Matelieff in 1606. To the bewilderment of Verhoeff and the members of his *breede raad*, the king was clearly hesitant to lend any direct military support for this ambitious enterprise. An explanation for the king's evident reluctance can be found in a letter from Cornelis Franck, the Dutch factor at Batu Sawar, written in December 1608. From this document it transpires that the king was facing a number of serious political and diplomatic challenges. Ala'ud'din Ri'ayat Shah's unwillingness to dispatch military support is explained on the grounds that his people were fasting during the month of Ramadan and consequently could not prepare for — or engage in — a war, at least until the fast had been broken.[44] Deliberations and negotiations resulted in the abandonment of the plan to attack Melaka. The city, as was expressly noted by an unnamed French defector,[45] was well-fortified and well-manned. There were also sufficient ammunition and stockpiles of food for the city to withstand a prolonged siege by the Dutch and their Malay allies. It was also contended that even if the king of Johor eventually dispatched some soldiers after the breaking of the fast on Hari Raya Puasa, he would not be in a position to muster a sufficient number to decisively enhance the power of the attacking forces.

The admiral's *breede raad* remonstrated to the king.[46] They wished to know whether the king had any intention of lending military assistance in a future attack on Portuguese Melaka. At the same time, they wanted to know whether the king would consent to the construction of a fort or citadel, and they used the opportunity to highlight the security that such a fort would provide for the kingdom and its trade.[47] The monarch's reply must have bewildered his Dutch visitors. He stated that the Portuguese did not detest him as much as his esteemed visitors generally assumed.[48] Were there plans for peace negotiations with the Portuguese, as rumour had it? The king thought that in the event the Lusitanian forces should again impose a naval blockade and cut off riverine trade to and around Batu Sawar, or indeed launch an attack on the capital, it would still be possible for him to flee farther upstream. The king also observed that the construction of a fort in his territory would inevitably mean that the Dutch would live in their midst. The monarch expressed his grave concern that since the Dutch were very much like the Portuguese, the Dutch men were likely to go out with local womenfolk. Evidently the monarch was concerned that the maidens of his lands would be deflowered by the strapping European sailors. The monarch also cautioned he would be aggrieved if he found it necessary to commence a war against his good friends, the Dutch.[49] The king expressed his distinct preference for direct assistance in the form of cash and ammunition.[50] He had made similar requests during the visits of Admirals Sebastiaanse and van Warwijk in 1605,[51] and again during Matelieff de Jonge's visit in 1606.[52] On these two earlier occasions, the Johor monarch received from his Dutch visitors five small cannons and ten vats of gunpowder, and in 1606 he also made a specific request for cash subsidies. Matelieff obliged and gave him 1,000 ryals-of-eight; he apparently did so personally, and purportedly out of his own proverbial pocket.[53]

Admiral Verhoeff and his *breede raad* resolved that they would comply with the king's request for cash and ammunition. Verhoeff thus abandoned his negotiations with the Johor monarch, which he knew would be fruitless.[54] The king was to receive a cash subsidy amounting to 3,000 ryals-of-eight. This cash, one should immediately add, had been seized earlier from the ill-fated *Nossa Senhora del Pare*[55] and was formally donated to assist the Johorean monarch in the construction of his "new city", which is presumably a reference to Pasir Raja.[56] The king was also to receive 20 vats of gunpowder and *tintinago*, or spelter, for the casting of metal cannonballs.[57] As a precaution, and at the request of the Johor monarch, the Dutch would station two vessels around the Johor River estuary. The crew was to ensure that trade was conducted "freely" immediately after the departure of Verhoeff's fleet.[58] It goes almost without saying that the true purpose of stationing these vessels was to ensure that the Portuguese would not again impose a punitive blockade on the Johor River as they had done after previous visits by Dutch ships. The *Roode Leeuw* and the cutter *Griffioen* were issued express instructions to hold guard in the Johor River estuary until July 1609. They should thereafter set sail for Patani and later head for Borneo and the Malukus, where they could rejoin the rest of the fleet. The remaining nine vessels of Verhoeff's fleet set sail on 6 February 1609 for Banten, where they arrived nine days later.

The two ships the *Roode Leeuw* and the *Griffioen* temporarily lent the protection that the proposed fort was meant to provide. While the ships were waiting for their mandate to elapse, the winds from Europe and Java brought information that would alter the commercial and political forces at work in the Straits. A sloop arriving from Banten brought news that the Dutch had drafted preliminary articles for a truce with the king of Spain and Portugal.[59] The markets of Asia, the report continued, were to be opened to the VOC for trade. The *Griffioen* and *Roode Leeuw* later raised their sails and headed for Japan.[60]

News of the provisional truce articles pending negotiations for a standing treaty in Europe raised considerable uncertainty among the Asian communities. The full accord, as it was finally agreed upon in April 1609, did not implement the open-market concept that had been originally touted in the epistolary reports dispatched to VOC servants in Asia.[61] In fact, the Twelve Years Truce (1609–21) was amended by secret clauses that assured the VOC free access to market places that were not subject to the Iberian powers. This effectively pre-programmed the continuation of war in the East Indies. But these clauses were not, and could not have been, known to VOC servants in Asia at the time. News of the transitional truce arrangements and the prospective open market policy conceded by the Iberian monarch was accepted with a considerable dose of optimism by the Dutch agents in Asia. Enthusiasm over a new open-market strategy led them to temporarily neglect their interests in Johor. This coincided with events that would unfold in the second half of 1609 and in 1610, and eventually push Johor to the brink of near destruction — not by its erstwhile enemy, Portugal, but by one of Johor's fiercest rivals, Aceh.

Documentary evidence suggests that the transitional truce arrangements negotiated in Europe were exploited in such a way so as to throw a spanner into Dutch diplomatic and political interests in Johor. Cleverly, the Portuguese would exploit the relatively long intervals between Dutch visits to Batu Sawar as an opportunity to launch a diplomatic offensive on the Johor court.[62] Their efforts to draw Johor back into the orbit of Lusitanian interests on the peninsula were backed by the now customary show of force.

Soon after the *Roode Leeuw* and *Griffioen* set sail for Japan,[63] the Melaka government dispatched a naval squadron with orders to impose a blockade on the Johor River. This latest blockade lasted from 1609 through 1610 and was one of the most devastating to the Johorean economy in recent memory. Food supplies were completely cut off, and trade with China as well as the surrounding regions in Malaya, Sumatra and the Riau ground to a complete halt. In previous instances, the arrival of Dutch or even English ships brought relief to Johor, as the Portuguese blockaders either lost in battle or simply fled when they spotted European vessels. This time, though, there were no visitors from northern Europe. Both Raja Bongsu, the Dutch Republic's staunch supporter at the Johor court, and King Ala'ud'din were clearly distressed that the Dutch had concluded some form of peace with the Lusitanian foe without consulting them.[64] They were also upset at the VOC's apparent abandonment of Johor's political cause. According to a letter from the Dutch *opperkoopman* (chief merchant) Jacques Obelaer, dated 25 November 1610, the king had repeatedly asked why the Dutch had not called on Johor for such a long

Section from a drawn hand coloured chart by Hessel Gerritsz, dated c. 1620, depicting the southern portion of the Malay Peninsula and part of the Riau Archipelago together with the Straits of Singapore and Melaka. (Staatsbibliothek Berlin-Preussischer Kulturbesitz, T.7567)

time. He also wondered aloud whether the Dutch might not be trading with Johor's commercial and political archrival Patani.[65] Obelaer did what could be expected of any good factor or diplomat. He probably had no answer to this truly burning question, and he therefore resorted to the only course of action at his disposal: damage control. Obelaer replied to the king that the Dutch traded in both places, implying that they also wished to maintain good relations with both rivalling powers, Johor and Patani.[66]

Adriaen van der Dussen's Mission to Johor, 1614

In the aftermath of the 1613 Acehnese attack on Johor (see Chapter 2) and the resumption of Johor's hostilities with Portugal, the plan for a Dutch fort in the Straits of Singapore and the Johor River estuary was revived. The new Johor monarch faced two pressing problems in his foreign relations management. First, he was seriously concerned that earlier actions, such as the commercial and political rapprochement with Portugal, might have alienated the Dutch and lessened their interest in Johor.[67] Second, the Acehnese attack on Batu Sawar confirmed what the Dutch had feared, and what they had warned the king's brother and predecessor of all along, that the capital was vulnerable to attacks and required some form of additional protection through a fort or citadel. While Batu Sawar was being reconstructed with the help of the Acehnese, who also garrisoned the city, the Johor monarch dispatched a letter to Banten. In this reportedly confused and muddled message,[68] the king expressed his sincere hopes of reviving former ties and claimed that he carried an important message for his friends and allies.[69] In a letter to the Heren XVII, Jan Pieterszoon Coen surmised that the king might now consent to the building of a fort despite his earlier reservations.[70] Two men were dispatched on 11 August 1614 from Banten to liaise with Raja Bongsu.[71] Jan Gommerszoon Cocq and Adriaen van der Dussen were invested with the authority to negotiate the construction of a fort in the event that the king was now willing to give his consent for such an enterprise. Shortly after arriving at Batu Sawar on 25 August,[72] Gommerszoon Cocq passed away suddenly and mysteriously, leaving van der Dussen to conduct the negotiations on his own.[73] At the time of their arrival, the king was waging war against Pahang and their Portuguese ally,[74] and he returned to Batu Sawar only on 3 September. The following day the Dutch envoy presented the VOC's gift, consisting of a piece of artillery and one vat of gunpowder.[75]

The members of the Johor court, including the king, were reassessing their options. A meeting was convened in Batu Sawar on 4 September that included noblemen, *orang kaya* and even members of the Chinese merchant community.[76] Apart from talking about losses estimated at 47,000 ryals-of-eight incurred by the VOC as a result of the Acehnese onslaught,[77] the issue of building a fort in the region of the Singapore Straits — four years after it was proposed and seriously pursued by Verhoeff — was placed as a key item on the agenda for discussion. In a letter to the Heren XVII written in late October, after the return of van der Dussen from Batu Sawar, Coen triumphantly exclaimed that the king had offered any location in his territory, be it on one of the Karimuns, around the Johor River estuary, or elsewhere.[78]

Negotiations appear to have been focused but encountered some obstacles. It transpires from the testimony of van der Dussen that the king, while apparently inclined towards consenting to the fort project, was concerned that this would give the Dutch the "keys to his river",[79] and the Johor monarch confessed that in any case such a decision could not be made rashly but only in consultation with his courtiers.[80] Van der Dussen assured the king that they would remain trustworthy allies and would not — as the monarch worried aloud — use the fort as a means of tyrannising the Johoreans.

The outcome of the king's consultation was not only swift, but also positive. He arranged for van der Dussen to inspect a few possible sites for the proposed fort. The latter was taken on 6 September 1614, with a number of Johorean prahus, to several locations in the broader region of the modern Singapore Straits.[81] Together with his Johorean hosts, van der Dussen inspected unspecified locations along the shores of the Johor River estuary, and on the islands of Bintan and the Karimuns.[82] The latter two islands, to the southwest of contemporary Singapore, were singled out as the best possible option.[83] Three considerations appear to have influenced van der Dussen in his search for the ideal location. First, the Karimuns were generally uninhabited due to the continuing hostilities with Portugal.[84] The king approved of the idea that on account of the constant threat of Portuguese raids, the inhabitants of the Karimuns be permitted to live with the Dutch within the perimeters of the fort.[85]

Second, one of the chief purposes of building the fort was to monitor shipping through the Straits. The Karimuns were ideally suited to this. According to old Portuguese naval charts, the northern shores of Karimun Besar marked the navigation point that brought ships

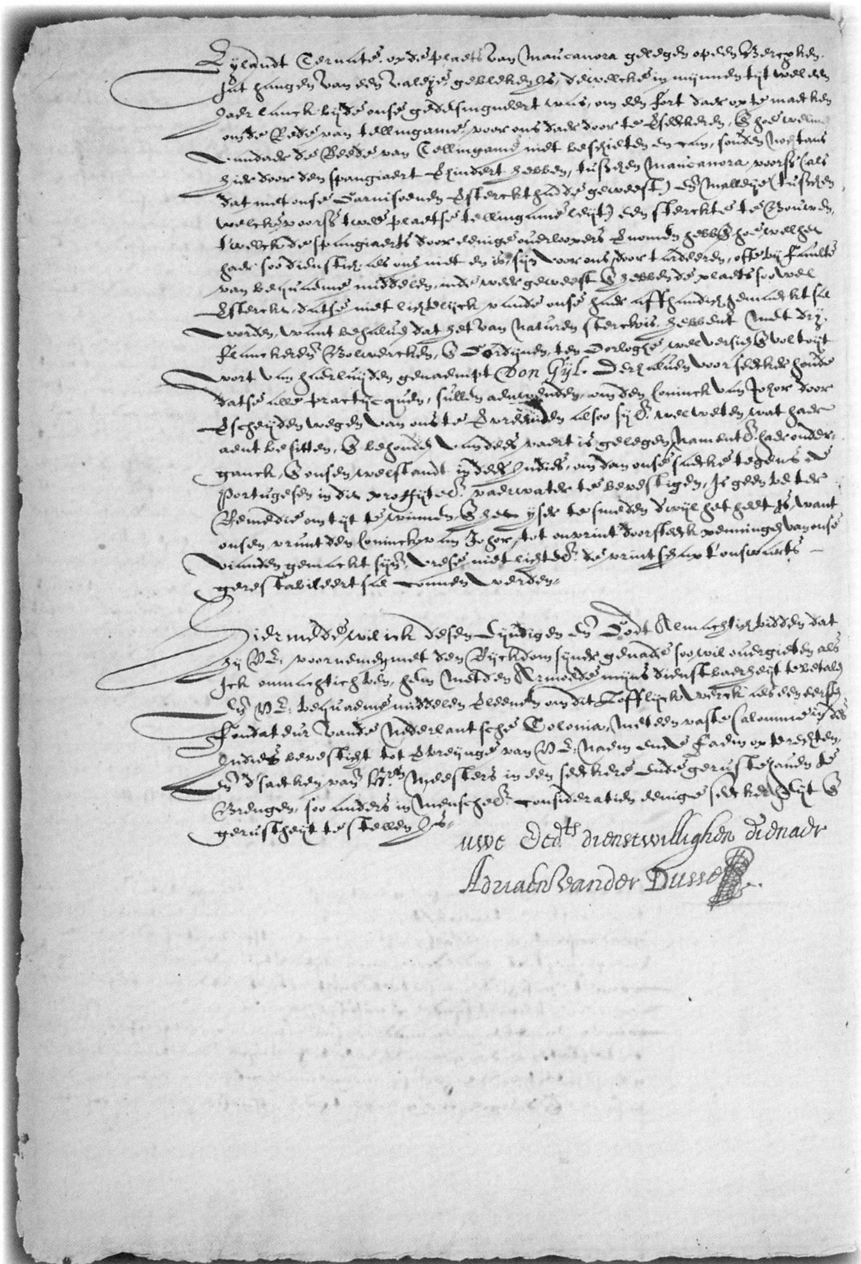

uwe Ed. dienstwillighen dienaer
Adriaen vander Dussen

Final signed page of Adriaen van der Dussen's *Cort Vertooch* of May 1615. (Nationaal Archief van Nederland, ms. VOC 1061)

from Japan, China, Cochinchina, Champa, Siam, Patani, Borneo and the eastern shores of the Malay Peninsula through the Singapore Straits. The Dutch would be able to impose control over the principal sea lane that brought ships to or from the Straits of Melaka and Sabam to ports in eastern Sumatra, Java, the Malukus and Timor.[86]

Third, the Karimuns were also a favoured destination of visiting European vessels, because the islands not only possessed sources of fresh water but were reported to have tall, straight hardwood trees. These trees were prized by sailors for repairing broken masts.

Van der Dussen returned to Banten and filed his *Cort Verhael* (Short Narration) with Governor-General Pieter Both on 10 November 1614. Further information derives from a hitherto unpublished document by van der Dussen titled *Cort vertooch* (Short Account), filed with the new VOC governor-general, Gerard Reynst, about six months later, on 19 May 1615.[87] In these, van der Dussen explains to the governor-general that the Portuguese presence in Melaka and Spanish retention of Manila remain the two principal obstacles to the pursuit of trade for the VOC. To turn this situation around, van der Dussen sees it as necessary to close the Straits of Singapore, Kundur (Sabam) and Melaka, to deprive the enemy of their ability to conduct trade in key places such as Java, Makassar and Macao. He explains that "Raja Bongsu, presently in the place of his brother the Jang di Pertuan" is lending crucial help in closing the Straits to Portuguese shipping by granting permission to construct a fort on "one of the islands around the Straits of Singapore" or somewhere around the Johor River estuary between Johor Lama and Batu Sawar.[88] Van der Dussen explains some of the principal advantages that derive from constructing the proposed fort on Karimun Besar. The location would not only serve as a general warehouse, but would also attract ships from around Melaka and even Chinese merchants. The latter would be attracted to Karimun because the tolls and imposts would be significantly lower than in either Banten or Patani. Also, thanks to the lumber industry in Johor, it would be possible to construct smaller craft such as galleys and foists on site.[89]

Van der Dussen also proposes the founding of a Dutch colony in Johor. He suggests that European soldiers of the VOC should be encouraged to marry women from different parts of Asia and Africa, who, he underscores, can be purchased on the markets in Makassar, Bali, Binia and Madagascar. Such marriages would not only assist the VOC in establishing itself on a sound foundation throughout the region, but would also contribute towards the spread of Christianity. The offspring from these marriages should ideally be bound to serve in the employ of the VOC.[90] In a more sinister vein, van der Dussen also exhorts the governor to station garrisons on Karimun Besar and along the Johor River estuary to "rein in" the new Johor monarch and to ensure that he does not take any actions (under duress or political pressure from Portuguese Melaka) that would be detrimental to Dutch interests.[91]

Plans, Financial Constraints and Changing Priorities

Despite the sense of enthusiasm among certain parties in the VOC, the fact is that the fort was never built.

First, rumours pervaded Lisbon that the Dutch were attempting to build a fort in the Straits of Singapore. It was first believed that the Dutch planned to construct the fort on the island located between the New and the Old Straits of Singapore — in other words, on de Coutre's *Ysla de Arena*, or present-day Sentosa. In a letter to Viceroy Dom Jerónimo de Azevedo in Goa dated 7 January 1614, the Iberian monarch, Philip III/II, vents his serious concern about this Dutch plan and places pressure on his servants in India to halt it at all costs.[92] The king underscores for his viceroy how important the Straits and the whole region really are to the prosperity of the *Estado da Índia*.

Two years later, the Iberian monarch again wrote to his viceroy in Goa. According to this letter, Archbishop Dom Frey Christóvão de Sá e Lisboa[93] had let His Majesty know that the Dutch rebels had struck an agreement to construct a fortress "between the Straits of Sabam and Singapura, [namely] on Pulau Karimun" and that Raja Bongsu of Johor had given his consent to such a project.[94] The king again emphasises what ruin such a Dutch enterprise would mean to Portuguese shipping and commerce in the Southern Seas, and consequently exhorts his viceroy, Dom Jerónimo de Azevedo, to do all in his power to ensure that this fort never be built. Similar instructions were issued to Azevedo's successor, Dom João Coutinho. The king instructed him in no ambiguous terms to thwart the construction of the Dutch fort in the Straits "by all possible means".[95] King Philip also expressed serious doubts that the Johor monarch had ever given his approval to such a scheme.[96]

From the correspondence between the Iberian monarch and his viceroy of India, it is clear that the crown of Portugal was intent on taking the necessary steps to prevent the Dutch from constructing their fort in the Straits. But that is only one side of the story. Within weeks

Printed portrait of Philip III/II of Spain and Portugal from Emanuel van Meteren's *Commentariën ofte Memoriën* (Commentaries or Memoirs), 1652. (Private Collection, Peter Borschberg)

of van der Dussen's return to Banten from Batu Sawar, Jan Pieterszoon Coen wrote to the Heren XVII — on 10 November 1614.[97] In this letter, the future governor-general of the Dutch East Indies explains that while it is important to find a stable rendezvous location in the region, the Sunda Strait are to be preferred over Johor.[98] He cites a number of reasons for this. First, a rendezvous point has to represent a safe and secure place where the company could store cash.[99] The attack on Johor, the chronic problems with Portugal, and the company's recent losses at Batu Sawar could be cited as evidence against Johor as a safe location. Second, Coen writes, the Chinese merchants would come and trade where it was safe. The marketplace may have been more predictable, given the regular imposition of Portuguese blockades on the Johor River. Certainly the waters around west Java and the Strait of Sunda were safer than the Straits of Singapore and the pirate-infested Riau Archipelago.

Add to these considerations the financial constraints faced by the VOC that very year. Pieter van Dam reports that the company received a cash subsidy from the States General in 1614 in order to continue the war against the "Spaniards in East India".[100] This was symptomatic of the growing concern over financial viability faced by the aggressive and expanding Dutch company. Lamenting high overheads and fixed costs, Dutch negotiators at the Indies Conferences held in London in 1613 and in The Hague in 1615 sought to break out of their financial constraints in their negotiations with the English, by proposing several cost-sharing schemes. These schemes included a possible merger of the Dutch and English East India companies, as well as carrying the financial burden incurred as a result of protecting native Asian princes against Iberian advances and generally sharing the cost of the war effort in Southeast Asia with the English.[101] Negotiations did eventually lead to a cooperation agreement on commerce and security, which in any case never functioned properly.

Afterthoughts

Initial enthusiasm over the commercial significance of Johor had already faded by 1615. Like many regional ports that were frequented by VOC ships in the opening years of the 17th century, Johor faded in its perceived significance as the company's operations were settled and became centralised in Batavia. Fewer Dutch ships called at Johor, a claim that can easily be substantiated by reference to Bruijn, Gaastra and Schöffer's comprehensive study *Dutch-Asiatic Shipping*.[102]

In view of the Acehnese invasions of Johor and Pahang during the second decade of the 17th century, and the move of Johor's capital from Batu Sawar to Lingga around 1618, the patterns of economic activity within Johor, as well as between Johor and its regional neighbours, were transformed. The move to Lingga also saw a shift in the security needs of the Kingdom of Johor. If the Dutch fort was to protect shipping through the Straits as well as the capital city from potential invasion by the Portuguese or any other enemy, then the latter was no longer a principal consideration after the shift of the royal residence to Lingga.

Another important factor was the Portuguese settlements on the Malay Peninsula and across the Indonesian Archipelago as well as the fierce competition with the Dutch over the control of the Malukus and the spice trade. But even joint efforts with the Spanish to expel the Dutch from the region — especially critical nodal points such as around the Straits of Singapore — proved increasingly futile. Admittedly, such moves were not initiated on the basis of perceived military strength. In retrospect, the Iberian powers recognised that they were beaten on a protracted retreat. The modern student of Iberian presence in Southeast Asia would probably conclude that the *Estado da Índia* was more fragile than most key players would have recognised at the time, but this may just be the benefit of judging with hindsight.

Finally, entrepôts such as Melaka, and particularly Macao, were seriously affected by Dutch activity in the region. This was reflected in the level and flow of trade to and from these ports. Ptak in his seminal study "Outline of Macao's Economic Development, 1557–1640" contends that the systematic targeting of Portuguese shipping around the Malay Peninsula seriously crippled Melaka's role as a centre of trade, but this view is admittedly not shared by all scholars today.[103] Its gradual decline "almost cut off Macao's ties to the West, and inasmuch as conditions worsened in India and Melaka, Macao preferred to trade with China and Japan, where profits were greatest anyway".[104] More recently, Boyajian also confirms that Macanese *casados* also became prominent players in the trade with Makassar.[105] But this proved a double-edged sword, for Macao now grew over-dependent on two regional markets — Guangdong (Canton) and Japan. The latter highly lucrative market completely vanished when Japan forbade all connections with the Portuguese in 1639. Less than three decades later, in 1667, the VOC conquered Makassar. Asian and European competitors, who were active in that important insular entrepôt, were expelled.

CHAPTER 4

Luso-Spanish Naval Intervention, 1615–6

Luso-Johor Relations, c. 1610–5

As has been evidenced in the preceding chapters, three developments across the region triggered Luso-Spanish naval intervention around the Straits between 1615 and 1616.

First, there were Dutch plans to construct forts around the Straits. VOC admirals routinely reminded their Johorean allies that key locations, including Batu Sawar on the Johor River, were vulnerable to retaliatory attacks by the Portuguese, and exhorted them to fortify their cities. The Dutch also sought permission to construct a fort in Johor around the Singapore Straits. This broader location was chosen by the Dutch because it represented a crucial nodal point in the *Estado da Índia*'s long-distance trading networks across Asia. As is known from correspondence between Goa, Lisbon and Madrid that these Dutch plans were known to senior officials there, and so were the consequences, should the Dutch succeed in their ambitious design.[1] The impact would certainly extend beyond Portuguese possessions in Asia. Spanish Manila, too, would not be spared from Dutch naval assaults. In the second half of 1614, permission was granted by the Johor monarch Abdullah Hammayat Shah (formerly known in Dutch and Portuguese sources as Raja Bongsu or Raja Seberang) to construct a Dutch fort. From official correspondence on the Portuguese side, however, it is clear that the planned Dutch fort became a major security issue for the whole region.

The second development was Acehnese ambition for territorial expansion. One of the principal reasons why the king of Johor yielded to Dutch demands for a fortification has to do with the invasion of Johor, in the massive Acehnese campaign of 1613. Johor had formally been made a client state (or "vassal") of Aceh, a deal sealed by the marriage of an Acehnese princess with the newly installed Johor monarch.[2] Rumours abounded by 1614 of an imminent attack by Acehnese and Johorean forces on Portuguese Melaka. The Dutch were formally requested by Aceh to dispatch naval aid for this purpose, but other rumours reaching VOC officials in Banten report that the Johoreans were secretly extending the olive branch to the Portuguese while paying lip service to Aceh's latest sabre rattling.[3]

The third development was Luso-Johor relations. The exact nature of these relations in the period 1614–5 is difficult to fathom, but they could be described as having been volatile at best. Relations between Portuguese Melaka and Johor were never happy; even at the best of times, they were cautiously strained. The Dutch faction at the Johor court appears to have been seriously weakened when, after a prolonged blockade of the Johor River and its upstream towns, a "peace deal" was finally brokered by the Prince of Siak and signed in October 1610 (see Chapter 2).[4] One recalls that the provisions of the 1610 Luso-Johor peace were eventually rejected by the viceroy in Goa, but some deal appears to have been in place, for it was precisely this peace that, according to sources consulted, triggered Acehnese intervention in Johor. This was addressed in Chapter 2. It is difficult to verify the validity of rumours circulating in 1614 that the Johoreans were pursuing a peace with Portuguese Melaka. On the basis of extant source materials, it is safe to conclude that some form of agreement was eventually struck.[5] In his report to the Heren XVII of 22 October 1615, Jan Pieterszoon Coen claimed that the Johoreans were at peace with Melaka (and therefore the *Estado da Índia*) and insinuated that Luso-Johorean trade was flourishing.[6] In his letter to the Heren XVII of 10 March 1616, Admiral Steven van der Hagen mentions the Luso-Portuguese peace deal on several occasions, and he specifically underscores that "although the King of Johor is at peace with the Portuguese, his heart is still with the Hollanders".[7] An anonymous Portuguese letter written in Melaka and dating from around 1615 claims that the King of Johor, described as a "great friend of ours", alerted the Portuguese to "seven Dutch ships and a *patache*" approaching Melaka to engage the colony in battle.[8] To demonstrate open Lusitanian commitment to the Johor ruler, the Portuguese provided a naval convoy when the king's son embarked for Pahang in 1615. The Johor monarch, however, was weakened politically, and because he was unable to withstand Aceh's fresh military onslaught, he "transferred" — or fled — to Bintan in 1615. A squadron of four Portuguese galleons rushed to Riau, engaging Acehnese forces off the western coast of the Malay Peninsula between Muar and the Rio Fremoso (the present-day Batu Pahat River). One of the galleons exploded when its powder magazine caught fire. In the confusion, the Acehnese succeeded in taking several prisoners, estimated by van der Hagen at between 50 and 60.[9]

Preparations for the Armada

At the behest of the Heren XVII, pressure was stepped up by the VOC to attack Portuguese and Spanish targets and later also seize all the spice-producing islands of the Bandas and Malukus.[10] But heightened aggression by the Dutch company and traders after the onset of the 17th century certainly did not go unnoticed in Manila or in Europe. The Portuguese dispatched several punitive expeditions to rein in Southeast Asian princes who entered into friendly relations with the VOC, but those met with little, if any, success. With the evident backing and permission of his patron, the king of Spain and Portugal, and with the cooperation of the Portuguese viceroy of India, Dom Jerónimo de Azevedo, Philippine Governor Juan de Silva launched a new forward policy that sought to contain, and eventually crush, Dutch power first in the eastern archipelago and ultimately all of Asia.[11] A cornerstone in this scheme was to garrison the fort in Ternate with Spanish troops; another was to embark on an ambitious plan to construct and equip a powerful armada that would be capable of dealing with the Dutch menace and also re-establishing security along major trading routes.[12] The Spaniards under de Silva's leadership initially scored some successes, including the (second) capture in 1610 of Admiral Paul van Caerden and the engagement of François Wittert's fleet in battle.[13] Hernando de los Ríos Coronel, an agent for the city of Manila, underscores in his *Memorial y Relación para Su Majestad* (Memorial and

Relation for His Majesty), published in 1621, that these military successes made de Silva very wealthy, with the king granting him the handsome reward of 200,000 ryals-of-eight.[14]

Iberian successes in the military campaign against the Dutch were short-lived and, not surprisingly, left the royal exchequer steeped in debt.[15] A series of letters and instructions from Spain to de Silva lamented the actions of the Dutch and exhorted the good governor to assemble an armada and strike back at the European enemy.[16]

And build an armada he did, over the course of four years.[17] The governor enlisted native labour, imposed high taxes on the Filipino population and even requested additional funds, men and ammunition from New Spain (Mexico) to fund his ambitious military enterprise.[18] The Spanish viceroy of New Spain responded positively by dispatching 3 vessels and 500 men to Manila.

A massive show of naval force also requires appropriate weaponry, powder and ammunition. As supplies were difficult to obtain in faraway Asia, and Mexico was not readily rushing supplies across the Pacific, weapons, including heavy artillery, had to be produced on the spot. Metal had to be imported from as far away as Japan, but the lack of expertise in Manila for casting artillery proved a serious obstacle, as is evidenced by the following excerpt from Hernando de los Ríos Coronel:[19]

> In two years he [de Silva] cast one hundred and fifty large pieces of [bronze] artillery; but he had no master who understood it, and consequently the pieces were so poorly made that none of them stood the test. I saw twenty pieces out of thirty-six burst into flames at the first shot, as the gunner, one Pedro Castaño … will tell; consequently they did not dare to test the cannon with the royal test.

Reporting on the failed naval expedition, de los Ríos Coronel renders an emotional account of the plight and hardship of the native workers, as if to drive home the inevitable message that the armada was the project of a madman and doomed to fail right from the start.

By December 1615, the Spanish armada — the largest ever seen in the Philippines until then — was being equipped and provisioned at Cavite.[20] But the *Audiencia Real*, the bishop of Manila, leaders of the religious orders and the *cabildos* (municipal councils) could not simply stand aside and do nothing in the face of a tragedy waiting to happen. They sat de Silva down and seriously remonstrated with him on the sheer folly of his venture.[21] They questioned the viability of the proposed naval expedition against the Dutch, highlighting that the ships were not properly equipped and, for their size, dangerously understaffed with sailors. They questioned the proposed maritime route, arguing that it was "foolishly chosen because the season and the monsoon … for seeking the enemy was already past; and he [de Silva] was going with a known risk of suffering shipwreck or accomplishing nothing".[22] Worst of all, perhaps, was the grave concern voiced by the members assembled that the governor was exposing the city of Manila to unnecessary and uncertain danger by having "dismantled the forts and walls of artillery", leaving no good piece to defend the city in the event of an attack or emergency. But de Silva was relentless in insisting that he was following orders emanating directly from the king, and he produced a document as proof of his claim. This document instructed de Silva that "the [Portuguese] Viceroy of India be advised so that both should join forces and go in pursuit of the enemy with their armadas, and that the viceroy should act as superior officer if he came in person".[23]

While views differed widely as to whether de Silva was negligent or indeed heeded the orders of the king in word and intention, he did in fact consult with the Portuguese viceroy, Dom Jerónimo de Azevedo, on the matter of the proposed joint offensive against the Dutch. According to Paulo Pinto's investigations, the Spanish governor extended invitations to the viceroy on more than one occasion, to which the latter responded.[24] Six craft comprising four galleons, one caravel and a patache were dispatched to the Spice Islands via Melaka on 29 April 1614 under Lopo Sarmento de Carvalho, to assist the decimated Spanish forces. Another five galleons in the company of two trading vessels under Gonçalo Rodrigues de Sousa left Goa on 21 September that year with express instructions not to call at the port of Melaka.[25]

To this end of securing tighter Luso-Spanish cooperation in the eastern archipelago, de Silva had earlier dispatched to India two Jesuits, Father Juan de Ribera, rector of the College of Manila, and Pero Gomes, the superior of the mission on Ternate.[26] They appear to have been in the company of one Diego de Miranda, a Portuguese subject.[27] The two emissaries set sail for Goa on 21 November 1614, passed through Melaka by December, and arrived in India early the following year. The viceroy was reportedly preoccupied with warfare against the Great Moghul at that very point in time, and appointed as Portuguese commander of the armada Francisco de Miranda Enriquez (spelt in certain sources as "Henriques").[28] The viceroy placed at the disposal of de Miranda Enriquez four galleons and 300 additional soldiers, who might well represent the group of "outlaws" mentioned by Manuel Faria y Sousa. This was less than the number of ships earlier promised to Manila.[29] The armada set sail from Goa on 12 May 1615, with the Spanish emissaries as well as Dom Gonçalo de Silva, the bishop of Melaka, and his (one assumes substantial) entourage.[30]

According to extant reports, the four galleons encountered several problems on their journey from India to the Malay Peninsula. Due to poor weather, the voyage to Melaka extended to a period of six weeks rather than the customary four. One is also informed that the "soldiers of India" had brought "many servants of their own and of other people" on board, so supplies of food and fresh water were quickly depleted at mid-sea. Father Ribera reports that on his vessel there were only 110 soldiers, but the conditions on board were terribly cramped with the presence of more than 700 persons reported. It should be no surprise to learn that there were many incidents of fires breaking out on board (some of them deliberately set) and diseases spreading like wildfire among the crew and passengers.[31]

After engaging the Dutch in combat off the coast of Aru, the four galleons from India arrived on 22 August in Melaka, where many of the aforementioned outlaws-turned-soldiers absconded. Generally, the crew was given a hostile reception by the local population.[32] One can only surmise why: Soldiers do not enjoy the reputation of exhibiting the best of behaviours, and certain urges could hardly be suppressed. The original plan was that the galleons would proceed from Melaka to Manila or the Strait of Makassar, where they would join with the armada of Juan de Silva and then set sail for the Maluku islands.[33] The evidence gleaned from sources proves confounding. Manuel Faria y Sousa and, in more recent times, Paulo Pinto inform that after engaging the enemy in battle, Francisco de Miranda Enriquez was charged at Melaka with disobedience for his "refusal" to sail on.[34] By contrast, van der Hagen, who cites cross-examinations of Portuguese sailors, testifies that the Lusitanian galleons attempted their onward voyage to Manila, but once they reached the Singapore Straits they decided to return to Melaka.[35] The reasons underlying this resolve are not sufficiently clear. Van der Hagen furnishes two different explanations exacted from captured Portuguese sailors, one stating that the galleons were simply not in a position to proceed through the Straits of Singapore (as the winds apparently failed), the other being that the crew shuddered at the thought of going to a place such as Manila and dreaded the idea of heading for the Malukus.[36] Is this really what happened to the galleons of de Miranda Enriquez, or might van der Hagen have confused them with de Mendonça Furtado's six galleons that proceeded to the Straits of Singapore to await the arrival of trading ships from China? On news of the attack by Aceh on Melaka, the Singapore-based squadron rushed back to lend the city armed assistance.[37]

The initially hostile reception of the squadron turned into a hero's welcome that, as shall be seen, lasted only a fleeting moment. In September 1615, the king of Aceh arrived and laid siege to Melaka with up to 300 craft and an estimated 30,000 to 40,000 men. He was spotted with his harem at the time of the attack.[38]

The Relief Squadron in Flames, 1615

The galleons from India were praised for having successfully repulsed the Acehnese onslaught and possibly saved Melaka from falling into enemy hands, albeit at the cost of one of four ships.[39] VOC reports have it that the Acehnese navy retreated to Bengkalis (across the Strait from Melaka), where they made preparations for their next attack, which would be against Johor rather than Melaka.[40] But the sense of relief in the famed city of spice and trade was not to last. A Dutch squadron under van der Hagen comprising five ships and one cutter arrived from Banten in the waters of the Melaka Strait.[41] Rumours had already been circulating for some months that the VOC might join an Acehnese offensive on Melaka, and it is known from Dutch documentation that invitations to join the military operations had been extended to the VOC by both the Acehnese as well as their Johorean allies.[42] It may seem bewildering that the crew and soldiers of the galleons could fend off a massive attack by Aceh but found themselves unable to hold their own against a medium-sized Dutch squadron. This may have had to do with the unfortunate circumstances that are described with a sobering dose of disappointment, tracking the change in mood that quickly swung from optimism to outright despair. After reconnoitring the waters outside Melaka harbour and finding two "large galleons" and a "carrack of war" at anchor, the Dutch launched an attack on the armada that resulted in the seizure by the VOC of one Portuguese ship and the complete destruction of the other two.[43] As the two galleons and carrack were positioned between a sandbank and the Ilha das Naus off the coast of Melaka, they experienced serious difficulty in returning fire, evidently because they were unable to use all their artillery.[44] One testimony claims that the Melaka officials did not want to take the risk of placing heavy artillery on the island, evidently for fear they may fall into enemy hands. Many of the pieces transferred on eight river rafts (of which only one was properly operational) to the Ilha das Naus were reported stolen by the local inhabitants.[45] The battle lasted for three full days and one Portuguese source laments that the galleons received little or no help from either the Melaka authorities or, indeed, the casados on land who only came to salvage the corpses of the dead.[46]

The three carracks were doomed. The Portuguese soldiers gradually abandoned ship and sought to row or swim to shore, but not before setting fire to the craft to prevent the enemy from seizing it. The fate of the Portuguese flagship is described in the following words:[47]

> It began to burn, to our very great sorrow, for it was an unusually fine vessel; it carried thirty six pieces of artillery and a quantity of ammunition. When the fire reached the powder magazine, so great was the noise made, that the island of Melaka trembled and the houses shook. A cloud of smoke arose to the heavens which hid the clouds, and in that instant we lost sight of the galleon.

The losses were substantial — including 100 men wounded or dead,[48] and 92 pieces of artillery taken, fished out of shallow waters by the Dutch, or simply lost to the sea. The Dutch themselves counted 21 casualties and 19 men crushed — a figure that is inflated to "300 men" in one Portuguese report.[49] In the course of the attack, van der Hagen's men shot 11,000 pounds of powder![50] The Portuguese squadron was annihilated. The soul searching in Melaka was considerable: "After the battle and disaster many quarrels arose among the nobles by land and sea, over the question who was to blame."[51]

Another source explains it thus:[52]

> In the city was little harmony, those of the fleet and those of the city accusing one another of the [defeat]. I reverenced the judgments of God, and considered that, although there was some excess on both sides, the chief cause of so great a loss was our sins. *Quia peccavimus tibi Domini, etc.* (Because we have sinned against Thee, Lord, etc.)

It was not just the degree of soul searching that was formidable — so was the outright anger and disappointment. It is reported that the distressed merchants of Melaka had to cede a one percent levy to provision the four carracks that were now destroyed.[53] De los Ríos Coronel could hardly contain his sense of embitterment. Reflecting on the fate of the Portuguese squadron before Melaka, he abandoned the Baroque poise of inflated praise and saccharine politeness so characteristic of his day and made the following comment:[54]

> The Portuguese gained little reputation — or better to say, lost much — in not defending themselves. But since it is not my intention to meddle with other jurisdiction, I shall not discuss that.

As far as formal 17th-century insults go, this one is considerable. But then de los Ríos Coronel is scarcely more positive about the military exploits of Governor Juan de Silva, who anticipated in vain the Lusitanian squadron's arrival in Manila. After much delay and news that the Portuguese galleons were "wintering" in Melaka, de Silva changed his original plan to head straight for the Malukus and resolved, instead, to set sail and meet up with the viceroy's ships from India in the Straits of Singapore.[55] De Silva "ordered the four galleons to await him in the Strait, saying that he had resolved to pass there, that all would go together to attack the factory of Xava [Java],[56] the chief factory of the enemy which had no fortress, thence they would go to Banda and to Maluco". That, de los Ríos Coronel adds, "would have been a very suitable idea if it could have been executed during the season of navigation".[57] But the obstacles and miscalculations did not end here. De Silva also set sail from Manila late in the season, ill-staffed, ill-equipped, under a barrage of criticism from the church, the orders, the bishop, the *cabildos* and the *Audiencia Real*. Worst of all, he left Manila heavily taxed, the exchequer steeped in debt, and a fort-city with no defences to speak of. As if the members of the church and secular government had more than just a hazy foresight of things to come, Joris van Spilbergen arrived with his fleet off the coast of Luzon on 19 February 1616, by way of Cape Hoorn and Peru, just days after de Silva had set sail with the Spanish armada for the Straits of Singapore.[58] In March van Spilbergen arrived in Manila, where he learned of the designs of the Philippine governor to attack Dutch positions in the Malukus. Horacio de la Costa succinctly makes the following observation in this context:[59]

> The consternation into which he threw the city [of Manila] may well be imagined; but Van Spilbergen had of course no way of knowing that the massive walls he scanned through his spyglass were practically destitute of usable artillery and had for their defenders only a raw militia of old men and youths. The Manilans had enough sense to return an arrogant reply to his offer of ransom (the [Dutch] officers had already been executed in any case) and van Spilbergen took his departure none the wiser.

Van Spilbergen's log entry of 8 March 1616 expresses hope that it would be possible to waylay and plunder Chinese trading vessels entering

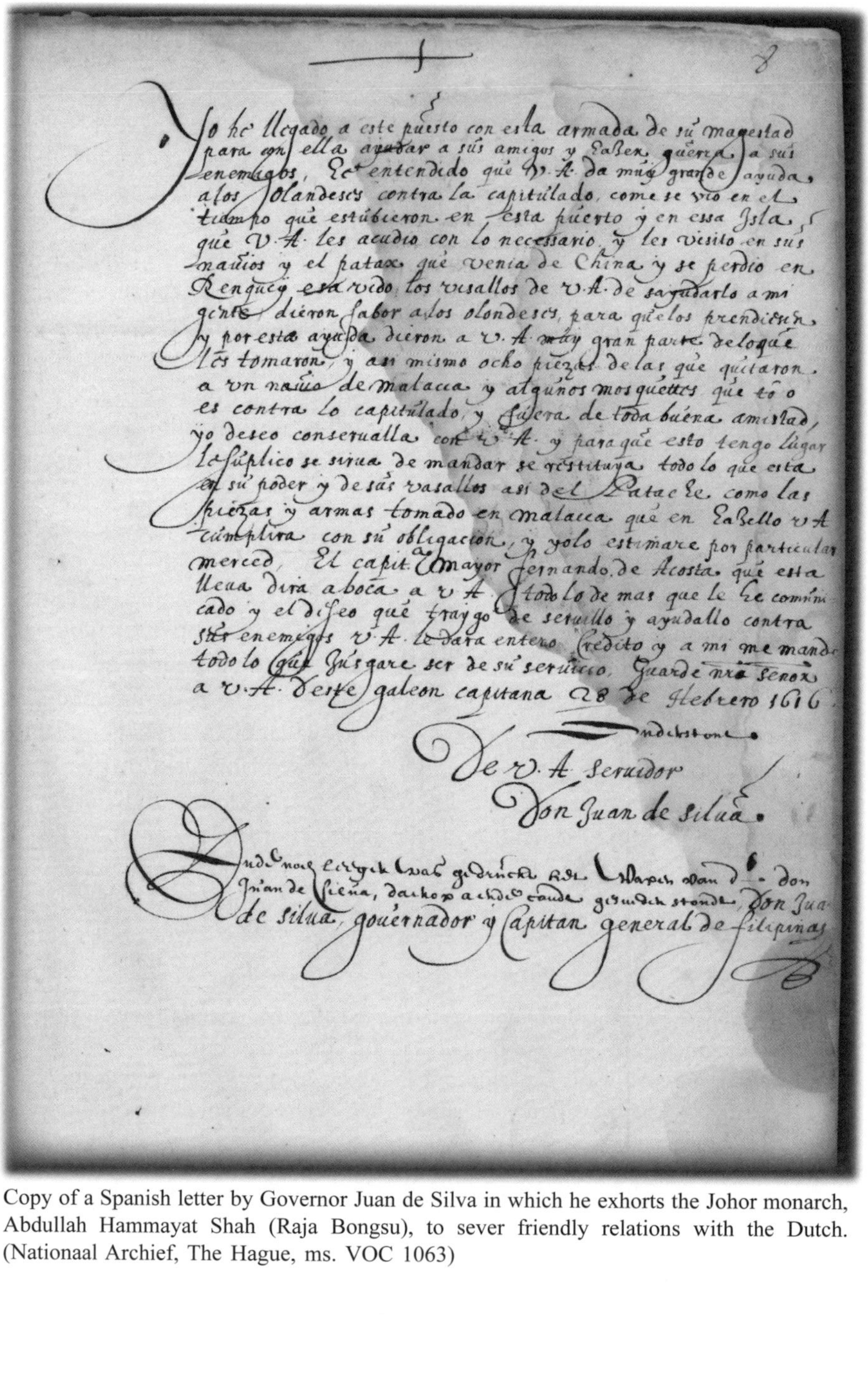

Yo he llegado a este puesto con esta armada de su Magestad
para con ella ayudar a sus amigos y hazer guerra a sus
enemigos, he entendido que V.A. da muy grande ayuda
a los Olandeses contra lo capitulado, como se vio en el
tiempo que estubieron en esta puerto y en essa Isla,
que V.A. les acudio con lo necessario, y les visito en sus
navios y el patax que venia de China y se perdio en
Renquey estando los vasallos de V.A. de sayudarlo a mi
gente dieron favor a los olandeses, para que los prendiessen
y por esta ayuda dieron a V.A. muy gran parte de lo que
les tomaron, y asi mismo ocho piezas de las que quitaron
a un navio de Malacca y algunos mosquetes que todo
es contra lo capitulado, y fuera de toda buena amistad,
yo deseo conservalla con V.A. y para que esto tengo lugar
le suplico se sirva de mandar se restituya todo lo que esta
en su poder y de sus vasallos asi del patache como las
piezas y armas tomado en Malacca que en hazello V.A.
cumplira con su obligacion, y yo lo estimare por particular
merced, El capitan mayor Fernando de Acosta que esta
lleva dira a boca a V.A. todo lo de mas que le he comuni-
cado y el deseo que traygo de servillo y ayudallo contra
sus enemigos V.A. le dara entero credito y a mi me mande
todo lo que juzgare ser de su servicio, Guarde nro señor
a V.A. deste galeon capitana 28 de Hebrero 1616.

Onderstont

De V.A. servidor
Don Juan de Silva.

Onder noch [illegible] was gedruckt het wapen van d[illegible] don Juan de Siena, daer op achter [illegible] stonde, Don Juan de Silva, governador y capitan general de filipinas

Copy of a Spanish letter by Governor Juan de Silva in which he exhorts the Johor monarch, Abdullah Hammayat Shah (Raja Bongsu), to sever friendly relations with the Dutch. (Nationaal Archief, The Hague, ms. VOC 1063)

Drawn and hand coloured bird's-eye view of the VOC "logie" (lodge or factory) in Aceh dating from the 17th century. According to the entry on the bottom left-hand side, it was situated next to the English "logie", and the two properties were separated by a narrow road or path. (Nationaal Archief, The Hague, 4.VEL 1150)

Manila Bay after about the middle of April. This marked the beginning of the annual trading season between Manila and China. But as the winds were about to shift, and rumours of an imminent attack on Dutch positions in the Malukus were making their rounds, van Spilbergen and his officers resolved to rush to the defence of the Spice Islands.[60]

Juan de Silva in the Straits of Singapore, 1616

After destroying the Portuguese naval squadron before Melaka, van der Hagen headed for the Straits of Singapore. He arrived towards the middle of December 1615 and had his ships dropped anchor at different key locations.[61] News arrived that there were two trading ships heading from China to Melaka, carrying "all the wealth of India", that means, very rich cargoes.[62] Given the state of Portuguese Melaka after the Acehnese and Dutch attacks, traders there thought it a foregone conclusion that the two trading vessels would be lost to the Dutch "thieves" and "pirates". The Portuguese viceroy had already issued written instructions to all inbound vessels to call at Tioman and ascertain whether the Singapore Straits were "safe"; should they not have been, one is told elsewhere, instructions had been issued to set the ships and cargo ablaze off Tioman or Bintan so as to prevent them from falling into the hands of the enemy. To the great fortune of the Portuguese traders concerned, this radical solution was not necessary, for while van der Hagen's men were awaiting the arrival of the two trading ships from Macao, they received a tip-off from a caravel that had run aground.[63] Hoping to extract information on inbound trading vessels from China and Japan, the Dutch were informed by the captured pilot that a large Spanish armada had set sail from Manila in January or early February 1616 and was now heading directly for the Straits of Singapore.[64] Similar but more detailed information was extracted from the crew of a captured Portuguese prahu.[65] This news was not entirely novel to van der Hagen. Prisoners taken at Melaka earlier in December had reported that the Portuguese squadron was destined to sail to Manila, and additional military assistance of unspecified magnitude had already arrived in the Philippines from across the Pacific.[66] Van der Hagen quickly abandoned his position, weighed anchor and set sail for Banten, where the ships arrived on 26 February 1616, and then sailed on to Ambon.[67]

De Silva's armada — consisting of ten galleons, four galleys, one patache and three frigates — arrived in the Singapore Straits on 25 February 1616.[68] They carried on board an estimated 5,000 soldiers — about

1,500–2,000 of them supposedly Spaniards — 500 Japanese mercenaries, 200 volunteers of indistinct origin and an unspecified number of private passengers.[69] The ships were armed with 300 cannons and 4,500 *arróbas* (or about 56 metric tons) of powder.

The following day, 26 February 1616, the carrack and galleon from Macao arrived at the eastern entrance of the Singapore Straits (only five days after van der Hagen abandoned his position) and proceeded unscathed to Melaka amidst great jubilation. With the arrival of the southwest monsoon in June, these two trading ships set course for Goa.[70]

Via his contacts and information channels in Johor and Jambi, Jan Pieterszoon Coen was kept well informed on the movements of the Spanish and their armada. In his report to the Heren XVII, Coen explains that when Governor de Silva learnt of the destruction of the Portuguese carracks at Melaka, he sent an urgent dispatch to the viceroy in Goa requesting additional naval reinforcements. It further transpires that he was intending to remain anchored off Singapore island for as long as it took for the Portuguese viceroy's ships to arrive from India.[71] Hans de Haze, who had earlier visited Aceh, explained to Coen in a letter dated 5 June 1616 that Acehnese informants reported the arrival of de Silva's armada in the Straits. Evidently alarmed by this development, Aceh's Iskandar Muda assembled his own fleet and prepared to strike targets around Johor.[72] The sense of panic was equally high at the Johor court. Van der Hagen underscores that direct discussions with the king on 8 February 1616 — literally days before de Silva arrived in the Straits — showed a clear sense of frustration. Abdullah Hammayat Shah, so one is informed, was desperately beseeching the admiral for military support, ammunition and artillery. But these supplications were turned down on the grounds that such intervention "would be taken very badly by the king of Aceh", of whom Johor was at that time a nominal vassal.[73] The VOC walked a precarious tightrope of diplomacy in the Malay world, especially at moments like this!

On 28 February 1616, just three days after casting anchor, Juan de Silva dispatched a note written in Spanish to the king of Johor, who in the past had been known as a trusted ally of the VOC and, as indicated above, may well have extended the olive branch to the Portuguese in 1614 or shortly thereafter. Coen confirms that some formal or informal peace deal had been struck at an earlier date, for the Spanish governor lectured the Johor monarch (who had earlier fled to Bintan) on good diplomatic etiquette. De Silva expressed his gravest disapproval that the king was generally known to have been lending "very great assistance" to the Dutch and urged the monarch to intervene to restore the arms and a patache seized at Melaka. This, he underscored, was something that clearly contravened the capitulation or treaty that the king had signed earlier with the *Estado da Índia* and, of course, such support did not foster amicable relations. One should read between the lines a serious warning that the good prince had better stick to his peace agreement with the Portuguese and not side with the Dutch during the impending show of military might.[74]

Given that Abdullah Hammayat Shah was "on the run" from the Acehnese (who were plotting their attack on Johor), and his reputation as a deeply loyal ally of the Dutch, it should scarcely surprise that a copy of de Silva's menacing note was rushed to Banten together with a written request for urgent assistance. The documents arrived at the VOC factory at the Sunda Strait on 10 April.[75] But was the VOC even in a position to lend assistance to Johor at that point in time? Apparently not, or at least not according to the testimony of Coen. In a report filed with his superiors, the Heren XVII, on 10 October 1616, Coen lamented that there were simply no vessels available for the relief of Johor. Had there been, he assures the directors in Europe, "we would have been able to accomplish something wonderful".[76] Most available naval craft had congregated around the Spice Islands for the defence of Dutch positions there against an imminent Luso-Spanish attack or further English encroachment in the Bandas. Due to unfavourable winds, it was simply not feasible to rush a request to the Malukus or Bandas for swift naval assistance. An actual attempt to do so ended in failure.[77]

De Silva's armada remained at anchor in the Johor River estuary between the northeastern coast of Singapore and Johor Hill for at least one month, from late February to 26 March 1616.[78] One surmises that it was during these weeks that de Silva, expressing his deep dissatisfaction with the Johor monarch's support for the Dutch, issued orders to have all the fruit trees felled around the settlements of Johor Lama and Batu Sawar.[79] This was deemed an unusual and also extremely cruel tactic by the Johor monarch, who needed no reminders of how vulnerable his upstream towns were to blockades and food shortages.[80] Andries Soury, reporting from Jambi, may not have been exaggerating when he claimed that the Johor monarch feared a blockade of his river like "a child fears the bogey man".[81]

Another incident that presumably falls within this period is the "discovery" of the Governor's Strait. Intra-Asian trade at that time used to pass either to the north of present-day Sentosa (Old Strait of Singapore) or to its south (New Strait or Strait of Santa Barbara). The discovery of this third and historically most significant maritime passage, however, does not appear to have been the result of deliberate exploratory efforts, but rather the fortuitous outcome of Juan de Silva's 2,000-ton flagship *La Salvadora* running aground while the armada was attempting to ply its way south of Singapore island![82]

Celebration and Mourning: The Arrival and Death of Juan de Silva at Melaka, April 1616

While the main portion of the armada appears to have remained at anchor off Singapore, two galleys of the Spanish armada proceeded to Melaka, where they arrived towards the end of March. In the aftermath of the seaborne Acehnese attack and the Dutch destruction of the Portuguese squadron (not so much by the cannon fire of van der Hagen's ships as by the fires deliberately set by the Portuguese crews who abandoned ship), the city was understandably engulfed in a sense of crisis and deep pessimism. It is against the backdrop of this gloom that one is to understand the excitement and newfound hope that accompanied the arrival of the Spanish governor in Melaka:[83]

> It was a most fortunate event, and was worthily celebrated by the public acclamations of the inhabitants of Melaka, who called Governor Don Juan de Silva their redeemer. They received him in their city under the pall, with demonstrations of joy and honours as if he were a viceroy, for as such did they regard him; and they assured themselves that with his valour and powerful fleet they were to deliver India from the inopportune war and the continuous pillaging of the Dutch.

This newfound optimism that the "locust plague of heretics" from the Netherlands might soon find their just retribution would evaporate within days.[84] Shortly after his arrival with pomp and ceremony, Governor de Silva fell seriously ill with a "mortal burning fever" that "killed him in eleven days". On 19 April 1616, Melaka was in mourning over the death of the governor from Manila who would deliver the city and its trade from the "Dutch menace".[85] If rumours circulating that year as far away as Japan are anything to go by — and these were just rumours — before expiring, Governor de Silva lost hope in the expedition's success and also in the

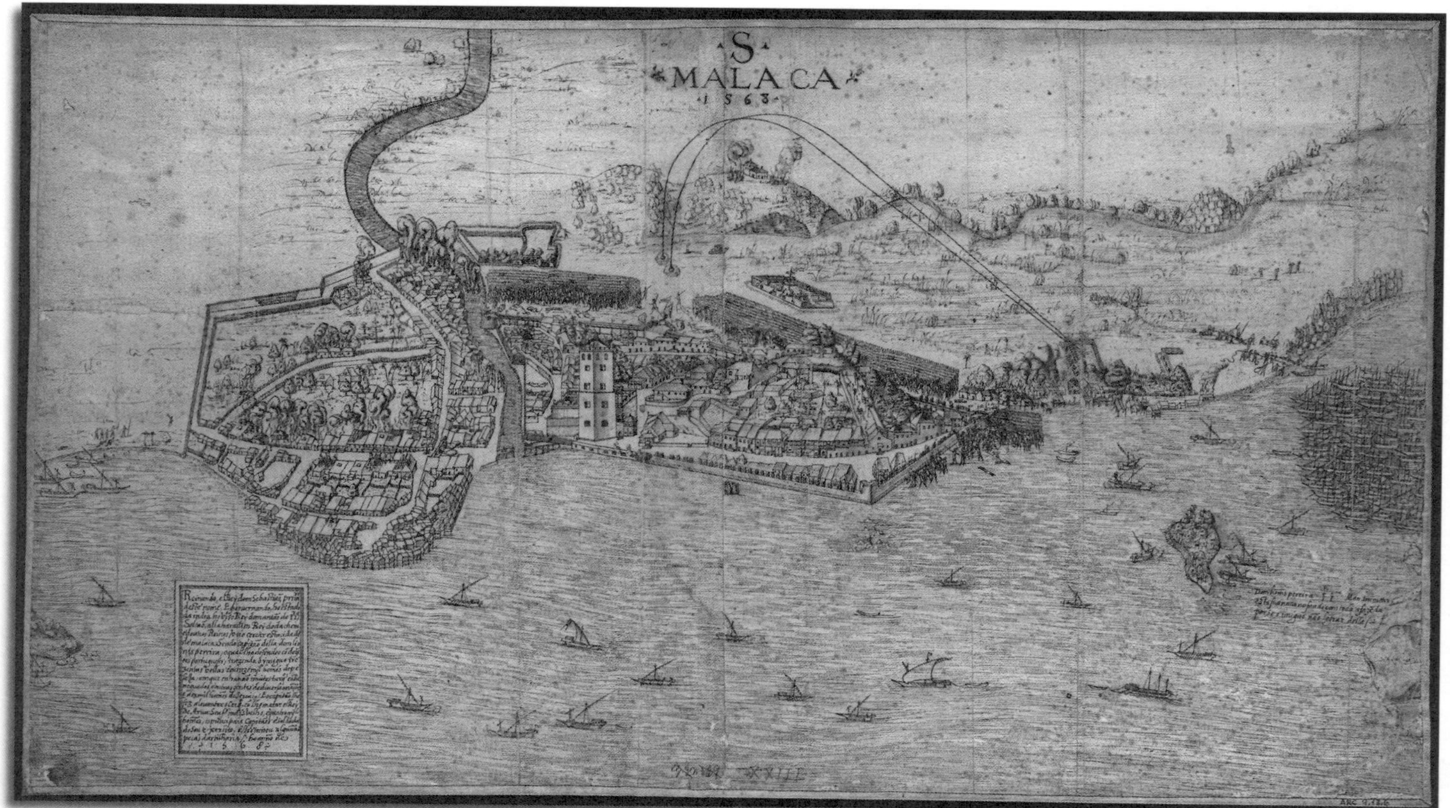

Bird's-eye view of the Acehnese attack on Melaka in 1568. The layout and ground plan of the city remained largely intact well into the 17th century. (Biblioteca Nacional do Brasil, Rio de Janeiro, ARC.009,13,006 cartografía)

prospect of incorporating the Spice Islands into the possessions of the king of Spain. He was also supposedly deeply disillusioned by the scant and haphazard support that was sent to him "from time to time from Acapulco", that is to say, from the Spanish viceroy of New Spain (Mexico).[86]

Retreat of the Spanish Armada, May–June 1616

Governor de Silva's death at Melaka — some rumours making the rounds among Dutch circles claim that he was poisoned — marked a sad end to an ambitious endeavour to oust the VOC by force of arms from the East Indies.[87] It was a military enterprise that was personally sanctioned by the king of Spain and Portugal, and directly supported by the Portuguese viceroy of India and the Spanish viceroy of New Spain (Mexico). The governor's demise marked in some symbolic way the fate of the entire expedition. There was to be no rendezvous of Spanish and Portuguese armadas. Nor would the proud Spanish armada engage the enemy in battle. Disease was decimating the crew and soldiers by the day. Some reports speak of casualties running into the hundreds,[88] and the blame was put squarely on the bad climate and foul water:[89]

> … at that part of the Strait where it [the armada] was anchored the air was so unhealthful and the waters so poisonous that the soldiers began to sicken immediately and to die swollen up and yellow and some days forty or fifty of them were thrown into the sea. All asserted that had they remained there one fortnight longer, not enough men would have been left to manage the sails, nor could they have brought back the galleons, which returned without anchors, for the few that they carried were lost in the currents, which are very strong.

The crew, however, did not need to remain there. One report claims that the Spanish governor, prior to his death, issued specific orders for the armada to return to Manila.[90] De la Costa, who touches briefly on this episode in his classic work *The Jesuits in the Philippines*, contends that "his [De Silva's] captains voted to return to Manila without striking a blow".[91] But there is evidence that also points to other, broader considerations. The Spanish were nervous about having left Manila with few men and defences; many of the Spanish soldiers on board were *casados* whose arms had been twisted to join the expedition.[92] Finally, there appears to be a connection with the arrival of the *armada de remo* (armada of oared galleys), which the viceroy in Goa had dispatched to Melaka at de Silva's urgent request of February 1616.[93]

After lying in state at the residence of the Society of Jesus at Melaka, the embalmed corpse of the governor was brought to the armada and received with a salute on 2 May.[94] Two days later, the ships set course for Manila and wrought havoc before their final retreat to the Philippines by setting ablaze the forests on Tioman.[95] Coen also reports that a contingent of 500 soldiers was left behind in Melaka by the Spaniards to help protect the city; but in a more cynical vein, Ernst van Veen sees them as de Silva's 500 Japanese mercenaries who were set ashore because they were deemed unreliable.[96]

The fear of the Spanish armada and its possible return to the waters of the Singapore Straits lingered for many months. Andries Soury, the VOC factor at Jambi, conceded to the uncertain and possibly unreliable news that the armada had in fact returned to the Philippines. He was keen to ascertain the reliability of this information from different sources. Even Laurens Reael, the new Dutch governor-general, expressed concern in his communication of 11 July 1616 that the Spaniards may dispatch warships to Tioman and the region sometime in the near future.[97]

With the benefit of hindsight, it is evident that Manila was not in a position to send out a punitive expedition but rather found itself under siege. De la Costa casts the following indicting verdict on de Silva's expedition as well as the attack on Manila and its surroundings:[98]

> The operation failed. Instead of accepting battle like gentlemen, the canny Dutch avoided the armada and sent a squadron to attack Manila instead. On their way there they stopped at Jolo and asked the Sulus to join them. It was too good an opportunity to miss. While the Spaniards made desperate preparations to meet the Dutch, a powerful Sulu fleet destroyed the shipyard at Pantao in Camarines, slipped into Manila Bay, burned the Cavite navy yard, and carried away a number of Spanish prisoners for ransom.

It must have been a sad sight. Juan de Silva's armada arrived in Manila by early June 1616.[99] Not only had the ships experienced an almost perilous decimation of crew and soldiers, the armada was in such "bad shape as if it had been a year at sea".[100]

Afterthoughts

On the basis of Spanish, Portuguese and Dutch source material, this chapter has sought to cast light on an interesting episode in Luso-Spanish security and sincere efforts at military cooperation in the East during the second decade of the 17th century. This mood of cooperation was made feasible to a certain extent by the Union of the Two Crowns, as well as the growing exasperation of the Iberian powers over the heightened contest for control of the Malukus and Bandas.[101] But Luso-Spanish cooperation even at its best was slow and cumbersome, usually involving separate channels of information, communication and financial support that arguably spanned the globe. Although Spain showed a consistent interest in East and Southeast Asia for most of the early 17th century, and always kept an eye open for trading opportunities, official action was seriously constrained by Portuguese claims to patrimony over most Asian lands and seas. These stakes were formally laid down in agreements such as the Treaty of Zaragoza (Saragossa). As time passed, Spain felt increasingly strained by its Asian exposure, not only on account of the garrisons that had to be maintained in the Spice Islands (particularly on Tidor), but also because of stepped-up attacks by the Dutch enemy on Manila.[102] The port was attacked no fewer than three times in 1620, and the harbour was blockaded between January 1621 and May 1622. Colonial officials were also seriously concerned over the staggering cost of maintaining security in the Malukus (technically Portuguese) and Manila. Van Veen calculated that between 1607 and 1620 the total cost to the exchequer of New Spain (which was responsible for providing subsidies to Manila) amounted to more than seven million ducats. To place that sum in context, it was equivalent to one-third of the amount spent by Spain to maintain the Army of Flanders in the same period — an army that, during the truce in Europe, was meaningfully "downsized" from the height of the Spanish-Dutch confrontation![103]

The story of Luso-Spanish cooperation in 1615 and 1616 provides a unique glimpse into the functioning of the two separate and distinct empires under the Union of the Two Crowns, the distrust and unease under which cooperation took place, the challenges faced, the manifold obstacles to success, and the ever-precarious nature of diplomacy, peace and warfare in the Malay world. From the very start, the naval intervention of Viceroy Jerónimo de Azevedo and Governor Juan de Silva was riddled with wavering commitments, slow communications, financial and logistical bottlenecks, serious miscalculations and perhaps even an inadequate understanding of the strategic task and military mandate at hand. Everything that could go wrong did — or at least so it may appear to the contemporary researcher — and the outcome of what might possibly be viewed as "a worst-case scenario" was clearly disheartening. On the

Spanish side of the equation, the expedition to oust the Dutch from the region not only ended in failure, but resulted in massive debt for the crown.

One might contend that had de Silva not suddenly passed away due to disease or poisoning in Melaka, the episode might have ended very differently. In the assessment of the author, the evidence from the sources does not support such a conclusion. The Dutch were prepared for the joint offensive in the Malukus. De Silva's ambitious and expensive enterprise left Manila virtually defenceless. The governor failed to listen to the grave admonitions and exhortations of ecclesiastical and government officials prior to his departure for the Malay Peninsula. Also, in the Straits of Singapore, de Silva's men were being decimated by disease at a truly alarming rate. By the time the armada set sail on its homebound voyage, without engaging the enemy in even a single confrontation, arguably half the men had already been carried away by disease. The Dutch appear to have somehow gained the upper hand, not so much on account of superior military hardware or even tactics, but simply because their channels of information and methods of information gathering were comparatively more efficient. To employ a modern term in this context, the VOC had command over a solid and reliable "intelligence network". One can only gape in awe at the wealth and diversity of information at the disposal of the company and its key servants in Asia.

The presence and intervention of the Spanish armada around Singapore marks a fascinating episode in the early modern history of the island. Snippets from this story have long been known, mainly in the context of de Silva's accidental "discovery" of the Governor's Strait, one of the main passages collectively known as the Straits of Singapore. It is curious why the story and fate of the expedition have remained obscure, undiscovered and under-researched.

CHAPTER 5

VOC Blockades in the Singapore and Melaka Straits: Diplomacy, Trade and Survival, 1633–41

Melaka and the VOC: Evolving Perceptions of a Colonial Prize, c. 1600–33

To many Europeans of the late 16th and early 17th centuries, the Portuguese emporium of Melaka was a place of almost legendary wealth, an undisputed "jewel in the crown" at the centre of the *Estado da Índia*'s far-flung possessions spanning from the eastern coast of Africa to the Japanese islands. Unbridled fantasies of prosperity far exceeded the reality on the ground. What is certain is that the Portuguese did not inherit either a hugely populated city or a vast empire that controlled much of the region around the Straits of Singapore and Melaka. These less fantastic realities may have been recognised on the ground, but they were not readily reflected in reports circulating in writing or, more often, by word of mouth around the trading centres of Europe's Atlantic seaboard.

At the dawn of the 17th century, accounts of Melaka's almost-legendary wealth still fired the imagination of traders in Europe. Melaka was still regarded as a "jewel in the crown" of the *Estado da Índia*, an assessment that made it a colonial possession of great envy. When the

Dutch arrived in the waters of insular Southeast Asia, inspired not least by Linschoten's *Reysgeschrift* and *Itinerario* (1595–6), Melaka was seen as a great, prosperous colonial prize. The VOC that sprung out of earlier regional trading firms inherited a dream to wrest control of Melaka from the Portuguese for the prestige of the Dutch company and the glory of the new Dutch Republic. The imagined riches in and from the East Indies inexorably drove policy-making in the VOC's boardrooms and in the republic's corridors of power.

As has been shown in Chapter 2, the *Santa Catarina* incident of February 1603 was to impact the European scenario in several ways, two of which merit further explanation in the present chapter. First, the auction of the carrack's cargo evoked considerable attention among the merchant communities of the Low Countries and beyond over the riches to be reaped from the East Indies commerce, and especially from the trade with China. Given the circumstances of the seizure in waters en route to Melaka, it can be little wonder that the *Santa Catarina*'s cargo sold by public auction served as visible, tangible evidence to validate the fantasies surrounding the Melaka legacy. Second, as will be recalled from Chapters 2 and 4, Admiral Jakob van Heemskerk returned to Europe with a Johorean ambassador, Megat Mansur, and his entourage. The purpose of this embassy has been subject to some speculation, but readers can be left with little doubt about the subsequent development of Dutch-Johor relations. Megat Mansur may have passed away during the voyage to Europe, but a member of his entourage, one Encik Kamar, made it to Europe and returned to Johor with the fleet of Admiral Cornelis Matelieff de Jonge in 1606.[1]

On the basis of materials consulted, the Johor embassy to the Dutch Republic appears to have served two specific ends. One was to pave the way for formalising budding VOC-Johor relations with a treaty. The second was to use the formal alliance to wrest control of Melaka from the Portuguese. Conclusions about the latter derive from snippets of information in the travelogue of Admiral Cornelis Matelieff de Jonge. On arriving with Matelieff's fleet in the waters at Melaka on 30 April 1606, Encik Kamar set ashore and proceeded to inform his ruler that the Dutch had returned and were ready to launch a seaborne attack on the Portuguese fort and settlement.[2] On learning of the arrival of the Dutch fleet, the Johor ruler dispatched the *shahbandar* of Singapura to examine the situation.[3]

Melaka was a jewel waiting to be plucked from the Portuguese, or so the Dutch thought at the time. Within just over three weeks of arriving off the coast of Melaka, Matelieff had signed a preliminary agreement with the Johor royals for the capture of Melaka and the division of the spoils of war.[4] The treaty of 17 May 1606 signed aboard the VOC ship *Oranje* made among other things provisions for the harvesting of wood, the repopulation by the Johor monarch of the suburb *Kampung Kling* (after it had been deliberately burnt down by the Portuguese),[5] and other specific matters pertaining to jurisdiction and extradition. In negotiating the provisions of the treaty, it is said that Raja Bongsu wished to be left control of the fortress 'A Famosa while concessions would be made to the Dutch to take up residence and have lodgings within the captured city.[6] The Dutch company and the Johor monarch were to act in unison to gain control of the settlement, Matelieff attacking by sea and Johor's troops on land. A second treaty was ratified in the royal capital of Batu Sawar on 23 September 1606, after earlier engaging the Portuguese armada off Cape Rachado and weeks of futile attacks on the fortress and colony of Melaka.[7]

Matelieff attacked Portuguese positions on several occasions between May and October 1606.[8] It is reported that he occupied an island off the coast of the town and fortress, which he used to set up a battery and control shipping in and out of the port of Melaka. In some sources this islet is identified as the Ilha das Naus, or present-day Pulau Jawa.[9] The Portuguese would remember this for years to come, and almost immediately after the withdrawal of the Dutch they constructed fortification structures and garrisoned the island.[10] At sea, in August and October Matelieff engaged the Portuguese armada that had been dispatched from Goa on 13 May 1606. In the words of Sanjay Subrahmanyam, this armada was "the largest that the *Estado da Índia* ever managed to put together in the entire course of the Luso-Dutch struggle in Asia".[11] A schematic depiction of one of the naval confrontations was printed by Johan Isaakzoon Pontanus in 1611.[12]

Melaka could not be easily wrested from the Portuguese, not least because the town was well-provisioned, security had been beefed up with Japanese and African mercenaries,[13] and, if certain Dutch testimonies are even credible, the Johoreans did not live up to their end of the preliminary agreement signed on 17 May 1606. These testimonies sharply contrast with the undated Portuguese account titled *Relação do sucesso que teve a armada do viso-rei Dom Martim Afonso* (Account of the course of events of the armada of Viceroy Dom Martim Afonso de Castro) according to which the city of Melaka had been besieged by the Dutch with the

Image depicting the arrival of Admiral Cornelis Matelieff de Jonge's fleet at Melaka in 1606. From J.I. Pontanus, *Rerum et Urbis Amstelodamensium Historia* (History of the City of Amsterdam), 1611 (Koninklijke Bibliotheek, The Hague, 136 B 20)

Schematic depiction of the naval confrontation between the fleets of Cornelis Matelieff de Jonge and Pedro Mascarenhas off Cape Rachado. The Latin entry "Matlivij naves 12" refers to the ships of Admiral Matelieff, while the "Lusitanicae naves" refers to the Portuguese armada. From J. I. Pontanus, *Rerum et Urbis Amstelodamensium Historia* (History of the City of Amsterdam), Amsterdam, 1611 (Koninklijke Bibliotheek, The Hague, 136 B 20).

support of 1,400 Dutch soldiers, "seven neighbouring rulers" and "about 16 thousand Javanese troops" for a period of four months.[14] Dutch claims that the Johor troops refused to engage the Portuguese in battle may have just served as a convenient excuse to avoid soul searching and to pin failure on someone else, but the wider context also lends support to the view that the Batu Sawar court was split into at least two powerful factions. As previously mentioned in Chapter 2, certain high-ranking nobles or officers of Johor, such as the Prince of Siak and the *laksamana*, were very sympathetic to the Portuguese cause — especially for the financial revenue it generated — while King Ala'ud'din and his younger brother, Raja Bongsu, supported the Dutch.

Matelieff's seaborne attacks of 1606 must be seen as a lost opportunity, for, as is known, the Portuguese would work to further split allegiances in the Batu Sawar court and also cultivate the pro-Lusitanian faction. These developments have been described in greater detail in Chapter 2. Importantly, the failed attack on Melaka served as an opportunity for the Dutch to sit back and stake out the goals of the nascent Dutch company and empire. Who was better qualified to do that than Matelieff himself?

In an epistolary report filed after his return to Europe titled *Discours van den stant van Oost Indiën* (Discourse on the State of the East Indies), Cornelis Matelieff de Jonge runs through a number of scenarios for a successful campaign of violence directed against the Portuguese, the Spanish and their allies in Asia.[15] It is important to bear in mind both the date and the addressee of the report. The *Discours* reached the desk of Hugo Grotius around the time he was revising *Mare Liberum* (The Free Sea) for publication.[16] Grotius was extremely well connected not only in government circles of the Dutch Republic, but also with the VOC. As recent research has shown, Grotius proved himself as one of the most enthusiastic supporters of the Dutch-Johor alliance and also emerged as one of the most outspoken advocates of freebooting, endorsing the use of violence against hard and soft targets of the Iberian powers in Asia.[17]

In his *Discours*, Matelieff identifies and spells out two priorities for the VOC in Asia. The first is to wrest Melaka from the Portuguese, possibly with the help of existing or future Asian allies, such as Siam but also Johor, Aceh, Kedah, Perak, Pahang, Patani and Jambi.[18] The second priority he identifies is the need to establish a rendezvous location as a base for the VOC's Asian operations, where goods could be collected centrally from around Asia and ships could assemble before setting off to, or returning from, other trading emporia in the East Indies.[19] This rendezvous, Matelieff

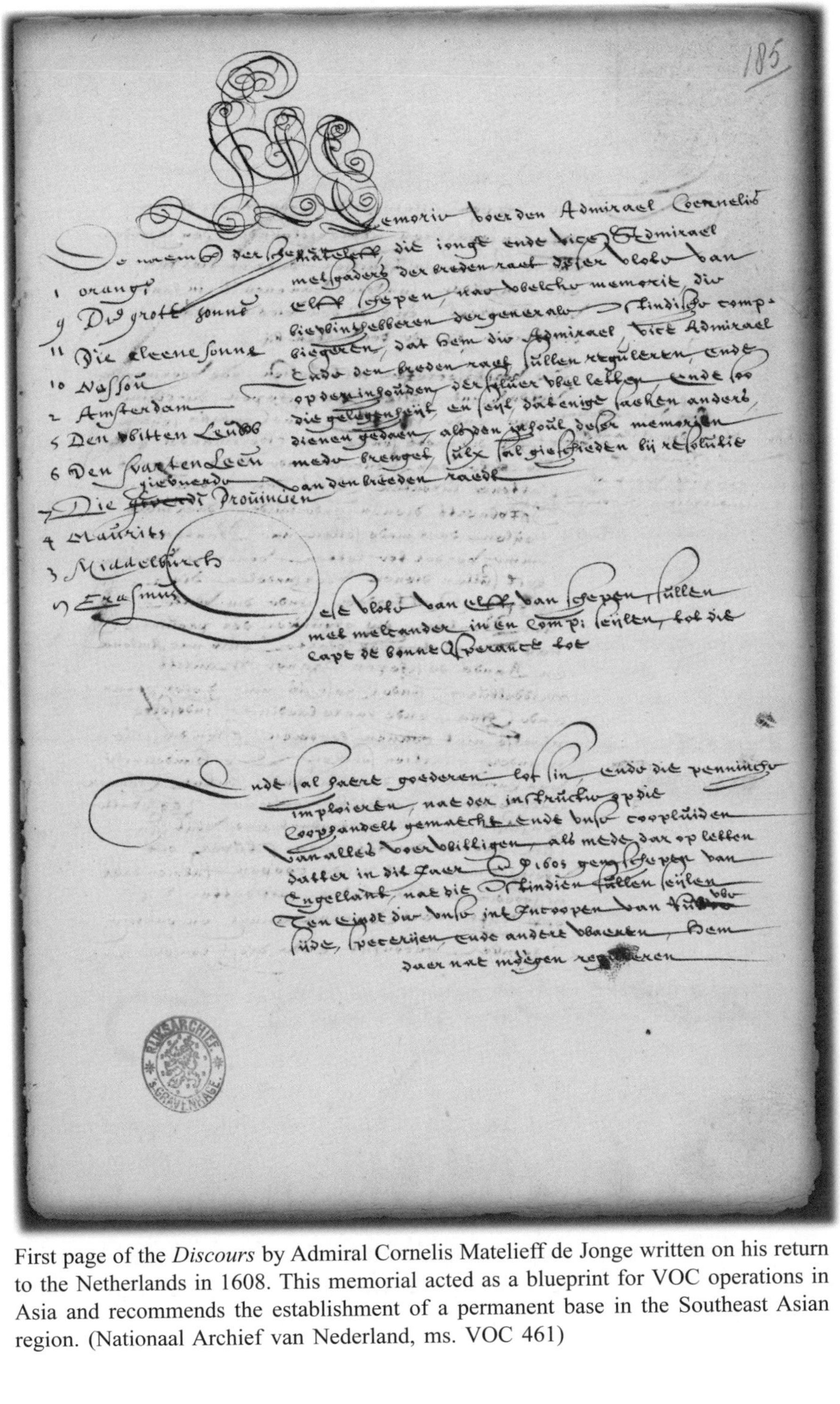

First page of the *Discours* by Admiral Cornelis Matelieff de Jonge written on his return to the Netherlands in 1608. This memorial acted as a blueprint for VOC operations in Asia and recommends the establishment of a permanent base in the Southeast Asian region. (Nationaal Archief van Nederland, ms. VOC 461)

cautions, would need to be readily accessible year-round and independent of prevailing monsoon seasons — and in this respect, Melaka's location was not ideally suited.[20] Possible (but clearly not ideal) locations included certain areas near the Strait of Sunda along the northern coast of Java, such as "Jacatra", as well as Palembang on the great island of Sumatra.[21] Matelieff recommended beefing up security around places such as Ambon, the Bandas and, importantly, Johor's royal residence of Batu Sawar. He encouraged intercepting enemy shipping in the Straits, around Ceylon (now Sri Lanka) and generally also around the Bay of Bengal. But he stressed that by far the most damage could be inflicted on the Portuguese by attacking commercial vessels outbound from Macao and taking them as prizes of war.[22] These recommendations proved seminal for the future development of VOC operations in Asia.

After Matelieff's ill-fated seaborne attacks in 1606, Melaka remained a focal point of attention for VOC directors and officers. The company maintained its wish to wrest the emporium of trade and spices from the Portuguese, and additional attacks were launched after the elapse of the Twelve Years Truce in 1623, 1627 and again in 1629.[23] It is also evident, however, that Melaka's standing and prestige in the eyes of the Dutch company's leading servants began to wane by the second decade of the 17th century. VOC directors and officers were growing aware that delays in wresting Melaka from the Portuguese came in the way of the rapidly evolving needs of the VOC in Asia. Asian operations were initially centred on the Dutch factory in Banten, but the long-term viability of the Sundanese port as a permanent residence for the VOC's new resident governor-general was seriously questioned. VOC materials echo Matelieff's two-pronged strategy and carefully weigh the merits of locations around the region for a rendezvous point. Among these, Johor was singled out as a serious candidate; it had already been identified as "a place where commerce and trade must be maintained at all cost".[24] This was quite understandable, given Johor's strategic location along important maritime arteries such as the Singapore and Melaka Straits, as well as the good relations forged by the VOC with the royals of Batu Sawar after 1606. But as the factionalism at the court became more exposed, and after the sudden political changes inflicted on the region as a result of Aceh's attacks (see Chapter 2), Johor disappeared from the shortlist of qualified locations. By 1621, it was resolved to establish a permanent base in Jacatra (renamed Batavia), a decision that served to finally push Melaka off the pedestal of desired locations.[25]

In the mid-1620s, the VOC's aim to wrest the colony from Portuguese control was no longer driven by dreams of huge profits, but by the need to bring stability back to a region that had seen decades of political, social and economic turmoil. The Dutch company walked a narrow political tightrope, carefully balancing the demands, interests and requests of both Johor and Aceh, while at the same time boosting efforts to isolate and eventually eliminate the Portuguese as an economic, political and military force in the region of the Straits. The early 1630s saw the enforcement of intermittent naval blockades against Portuguese interests in the Straits of Singapore and Melaka that proved costly. These yielded few prizes of war from freebooting activities, and in the end failed to weaken the Portuguese at Melaka financially, or even isolate them diplomatically. The endeavour, however, eventually came to fruition when Melaka's population, decimated by the plague and starvation, surrendered to the Dutch on 14 January 1641. The Portuguese emporium had not so much fallen to the force of Dutch arms as become the humiliated victim of a "black trinity" comprising war, famine and the plague.[26]

The Blockade of the Singapore and Melaka Straits after 1633 and the "Bigger Picture"

Between 1633 and 1641, the VOC imposed an intermittent blockade in the Straits and on the Portuguese-held emporium of Melaka. This represents part of a broader strategy, echoed in many VOC-generated documents, including the *Discours* of Cornelis Matelieff de Jonge, to disrupt trade between the far-flung ports of the *Estado da Índia* and starve the Portuguese administration of revenue.[27] A financially weakened *Estado*, it was rightly opined, would find it difficult to meet the security needs of traders on whose wealth and tax-generating activities the future of the Portuguese colonial enterprise ultimately rested.

The VOC positioned its sparse naval and military forces carefully by singling out crucial nodal points around the *Estado da Índia*'s possessions along the rim of the Indian Ocean and the coast of the South China Sea. As has been seen across all chapters of the present book, the Singapore and Melaka Straits, together with the Portuguese-held emporium Melaka, had always played a major role in the security calculations of both the *Estado da Índia* and its northern European enemies. The reason is clear: the Straits represented a principal artery of seaborne commerce in the regional and long-distance networks of trade. Disrupting maritime traffic destined for

Melaka and other Portuguese ports in effect severed the *Estado*'s far-flung network of settlements. Concurrently, the VOC blockaded several nodal points and ports, including Portugal's Asian capital, Goa. Historians should not be surprised to unearth important parallels in the way the blockades of Melaka and Goa were handled. Planning for both took place in Batavia, and there was also an important continuity of key personnel supervising the two operations. Of special interest in the present context is Jakob Cooper,[28] who first acted as the commander-in-charge of the blockade operations in the Straits of Singapore and Melaka. He was later transferred to the blockade of Goa[29] and reassigned to Melaka,[30] where he supervised military operations for the final assault on the town and fortress in the second half of 1640.[31]

Though of considerable interest for the history of the region during the first half of the 17th century, the crucial VOC blockade of the Straits between 1639 and January 1641 finds only passing mention in several histories of Melaka, including Barbara Andaya's *Melaka under the Dutch, 1641–1795* as well as Dianne Lewis' *Jan Compagnie in the Straits of Malacca*.[32] The blockade is also broadly mentioned by Afzal Ahmed, Glenn Ames, James Boyajian and Ernst van Veen, usually in conjunction with similar operations around Asia, such as the VOC blockade of Goa.[33] Two older contributions that address the military campaigns at large also mention the blockade: P.G. Leupe's *Siege and Capture of Malacca from the Portuguese in 1640–1641* (1936) and David Bassett's *Changes in the Pattern of Malay Politics, 1629–1655* (1969).[34] One might also wish to include here the excellent study of René Barendse, *Blockade: Goa and Its Surroundings 1638–1654*, which can serve to meaningfully extend the picture from the region around the Singapore and Melaka Straits to also encompass the Indian subcontinent.[35] Barendse's paper offers a model for the present chapter, with the noteworthy difference that this account places greater emphasis on specific strategies devised by the two enemies, the Portuguese and the Dutch, as well as their respective treaty partners and supporters.

Before delving into the dynamics of the naval blockade, it would be worthwhile to sketch the bigger picture around the Straits, the Malay Peninsula, Sumatra and Southeast Asia. For a better grasp of the issues at hand, one can point to the aforementioned articles of Basset and Leupe as well as Lombard's now classic *Le Sultanat d'Atjéh au temps d'Iskandar Muda* (The sultanate of Aceh in the age of Iskandar Muda) for further reference.[36]

As is known from that pioneering work of Lombard, together with some more recent studies such as those by Jorge Alves and Paulo Pinto, the

Hand coloured printed scene of Goa from J.H. van Linschoten's first edition of the *Itinerario,* 1596. (Koninklijke Bibliotheek, The Hague, 1702 B 4)

Hand coloured map of Goa from J.H. van Linschoten's first edition of the *Itinerario,* 1596. (Koninklijke Bibliotheek, The Hague, 1702 B 4)

kingdom of Aceh embarked on a trail of expansion in the first half of the 17th century and emerged as the dominant power in the region around the Singapore and Melaka Straits. Its cultural and military rival, Johor, was attacked together with other Malay states on the peninsula, including Perak and Selangor. The Portuguese were traditionally hostile to Aceh (and vice versa), and their relations with Johor were mixed, but their ties to Pahang were generally on sounder terms.[37] The VOC was an ally of both Aceh and Johor, but after 1613 it was caught in a serious tussle between the two parties — a delicate situation diplomatically, as is evidenced by VOC-generated documentation, amongst other sources. These materials reveal that Aceh maintained the balance of power around the region, but caution ruled after the death of Iskandar Muda in December 1636 and the ascent to the throne of his son, Iskandar Thani.[38] Several promises by the Acehnese (as early as 1633)[39] to assist in military operations against Melaka remained unfulfilled, and gradually the Dutch lost all hope of securing any military support from the Sumatran ruler.[40]

In mainland Southeast Asia, Siam entered a period of political instability during a succession crisis that brought King Prasat Thong to the throne in September 1629.[41] Evidence suggests that the Siamese sought the active assistance of Aceh in quelling the unrest in their lands, but King Prasat Thong reportedly acted with "brutal force" by throwing the Acehnese envoy "into prison".[42] Other sources mention ill-conceived Spanish schemes to destabilise and perhaps even overrun the Siamese kingdom, possibly with the help of the "king of Cambodia".[43] Such schemes were concocted after the Spaniards "defied the [Siamese] king's sovereignty" in the mid-1620s by attacking a Dutch trading vessel in the Chao Phraya River.[44] Despite pressure from officers of the *Estado da Índia* to exclude Dutch traders from Siam, Portugal's commercial and diplomatic relations with the kingdom as well as with Pegu and Makassar were generally sound. But news of an embassy of Mataram to Portuguese Melaka in 1636 and again in 1639 was received with considerable suspicion by Dutch officials in Batavia. In fact, a flurry of Luso-Siamese diplomacy in 1636 alarmed the Dutch in Siam and, in the words of Ruangsilp, turned the court of Ayutthaya into a "virtual battlefield".[45] It is known that the Portuguese sought the assistance of Mataram,[46] which was reported to not only have rushed food supplies to Melaka, but also considered the dispatch of military assistance.[47] Farther to the east, the Dutch established themselves on the island of Taiwan in 1624. In 1635 the Tokugawa Shogunate forbade the Japanese from leaving the archipelago, and in 1639 it closed its doors entirely to the Portuguese.[48] The latter decision dealt a serious blow to trading centres such as Macao, which relied heavily on the Japan trade.[49] These developments in Northeast Asia are well-documented and form the subject of several scholarly discussions.

Against the backdrop of this constellation of forces one needs to place the conflict between the *Estado da Índia* and the VOC, the latter representing a technically private enterprise acting as an arm of the Dutch-Iberian war effort in Asia.[50] The Dutch company adopted a two-pronged approach in dealing with the Lusitanian foe: the first was disrupting networks of trade and strangling the flow of goods between Portuguese-held ports; the second was attacking both hard[51] and soft Portuguese targets. Attacks on soft targets translated in practice into intercepting and plundering commercial trading vessels.[52] Both strategies aimed at starving the *Estado da Índia* of financial revenue so as to weaken its ability to carry out swift and decisive military responses. Imposing a blockade was one means of enforcing these objectives, particularly when the blockade could be effectively imposed over a sustained period. Blockades were organised and enforced at points of strategic and commercial importance, especially in the Straits of Melaka and Singapore.

Source Materials: Dredging for Clues

At this juncture, a look at the extant source materials is warranted. For information on the Dutch side, the present author has relied chiefly on published and unpublished documentation deriving from the VOC, including reports and letters by Commander Jakob Cooper,[53] correspondence from the Sumatra outposts to Batavia (especially from the factory in Jambi),[54] the *Generale Missiven*, as well as that treasure trove of gossip and information for the Indonesian Archipelago and beyond, the *Dagh-Register Batavia.*

For information on the Portuguese side, the author has consulted the *Assentos*, edited and published by Pissurlencar,[55] and individual pieces of correspondence that were intercepted by the VOC during the period of the blockade have been consulted.[56] The *Livros das Monções* (Books or Letters of the Monsoon) proved useful for gleaning responses to the blockade and VOC aggression in the East Indies in general from an institutional, or at least official, perspective.[57] For the earlier period of the blockade — 1633 to the middle of 1635 — there is also the published diary of the Portuguese viceroy of India, the Conde de Linhares. It contains interesting and useful information on issues pertaining to security and trade.[58] While admittedly far from complete, the materials paint a rewarding account of the situation within the walls of Portuguese Melaka (together with some other port cities of the *Estado da Índia*), and also reveal strategies devised by Lusitanian traders to circumvent the Dutch blockade.

In reviewing sources, the following questions stood at the forefront of attention: How did the parties on the ground act to enforce the blockade? What specific steps were taken to break, evade and circumvent the VOC blockade? What were the immediate factors on the ground that induced the defeat and surrender of Portuguese Melaka in January 1641?

On the Dutch side, it is possible to detect a reliance on maritime power and artillery along with the signing of new treaties, or invoking of existing ones, with princes in the region. The Dutch also co-opted local merchants and political elites to support their cause.[59] The co-optation of indigenous elites is paramount for two reasons: first, because looking at the bigger picture, it was evident to VOC servants at the time that they did not control the balance of power. It was clear that the key to holding the balance of power was firmly placed in the hands of Aceh. In mobilising their (regional) treaty partners, the Dutch naturally also had to cast an eye on the Acehnese, and preferably also persuade Aceh's monarch, Iskandar Muda, and his successor, Iskandar Thani, to lend active military support to the Dutch cause.

On the ground, it proved almost impossible to seal off the Singapore and Melaka Straits with anything between five and nine cutters together with an undisclosed number of sloops. The vessels and men at the company's disposal were simply insufficient to impose a tight naval blockade on Melaka, or to solicit information from local agents or passing vessels. But the control of specific nodal points in the waters of the Straits facilitated the interception and seizure of craft destined for Melaka and other Portuguese-held ports. Freebooting was certainly not a new strategy adopted by the VOC; still there is documentation to prove that such activities were successfully pursued in the Singapore and Melaka Straits between 1636 and 1639.

Portuguese Responses to the VOC Blockades in the Straits

Lusitanian counter-strategies were generally conceived as responses to specific Dutch aggression. The co-optation of regional elites is important for appreciating and understanding the historic unfolding of events. It should be noted, however, that in times of distress it was not uncommon to devise forward strategies that consciously aimed at upsetting the balance of power in the region.

In the period under review, the Portuguese offered to improve relations with their long-time enemy and commercial rival, Aceh. For a short span, notably in the months preceding the death of Aceh's Iskandar Thani in February 1641, some progress was arguably made by the *Estado da Índia* by radically changing tack on the diplomatic front.[60] The matter is admittedly shrouded in obscurity and difficult to reconstruct in detail. Source materials reveal that Lusitanian officials sought to grease the wheels of diplomacy in September 1638. On that occasion the embassy, led by Francisco de Soza de Castro, ended in an unmitigated fiasco, resulting in the burning of Aceh's royal palace and triggering the massacre of almost all those associated with the Portuguese mission.[61] De Soza de Castro survived, but he was held prisoner by the court in Aceh and returned to Goa only upon Iskandar Thani's death a few years after the ill-fated diplomatic offensive.[62] Despite this setback, Viceroy Pedro de Silva arguably scored success.

In October 1638, just one month after the ill-fated diplomatic mission, the Acehnese dispatched their own embassy, comprising 200 men, to Dutch Batavia. The Acehnese envoys recounted that the Portuguese sought to forge a deal with Iskandar Thani by offering him nominal sovereignty over Melaka in return for Aceh declaring war on the VOC. This enticing offer was accompanied by the sale of jewels to the Acehnese monarch at what is disclosed as a "friendship price".[63] Perhaps the Portuguese offer of nominal sovereignty over Melaka amounted to little more than rumour, and it is possible that the Acehnese envoys were toying with the worst fears of their Dutch hosts.[64] Or they might have been fishing for rival offers from Batavia. Whatever the case may have been, it is reported with evident relief by VOC sources that Iskandar Thani turned down the *Estado da Índia*'s offer.[65]

Were the responses or counter-strategies of the Portuguese new or innovative, and in what ways? Was there something unique or unusual about them? Or were they just knee-jerk, street-smart reactions to a growing crisis situation in and around the Straits? To facilitate the reconstruction of decisions and events, it is advisable to start with the Dutch side, not least because it was to their acts of aggression that the Portuguese of Melaka and farther afield ultimately responded. The present chapter sketches a broad reconstruction and is not strictly shackled by chronology.

Dutch Strategies, c. 1633–41

VOC officers identified key ports and choke points in the Portuguese networks of trade. The company launched a concerted series of blockades aiming at controlling these nodal points. A VOC document found in the Nationaal Archief van Nederland in The Hague provides a snapshot of how the Dutch company carefully distributed its limited naval forces across the waters of the South China Sea and the Straits. The targets of Dutch maritime hegemony were not just the colonial port strongholds of the Portuguese and the Spanish in East and Southeast Asia, but also select emporia that remained under the control of local rulers, such as Makassar. The latter openly traded with both Iberian powers, and indeed other northern European competitors of the VOC, such as the Danes and the English.

Judging from specific documents such as ms. VOC 1108,[66] it also transpires that the Dutch dispatched only a handful of small- to medium-sized vessels to impose a stranglehold on the Singapore and Melaka Straits. Given the state of technology of the day, it was difficult, if not impossible, to exercise a tight control over the commercially important waters of the Straits with so few ships and such sparse manpower. For this reason, the Dutch positioned their ships and men at specific nodal points of maritime traffic, and at the same time sought to co-opt the local population in amassing information on the movements of the Portuguese around the Indonesian Archipelago and the Malay Peninsula at large. In the Straits of Singapore, there were three such points of special interest: the most easterly was the entrance at the Singapore Straits around Pedra Branca;[67] the second was at the mouth of the Johor River, opposite the northern entrance to the Riau Strait known as the Hook of Berbukit (October through May);[68] and the third was on the north-northeastern coast of the Karimuns.[69]

Pedra Branca is situated at the eastern entrance of the Singapore Straits, and from the waters around this navigational landmark it was possible to monitor maritime traffic in and out of the Singapore Straits, as well as ships skirting the eastern coast of Bintan en route to Java, Makassar, the Malukus and Timor. The Hook of Berbukit is situated at the mouth of the Johor River. From here it was possible to monitor ships entering the river or passing through the Singapore and Tebrau Straits.[70]

The Hook of Berbukit is also situated opposite the northern entrance of the Riau Strait. The latter connects the principal port on Bintan with other islands of the Riau Archipelago and eastern Sumatra. From the northern coast of the Karimuns, it was possible to monitor all traffic passing through the Melaka Straits into the Sabam[71] and Durian Straits, as well as ships heading for one of the four routes near or around Singapore. In fact, by 1614–5 the Dutch had already recognised the northeastern shore of Karimun Besar as being the single most important nodal point in the region, as can be evidence from the proposal of van der Dussen to construct a fort there (see Chapter 3).[72] During the entire period under review, the VOC used the island's sandy eastern shoreline as a camp, a depot for supplies from Batavia, and also as a place to beach, careen and repair their weather-beaten vessels.[73] Apart from food supplies, vessels were in constant need of pitch and new anchors, the latter not least because of the very strong currents in the Straits and especially around the Karimuns. During the change of tides, the waters around the islands resemble a flowing river.

To the north, in the Strait of Melaka, the Dutch assumed positions in two key locations: outside the port and colony of Melaka, on a small island commonly referred to in Portuguese and Dutch documents as Ilha das Naus; as well as in the waters off Cape Rachado. The Ilha das Naus was reportedly out of the range of cannon fire from the fortress 'A Famosa and had been used by, amongst others, Admiral Cornelis Matelieff de Jonge during his seaborne attack on Melaka in 1606.[74] Based on the sources consulted, it remains insufficiently clear how long the Dutch were able to hold their artillery position on the Ilha das Naus during the blockade of the 1630s.

Cape Rachado represented the most northerly strategic point for the VOC blockades and offered a view across the Melaka Strait. This position enabled the Dutch blockaders to monitor, control and intercept maritime traffic from north Sumatra and ports around the Bay of Bengal during the southwest monsoon between June/July and September each year.[75]

As there were only a handful of cutters with a few hundred men to control this yawning pelagic space littered with shoals and islets, intelligence on expected supplies of goods, food and weapons earmarked for Melaka proved vital for the success of the blockade operations. It was always beneficial to keep one's ear to the ground to ascertain the mood inside the stronghold of Melaka. According to sources consulted, there were three methods used for obtaining information about the Portuguese and their activities at large. One was to intercept ships carrying correspondence to and from the Lusitanian port and colony. Correspondence and instructions taken from the captured ships by the Dutch from other parts of the far-flung *Estado da Índia*, especially Portuguese India's capital of Goa, gave the blockaders a tremendous advantage. A second tactic involved the cross-examination of mariners whose vessels were stopped and boarded around the aforementioned strategic nodal points in the Singapore and Melaka Straits. One should not forget here the prisoners and defectors, whose testimonies should always be read with a sound dose of caution.

The third, and probably the most important, source of intelligence consisted of the testimonies solicited from Asians whose sovereigns were bound to the VOC by alliance or formal treaty. Information could be sourced across a wide spectrum of society and using a broad range of pretexts. For example, Commander Cooper visited Johor's upstream town, Batu Sawar, under the pretext of purchasing provisions for the Dutch naval squadrons stationed in the Straits, but the visit also offered a tremendous opportunity to exchange information and gossip on the state of affairs in Melaka.[76] VOC vessels in the Straits also garnered useful information on the general mood in Melaka by entertaining flying vendors in sampans who routinely pulled up to the side of the Dutch vessels offering fresh fruit, vegetables, eggs and live chickens for sale. These vendors knowingly or unknowingly played an important role in feeding the blockaders with information on the movements around the port of Melaka and the region around the Straits at large. Sometimes they even entertained VOC crews with tales of Portuguese merchants who had successfully evaded the Dutch blockade. Needless to say, many of the stories were almost certainly exaggerated or embellished with dubious details as they were passed on from mouth to mouth, so reason and caution are advised when reading the Dutch reports.

Today, naval blockades are understood to be a matter for naval forces, but this was clearly not the case in the early modern period, especially when blockades were imposed by an integrated trading company such as the VOC. Sources reveal that the Dutch blockades of the 1630s were also taken as an opportunity to strike up deals. An incident taken from the *Dagh-Register Batavia* of 1634 serves as a classic example.[77] The *Texel*, belonging to the fleet of Commander Cooper, was dispatched to Arakan (present-day Mrauk-U, Myanmar) carrying two ambassadors and an unspecified consignment of cargo. Instructions issued to the *Texel* were to strike business deals for the Dutch company in Arakan and procure rice, benzoin, red lacquer (*gummalacca*),[78] as well as 300 slaves of both sexes aged between 10 and 25. The VOC first opened trade with the peoples of present-day Myanmar in May 1634, and by July the following year the king of Arakan requested the Dutch for "assistance in his struggle against the Burmese" of Ava.[79]

Last but certainly not least, the Dutch engaged in what could be generously dubbed "public relations exercises", especially with the Iberian enemy. Judging from the interviews conducted with Portuguese officers, traders and defectors, the Dutch became aware that rumours in Melaka and around the region had painted them as faithless scoundrels, rebels and ruthless slave traders. Merchants widely believed that the Dutch would not only seize ship and cargo, but that they would enslave the crew and dispose of their human cargo on the local slave markets. This accusation, while technically false, was not entirely unbelievable, for Commander Cooper, frustrated with the common Portuguese practice of immolating ship and cargo, issued instructions to drown those who sabotaged their own vessels and shower generosity on those who surrendered.[80] In order to rehabilitate themselves and also boost their credentials in the eyes of their Lusitanian foe, and with an eye on mollifying the Portuguese into forfeiting their ship and cargo rather than setting them ablaze, the Dutch engaged in a sporadic number of cash-for-prisoner exchanges meant to counterbalance negative impressions and rumours.[81] The sums involved in these cash-for-prisoner exchanges were by no means paltry, and residents of Melaka were known to send out sampans laden with fresh fruit and other provisions as a token of genuine gratitude for the release of Portuguese prisoners.

Portuguese Responses and Counter-Strategies, c. 1633–40

One has now entered into the subject of Lusitanian responses to the Dutch blockade. From the vantage point of the Portuguese, it was imperative not only to mollify the Dutch aggressors as far as possible, but also to forestall locals from being drawn into the circle of the VOC and ultimately being co-opted by it. Secondary studies by English and Dutch authors frequently dwell on heavy-handed blunders of the *Estado da Índia*'s leading officers and rarely delve into the deft manoeuvres that are also evidenced from period materials. Diplomacy in the early modern Malay world was beset with scandal, bribery, sex and intrigue, which certainly add spice and infuse a good dose of entertainment value into the narrative. As for co-opting locals for their own political, strategic or commercial ends, the Portuguese proved very capable. From time to time, VOC servants begrudgingly conceded to their superiors in Batavia or Europe that they had been outsmarted, outwitted and outmanoeuvred by their Lusitanian counterparts.

No amount of intelligence could place a handful of craft and a few hundred men in a position to establish and maintain a tight stranglehold on maritime activity in the Straits of Singapore and Melaka. The fact remains that VOC blockades only scored uneven successes against the imagination and ingenuity of the Portuguese traders. On the Dutch side, one learns of efforts to evade the VOC blockade mainly from recorded cross-examinations of persons who had failed and been captured. The picture, therefore, is not a complete one, and the evasive strategies revealed by period documentation are neither complete nor genuinely representative. When the numerous accounts are put together, however, four basic strategies are uncovered.

The first was to divert cargo beyond the maritime stranglehold of the Dutch, such as along overland and riverine trading networks. One move was to station an agent on the island of Tioman,[82] which is located off the southeastern coast of the Malay Peninsula. For centuries before the arrival of the European traders and colonists, this island served as a provisioning and watering station for passing ships. The said agent was charged with duly informing captains of the presence or activities of Dutch naval squadrons in the Straits. Ships were subsequently diverted along other maritime routes (if that was possible) or (as was usually the case) urged to call at friendly ports such as Pahang.[83] This port served intermittently as a rendezvous where Portuguese-flagged ships from different parts of East Asia and the Indonesian Archipelago could assemble and then sail in convoy to Melaka.[84] Sometimes the Portuguese-owned cargo was unloaded and transferred to smaller vessels. This had several advantages: spreading the cargo over different vessels substantially reduced the risk of loss to the enemy — or, more rarely, to the forces of nature. The cargo was then brought along the Pahang River, via its tributaries, the Bera and Serting, across the *penarikan* and then downstream to Muar. Sometimes other inland trading routes were taken; these are mentioned only in passing.

Another attested strategy for evading enemy squadrons was to sail and row smaller vessels very close to the shoreline during the darkness of night, preferably at high tide. Hugging the shoreline during the wee hours in the moonlight sometimes also worked for larger vessels, as at least one account can attest.[85] As a rule, small vessels are difficult to detect

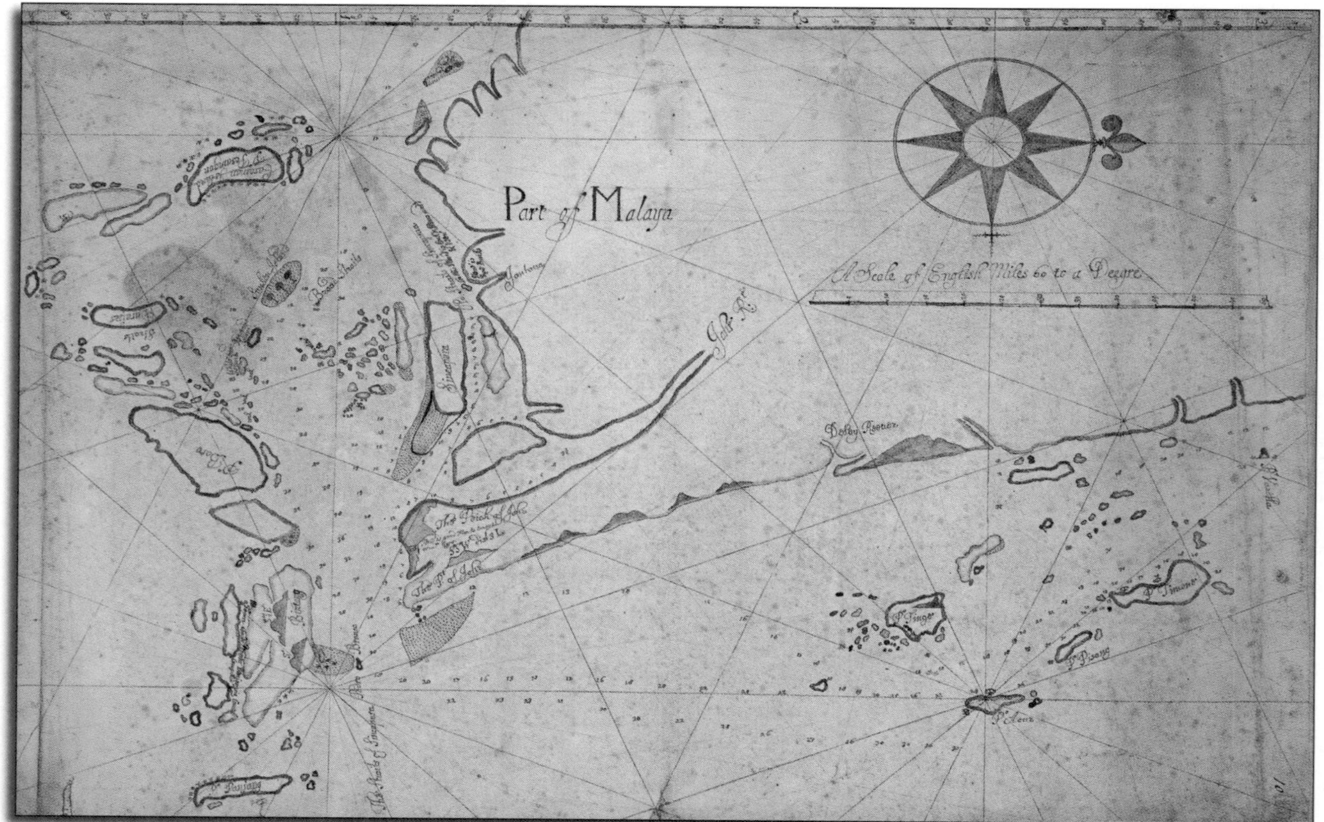

Hand drawn and coloured chart of the southern portion of the Malay Peninsula, the Singapore Straits, and part of the Riau Archipelago by Thomas Bowrey, 1690. (© The British Library Board, Add. Ms. 5222-10)

at night, and even when they were spotted, the shallow waters in close proximity to the shore were not accessible to sailing craft armed with cannons such as the ones used by the VOC during the blockade. Even if they were spotted, the smaller, low-lying Malay craft, such as sampans, were often beyond artillery and gunfire range or were at least difficult to hit by artillery fire because of distance or poor visibility. By the time the Dutch had launched a sloop to further reconnoitre the situation, the sampans could hide in narrow estuaries and coastal mangroves or simply get a good head start by rowing.

When Portuguese vessels entered the Singapore Straits but could not proceed without danger of attack and seizure by the Dutch, they sometimes called at Bulan and, as mentioned in the case of Pahang, redistributed their cargo among several smaller craft.[86]

The second major strategy adopted by the Portuguese was to open up new sailing routes through and around the sprawling Riau Archipelago. A report from Dutch Governor-General Hendrik Brouwer to his superiors in Europe, dated 15 August 1633, discloses the presence of two cutters, the *Dieman* and the *Daman*, patrolling the waters around the island of Lingga "since July".[87] One Portuguese vessel was spotted in the same area the following year.[88] Its captain abandoned ship and sought to flee to Melaka in a dinghy. The Dutch intercepted him as he was about to enter the harbour, and he was taken prisoner.[89]

The presence of patrols around Lingga since the middle of 1633 was most certainly no coincidence. Pedro Bertollo, a name that surfaces in several letters by the contemporaneous Portuguese viceroy, the Conde de Linhares, is seen to have "discovered" — or at least opened up for more regular maritime traffic — a new passage that ran to the south of Bintan and Galang and west to the Karimun islands.[90] This previously uncharted route ran straight through the heart of the Riau Archipelago and found its historically earliest and most important cartographic entry on two surviving maps penned by André Pereira dos Reis. One is currently in the Casa da Bragança at Vila Viçosa,[91] while the other forms part of the Dr. W.A. Engelbrecht Collection at the Maritiem Museum Prins Hendrik in Rotterdam.[92] The two hand-drawn charts are very similar but, crucially, not identical. Only the Rotterdam specimen credits the "discovery" of the new maritime route across the Riau Archipelago to Pedro Bertollo in 1633. That year also marked the beginning of the maritime blockade of the Straits by the VOC. The new maritime passage, named the *Derrota de Conceição de Nossa Senhora* (Route of the Conception of Our

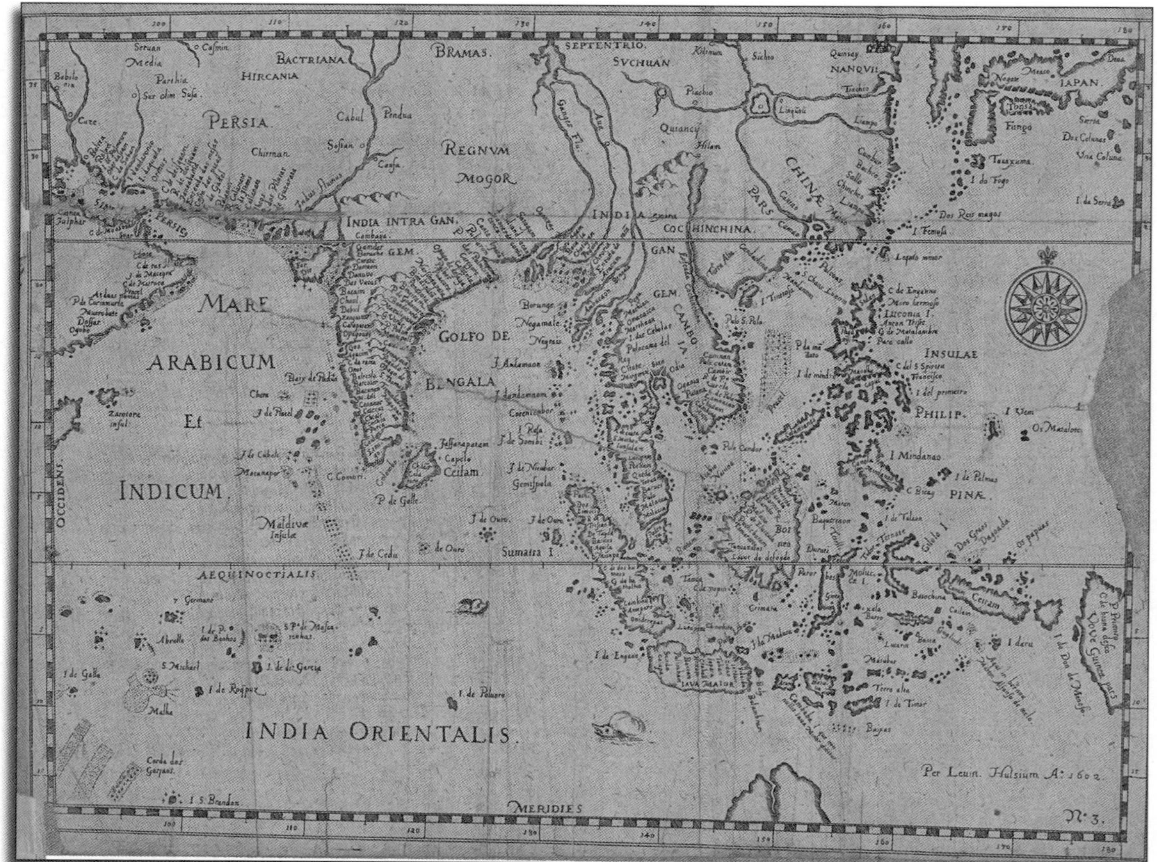

Printed map of Asia from Isaac Genius and Levinus Hulsius, *Neundte Schiffart* (Ninth Voyage to the East Indies), 1612. (Koninklijke Bibliotheek, The Hague, 2112 C 4)

Lady), was not used for long before local fishermen from Bintan tipped off the Dutch. Indeed, members of the same family lent assistance to different parties: the father acted as a pilot for the Portuguese, while the son alerted the Dutch squadrons. The following testimony, dating from the beginning of the maritime blockade, evidences the use of this new maritime route.[93]

> "Item, our [people] have learnt from a Malay of [the island] of Bintan that four Portuguese navettes arriving from Macao took their passage through the islands and shoals of Bintan for fear of encountering our cruising cutters. Our people, being advised of this, pursued these craft with the entire fleet through the aforementioned islands and shoals. They used as their guide the aforementioned Malay, who not only possessed good knowledge of said islands and shoals, but also because he had an arrangement with his father (whom the Portuguese had hired as their guide) to keep the Portuguese navettes cruising among the islands and the shoals until our ships arrive. Then our [men] chased after the said Portuguese navettes and cut off the route (which they would have to ply). When the Portuguese discovered that [our ships] were closing in on them, and realising that they were too weak to withstand our might, they laid fire to their navettes which were loaded with all sorts of flammable materials and fireworks, without being able to salvage anything in particular, except for the ready gold. The ships burned so furiously that neither our men nor the natives of the aforementioned islands (who in large numbers plundered the said vessels and obtained great booty) were able to extinguish the flames."

Another maritime passage situated to the south of the Singapore Straits ran between the present-day islands of Batam, Rempang and Bulan. This is also marked as a viable passage on the two aforementioned Portuguese naval charts.

In addition to prompting them to explore the islands of the Riau Archipelago, the blockade of the Singapore and Melaka Straits led the Portuguese to ply the waters off the eastern coast of Sumatra. One report testifies to the bewilderment of a Dutch crew on learning that a Portuguese ship had managed to evade their attention. How was it possible for a sizeable Portuguese vessel to pass undetected? The Portuguese followed a group of Malay or Javanese traders who had evaded the Dutch blockade by sailing between the islands off the eastern coast of Sumatra.[94] According to a report from Governor-General Brouwer to the Heren XVII dated 27 December 1634, this "nice channel", measuring "at least three *vadem* [fathoms] deep", found its entry at the estuary of the Kampar River and exited just "across from Melaka". This passage, referred to as the Strait of Bengkalis — and subsequently in Dutch sources as the Brouwer Strait — was frequented by several Javanese and Malay vessels that, evidently for quite some time, plied the waters of the channel in the dark of night and thus evaded the Dutch blockade undetected. The governor-general informed his superiors that measures had been taken to plug this back-door channel, and it became part of the regular "beat" of the VOC patrols for years to come.[95]

The third strategy adopted by the Portuguese to evade VOC blockades was to use proxies for trade and transportation. As for European parties, the Portuguese made use of the Danes, and on at least one occasion they chartered an English vessel to transport supplies from Portuguese India to Macao. The use of the Danish flag to safely transport Portuguese goods through waters controlled — or at least patrolled — by the Dutch appears to have survived well into the period after the blockade, as Charles Boxer's synopsis of the Goa archives wonderfully testifies.[96] The Dutch were painfully aware of such European proxies, and even if they did not intercept and impound craft and cargo, they did closely monitor the movements of these proxies very closely. Officers in Batavia and on the ground feared — with some justification, no doubt — that strong action taken in the East Indies against European-flagged vessels other than the Iberian enemy would almost inevitably have serious diplomatic and economic repercussions back in Europe. Fears were expressed that, if the VOC harass Danish shipping in the Melaka Strait and other Asian waters, Denmark might retaliate by closing off the Danish Sound to Dutch shipping. Skippers from the Low Countries were the biggest players in the long-distance seaborne trade in the Baltic. Understandably, no officer wanted to precipitate a serious crisis in Europe, so the VOC patrols turned a blind but wary eye on Portugal's northern European proxies.

Proxies may also have been used to conduct trade at ports that were either hostile to Portugal, or at least not tied to the stringent conditions of a Dutch commercial contract. Sometimes Dutch allies were courted as well. The VOC had to repeatedly remind treaty parties, such as Johor, that they were to abide by their agreements and sever all commercial relations with the Portuguese. This was not unique to the blockade of the 1630s; the Dutch had given the Johoreans similar reminders earlier, between 1610 and 1623. It was an open secret in the Malay world how Luso-Johor commercial ties painted a completely different picture from the on-again, off-again diplomatic and military relations. In order to satisfy

Dutch demands for tighter cooperation under the alliance agreement struck in 1606, the *laksamana* of Johor had some Portuguese trading vessels impounded and surrendered them to the VOC as prizes of war. Even then, after rounding up the proverbial "usual suspects" firmly engaged in Luso-Johor trade, commercial relations quickly "normalised" and returned within a short period to the more familiar patterns of trade, exchange and interaction.

The fourth strategy adopted by the Portuguese — if this can be deemed a strategy proper — was to enter Malay ports that were not under contract with the Dutch, chiefly on the pretext of making a distress call. It then just so happened that in order to pay for the supposed repairs, the captain had to sell off some of his cargo. Some instances may have been genuine, but when the Dutch learned of one such incident, they concluded that this was just another cunning ploy of Melaka merchants to dispose of their cotton pieces and clothing under false pretexts. But sometimes a pretext was not even necessary. The *Generale Missiven* for 1638 have the Portuguese selling cloth and textiles in Perak and highlight that the sales went down very well with the local population.[97]

The Eclipse of Portuguese Melaka, c. 1633–41

This was the wider state of affairs in and around the Straits of Melaka and Singapore. The actual Portuguese entrepôt and colony of Melaka, meanwhile, was subjected to oscillating fortunes. According to a report from Governor-General Antonio van Diemen to his superiors in Europe dated 28 December 1636, a blockade had been continuously in force for just over three years. He observed for the benefit of his superiors in the Netherlands: "As a result of our constant cruising outside and around Melaka since the year 1633, this city had become very depressed and fallen into a dire famine."[98] Maintaining a stranglehold on Melaka emerged as a costly undertaking. With ever a vigilant eye cast on the company's bottom line, Governor-General van Diemen lamented that despite the presence of eight cruisers and 412 men to enforce the blockade, few prizes of war were taken. In other words, hopes that the blockade of Melaka might become self-financing — or even turn in a profit — through the seizure of Portuguese-flagged vessels were dashed.

The cost of the blockade in terms of ships, manpower and funds had to be justified financially by the taking of prizes. This was not just a war involving the force of arms, but a war of nerves, patience, survival and timely supplies. In December 1637, van Diemen dryly acknowledged the munificence of some vessels rushed from Goa to relieve Melaka and underscored the serious damage inflicted on Portuguese shipping in the Melaka Strait. The following year, 1638, saw no naval assistance whatsoever arrive from Portuguese India.[99] Rumours and gossip swirled in Batavia that the "constant cruising in the waters of Melaka" had critically reduced the level of trading activity and that serious tension had emerged between the city officials and the *casados*. Even the city officials had got in each others' hair, as the famed chronicler Faria y Sousa observed with evident alarm: "At Melaka the Feuds were so great between the Commander of the Town and the Admiral of the Coast, that the latter shot an Uncle of the other."[100] Such confusion, rivalry and tension, as Governor-General van Diemen patiently lectured to his superiors in Holland, offered the opportune moment to "attack our enemies and make us masters of the city".[101]

The final push on the besieged Portuguese enclave followed in June 1640, with military operations stepped up after September that year when Commander Cooper was redeployed to the Melaka Strait.[102] According to the 17th-century VOC historian Pieter van Dam, Cooper and other officers played a meaningful role during the Dutch ground assault on Melaka. Van Dam also reports that many Dutch troops and officers succumbed to the plague,[103] which was hopping from bed to bed in the Dutch military camp as well as within the walls of the Portuguese stronghold.[104] Cooper himself eventually succumbed to the black death and passed away just days before Melaka surrendered on 3 January 1641.[105] The final stand drew closer when Melaka's officials expelled all women and children from the city, a move that doubtless accelerated the contamination of libidinous Dutch troops with the plague. Melaka surrendered on 14 January 1641, after what Valentijn reports was a tough stand by the last few hundred men.[106]

Looking back to the years immediately preceding the fall of Melaka to the Dutch, the following questions merit further exploration: What did the *casados* and city officials do in order to circumvent the Dutch blockade and its objective to starve the colonial port city of financial revenue and food supplies? Period reports are beset with contradictions as to the actual state of Melaka during the blockade. Attention shall first be cast on the food supply situation.

Melaka was highly dependent on food imports, not just during the Portuguese colonial period of 1511–1641 but, according to several testimonies — including the oft-cited *Suma Oriental* of Tomé Pires — well before European colonial rule. Staples such as rice were key imports into the city. In the late 1630s, prices of this staple food rose persistently to 70, 80 and then 120 ryals-of-eight per *last*.[107] That rose to 10 rijksdaalder for one *gantang* of dry rice towards the end of the siege, in December 1640.[108] To the ordinary ship boy serving in the VOC, for example, this sum was equivalent to at least six months' salary.

Judging by the price and its wild fluctuation across the period of the maritime blockade, supplies were naturally very tight but not entirely severed. The *Dagh-Register Batavia* entry of 22 October 1640 reports that nine vessels had successfully slunk out of Melaka harbour under the cover of night. The crew had been charged with the task of procuring sago and rice and transporting these overland into the city.[109] With reference to maritime trade, it is evident that supplies of rice and other foodstuffs continued to arrive, even if some of the ships were intercepted or captured by the Dutch.[110] The *Dagh-Register Batavia* reports for 10 December 1634 that 12 prahus from Mataram bearing a cargo of rice and destined for Melaka were intercepted by the Dutch in the Strait of Sabam.[111] Supplies of flour and wine arriving from Goa and Cochin were intercepted off Cape Rachado; both these locations were among the nodal points of control used by the Dutch.[112] More supplies were rumoured to have arrived that very year.[113] In 1634, sloops belonging to the cutter *Nassau* caught up with some smaller vessels carrying provisions of rice to Melaka that were sailing very close to the shore in order to avoid detection.[114]

A report by Governor-General Antonio van Diemen dated 18 December 1639 reveals how the Dutch solicited Aceh's assistance in interrupting Melaka's food supplies. At the request of the VOC, Aceh dispatched 4 rowed galleys and 16 banteens for this very purpose. They never arrived at Melaka, for the Acehnese vessels were quickly redeployed to relieve Pahang from a joint attack by Johor and Patani.[115] It is also reported that the Portuguese participated in this attack on Pahang, or at least lent their support to it.[116]

Melaka did not rely on seaborne trade alone, and this was particularly true with regard to food supplies. Several documents dating from the year 1639 speak of consignments of food brought in overland from Johor, supplies, one is informed, upon which Portuguese Melaka had become more dependent than ever.[117] Despite all the rhetoric to the contrary, especially in Dutch sources, Johor's relationship with Melaka in the late 1630s was probably far better than appears at first glance, and the on-again, off-again relations between the two parties were certainly nothing new.[118] In fact, all powers around the Singapore and Melaka Straits were playing hard political games. While the VOC was actively soliciting the military assistance of Aceh in its war effort against the Portuguese,[119] Johor was drawn closer into the orbit of Lusitanian interests. Shortly before the final assault on Melaka in 1640, this constellation of forces appears to have entered a radical reversal when the VOC began to tighten its relations with Johor.[120]

On 18 December 1639, Governor-General van Diemen openly conceded to his superiors in Amsterdam that any seaborne assault on, and conquest of, Melaka could no longer be cleanly separated from the entrenched rivalry between Aceh and Johor. In order to move forward, it was important to identify and stake out clear priorities: First "Melaka has to be won, and [then] the Acehnese brought into a balance of power with Johor."[121] And indeed, thus it came to pass. Valentijn and Netscher both underscore that the Aceh monarch failed to dispatch any military assistance to the Dutch, but in his stead, the Johor monarch dispatched "40 vessels" in late July and early August 1640.[122] Barbara Andaya deemed the effectiveness of the Johorean troops in the final assault on Melaka absolutely "vital" and, in casting her verdict, took serious issue with Netscher's earlier position that the Johoreans proved utterly useless in the onslaught on Melaka in late 1640.[123]

During the period of the blockade, Portuguese Melaka's trading relations with the outside world broadly mirror the problems and dynamics of food supplies. Again, there are conflicting testimonies as to the state of trade and commerce in the Lusitanian entrepôt. Dutch reports, based on rumours together with the testimonies of defectors and prisoners, paint a picture of a Melaka that had ground to a complete standstill, a pathetic ghost of its far more glorious past. As one testimony of 1639 had it, "It is certain that Melaka, Macao and other fortresses on Ceylon will not be able to withstand much longer."[124] The absence of larger carracks plying the waters of the Singapore and Melaka Straits was further taken as a clear signal that the emporium was in serious distress. In a self-congratulatory tone, Governor-General van Diemen informed his superiors in December 1639 that as a result of "constant cruising of our cutters in Melaka's navigable waters the city has been almost reduced to the outer extremities" and merchants generally avoid the port.[125] Portuguese (and probably also Spanish) merchants inbound from Macao or Manila, the governor-general further highlighted, often altered their familiar course and invested great pains in discovering, or opening up, alternative maritime routes to the Indian subcontinent and ports farther beyond in the western Indian Ocean. Such alternative routes were often a substantial diversion from the original path, including the Straits of Sunda and Bali, and as far south as Solor and Timor.[126]

In another report, filed in August 1633, VOC servants informed of "Makassarese and Javanese junks in Melaka". In December of the same year they informed also of heightened maritime traffic of the Makassarese to the ports of Melaka, Macao and Manila. Such reports fanned fears in Batavia that commercial activity in enemy ports could only serve to fill Spanish and Portuguese coffers.[127] Still, ships continued to call at Melaka, as even van Diemen was forced to concede in late 1639. Several smaller craft described as foists had arrived from Goa, Nagapatnam and Java, and one vessel completely evaded the attention of the Dutch blockaders before setting sail for Macao.[128]

Spreading the cargo over several smaller vessels reduced the risk of seizure and therefore of loss and forfeiture to the enemy. Whilst it is true that large carracks and galleons were not sighted or seized by the Dutch, Portuguese Melaka's business continued. In fact, James Boyajian appraised the annual average value of trade in Melaka throughout the period of the blockades under review at 500,000 cruzados, mainly from its trade with ports around the Bay of Bengal. That sum is far greater than the paltry 150,000–170,000 guilders reported by the VOC for much of the 1640s and 1650s![129]

Afterthoughts

Secondary literature has placed considerable emphasis on the *military* aspects of the victory and less emphasis on the diplomatic, social and economic effects of the blockade. In her book *Jan Compagnie in the Straits of Malacca*, Dianne Lewis writes: "On 14 January 1641, the forces of the United Netherlands East Indies Company victoriously entered the Portuguese fortress of Melaka."[130] Like Barbara Andaya, Lewis shows surprisingly little interest in why Melaka surrendered, but both hasten to underscore that hopes of inheriting the "enemy's commerce" proved illusory and efforts in justifying the high cost of the blockade and military campaign to the Heren XVII proved problematic, if not utterly futile.[131]

From the documentary sources reviewed, including especially the report of special commissioner Joost van Schouten, it is clear that the Lusitanian stronghold — that erstwhile "Queen of the East" — was defeated by the inability of Goa to rush men and supplies[132] as well as by war, famine and the plague. The long blockade, while very costly, reduced but did not entirely quash commercial activity. Food supplies, while always a problem throughout the period of the blockades, began to run seriously short only at the time of the final onslaught. The ensuing famine, together with the plague epidemic of late 1640 and January 1641, pushed the city authorities to expel women and children outside the city gates. Decimated numbers, disease and starvation — and, probably to a lesser extent, the force of Dutch arms — led Melaka towards surrender.

The costs associated with the Melaka blockades of 1633–41 may have been high, and plunder taken from Portuguese traders may have been disappointingly low. But one of the now long-forgotten legacies of the blockade is that the region around the Straits of Singapore and Melaka became one of the best-explored and best-mapped pelagic spaces in Southeast Asia.

Conclusion

The Singapore and Melaka Straits were historically, and still remain, a nexus of security and commerce. This is not retroactively reading present-day priorities and concerns into the more distant past. This book has shown, for the period under review (c. 1600–40), that the Straits were a focal point of competition not only among regional players such as Johor and Aceh, but also among the early European colonial powers.

It is appropriate, in the present context, to tease out some conclusions about a few "big themes" that derive from the history of early modern European expansion. These include the strategic location of Singapore island and the adjacent Straits, the sovereignty of the Asian princes and the dynamics of cooperation between Asian princes and the early European colonial powers.

Strategic Location

What factors significantly shaped and determined a strategic location in the maritime context of the early modern period? The first ingredient was the presence of seaborne trade. In the maritime context, there can be sparse value to a strait or a promontory where little or no commercial interaction takes place.

In the age of sail, oceanic currents, weather patterns and wind conditions greatly shaped the patterns of seaborne trade. Familiarity with and knowledge of these conditions were prerequisites to mastering the maritime sea lanes, which in many instances did not — and could not — follow the shortest, most direct route.

The region between the Malay Peninsula and Sumatra marks a point where the two Asian monsoons overlap. Singapore, Melaka and the Straits are situated in this region, and over the centuries they have supported the rise of several historically important trading emporia along their shores. In the age of sail, Asian traders did not favour long-distance intra-Asian commerce, as waiting for the monsoon winds to shift extended the turnaround time of ships, crew and cargo. This consequently cut into potential profits. Thus, long before the arrival of the early European colonial powers, the ports and emporia located around the Singapore and Melaka Straits had firmly established themselves as meeting grounds and forums of commercial exchange. Produce from ports around the Bay of Bengal, Persia, Arabia and East Africa was exchanged for goods from around the Indonesian Archipelago, the Malay Peninsula, Siam, Cochinchina, Champa, China, Korea and Japan.

The strategic significance of Singapore and the adjacent Straits was thus determined by the convergence of numerous trading networks that were, in turn, conditioned by the two monsoonal weather systems, by geography and, of course, by the desire of traders to maximise their profits. Sumatra and also, to a lesser extent, Java, staked out both the land-based meeting grounds as well as the physical barriers to maritime trade that straddled the ports of the Indian Ocean rim and the South China Sea.

The advantage of location, however, only partially helps to reconstruct the parameters underpinning the "strategic location" of Singapore, Melaka and the region around the Straits at large. The second — and arguably far more important — facet is political stability. For a region or emporium to succeed, it is not sufficient for it to be situated at the convergence of important regional trading networks. Location is only one aspect within the bigger scheme of things, and in order to both attract and maintain trade it is imperative to optimise conditions of trade with regime stability as well as commensurate fees and imposts. The history of the ports and polities around the Straits of Singapore and Melaka is replete with stories of success and failure. This book has focused on a relatively narrow period within this wider history, namely, the first four decades of the 17th century. The evidence presented, however, demonstrates how regime change, the arrival of new "players" in the region, the shift in the balance of power and successive changes in policy greatly impacted the fortunes of a given port or polity. The arrival of the VOC as a commercial and political force in the region, the rise of Aceh as an imperial power and the resulting fates of important settlements and trading centres such as Johor Lama, Batu Sawar and Portuguese Melaka merit specific mention in this context. The jockeying for political supremacy by Johor and Aceh; the legacy of their respective relations with Siam, Patani and Pahang; as well as Portuguese and Dutch commercial, military and diplomatic activity converged into a destabilising mix that would influence regional historic developments for decades, if not for centuries. As is known, traders dislike instability, sudden or unpredictable change and, of course, threats to the security of their cargo. Perhaps nowhere are such concerns more pronounced than in Dutch and Portuguese documentation dating from the first half of the 17th century.

Strategic location at the crossroads of trading networks could prove to be a double-edged sword. Tipped off by their new-found Johorean allies, the Dutch came to learn about the different nodal spots around Singapore island and the nearby Straits. These nodal spots were initially used as points to attack Portuguese shipping, as is evidenced pre-eminently by the "*Santa Catarina* incident" of February 1603. Historic nodal points of strategic and military significance identified in this book include the "Hook of Berbukit" off Johor Hill, the northwestern tip of present-day Sentosa, the northeastern coast of Karimun Besar and the waters off Cape Rachado.

Awareness and effective use of these maritime nodal points, especially those near Singapore island, enabled the Dutch to impose, with relatively modest naval forces, an effective grip on Portuguese trade through the Straits. This spurred, amongst other developments, the deeper European exploration of the Riau Archipelago and the eastern coast of Sumatra. This, in turn, is reflected in the evolving cartography of the region. More detailed knowledge of the region's topography became important not just for opening up alternative maritime passages across the Riau Archipelago and the Malay Peninsula, but also for purposes of establishing and maintaining control over the Straits.

Knowledge of regional geography and of the Riau Archipelago emerged, for the early European colonial powers, as a means of projecting and consolidating maritime hegemony, commercial prowess and an evolving political agenda for the region. Taking a sweeping perspective, a tight grip on the Singapore and Melaka Straits proved devastating to the

Portuguese trading communities and the *Estado da Índia* at large, the latter comprising chiefly a far-flung string of ports and emporia between Japan and East Africa. The VOC's tight (but by no means full) grip over the Straits severely hampered, but did not completely sever, communication and the flow of vital supplies between the eastern and western ports of the *Estado da Índia*.

Portugal's answer was to combine naval forces with the Spaniards, as is evidenced by the plan to join the *Estado*'s men-of-war with the armada of Juan de Silva in 1615 and 1616. Plans to construct two fortresses on Sentosa and Singapore island, as well as the deployment of escort fleets for westbound Portuguese vessels from China, Japan, Cochinchina and Makassar, were devised to counter a growing number of attacks by Johor, Aceh and, formidably, the Dutch, on their lucrative seaborne trade. Against the backdrop of all these developments, the *Estado da Índia* remained diplomatically alert and sought to mend fences with regional Malay powers as far as this was feasible and possible.

Sovereignty of the Asian Rulers

The second "big theme" that merits further exploration concerns the position of the Asian rulers. The early European colonial powers' explicit acceptance of the sovereignty of Asian rulers marks a sharp contrast to the behaviour of the Spaniards, Portuguese, Dutch, French and English during the early colonisation of the Americas.[1] It can also be juxtaposed to the East Asian tributary system, which assumed a civilised centre and a barbaric periphery of inferior and subordinate polities.

Scholars and politicians of the 16th and 17th centuries who had a hand in formulating early colonial policies, or actually commented on early colonial institutions and mechanisms, acknowledged that the East Indies and the West Indies offered very different contexts and scenarios for trade, war and colonisation.[2] Among the most celebrated individuals is the Dutch humanist and polymath Hugo Grotius, who acted as a lawyer for the VOC and, in 1609, anonymously published the pamphlet *Mare Liberum*, or "The Free Sea".[3] In this treatise, Grotius pleaded before an essentially European audience for unimpeded access of the VOC to the great trading emporia in Asia, against the Portuguese and Spanish policies of exclusion. However, it would be utterly fallacious to conclude, as some authors have done, that Grotius was an advocate of (universal) "free trade" across the high seas.[4]

Hand coloured print showing "Malays" (left) and "Javanese" (right) from J.H. van Linschoten's first edition of the *Itinerario,* 1596. (Koninklijke Bibliotheek, The Hague, 1702 B 4)

Hand coloured print of peasant and affluent "Chinese" from J.H. van Linschoten's first edition of the *Itinerario,* 1596. (Koninklijke Bibliotheek, The Hague, 1702 B 4)

Hand coloured print depicting the fruits and produce of Asia from J.H. van Linschoten's first edition of the *Itinerario,* 1596. (Koninklijke Bibliotheek, The Hague, 1702 B 4)

Hand coloured print of a "junk" featuring sails of reed or bamboo, a wooden anchor, and a drummer, from J.H. van Linschoten's first edition of the *Itinerario,* 1596. (Koninklijke Bibliotheek, The Hague, 1702 B 4)

As has been evidenced by this book, the VOC, as an instrument of trade, war and diplomacy in the East Indies, served as a crucial projector of the Dutch Revolt into the Asian theatre. The projection of the war effort from Europe into the East Indies was governed by two fundamental tenets. During the Union of the Two Crowns that merged Spain and Portugal in the person of the monarch, the two Iberian powers became the principal victims of VOC aggression across Asia and the Indian Ocean rim. The VOC's earliest territorial acquisitions, such as Ambon, were possessions and forts plucked from the Portuguese; and additional Dutch attacks were subsequently also launched on Spanish Manila and Tidor in the Malukus. Of special interest to the reader, as discussed in Chapter 5, are the successive attacks on the Portuguese-held port and settlement of Melaka, which the Dutch first attacked in 1606 but could not take over until January 1641.

The second tenet of early VOC policy was to engage Asian princes diplomatically so as to contain the commercial activities and diplomatic prowess of the Iberian powers. The Spanish and the Portuguese were not the dominant players in Asia in terms of trade and diplomacy, but they were certainly discernible players. Engaging the Iberian enemy in war in the East Indies, coupled with concerted efforts to isolate the Spanish and the Portuguese diplomatically, came at a huge cost to the VOC. Legitimate trade, along with aggressive plundering of enemy trading vessels — as exemplified by the seizures of the *Santa Catarina* and *Santo António* — failed to improve the company's bottom line over time. Also, manpower and naval infrastructure such as warships, naval artillery and military hardware were scarce resources of the Dutch company, as the maritime blockades of the Singapore and Melaka Straits during the 1630s clearly demonstrate. It was thus clear, almost from the time of the first VOC voyages to the East Indies, that in order to access marketplaces and contain the Iberian enemy in Southeast Asia, the company would need to secure allies. From the very beginning of its corporate lifespan, the VOC (rhetorically) upheld the sovereignty of the Asian rulers against Iberian naval hegemony and pretensions of economic exclusion. Most certainly, this "mission" of the VOC was not driven by considerations of economic, let alone political, altruism. Not unlike its clever advocate Grotius, the Dutch company found itself expounding an almost circular argument: In order to underpin its pleadings in Europe for free access to emporia in Asia against Iberian attempts at exclusion, the VOC upheld the sovereignty of Asian rulers on whose survival the Dutch case for unimpeded commercial access ultimately rested.[5]

Having staked out the above conclusions, some important caveats are now in order. First, the idea of sovereignty, as it is used today, is essentially a concept dating from the second half of the 16th century that has been subjected to intense debate and revision over the past four centuries. Before the birth of the modern nation state, sovereignty within the family of nascent nations was clearly variegated. The monarchies of England, France, Denmark, Sweden, Spain and Portugal offered a sobering contrast to the waning of central power in the Holy Roman Empire. Central European nations such as Prussia, Austria, and arguably even the Dutch Republic and the Swiss Confederation, emerged from the erosion of central authority within the Holy Roman Empire. Even in Europe, sovereign polities might have been formally and legally placed on an equal plane; but in reality, much depended on their territorial expanse, population and national wealth.

An analogous picture can be offered for the princes and polities of Southeast Asia. As has been seen in this book, both the Portuguese and the VOC had often — but not always — realistically assessed the constellation of power on the ground. It might have been possible to behave more aggressively towards princes and rajas of lesser polities, but the Portuguese and the Dutch — and indeed, all the other players in early modern colonial expansion — as a rule were very cautious when negotiating with the sovereign lords of expansive and populous polities. If caution did not reign, the consequences for trading opportunities could be very serious. To put it bluntly, it was probably possible to get away with bullying the "small fry", but it was certainly not advisable to mess with the "big boys". Besides — and this is a point the historian Michael N. Pearson also underscores — Asia's expansive land-based empires showed only sparse interest in seaborne trade and thus did not enter into intense competition with the early European colonial powers.[6]

Admittedly, the realities on the ground did not always lend support to this maxim. The Dutch, and to a lesser extent the Portuguese of the early 17th century, showed some difficulties in grasping the wider dynamics of the tributary trading regime. Far from facilitating interaction as sovereigns and equals, the tributary system demanded subordination as "tributaries" and "barbarians", and this in turn affected the diplomacy and trading relations of the early European colonial powers with Southeast Asian princes.[7] Still, the jockeying for regional supremacy and dominance among the Southeast Asian rulers offered opportunities to the European parties to rally behind the weak in the hope of gaining improved trading conditions.

This leads to a second caveat that addresses the impact of European alliance policies on the regional balance of power. The region around the Singapore and Melaka Straits during the 16th and early 17th centuries was characterised by intense rivalry among the polities of Sumatra as well as the Malay Peninsula and the Riau Archipelago. This rivalry existed long before the arrival of the first early modern European colonial powers in the Straits. But one can be left with little doubt that the establishment of European presence in the region after 1511 did affect regional dynamics of interaction and the balance of power. Portugal's diplomacy was determined by a mix of commercial considerations, its positioning as a maritime power in the Straits as well as its desire to spread the Christian faith. As a rule, commerce took precedence over religious zeal, and in practice this meant "blending in" as far as possible. "Blending in" should not be immediately taken as a manifestation of Portuguese backwardness, decadence or even weakness, as some historians have hastily concluded, but as a process of accommodating to local realities. In the words of Steensgard, "In the old and sophisticated world of Asian trade nothing was to be had for free, and not much was left to be created."[8] Many of the practices adopted by early Portuguese Melaka were a continuation of customs, arrangements and institutions inherited from the fallen Melaka Sultanate. These have been staked out by Tomé Pires and other early Portuguese chroniclers. In fact, it is well known that in forging and maintaining diplomatic relations with local rulers, the Portuguese broadly conformed to established Asian customs and protocol.[9] Still, the interests of the merchants, the *Estado da Índia* and the Roman Catholic Church often proved to be a source of considerable friction, which in turn led to (what at least on the surface appear to have been) unpredictable or even erratic policy decisions.

As a trading company dedicated to generating profits and with no formalised religious ambitions,[10] the VOC did not experience tensions along these particular lines of organisation, although, admittedly, the Dutch company inherited its own unique set of problems that chiefly derived from the "imperfect merger" of the six *voorcompagniën*, or "predecessor companies". The early VOC was beset with rivalry from the remains of the predecessor companies (institutionalised as the six chambers) that continued, after 1602, to organise their own voyages on a joint company account. Also, the VOC was to act as the agent of war, peace and trade in Asia for the young Dutch Republic.

The *Estado da Índia*, the VOC and the Malay courts with which they forged alliances, waged war and traded were, of course, all but tightly organised, monolithic agents. The situation on the ground was actually quite messy, and this book has sought to offer a glimpse into the different factions and power brokers on all sides. There were the inevitable deals that were struck, errors in judgement, bewildered groping in the dark, policy reversals and enticing opportunities that suddenly moved into the foreground. For all parties concerned it was all about recognising and seizing the moment, or identifying opportunities when they presented themselves. But the important question one needs to ask here is: Amidst all this jostling for supremacy, did the alliance policies of the Portuguese and the VOC meaningfully alter the balance of power in the region? In allying with the strong or the weak regional powers, did the Europeans alter the lifespan of polities such as Johor or even Aceh?

Johor's ever oscillating relations with the VOC and the Portuguese were indicative not just of intense factional rivalry within the Batu Sawar court, but also of a struggle to position Johor as a key regional power *vis-à-vis* its counterparts Aceh, Pahang, Patani and probably also Siam. The diplomacy, alliance policies and trade supplemented by the Portuguese and the Dutch partially played on these manifest internal divisions at the court, and partially also deepened pre-existing factional divides. Thus, the question that almost inevitably arises is: Did this interference ultimately serve to weaken Johor internally and externally, or did it, by contrast, perhaps even extend the lifespan of this complex Malay polity?

The evidence expounded in this book shows how European policies of alliance making and trade almost certainly did influence internal developments and altered the lifespan of Malay polities, notably Johor. But it is also clear that European agents on the ground did not fully comprehend or even recognise the forces that held together as complex a polity as Johor. Against the backdrop of fresh conflict with Aceh, VOC Governor-General Pieter de Carpentier wrote a letter on 29 January 1624 to his superiors in Amsterdam, the Heren XVII. He reported on the death of Abdullah Hammayat Shah (Raja Bongsu, Raja Seberang) and the disintegration of Johor.[11] With hindsight, one knows that he hastily pronounced the virtual demise of what, in the history of the Malay world, doubtless proved one of the most enduring and resilient polities. It is clear that VOC military and diplomatic support prolonged the lifespan of Johor in the period under review, and arguably beyond. According to Leonard Andaya, "a decisive factor in Johor's resurgence as a power in the area was its long and friendly relations with the Dutch, dating back to 1602".[12]

Aceh, and its political, cultural and economic rival Johor, seemed almost as affected by the tumultuous and hostile relations between the Portuguese and the Dutch as the latter were, seeking to comprehend the dynamics of the Johor-Aceh rivalry. With hindsight, it is clear that once the *Estado da Índia* was eliminated in 1641 as a regional, political and military entity, a dramatic realignment in the balance of power followed. However, judging from the historical developments during the opening three decades of the 17th century — Aceh's dramatic rise to pre-eminence, Johor's defeat at the hands of Iskandar Muda as well as Johor's status as a "client polity" of Aceh after 1613 — Johor's long-term political survival was far from self-evident.

The final question is: Had the European powers not interfered with the polities around the Singapore and Melaka Straits, would another regional Asian power have behaved differently over the longer term? Temporarily extending the timeline to cover the late 17th and early 18th centuries, the answer must be in the negative. By the middle of the 16th century, Portuguese interaction with regional powers had been greatly assimilated to accepted Asian practices; and in any case, by the middle of the 17th century the *Estado da Índia* ceased to be a regional military and political force. As is well known from a number of important studies such as those of Ames, Boxer, de Souza, Subrahmanyam and Winius, the Portuguese, as a discernible community, survived as a player in Asia's seaborne commerce either as independent traders, as members of far-flung Luso-Asian commercial networks or as employees of the various northern European East India companies.

A strikingly different picture presented itself with the VOC. For as long as the Dutch company at home focused on gaining access to Southeast Asian marketplaces against real and perceived Iberian exclusion, the VOC was willing to support and uphold the sovereignty of Southeast Asian princes. It used the argument of sovereignty to create and legally justify a web of exclusive trading contracts that underpinned and ultimately sustained its aspirations to create a trading monopoly in spices and other select products. Once the Portuguese had been eliminated as a political force in the region of the Straits, and once the VOC had begun to expand its territorial presence across the Indonesian Archipelago and the Indian subcontinent, the company's parameters of basic interaction and diplomacy were also transformed. By the close of the 17th century, or perhaps even as late as the mid-18th, the VOC no longer regarded its allies and treaty partners as "equals" within a larger family of sovereign entities but as territorially largely undefined polities. Clearly, the company had regarded them as equals in the early decades of its corporate lifespan, but during the course of the 17th century it treated them increasingly as politically crippled and economically compromised dependents. The latter had become bound to the company in a semi-tributary relationship.[13] Holden Furber has previously discussed these themes in the context of prescription and attrition of sovereign rights, a process, he argued, that did not follow a steady, progressive trajectory but certainly accelerated after 1750.[14] The VOC — like the Portuguese *Estado da Índia* well before it — behaved increasingly like an Asian patron state that engaged its allies and treaty partners as dependents or client polities. The evolution of this semi-tributary relationship marks an important transformation in the company's diplomatic engagement with Asia. Significantly also, this insight marks the great divide, separating the colonial experience in Asia of the early modern period from the age of high imperialism of the 19th and 20th centuries.

For the period 1600–40, covered in this book, it must be remembered that the VOC was still in its diplomatic infancy. As far as the company was even capable of acting as a monolithic entity in trade and war, it should be strictly treated as a European agent within a Southeast Asian cultural and political setting. It played a dual role as a trading company and as a projector of the Dutch war efforts against Spain and Portugal into the East Indies.[15] The one advantage that the VOC seemed to possess was its superiority in offering naval and military might in exchange for the goods and commodities it needed to sustain its trade with Europe and also within Asia.

Tributaries and Partnership

When J.C. van Leur wrote his groundbreaking work on the commerce of the Indonesian Archipelago in the 1930s, he was reacting to a genre of imperial history, pre-eminent in the late 19th and early 20th centuries, that highlighted milestones of the nation, exalted national achievements and proclaimed military hegemony across the globe.[16] Above all, the imperial narratives celebrated European cultural and technological superiority almost to the complete exclusion of their Asian counterparts. One can certainly extrapolate, from early modern documents, snippets of information that support some of the conclusions of high imperial narratives — but the sources also offer a spectrum of ideas, attitudes and opinions that the narratives of high imperialism shrug off, ignore or misinterpret. In fact, many of the documents dating from the late 16th and early 17th centuries express open admiration for and genuine interest in the societies and polities of Southeast Asia and, more often than not, impart a sense of fascination for and also a willingness, on the part of their European authors, to learn from Asia. Such a sense of admiration and willingness to learn are largely absent from later imperial narratives.

Van Leur was not alone in his disdain for the conclusions of the high imperial historical narratives. He provocatively turned these on their heads by denying the predominance of the European colonial agents in terms of political power and commercial prowess. In the post-colonial era, historians have sought to place Southeast Asian history within its own proper context, notably by upgrading Asian sources and sometimes by downplaying or even marginalising European materials from the age of colonial rule. In celebrating the achievements of the American historian Holden Furber, Kling and Pearson compiled an important collection of studies titled "The Age of Partnership", which has, amongst other achievements, served to inspire and critically re-engage the contemporary historian with sources dating from the period of early European expansion into Asia.[17]

This book brings into the picture a wide range of source materials, including cartography. The latter has been interpreted both as expressions of European knowledge about regional topography, as well as projections of an expanding commercial prowess or an evolving political agenda. For sure, the Portuguese and the Dutch, as well as the English, Danes and the French, were greatly concerned about each other as trade competitors, both in Europe as well as within Asia. For the period under review, Southeast Asian polities were generally treated not as primitive, ephemeral or naturally inferior, but as important partners and allies in the broader scheme of arrangements. It almost seems common sense to emphasise that the different actors around the Singapore and Melaka Straits were anything but monolithic; rather, they were characterised by deep internal divisions that could not, and were not, easily overcome. By consulting a wide array of known and previously unknown source materials, the present book adds meaningfully to what has been researched and discussed on the evolving relationships between Asian and European actors in the early 17th century and in tracing continuities and discontinuities of policy. It is clear that the early European colonial powers survived because they learned to adapt and to appease, to engage in war or diplomacy, and co-opted or were in turn co-opted by individuals and office holders across a wide spectrum of Malay society and the Southeast Asian trading élite. Like the shifting pelagic waters that wash the Singapore and Melaka Straits, the *Estado da Índia*, the VOC as well as the polities on Sumatra and the Malay Peninsula found themselves swept by the tides of factionalism, alliance making and diplomacy in a region sustained by commerce and greatly impacted by political instability during the first four decades of the 17th century.

Appendices

APPENDIX 1

Challenges from Early Modern Source Materials: Melaka and Adjacent Regions

[The present appendix forms a side discussion of Chapter 1 and addresses some of the major problems of handling early modern sources of European and Asian origin. Special attention is paid to the *Suma Oriental* of Tomé Pires, as well as to printed materials that contain accounts of chiefly Portuguese, Italian, and Malay origin. These include Gaspar Corrêa, Duarte Barbosa, Francesco Carletti, Giovanni da Empoli, Manoel Godinho de Erédia, Gianbattista Ramusio, Ludovico de Varthema, as well as the *Sejarah Melayu* and the *Undang-undang Melaka*.]

Almost every modern historical account touching on the history of Melaka and adjacent regions during the early modern period has mentioned the *Suma Oriental* of the apothecary and diplomat Tomé Pires. It is now widely believed to have been written between 1512 and 1515.[1] However, work conducted over the past five decades has not only made great headway, but also posed a series of questions about Pires' integrity and the transmission of the text.[2] It is extremely important to display a critical mindset when contextualising and translating the terminology Pires employs,[3] and to the best of the present author's knowledge, no recent studies have cross-referenced the text of the *Suma Oriental* with Pires' published letters of 1512 and 1513.[4] In the same vein, his *Rol de Drogarias* (1516), a list of pharmaceutical substances used in the context of Asian, specifically Indian medicine, has evoked very little interest and remains virtually unknown in modern scholarly circles.

Researchers have grown increasingly aware — and wary — of the differences among terms and toponyms between the "Paris manuscript", published and translated by Armando Cortesão in 1944, and the far shorter "Lisbon manuscript", edited and first published as a self-standing text by Rui Manuel Loureiro in 1996.[5] The Paris manuscript is thought to date from the second half of the 16th century,[6] while the Lisbon manuscript represents a 16th century copy of the original sent by Pires to the Portuguese viceroy of India, Dom Duarte de Meneses.[7] Linguistic style, nomenclature and specialist terms found in the latter, shorter text are certainly more authentic, and one cannot help but shudder at Cortesão's own frank admission, found in the foreword to his English translation, that he sometimes had to "guess" what Pires was trying to say.[8]

Other early Portuguese texts fare little better. Duarte Barbosa serves as a case in point. One has a hard time appraising what parts were frivolously added by Giovanni Battista Ramusio in his collection *Delle Navigazioni e Viaggi* to "exoticise" the story for European readers, or alternatively, reconstructing the parts that were censured by the Portuguese authorities from the original manuscript(s) because the text revealed commercially sensitive and therefore classified information.[9] A third classic Portuguese text, the *Declaraçam de Malacca* by Erédia, is also not without serious problems. First, it dates from a much later period, namely, the early 17th century. A comparison of this text with Erédia's earlier treatise, the *Informação da Aurea Chersoneso* (about 1597–1600), reveals considerable inconsistency in the way terminology is employed and also in some of the basic insights expounded. Take, for example, what Erédia says about the home of the Malays. In the *Declaraçam de Malacca* he claims this to be Pahang, but in his earlier text, the home of the Malays is placed unconventionally in Patani.[10] Did Erédia change his mind? Or was there genuinely no consensus on this very issue? Other authors claim that the Malays are from Melaka, Sumatra or Lingga. Who really knew? Although the view may well be sustained that Erédia's treatise ultimately represents an honest effort, there are several, still inadequately researched, discontinuities of argument (terminological and otherwise) between the text dating from around 1597–1600 and the final version of 1613.[11]

Historians of early modern Melaka as well as the Singapore and Melaka Straits broadly concur that some important accounts have perhaps relied too strongly on Pires and the handy English language translation published by Cortesão at the height of World War II.[12] It is perhaps against the backdrop of this discomfort and acknowledged over-reliance that one needs to specially appreciate the document translations prepared by Manuel Pintado and published by Malaysia's National Archives in the early 1990s.[13] Despite some problems with Pintado's translations, there can be little doubt that his labours represent an important first step in weaning the modern historian away from an over-reliance on Pires to meaningfully broaden the range of early Portuguese colonial sources that are readily available in the English language.

Asian — and specifically Malay-language — texts, as far as they exist, present the modern historian with a different set of textual obstacles and hermeneutical challenges. First, there are very few sources that date, or claim to date, from the period around the fall of the Melaka Sultanate (1511). Most of these represent later codified version(s) of oral tradition and/or public memory. The meaning and intention of the text is by no means consistent; one may speak here particularly of such texts as the *Sejarah Melayu* or Malay Annals.[14] This text, as it stands today, is believed to date from the period after the fall of the Melaka Sultanate to the Portuguese, and evidence from the 17th Acehnese chronicle *Bustan-as-Salatin* (The Garden of Kings) and more recent scholarly contributions hold that the text of the *Sejarah Malayu* dates from 16th up to the early 17th century.[15] The famous ms. Raffles 18 is dated 1612, that is during the period under review in the present book.[16] The core objective of the *Sejarah Melayu* is to rally the Malays behind the deposed sultan by stressing lineage, providing prophetic statements or testaments, stressing the benefits of mutual obligation as well as employing moral suasion and the language of obedience.[17] Modern historians often find that the *Sejarah Melayu* has the important benefit of being a source of historical geography.[18]

The two legal digests of Melaka, *Undang-undang Melaka* (Laws of Melaka) and *Undang-undang Laut* ([Melaka] Maritime Code), are also of considerable historical interest, but they have until now remained peripheral to studies on Melaka from the late 15th until the late 17th century.[19] Both purport, and are widely accepted, to trace their origins to the period of the Melaka Sultanate. Like any other legal text, these digests now represent different strands of thinking from different periods of time, both pre-colonial and colonial Melaka as well as their claimed successor states. The Malay Concordance Project at the Australian National University traces the origin of both texts to the 15th century but advises caution.[20] On the surface, this caution is justified for the text of the *Undang-undang Laut*, where certain clauses incorporated into the main body of the text bear specific dates from the 17th century. As a digest, the *Undang-undang Melaka* is far less transparent. The editor, Liaw Yock Fang, simply observes that the digest is strung together from different texts and most likely across the reign of several Melaka rulers.[21] The question inevitably arises: Exactly which laws belong to which period? And for a polity that thrived on commerce, why were there "no specific laws to protect the trader and the entrepreneur?"[22]

Liaw, like Winstedt well before him, traces the digest to the rule of Muzzaffar Shah (1445–58), a period that may be considered the Golden Age of the Melaka Sultanate.[23] By this stage the erstwhile "pirates lair" of Parameswara[24] (to borrow the terminology from Paul Wheatley) had grown from a fishing village under the influence of Pasai on Sumatra and nominal suzerainty of the king of Siam[25] to a separate kingdom in its own right.[26] Admiral Zheng He's famous visit, on which occasion the ruler of Melaka's status was elevated from chief to "king", was almost a half-century in the past. Melaka was the emporium that Portuguese and other early European visitors, including also Giovanni da Empoli, described with admiration in their letters and accounts dating from the early 16th century.[27] Wheatley estimates a population of around 6,000 inhabitants in the year 1424, a figure that supposedly had swollen by "later arrivals [of *orang laut*], scavenging along the coast and lured by the promise of early gains. [They] had taken up their preferred site, close against the water's edge".[28] Agriculture was not the preferred activity of the immigrants, and as a result, food remained in short supply.[29] Sago, vegetables and fruit were the staple foods in Melaka at this time.[30] Under Sultan Muzzaffar, Melaka also began to expand from a city-state to an "imperial power" — or at least so one is told. The peoples of the western Peninsula, and also Pahang, Siak on Sumatra and the Riau Archipelago are believed to have been absorbed into an expanding polity centred in Melaka.[31]

If one compares these insights with information gleaned from early Portuguese colonial documents and chronicles, one scarcely fares any better. Certainly, the claim advanced by Corrêa in his *Lendas da Índia* that Melaka was a great trading city since the eighth century AD cannot be sustained by any stretch of the imagination. Medieval Arabic sources reproduced by Gabrial Ferrand certainly make no mention of the entrepôt.[32] Nor is it expressly mentioned by Nicolò de Conti in the account of his voyage to the East (1414–39), *Historiade Varietate Fortunae*. However, the fact that Fra Mauro of Venice made two entries on his world map of 1459 for Melacha (Melaka) has led to some speculation that de Conti shared his first-hand knowledge of the East personally with Fra Mauro. Certainly, Fra Mauro perused de Conti's written account which, in the words of curator Piero Falchetta, was available "to the reading public" by 1447.[33] The *Mohît* (or Muhît), an Ottoman-Turkish rutter for the Indian Ocean, may have synthesised geographic knowledge of the region compiled anytime between the 14th and 16th centuries,[34] but the two surviving manuscripts in Istanbul and Vienna date from 1554 and 1558 respectively, and they acknowledge the incorporation of information gained from the Portuguese.[35]

Nor should one give much credence to the testimonies of so many of Europe's scholars from the age of Renaissance and Humanism, especially those who were mentally shackled by the tenuous and mostly unverifiable names linked to Ptolemaic geography, dating from the second century AD, or even Isidore of Seville's voluminous *Etymologies* dating from the early seventh century. Erédia's widely acclaimed *Declaraçam de Malaca*, and perhaps also his earlier *Informação da Aurea Chersoneso*, should be mentioned in this context. Rather, one should be drawn to the more sobering scholarly enquiries of Rouffaer, Obdeijn and later Wheatley,[36] none of whom opine that Melaka was much more than a fishing village — in fact, little more than a wretched "pirate's lair" — before the eve of the 15th century. Melaka early on was a marketplace for all sorts of merchandise, including the ill-gotten ones, and it was only after the marriage of Melaka's ruler with a Pasai princess,[37] and later the arrival of Chinese merchants following the Zheng He expeditions, that the port polity emerged to great regional prominence.

As has been argued in the case of *Singapura*, early modern sources are not always clear what they mean when they mention "Melaka". Is it a reference to the port, city and emporium? Is it a reference to a territory, an empire, a cultural sphere or the complex economic relationship between centre and periphery? Is it a reference to the whole of the Malay Peninsula? The level of confusion raised by early modern source materials is considerable. Still, Melaka is celebrated as one of the prized possessions of the *Estado da Índia*, an emporium unlike any other in Asia and probably the world.[38] Correspondingly, early Portuguese colonial sources show a propensity to harp on the grandeur and glory of Melaka, and also provide figures that are hardly credible. Rui de Araújo estimates the number of households at 10,000, a number that was probably as great as many of the largest European settlements of the 16th century. Corrêa estimates the population at well over 200,000 (elevating Melaka to the largest city in "all of the Indies").[39] According to Pires, Melaka could muster 100,000 men-at-arms, which of course implies a population significantly greater than 200,000![40] Castanheda gave a more modest estimate of 120,000. Perhaps this is a reference to the whole Malay Peninsula and not just the city. Describing the period of the sultanate, Damião de Goes (also de Góis) estimated the population of Melaka town at 30,000, while the eyewitness Rui de Araújo spoke of 10,000 households.[41] Then again, at any one point in time, there were reportedly many craft and ships of various sizes plying the waters of Melaka harbour and the river. Contemporary commentators have confused estimates of maximum capacity with actual figures of maritime activity. True, Giovanni da Empoli estimates that the harbour of Melaka could accommodate two thousand vessels — and more still in the river. But his estimate of one hundred sail actually in port together with an unspecified number of smaller vessels that he calls *calaluzi* (kelulus, an oared vessel) and *ciamparie* (sampan) and yet more craft of still lesser significance yield far more sobering estimate of maritime trading activity at Melaka at the beginning of the 16th century.[42]

Yet the overly generous if not exaggerated numbers for Melaka quickly found their way into print, such as on the two world maps of Martin Waldseemüller and Laurent Fries that feature special explanatory text boxes in both the German and Latin editions.[43] It would be foolish to take these sources uncritically and at face value, as some authors have done in more recent decades, but what they do express are the views of foreign observers who were evidently impressed. Over time, Melaka appears to have diminished in size and population. The Flemish diamond merchant Jaques de Coutre, who lived in Melaka at the end of the 16th and beginning of the 17th centuries, reports that it was still possible to identify stakes or poles from former houses. Orchards that once surrounded residential areas extended some "two or three miles" from the Portuguese city centre. This area, where evidently a larger and more expansive city had once stood, was overgrown with tropical thicket. De Coutre estimates that a couple of hundred craft of various sizes called annually at the port.[44]

Francesco Carletti, the intrepid merchant from Tuscany whose travels at the eve of the 17th century brought him to the port of Melaka, and indeed around the world, explains to his readers that the houses of this city of spice and commerce were constructed of wood and located under shady trees.[45] This description does not differ significantly from Chinese accounts written one and a half centuries earlier.[46] Carletti also observed how the sailors of vessels at anchor spent the night on board, rather than on shore. This does not differ significantly from the observation Varthema made towards the end of the Melaka Sultanate's life span. According to Carletti's fellow Italian, the merchants at Melaka faced considerable dangers, and Varthema may have spoken the truth when he claimed that during the Melaka Sultanate, scores of merchants were killed in cold blood, "like dogs".[47] It can be presumed that with so many ships arriving and departing, and with the *orang laut*, Bajau, Aru and Batak scouring the waters outside the port, merchants had to be very alert.[48] In any case, the Portuguese authorities — just like their Malay counterparts around Sumatra and the Peninsula — reportedly sealed off the waterfront every night by trawling a series of logs linked by chains across the mouth of the port.[49] This was to stop merchants from setting sail under the cloak of darkness without paying their dues, and also to prevent ships from vanishing into the night without a trace. The logs and chain may also have served the purpose of forestalling an attack on the port facilities from the sea by *orang laut* and rapacious tribes that — so one is told — regularly engaged in plundering and slave raiding.

APPENDIX 2

[The Portuguese document transcribed here in appendix 2, together with its modern English translation, is a letter by Dom Paulo Lima de Pereira written to King Philip I of Portugal who also ruled as Philip II of Spain. This letter was written at Melaka on 28 November 1587, only weeks after Dom Paulo Lima de Pereira and his men destroyed the Johorean capital Johor Lama together with the fortress Kota Batu. It provides an account of his voyage by sea from India to Johor, details of the campaign, a list of noteworthy participants on the Johorean side, and briefly touches on an attack on Bintan later in the same year. There are strong parallels to the known accounts published by the Portuguese chronicler Diogo de Couto. The transcript provides readings from two manuscript copies of the letter preserved in London and Madrid and makes cross references to the published works of de Couto. It

Image of King Philip II/I of Spain and Portugal riding a horse and bearing his royal scepter taken from Emanuel van Meteren's *Commentariën ofte Memoriën* (Commentaries or Memoirs), 1652. (Private Collection, Peter Borschberg)

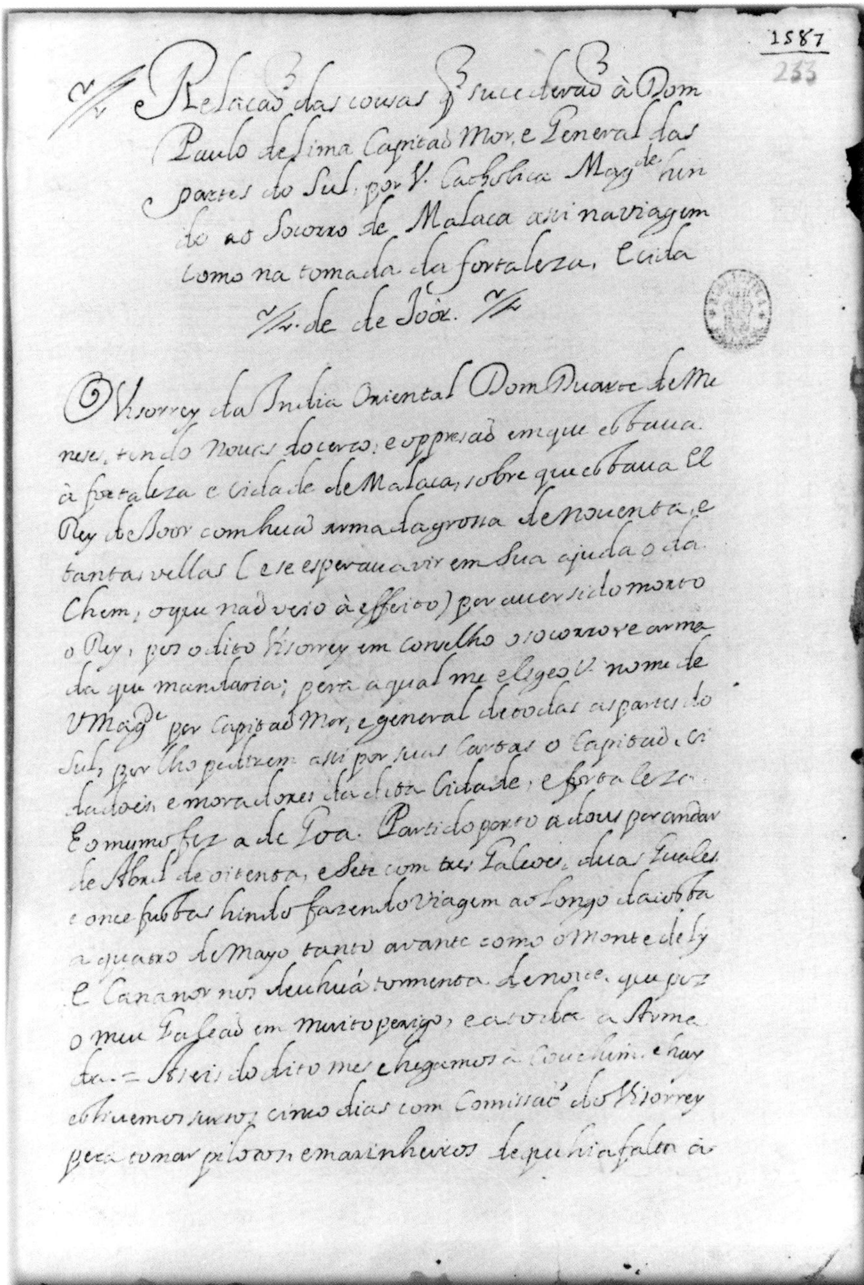

1587
233

Relação das cousas que sucederão a Dom Paulo de Lima Capitão Mor e General das partes do Sul, por V. Catholica Mag.de hindo ao Socorro de Malaca assi na viagem como na tomada da fortaleza e Cidade de Jor.

O Visorrey da India Oriental Dom Duarte de Meneses, tendo novas do aperto e oppressão em que estava a fortaleza e Cidade de Malaca, sobre que estava el Rey de Jor com huã armada grossa de noventa e tantas vellas (e se esperava vir em sua ajuda o da China, o que não veio a effeito) por aver sido morto o Rey, por o dito Visorrey em conselho o socorro e armada que mandaria; pera a qual me elegeo em nome de V Mag.de por Capitão Mor e general de todas as partes do Sul, por lho pedirem assi por suas cartas o Capitão, Cidadoens e moradores da dita Cidade e fortaleza. E o mesmo fez a de Goa. Partido do porto a dous por andar de Abril de oitenta e sete com tres Galeões, duas Galles e once fustas hindo fazendo viagem ao longo da costa a quatro de Mayo tanto avante como o Monte de ly e Cananor nos deu huã tormenta de noite que poz o meu Galeão em muito perigo e a costa a Armada. A seis do dito mes chegamos a Cochim e nas [illegible] estivemos cinco dias com Comissão do Visorrey pera tomar pilotos e marinheiros de que havia falta a

First page of the letter by Dom Paulo Lima de Pereira to King Philip II/I of Spain and Portugal of November, 1587. (Biblioteca Nacional de España, Madrid, ms. 1750, fol. 233 recto)

is important for understanding different aspects of Portuguese-Johor relations during the second half of the 16th and first decade of the 17th century addressed in Chapters 1–3.]

British Library, London, Ms. Add. 28461, fols. 10 recto–16 recto (Source L) and Biblioteca Nacional de España, Madrid, Ms. 1750, fols. 233 recto–239 verso (Source M), incip.,[50] "Relação das cousas que sucederão à Dom Paulo de Lima Capitão Mor e General das partes do Sul por Vossa Catholica Magestade hindo ao Socorro de Malaca assi na viagem como na tomada da fortaleza e cidade de Joôr".[51]

O Visorrey da India Oriental Dom Duarte de Meneses tendo novas do cerco, e oppresão em que estava à fortaleza e cidade de Malaca, sobre que estava El Rey de Joor com huma armada grossa de noventa e tantas vellas (e se esperava vir em Sua ajuda o da Chem,[52] o que não veio à effeito) por aver sido morto o Rey, pos o dito Visorrey em conselho o socorrese armada que mandaria; pera a qual me elegeo o [Vosso][53] nome de Vossa Magestade por Capitão Mor, e general de todas as partes do Sul, por lho pedirem assi por suas Cartas o Capitão cidadoes, e moradores da dita Cidade, e fortaleza E o mesmo fez a de Goa. Parti do porto a dous por andar de Abril de oitenta e Sete com tres Galeoes, duas Guales e once fustas hindo fazendo viagem ao longo da costa a quarto de Mayo tanto avante como o Monte de Ly[54] e Cananor nos deu homa tormeta de noite que poz o meu Galeão em muito perigo, e a toda a Armada. A seis do dito mes chegamos a Couchim[55] e hay estivemos surtos cinco dias com Comissão do Visorrey pera tomar pilotos e marinheiros de que hia falta à /[56] Armada de remo, e mandei refazer os Galeões e os mais navios dagõa para não faltar no golfão.[57] Partimos de Couchim a diez dè Mayo puzémos na travesa e golfão de Ceillão em Cobar tè chegar a vista de[58] Daia, que he na ponta de Samatra, quince dias com vento prospero, e do Rio de Achem the o de pedir[59] e ponta de Paiem[60] com correntes e calmarias grãdes andamos trinta e cinco sem passar adiante em que se gastou todo o mes de Junho.

Os Capitães das Galès, e mais navios de remo me requererão /[61] lhes desse licença para fazer aguo a da na mesma Ilha de Samatra, ou na de Polvareira, por perecem os soldados e chusma de sede depois de o por em Conselho e feito examen lho concedi, pera o qual effeito mandei por Capitão Mor dos navios de remo a Simão da Breu[62] de Mello homem esperto e bom soldado com Regimento do que avia de fazer despois de ter despedidos os navios, vendo que não podia passar avante. Estando ja em extrema necessidade daguoa juntamente com Dom João Pereyra e Francisco da Silva Capitães dos Galeões nos afastamos da costa, e cortando largo fomos a Polubutum[63] aonde fizemos aguoada, e no caminho chegarão algums soldados, e moços de Soldados pella pouca regra que se davão abiberem[64] na salgada.

As Gales e fustas forão ao longo da costa de /[65] Samatra fazendo aguoada nos lugares acomodados aonde apezar dos enemigos a fizerão, que a querião impedir. No caminho emcontrarão tres galiotas em que hia o Embaixador del Rey de Joor com cartas e dinheiro, em que pedia gente e socorro d'armada ao Dachen huma se tomou com todo o Recheo, a qual Dom Pedro de Lima emvestio, e a meterão no fundo, e outras vararão em terra, a que com a artelharia, e arcabuzeria fizerão dano, e catinarão[66] ao Capitão Mor das Galiotas E ao Embaixador, e tomarão alguns balos e somas a que puserão fogo, e as queimarão.

A armada de remo chegou a Salvamento A Malaca; mas por fazerem alguma detença os Galiões dè Pulobutum tè o porto a requerimento da Cidade e Bispo que hora he Capitão em lugar de João da Silva dando lhe o provimento necessario partio pera Jor com o regimento, /[67] no qual mandava o Capitão dos navios se ajuntasse com Dom Antonio de Noronha,[68] e que não desse em terra, nem fizesse mais que impedir os mantimentos ao Rey tè chegar com o restante da Armada, que erão os tres Galiões e huma naveta de Couchim, que veio de Socorro a Malaca. E assi forão mais vinte bantins, que o Bispo armou com muita brevidade. Estes Navios de Remo acharão Dom Antonio de Noronha surto fora da Barra na Romania com dous galeões e dous bantins de que era Capitão Mor, e a elle mandei despois obedecessem atè chegar e que estivessem em meu lugar e juntos /[69] todos forão emtrando o Rio de Joor, aonde emcontrarão duas Galiotas, que vinhão da cidade, o que parece fizerão os negros de industria pera se tornarem a recolher, e levarem os nossos navios debaixo da artelharia pera com ella os meterem no fundo, mas as fustas, e Galès com pouco dano as forão siguindo tè as fazer varar defronte da Cidade, e as queimarão, e outras quarto, ou cinco Galiotas, que estavão varadas na praya de xabandaria juntamente com os bantins, e derão em huma tranqueira, que esta a tiro de Camellete do lugar adonde do lugar adonde se fazião os dinheiros e que estavão alguns Mallajos, e Jaos que a defendião, na qual se tomarão alguns Chicorros, e outras peças de artelharia, que Serião quince o vinte por todas. O dia seguinte tomou Conselho contra Regimento Dom Antonio com os Capitães se darião em

Joôr, sendo os mais delles ou casi todos de opinião, /[70] que o não fizessem. E alguns Religiosos, que a isso chamou salvo hum so e os mais que se não sabe não tendo gente pera este effeito o pos por obra sem avisar aos Capitães os quais vendo a bandeira do dito Dom Antonio desembarcarão em terra, e o acompanharão por opinião, donde despois de lhe terem mortos e feridos alguns homens sem conseguir o que pretendia. Por que nisto vem a dar as cousas mal consideradas pondo a risco toda armada se recolheo com muito trabalho e perigou sendo poucos os enemigos, que vierão em Seguimento dos nossos o que /[71] pudera ser causa não somente de Se perder a armada mas de se não fazer empresa, à que o Visorrey me mandava com aquella consideração comselho, e recado que semelhantes cousas requerem.

Parti de Malaca a vinte e seis de Julho, e dahi a quince cheguei a Joôr com os galeões, que levava, e em sete repareci, e me apercivi do necessario, e achendo as cousas neste termo, e o enemigo fortificado, e apercevido tomei parecer dos Capitães conforme ao Regimento, que levava do Viso Rey se daria em Joor, ou não pondo a todos diante o muito que importava a destruição deste enemigo por ser ya tão poderoso, e ter intupido o estreito de Sincapura, e o detrimento, e perda grande que o estado receberia tendo os nossos naquelle lugar alguma rota e fiz lembrança se seria milhor fazer a guerra com o tempo tendo o de cerco, e impedindo lhe o mantimento ou com as armas forão todos de parecer, que determinadamente desse em terra porque nos não poderia fa-/[72] zer tanto dano o enemigo no assalto, quanto os nossos receberião em se dilatar a guerra por as[73] muitas emfermidades, que ha naquelle lugar por estar o Rio, e a cidade debaixo da linha quinocial, o que aconteceo a outros Capitães que estiverão em aquella paragem em que morreo, e adoeceo muita gente.

Quinta feira a tarde a trece de Agosto mandei com intento de dar em terra, e estar ya feito disto asento tirar os mastareos aos Galeões, e surtos defronte das es/[74]-tancias, e forte da cidade com seus repairos a comerçarão a bater, e a bateria se continuou sesta feira por todo a dia tè sabado pella menhã dia de Nossa Senhora do Rosario em que o assalto se deu, e a cidade se tomou, e abrazou; os galeões, que estiverão a bateria forão cinco, e a novata de Couchim — a saber — o de Dom Manoel Dalmada, e o de Dom Antonio de Noronha, e o de Dom João Pereyra, e o de Francisco da Silva, e a naveta de Luis Martins todos em ordem, e o galeão São Thome em que vi de Goa, que por ser novo e forte, e vir bem artilhado o mandei por defronte do Cotabatu, deu isto, e determinação muito emfadamento ao enemigo porque depois que a bateria se começou entre homens, e mulheres matou a nossa artelharia sessenta, ou setenta pessoas.

Ao outro dia pedi aos Religiosos, que hião na armada disessem missa em terra da outra banda pera toda a gente se confessar, e comungar, o que se fez, e vendo alguâs pessoas, que não era tanta, quanto se presumia assi /[75] Capitães como soldados arreceosos, me querião persuadir, que não desembarcasse segundo depois se soube mas me ousarão a dizer naceo esta alteração, e descomfiança de verem hum dia de antes trinta, e cinco vellas na barra entre bantins, e lanchas que os navios d'armada fizerão fugir, os quais por mandado do Rey nos vinhão adivertir. E tambem se dezia que doze Turcos dos Jaós, que estavão metidos no estreito da cidade (mas não ouve tal determinação) tinhão intento despois de nos desembarcados /[76] virem abalrroar os Galeões aonde estava a defensa necessaria, mas save Deos Nosso Senhor se se fez isto com malicia por algum respeito humano dada a ordem necessaria passei a gente aos navios de remo pera desembarcar em terra, mandei a Dom Antonio de Noronha e Dom João Pereyra, Dom Manoel dalmada (sic) e Dom Nunalverez tomasse a dianteira com presuposto de não desembarcarem tè lhe fazer sinal com huma trombeta, hindo recolhendo os navios sem esperarem o sinal desembarcarão os Capitães da dianteira, e derão na tranqueira da xabandaria, e em breve espaço a tomarão; despois que vi a determinação por ser assi forçado desembarquei em hum bantin em que hia com muita brevidade me fui meter na tranqueira por impedir aos nossos que não fossem avante por não aver algum desarranjo tanto que cheguei mandei fazer alto as bandeiras e a Dom Antonio recolher a gente que ficava nos navios, e na praya, porque alguns delles ficarão /[77] em sequo e afastados da praya por falta da mare, despois de ter a gente junta fui peleijando ao longo dos palmares com os enemigos que me Sairão da cidade ao emcontro os quaes rebati por muitas vezes combatendo elles[78] com muito impetu, e ouve da sua parte muitos mortos e feridos assi Capitães, como soldados, e da nossa alguns mortos e feridos trinta, ou quarenta, cometiendo os soldados a cidade pello mais forte, não sendo aquelle lugar por onde determinava de a entrar, os mandei recolher por Francisco de Sousa Pereyra è Dioguo Soares Dalvergaria Capitães de duas galio/[79]-tas e assi hindo proseguido o caminho pera a cidade me foi dito por Dioguo Soares, que Dom João Pereyra, e Dom Antonio hião caminhado pera a cidade e que estavão por toda tranqueira. Com este aviso mandei caminhar a bandeira de Christo as mais bandeiras, que hião em minha companhia todas em hum corpo, e tomando por hum atalho ao longo do muro com muita brevidade fui ter ao lugar por onde a cidade se havia de entrar hindo avante pella rua entrei logo o primeiro baluarte, e o tomej, e fui peleijando com os enemigos, que defendião o muro a mão esquerda, e com a gente, que estava pellas ruas casas e travessas a mão direita, e achando a Dom Antonio sò o recolhi a minha bandeira, e assi chegamos à porta principal, que estâ defronte da Rua do Rey, aonde os enemigos peleijando esforzadamente nos detiverão hum bom /[80] pedaço.

Em todas estes trances me acompanharão Francisco da Silva Dom Pedro de Lima, Diogo Soares Dalvergaria, Francisco Sousa Pereyra, Simão da Breu, Dom Fernando Lobo que hia por soldado ferido de huma espingardada afora duas ou tres que lhe derão, que lhe não fizerão nojo. Em hum Antonio Dandria Capitão Mor dos bantins bom soldado nacido nestas partes, en este lugar matarão a dous Capitães de Bandeiras, Dom Bernardo de Meneses, e Dom Manoel Dalmada, e outros dous soldados, e hum homen da terra, e ferirão tres, ou quarto, e a Dom Antonio com huma frechá de Zaravatana no rosto, neste comenos não sei /[81] se algem o mandou ou fez hum negro de seu proprio motu se abrio esta porta, que vay dar ao mar por la qual de Cansados se sahirão alguns soldados, e se forão asentar mi[82] palmar que estâ junto della; e Dom Antonio juntamente, que os hia recolher, e curar se da ferida avendo que a frecha era de peçonha; este refugio, e descanso, que os homens tomarão por o negocio estando emfermos de Se acabar em grande, e manifesto perigo. Tanto que isto vi com extrema necessidade, por não ficar cobrando animo o enemigo me fui pella Rua do Rey abaixo com a bandeira de Christo, não levando em minha companhia mais que Vinte pesoas, entre Capitães, e soldados e com estes; (porque assi o permitio a divina providencia) o desbaratei; e pus em fugida, e o Rey dezesperado virou as costas, de maneira que nunca ma-/[83] is nos tornarão acometer; nem aparecerão na cidade, em que tantos annos tiverão sua morada. E daqui me detube hum pedaço tè tudo se aquietar, mas tão cansado, e quebrantado destes e outros muitos trabalhos, que afirmo a Vossa Catholica Magestade que se os enemigos se reforçaraõ, e tornaraõ a peleijar que não pudera Eu fazer mais com tão pouca gente segundo a determinação que levava, que acabar em meu officio. Estando isto nestes termos mandei por fogo a cidade, ventando nesta conjunção o terrenho que não servia pera o incendio se passou em hum instante milagrosamente ao Sul o vento, e ventou com tanto impetu aquelle dia e outro, que nelles se queimarão todos os muros de madeira e cidade sem /[84] ficar nada em peê, a qual seria de meya legoa em comprido, e huma em redondo de maneira que Deos nesta batalha venceo, e da victoria forão instrumentos os Capitães, e soldados, e o foguo foi seguindo o alcanse. Matheus Pereyra caminhado pellos andaimos do muro, que vay dar ao baluarte do Catabatu com alguns soldados das companhias, que o seguirão entrou elle achou o ya despe jado, mas de creer he que se o achara com gente, que o tomara, e acabara na demanda tanto que mo fez, a saber, que foi tudo quasi em hum tempo, o mandei prover de mais gente, pera assegurança da vitoria. E dahi a pedaço estando alguma cousa aliviado do trabalho me fui meter nelle, e o sustentei seis dias nos quais os soldados continuarão o saquo, e acharão muita fazenda emterrada, e pessas douro, nestes recolhi a[85] artelharia grosa, em cuda em que avia quatrocentas, ou quinhentas pesas de bronce, /[86] em que entrava hum basalisco mourisco, hum liab, e huma serpe reforçada de vinte e seis palmos de comprido, hum camello de marca mayor, alguns cameletes, falcões, meyos falcões, cães e meias esperas, e chicorros que he artelharia meuda. Dom João Pereyra, que acaso se apartou de Dom Antonio e seu Irmão Dom Nunalverez tomarão por huma Rua, que vay ao longo do muro a mão direita, tinha[87] em Sua companhia cento e sincoenta soldados, ahi peleijarão todos esforçadamente, e estiverão a pee quedo o que foi de muita importancia; porque se por aquelle lugar vierão os enemigos, e nos sairão nas costas derão nos muito trabalho. Pero Coelho, /[88] e Lourenço Frões Capitães de dous navios de remo forão em Sua companhia, e costerão digo contestarão com sua obricação.

No estreito, e nas estancias defronte da cidade se queimarão passante de mil embarcações entre Juncos, ballos, e somas, e muitos balões, queimarão mais dous galeões, oito Gales, e algumas fustas, e lancharas, e tinha o Rey pera sua defensa mais de tres mil espinguardas, as mais dellas compravão aqui os Quelins a soldados necessitados, e as mandavão vender a Joor.

Tinha El Rey de Joor entre Jaós, menecabos e Malaios, pera defensa da cidade oito milhones porque lhe veio socorro de muitas partes os soldados Portugueses que a ganharão serião por todos quatrocentos, os mais ficarão na guarda do mar, e havia muitos doentes destes morrerão [os que assi mas digo][89] assi Capitães, como soldados; dos enemigos, se não sabe a copia certa mas na verdade morrerão muitos no combate e afoga- /[90] dos e os Jaos, que estavão nos Juncos, que dantes os ayudarão no mato por os roubarem fizerão grande matança nelles — porque o Rey lhe não tinha dado certa copia dinheiro, que lhe devia daroz que lhe tomarão, e outras muitas fazendas.

Estes são os Reys que Vierão de Socorro e se acharão no socorro da cidade

Rayelle Rey de Joor e com titulo entre os Reys do sul de Emperador dos Reys Mallaios[91]
O rey de Tucal[92]
El rey Dandreguj[93]
El rey de Bintan[94]

Capitães mortos e vivos
Quiaylante morto.
Raya[95] Macote vivo este anda fora dagraça do Rey e fugido.
Adipata Campar vivo
Rayalella vivo.
Sirina[96] morto.
Sirima[97] de Raya morto.
Sirindia[98] morto.
[Sirima Rayalella morto][99]
Hum Irmão par seu nome Emchegala morto.
Ninalante, que se não sabe se morto, o vivo, torno a dizer que he morto.
[Sy Mirabanca morto].[100]

Rayalle por descuido nosso era o mais poderoso Rey que avia no sul por liança que tinha com muitos Reys — a saber — Com o da Chém,[101] o com o Rey de Pão e Patane, e com outros muitos Reys de Jaoa, e carteava se com o de Tarnate afora /[102] os mais, que assima digo que tinha debaixo do seu Imperio, e a cidade de Joor [103] mais acomodada que todas as outras pera se empedirem os estreitos, e a navegação aos Portugueses, e /[104] pera por cerco, a Malaca todas as horas. E ainda que o da Chem parece que em gente e armada he mais poderoso como de feito he pellas alianças, e inconvenientes assima ditos ficava sendo estoutro mais enemicissimo da Feê de Christo depois de ser desbaratado. E o da Chem morto.

Mandarão a este porto o Rey de Pera e de Queda muitos navios de mantimentos e alguma pimenta não tendo estes annos atras nenhum comercio comnosco por alguns respeitos, e assim tem vindo mais de trezentos Juncos de Jaoa. Valem quorenta guantas daroz ao cruzado e dantes vendiase huma so por hum cruzado.

Depois de me recolher a esta cidade de Malaca mandei a Dom Pedro de Lima meu Irmão com duas Guales, cinco fustas, e oito bantins ao estreito de Sincapura, e de Sabão pera dar guarda aos Juncos dos Jaos, e emtrar em Joor, e saber do estando, e determinação do Rey, na boca do Rio tomou uma galiota em que vinha o Capitão de Sabão, que com tromenta desgarrou da companhia do Rey, meterão toda a gente à espada, na companhia desta vinha um Navio pequeno, que escapou, e deu rebate ao Rey que anda no mar com vinte e cinco embarcações pequenas e duas /[105]

Galeotas, se isto não fora ouverão no de tomar, puserão fogo a cidade de Bintão, nella queimarão huma galle muito fermosa que o Rey fazia pera si; Tomarão seis ou Sete balos, em que /[106] la tiverão e matarão muita gente; a cidade de Joor esta despovoada chea de mato, e de frutas silvestres, e o Rey sem cabedal, nem poder desamparado dos amigos aliados. Isto he o que ate qui tem sucedido. Tenho dito em hum dos capitulos atrás que são as pessas de artelharia quinhentas, tenho sabido por negros Cativos, que despois vierão, que são o dobro; mas as mais dellas são furtadas e sonegadas. Feita em Malaca a vinte oito de Novembro de 1587.

E assi queimarão mais de dento e cincoenta embarcações que estavão varadas.

Dom Paulo Lima de Pereyra

English Translation

"Account of the events that occurred to Dom Paulo de Lima, captain-major and general of the Southern region [appointed by] His Catholic Majesty, while going to assist Melaka both during the voyage as well as during the conquest of the fortress and settlement of Johor".[107]

The [Portuguese] viceroy of India, Dom Duarte de Meneses, had received news of the siege and of the oppression that the fortress and settlement of Melaka was suffering, because the king of Johor was besieging it with a vast armada of about 90 vessels. It was [widely] expected that the king of Aceh would come to his assistance, but this did not happen, since the king [of Aceh] was killed. As the captain, citizens and residents of the said settlement and fortress [of Melaka] and also the city of Goa had petitioned him to do so in their letters, the aforementioned viceroy met with his council and resolved to send relief by dispatching an armada. To this end he appointed me in the name of Your Majesty to serve as captain-major and general of all the Southern regions.

I set sail from the port on 28 April 1587, with three galleons, two galleys and 11 foists travelling along the coast.[108] On 4 May we had sailed as far as Monte Delly[109] and Cannanore when at night we ran into a storm that posed a great danger to my galleon, and [indeed], the entire armada. On 6 May we arrived at Cochin and anchored there for five days because the viceroy had instructed us to take pilots and sailors on board. Since the armada [also] lacked rowers, I ordered the galleons and other ocean-going vessels to be repaired so they would not falter in the gulf and beyond. We departed from Cochin on 10 May, [and] at Cotiar[110] set across the

Gulf of Ceylon until we were within sight of Daya, which is situated at the [northwest] tip of Sumatra 15 days' sailing with good wind.[111] Due to currents and great lulls we wasted 35 days at the river in Aceh, the river of Pedir, and the promontory of Pasai without making much progress. The whole month of June passed by in this way.

Since the soldiers and crew were perishing of thirst, the captains aboard the galleys and other oared vessels requested from me permission to stop and bring on fresh water on the said island of Sumatra and[112] on the island Polvoreira.[113] After holding council on this matter, and also having examined the situation, I granted them permission to do so, for which purpose I dispatched Simão d'Abreu de Mello,[114] an able man and a good soldier, who served as captain-major of the oared vessels, and instructed him what to do after leaving the ships and how far he could go.[115] Since we were already in dire need of [fresh] water we moved away from the coast together with Dom João Pereira and Francisco da Silva, [both] captains aboard the galleons, and cut across open sea towards Pulau Butang,[116] where we took on board supplies of fresh water.[117] Along the way, due to a lack of discipline, some soldiers and among them young soldiers caved in and drank salt water.

The galleys and foists sailed along the [eastern] coast of Sumatra, taking on board [fresh] water at suitable locations, even though the enemy sought to impede them from doing so. Along the way, they encountered three galliots that were carrying the ambassador of the king of Johor who bore money and letters in which the [Johor monarch] requested Aceh to dispatch men and naval assistance. One of these [Johorean] galliots was captured [together] with its entire cargo. It was attacked and sunk by Dom Pedro de Lima. The other galliots were run aground, inflicting great damage through their[118] artillery [fire] and volleys of harquebuses.[119] They apprehended the commander of the galliots as well as the [Johorean] ambassador and [also] captured some *bâlos*[120] and *somas*,[121] which they set on fire and burnt.

The oared armada arrived safely at Melaka, but the galleons [that had proceeded to] Pulau Buton were somewhat delayed in reaching the port. At the request of the settlement and the [resident] bishop (who now serves as captain-[major of Melaka] in lieu of João da Silva) the vessels were supplied with the necessary provisions and set sail for Johor.[122] The bishop ordered the captain of the ships to join forces with Dom António de Noronha, directing him not to land or to do anything other than block supplies for the king [of Johor] until the rest of the armada had arrived.

This was a reference to the three galleons and a *navette*[123] from Cochin that was on its way to assist Melaka. Thus, 20 additional *bantins*[124] set sail, which the bishop had hastily outfitted. These oared vessels discovered Dom António de Noronha, of which he served as captain-major, anchored with two galleons and two *bantins* off the harbour at the Romania Peninsula.[125] I subsequently placed them under his command, indicating that they served under me, and together they all entered the Johor River. Here they encountered two galliots that had come from the city,[126] and the Malays[127] did their best to return, regroup and place our ships under [their] artillery [fire] with the aim of sinking them. But our foists and galleys suffered [only] minor damage and continued to pursue [the two galliots] until they ran them aground before the settlement and set them ablaze together with four or five other galliots and some *bantins* that had run aground near the shahbandar's compound.[128] They discovered a stockade[129] situated a stone's throw away from the location where coins were struck and that was [also] defended by some Malays and Javanese. Here [our men] captured some *chicorros*[130] and other pieces of artillery, some 15 or 20 pieces in all.[131] The following day, contrary to his instructions, Dom António conferred with the captains on whether or not they should land at Johor.[132] The majority, or almost all of them, were of the opinion that they should not do so. The ecclesiastics, with a single exception, and others, who are not known [by name], were not in favour of this, because there were not sufficient men for this purpose. He [still] went ahead without warning the captains who, spotting the flag of the aforementioned Dom António, disembarked and headed to shore, dutifully accompanying him. Some of his men were later killed or wounded without managing to achieve [any of] their objectives. Since this was poorly considered and [also] placed the whole armada at risk, we[133] retreated under great duress and danger. Only a handful of enemies pursued our ships. Not only could this have led to the loss of the armada, it could have also led to the failure of the [very] mission that the viceroy, on the advice of his council and the [proper] procedures that such things require, had charged me to fulfil.

I set sail from Melaka on 26 July, and 15 days later I reached Johor with the galleons that I had taken with me, and did repairs on seven vessels. I sized up the situation, and finding things in their state and [noting that] the enemy [was] entrenching himself and preparing [for battle], I conferred with my captains according to the instructions given to me by the viceroy, about whether or not we were to land in Johor.[134] I impressed upon all present the importance of destroying this enemy. Since [the king of Johor] had already become so powerful and had imposed a blockade in the Strait of Singapore,[135] the *Estado* would suffer damage as well as tremendous losses since we[136] maintain trad[ing interests] in the region. I reminded them that it would be better to wage war opportunely, aiming for a siege and [thus] severing supplies and arms to the enemy. Everyone concurred that we should make a determined landing, as the enemy could [actually] inflict little damage [on us] during an assault, and also because our men would suffer if the conflict was drawn out for too long, owing to the many diseases prevailing in these regions. This is because the [Johor] river and [its capital] city are situated south of the equator.[137] Other captains who had stopped there suffered considerable misfortunes, as a result of which many [of their] men died or fell ill.

Thursday afternoon on 13 August, it was agreed that we head for land. I ordered the masts to be removed from the galleons and that the latter be anchored in the waters before the city's fortress and defences. Shelling commenced, and the battery continued throughout Friday up until Saturday morning, the day of Our Lady of the Rosary, when the city was stormed, captured and [subsequently] surrendered. Five galleons participating in the shelling, and the new ships from Cochin — namely, the ones [placed under the command] of Dom Manoel d'Almada, Dom António de Noronha, Dom João Pereira, Francisco da Silva and [also] Luís Martins' small ship [respectively] — all lined up in a row. Since the galleon *São Thomé*, on which I had travelled from Goa, was new, strong and well-equipped with artillery, I placed it before Kota Batu.[138] This [tactical move] and [also] our determined attack struck a serious blow at the enemy, because [shortly] after the shelling began, our artillery [fire] killed 60 or 70 people, among the casualties both men and women.

The following day I requested the priests aboard the [ships of the] armada to celebrate Mass on the opposite shore [of the Johor River] so that everyone could give confession and receive communion. This was done, but my captains and soldiers beseeched me apprehensively not to proceed to land, since some[139] had observed that there were not as many men [aboard the ships] as had been [originally] thought. The reason for this later became clear. [The captains and soldiers] ventured to inform me that this confusion and doubt had arisen because, on the previous day, they had spotted 35 sails in the harbour, among them *bantins* and *lancharas*,[140] which had been sent by the king [of Johor] to divert our attention and which the ships of the armada chased away. It was also rumoured that 12 Javanese Turks[141] were [at anchor] in the roadstead and

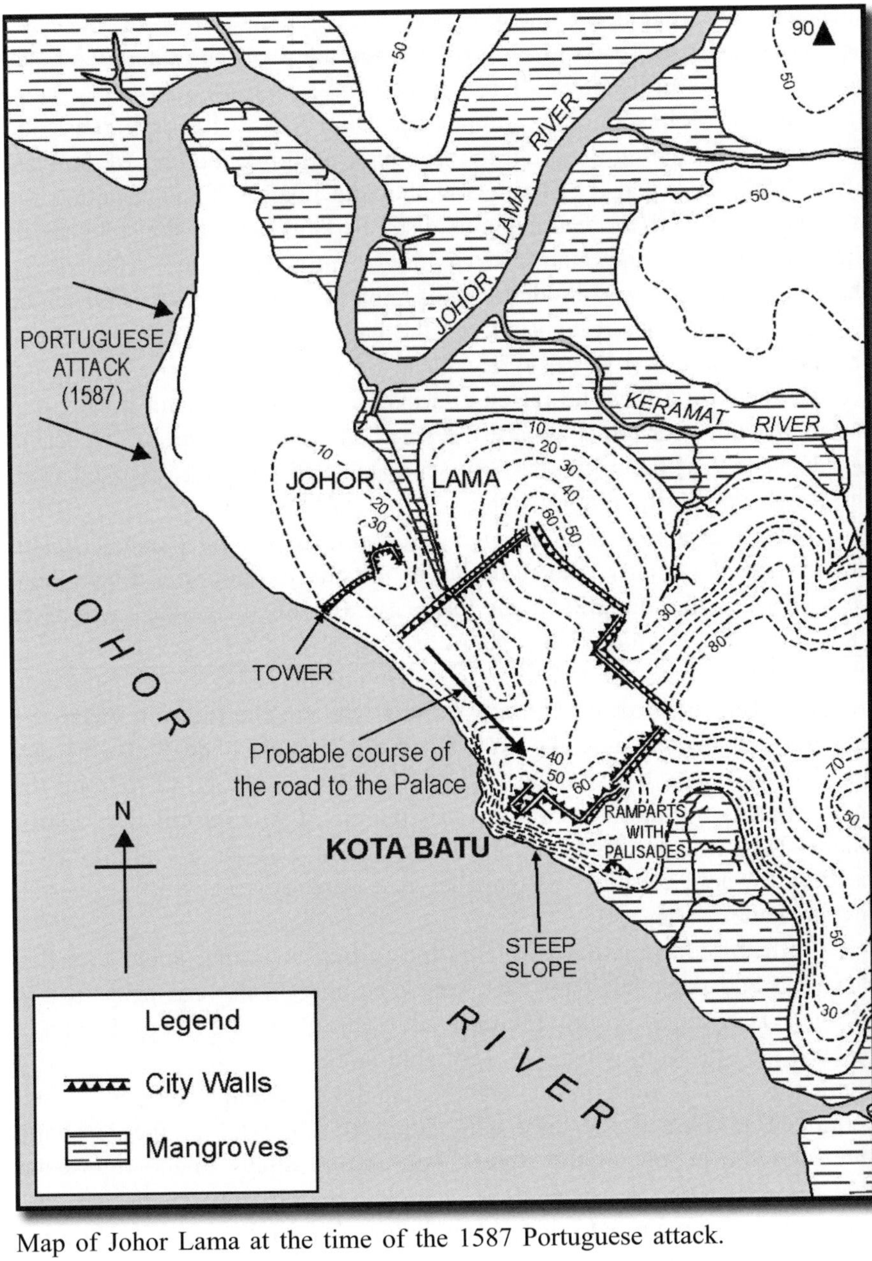

Map of Johor Lama at the time of the 1587 Portuguese attack.

intended, after we had disembarked, to come and crash into our galleons where the necessary defences were, but our Lord God spared us from such malicious damage being inflicted. As a matter of respect, once the necessary order had been given, I transferred the men onto the oared boats so that they could head for shore. I sent Dom António de Noronha, Dom João Pereira, Dom Manoel d'Almada and Dom Neno Álvares[142] to assume leadership, instructing them not to disembark until they had heard the blast of the trumpet signal. Gathering together the boats without awaiting the [trumpet] signal, these lead captains disembarked, entered the stockade of the shahbandar's compound, and captured it in a short time. After seeing their determination and boldness I disembarked on a *bantin*, with which I quickly reached shore and entered the palisades so as to stop our men from proceeding and [also] to thwart any mishaps. As soon as I arrived, I ordered that the flags be raised and instructed Dom António to regroup the men who were [still] aboard the ships as well as those on the beach, because some of them had become separated and were far removed from the beach due to the outgoing tide.

After regrouping my own men, I continued to fight along the palm groves with the enemy who came out of the city to battle me. I beat them back many times, fighting them furiously, and on their side there were many dead and injured, both captains as well as soldiers. On our side there were some dead and wounded, 30 or 40 [in number], the soldiers attacking the city from its strongest [point]. As this was not the location where we had decided to penetrate the city, I ordered Francisco de Sousa Pereira and Diogo Soares de Albergaria, captains of two galliots, to regroup the men. Thus continuing our way towards the city, I was informed by Diogo Soares [de Albergaria] that Dom João Pereira and Dom António were heading towards the city and that they had [already successfully] overrun the stockade.

With this information I ordered the [group marching under the] flag of Christ and the other flags that were marching in my company to join together as a single group. Taking a short cut along the walls, I quickly reached the site from where we were able to enter the city. Moving ahead along the road I immediately entered the first bastion, captured it, and continued to fight the enemy who defended the wall at the left-hand side, and the people in the streets, houses and alleys to the right-hand side. Finding Dom António alone, I took him into my flag group, and we reached the main gate that stands before the king's street.[143] Here the enemy, fighting resolutely, held us back for quite some time. In all these skirmishes I was accompanied by Francisco da Silva, Dom Pedro de Lima, Diogo Soares de Albergaria, Francisco Sousa Pereira, Simão d'Abreu and Dom Fer[n]ando Lobo, who had been wounded by a soldier by a shot, apart from two or three others that however did not harm him. In one of the [skirmishes I was accompanied by] a certain António d'Ándria, captain-major of the *bantins*, a good soldier born in these parts. Here two flag captains were killed, [namely] Dom Bernardo de Meneses and Dom Manoel d'Almada, together with two other soldiers, a local, and three or four [more] were injured. Dom António was shot in the face by a blowpipe arrow. Now I do not know whether a [local Malay] was instructed, or whether he did it of his own accord, [but] the gate that leads to the sea was opened. Through it some soldiers left out of sheer exhaustion. They went and rested in a palm grove that is located next to the gate. Dom António went there to rally them and [also] cure himself of the wound, since the arrow was poisoned. This refuge and rest that the men took, being ill from ongoing battle, could have got them into serious and manifest danger, and so I saw it was of utmost necessity not to let the enemy take heart and be given another opportunity to push forward. I went down the king's street bearing the flag of Christ, taking no more than 20 men with me, among them captains and soldiers, and by Divine Providence with these men I defeated the enemy and set him into flight. The desperate monarch turned tail and never returned to attack us, nor did he re-enter in the city in which he had lived for so many years. Here I waited a while until things subsided, but [I was] so exhausted and debilitated from these and many other deeds that — and I can assure Your Catholic Majesty — had the enemy succeeded in mustering reinforcements and returned to battle, I would have been [quite] unable to accomplish any more with so few people, notwithstanding my [firm] resolution to complete my mission. This being the case, I ordered that the city be set ablaze. Now the breeze that [normally] blows from the land to the sea arose, which did little to fan the flames, [but] suddenly, the wind miraculously shifted in a southerly direction. On that day and the next it blew so fiercely that all the wooden stockade and the [whole] city burnt and nothing was left standing. It was about half a *legoa* in length and one in circumference so that God, thus, triumphed in this battle. His instruments of victory were the captains and soldiers, and the fire extended as far as the eye could see. Matheus Pereira, with some soldiers from the companies who followed him, moved on the walkways along the wall that leads to the bastion of Kota Batu. He entered [the city] and found it already abandoned — but I believe that he found it full of people — captured it, and finished the mission since he told me that it ended in an instant. I ordered him to muster more men so as to ensure [our] victory. Some time later, as the fighting subsided, I entered inside and held it for six days, during which the soldiers continued their sacking and discovered a lot of buried goods and gold pieces. Among these I recovered the heavy artillery train, which comprised some 400 or 500 bronze pieces, including a Moorish basilisk, a lion, a reinforced serpentine measuring 26 *palmos* in length,[144] a camel of a larger calibre,[145] some cameletes,[146] falcons, falconets, ten pounders,[147] half-cradles,[148] and *chicorros*, which is light artillery.[149] Dom João Pereira, who by chance became separated from Dom António and his brother Dom Neno Álvares, went down a street that ran along the wall to the right-hand side. [He] had 150 soldiers in his company. There they all fought valiantly and were on their feet unflinchingly. This was very important, because if the enemy had stormed through that place and attacked us from the rear, it would have been very difficult. Pero Coelho and Lourenço Frões, captains of two oared ships, accompanied him, fought, and performed their duty.

In the Strait[150] and the anchorage before the city, more than 1,000 vessels were burnt, among these junks, *bâlos*, *sômas* and many *balões*.[151] [The enemy] burnt two more galleons, eight galleys, some foists and *lancharas*. The king had more than 3,000 muskets for his defence; most of them had been bought here [to Melaka] by the *klings*[152] from impoverished soldiers, and they then sent them to be sold in Johor.

The king of Johor had some 8,000 men to defend the city, among them Javanese, Minangkabau and Malays, because he received assistance from many places. The Portuguese soldiers who captured the city numbered about 400 men in all. Most of them held guard at sea, and there were [also] many sick among them. As a result, [and mentioned previously] captains and soldiers perished alike.[153] As for the enemy, the exact number [of fatalities] is not known, but in truth many perished in combat or taking flight.[154] The Javanese, who had earlier helped them in the jungle had now become incensed, and slaughtered a great many in the hope of looting the [dead], because the king had failed to repay a certain sum of money that he owed [to the Javanese] for rice. This they [simply] robbed along with many other goods.

These are the kings who came to help and participated in the defence of the city [of Johor]:

> Raja Ali, the king of Johor, who, among the monarchs of the South, bears the title of Emperor of the Malay Kings[155]

The king of Tukal[156]
The king of Indragiri
The king of Bintan[157]
Captains, dead and alive:
Kiai Lante, dead.[158]
[The] Raja Makota, alive.[159] He has fallen from favour with the king and is now a fugitive.
Adipati Kampar, alive.
Raja Lella, alive.[160]
His younger brother, dead.
Sri Nara'diraja, dead.[161]
His younger brother, dead.[162]
One of his brothers called Encik Gala, dead.[163]
Ninalante,[164] [initially] it was not known whether he is dead or alive, but it was subsequently learnt that he is dead.
Sri Mirabanca, dead.[165]

Due to our negligence, Raja Ali was the most powerful king in the South because of his alliances with [so] many rulers: with Aceh and with the king of Pahang and Patani, as well as with many other kings of Java; he corresponded with the king of Ternate in addition to the others I have mentioned above, whom he had under his empire. The city of Johor[166] was better placed than any other to blockade the Straits, impede Portuguese shipping, or besiege Melaka at all times. Still, it seems that Aceh is more powerful in terms of people and fleets, as in effect it is, judging by the alliances and inconveniences mentioned above. The former [Johor] emerged as a great enemy of the Christian faith following its defeat [by the Portuguese] and after [the king of Aceh] was murdered.

The king of Perak and [the king] of Kedah dispatched many ships bearing supplies and some pepper to this port [of Melaka, after] failing to conduct any trade with us in recent years for various reasons. Thus, more than 300 junks have arrived from Java; a cruzado [now] buys 40 *gantang* of [uncooked] rice, but before a cruzado would only buy you one.

After returning to this city of Melaka, I dispatched Dom Pedro de Lima, my brother, with two galleys, five foists and eight *bantins* to the Straits of Singapore and Kundur to protect the Javanese junks [coming to trade], to enter into the Johor [River] and reconnoitre the location and strength of the king in the river estuary.[167] He captured a galliot, aboard which the captain of Kundur was travelling and which, on account of a storm, had become separated from the king's fleet. Everyone [aboard the captured vessel] was put to the sword. The galliot was accompanied by a small ship that [managed to] escape and warned the king who was patrolling the seas with 25 small vessels and two galliots. Had this not happened, [the king] might have been captured [as well]. [Pedro de Lima and his men] set fire to the city of Bintan,[168] where they burnt a very beautiful galley that the king had built for himself. They captured six or seven *bâlos* that were [anchored] there, and [also] killed a lot of people. The city of Johor is [now] deserted; it has been subsumed by the forest and is full of wild plants. The king has no [more] wealth or power and has been forsaken by his friends and allies. These are the events that have occurred up until now. I mentioned in one of the passages that there were 500 pieces of artillery. I have [since] learnt from captive Malays,[169] who arrived later, that there were [originally] twice that number but most of them had been stolen or hidden away. Written in Melaka on 28 November 1587.

And in this manner they burnt more than 150 vessels that had run aground.[170]

Dom Paulo Lima de Pereira

APPENDIX 3

[The text featured in appendix 3 represent the navigational instructions for sailing from the Strait of Melaka to the South China Sea through the Old Strait of Singapore which according to some early modern sources of European origin is also known as the Varella Channel. The original Dutch text featured here has been taken from Jan Huygen van Linschoten's *Reysgeschrift* which was first published in 1595 and is considered to form an integral part of his work known as the *Itinerario*. Because of the important information contained in this publication, Linschoten's work was quickly translated into many European languages and was used by the first navigators who sailed from the Netherlands and other ports in northern Europe to the emporia of Southeast Asia. The original Dutch text and its English translation featured in Chapter 1 form part of the discussion in Chapter 2 of the waterways that during the early modern period and beyond were collectively known as the Straits of Singapore.]

Navigational Instructions for the Old Strait of Singapore according to Jan Huygen van Linschoten (1595), *Naer Oost Ofte Portugaels Indiën*, pp. iv, 97–9. Transcript of the original 16th-century Dutch text. A modern English translation is reproduced in Chapter 2.

De mont ofte inkomste van dese Straet, comt tusschen twee hooghe berghen in, wesende ontrent een steenworp inde breede, ende streckt oostwaert aen, mach hebben in de lenghte ontrent een schuet van een guetelingh. Het Canael van dese Straet heeft op het leeghsten 4½ vadem diepten. In 't incomen aenden voet van den bergh vande noordt zyde, is geheleghen een steen-clippe, welcke inde vorthooninge een Pylaer schijnt te wesen; Dese wort in gemeen van alle Natien (die dese passagie bevaren) ghenaemt die *Varella* vande Chinen, ende vande zuyd zyde, te weten, een stuck weeghs vande mont, van de Straet voort aen maectet eenen Inwijck. Int midden van desen Inwijck leyt een Clippe onder water, van welck een bancke af loopt nae het midden van het Canael toe. Wat voorder aen, aende selfde zyde, de lenghde van een Roer schuet, heeftet een open, het welc tot inde Zee aen d'ander zyde door loopt, makende een Eylandt. Dit open is over al vol ondiepten; dient alleen om met cleyne Fusten door te passeren. Te middelweghen van desen Inwijk daer dit open staet, leyt een Clippe ofte steen-plaet, twee vadem onder water, welcke steen plaet soo verder buyten den Inwijck comt, als de punten van het landt uytsteken, ende wat meer nae het midden van het Canael toe. Voor by desen Inwijck wesende, soo heeftet landt eenen hoeck ofte punt van eenen steylen afgebieckten huevel, alwaer de Straet voleyndt; ende int omloopen van dien, heeftet eenen rooden huevel, by de welcke men diepe ende suyvere grondt heeft, ende alsmender om geloopen is, so strect hem het landt vandaer af z.o. waert aen.

Men heeft aende noord zyde van dese straet, te weten, van 't beginsel tot het eynde toe drie inwijcken, waer van die twee eerste cleijn zijn, wesende de derde groot, welck is gheleghen recht teghens over den hoeck ofte punt vanden rooden huevel, daar de straet voleyndicht; Desen derden inwijck heeft een bancke van steen, die mettet leegh water van een sprinckvloet ontdeckt is, ende streckt van d'een punt tot d'ander; men sal hem wachten daer op te vervallen, alle 'twelcke vande noordt zyde is, ende buyten den Inwijck ist over 't gheheel Cannael van d'een punt tot d'ander suyver ende schoon.

In 't uytloopen vande Straet, soo heeftmen daer buyten zijnde, twee Riffen, waer van d'eene recht teghens over den uytganck vande straet leyt, een schuet van een lepel-stuck nae het oosten toe, comende van 't land vande noordzyde af, streckende zuyen aen; D'ander is geleghen in 't zuyen, te weten, een schuet van een goetelingh, vanden uytganck van 't landt, van de Straet af, streckende oostwaert aen, soo datse beyde gaer duer den anderen een cruijs maken, ende tusschen dese twee Riffen doorloopt het Cannael heen, ende men mach beyde dese Riffen (mettet leegh water van een sprinckvloet) ondeckt sien. Dit Cannael, welck tusschen beyden door loopt, heeft schaers 4 vadem diepte; De gront binnen in 't Canael is modder, ende buyten 't Cannael sandt; Hebbe dit alles also in 't particulier willen verhalen, tot dienst ende gherif voor den genen die daer van nu voort aen begheert door te passeren: want die deschriptie vande oude Derouten ofte Navigatie voor dese ghemaeckt, zijn seer cort ende duyster te verstaen, voor de geen die daer noyt door geweest en hebben, door welcke oorsake daer veel schepen aende grondt gheraeckt, ghestooten, ende groot perijckel ghepasseert hebben, jae etlicke verloren.

APPENDIX 4

[In 1575, the André Thevet, a geography and cosmographer under the patronage of the French crown, published his *Cosmographie Universelle* in 2 volumes. Volume 2, which is dedicated to Asia, features in book 11, chapter 24, a discussion on the "Island of Cingaporla near Melaka and of some other islands towards China". Reading this chapter, it is soon evident that by the "Island of Cingaporla" Thevet does not have the present day island of Singapore in mind, but a fictitious island that is separated from Peninsular Malaysia roughly along the course of the present-day Pahang and Muar Rivers, and broadly covering the present-day Malaysian State of Johor. Thevet's account is important in the context of Chapter 1 in highlighting the difficulties in both tracing the cartographical origins of the greater island of Cingaporla as well as in decoding early modern European toponyms around the Malay Peninsula at large.]

André Thevet, *Cosmographie Universelle*, vol. II, Paris, 1575, Livre XI, chapitre XXIIII, fol. 413 recto ff., *De l'isle de* CINGAPORLA*, pres de Malaca, & de quelques isles tirans à la Chine.*[171]

QUI VOUDRA adviser de pres l'assiette de *Cingaporla,* et comme elle est separee de Malaca, et quelle distance il y a de l' une à l'autre, qu'on regarde comme la Sicile est faite, et comme elle est divisee d'avec le païs de Calabre, quelles sont ses poinctes et Promontoires, et ainsi on pourra voir que l'espace et distance qui est de la Sicile à la Calabre, est toute pareille, et d'aussi peu d'intervalle, que celuy de Malaca à Cin-/[172] gaporla. Qu'on voye puis apres la poincte, qui regarde en Sicile l'isle de Malthe, et soudain on cognoistra, que c'est tout ansi que la poincte de

Cingaporla regarde l'isle de Burne, de laquelle et peult estre esloignee quelques soixante lieuës. Que si lon croit ce que les Anciens disent, que la Sicile fut jadis terre ferme avec le païs de Calabre, et que depuis par un tremblement de terre elle en fut separee, on pourroit amener une mesme fable de ceste isle, et du Royaume de Malaca, veu qu'elle n'en sçauroit estre esloignee de deux à trois lieuës de mer, et par un petit canal. Mais je vous veux bien advertir, qu'il ne fait guere asseuré s'engoulfer dans ledit canal: ains ceux qui sortent du port de Cingaporla, appellé *Muare,* du nom d'une ville bastie sur la marine, fault qu'ils entrent en pleine mer, et laissans le canal à main droite, prennent la route de Malaca, qui fait le voyage un peu plus long,[173] tout ansi que si on laissoit en nostre mer le destroit de Calais, pour crainte de la tempeste et orage, et on s'alloit mettre en haulte mer, pour descendre et prendre port en Angleterre. Ceste isle est grande, comme celle qui contient plus de trente lieuës de tour, assise en longueur, belle, et riche, sauf que vers le milieu elle est fort montaigneuse: qui cause que les vallons sont assez gras pour les ruisseaux et petites rivieres qui en sourdent. Le temps passé, avant que la ville de Malaca fust bastie, e lors que le Roy de Sian, nommé *Chamos,* nom d'une Idole jadis du peuple Moabite, en estoit Seigneur, en ceste isle se tenoient le plus riches du païs, et y faisoient leur trafic avec ceux de Sumathre, Burne, et isles de Moluques, non tel que à present, pource que ceux seulement du païs voisin y venoient troquer ce qu'ils avoient affaire l'un de l'autre. En ce temps là donc ils avoient un Gouverneur, qui estoit comme un Roytelet du païs, nommé *Perchoa*, qui signifie Seigneur de tous, à cause que ceste isle et le païs voisin, où est maintenant assise *Bumatta,* luy obeissoit. Apres ce *Perchoa,* estoit un autre, nommé *Aiam Campetit,* qui estoit comme Viceroy és parties plus haultes, tirant vers le Pegu. Le Gouverneur de Cingaporla avoit aussi bien que le Roy de Sian son maistre, un *Paraà,* qui est à dire Secretaire, et un *Concussaà,* qui estoit le Thresorier, levant les daces et peages, tant pour le Roy que pour son Seigneur. L'isle est abondante en Poivre: qui vous sera cognoistre qu'elle est fort chaulde, et exposee aux ardeurs du Soleil. Il y a en l'isle de Cingaporla des poissons fort monstrueux, qui meritent plus le nom de monstre que de poisson: entre autres un qu'ils appellent *Tiburon,* lequel a plus de douze pieds de long, et gros à la proportion de sa longueur, la teste fort grosse, et le bec long, les dents à deux rangees comme un animal terrestre, furieux outre mesure, et qui ne voit rien sur mer, qu'incontinent il n'engloutisse. Es rives où il descend, c'est le malheur du bestial qui y paist, ou des hommes qui s'y arrestent: veu que ceste bellue marine les occit, et devore: toutefois estant prins à un hameçon, gros de trois doigts, attaché à une grande corde, et y mettant quelque chose pour l'amorcer, apres qu'on l'a fait mourir, c'est bien la meilleure viande que lon sçauroit manger: et de ce poisson se fournissent de navires de ce païs là, apres qu'il est salé. Au reste, il n'est sans porter vertu sur soy, veu que son foye et cœur profitent grandement à ceux qui sont attains de fievre chaude, leur ostant l'ardeur de l'accez, et empeschant la resurie. Il a aussi un oz en sa teste, qu'on diroit estre de pierre: lequel est bon et utile à ceux qui sont tourmentez de la gravelle et pierre: et ce a esté experimenté en ceste sorte. Lon broye cest oz, est estant pulverisé, fault prendre de la pouldre, autant qu'il en tiendroit dans une coque d'Avelaine, le matin à jeun, avec du vin de Palmier, qui est leur breuvage, ou en un bouillon, et en ayant usé le patient deux ou trois matins, ne fault à se trouver fort bien. Les Indiens portent ces oz penduz à leur col, pour quelque superstition qu'ils ont, dequoy je ne vous sçaurois dire l'occasion: ce que j'ay aussi veu faire en quelques endroits d'Afrique. Et n'est seul ce poisson hideux en ceste mer, veu /[174] qu'il en a tel, qui de sa queuë, s'il attaint le timon de quelque barque, ne fauldra de le rompre, et renverser bien souvent le vaisseau en mer, tellement que plusieurs *Paroz,* c'est à dire Vaisseux en langue des Indiens, sont tournez c'en dessus dessoubz par l'effort de ces bellues. Ce poisson de vault rien à manger. De sa graisse, les Indiens allans en guerre, en oignent leurs lances, espees, e flesches, avec une autre drogue venimeuse: que si quelcun en est touché, à grand' difficulté en pourra il eschapper. Son sang est bien recueilli, pource qu'il est propre à la maladie des femmes: de sorte que quand elles se voyent detenues de ceste maladie, elles boivent du sang dudit *Tiburon,* par six matins:[175] et lors elles en cognoissent l'operation naturelle, ausssi bien que du sang d'Elephant. Ce peuple vit assez longuement: mais je pense que leur sobrieté et peu de manger les tient en vie si longue. Ceux qui sont proches des montaignes, se tiennent dans les grotesques et spelonques, soit pour eviter les chaleurs, ou qu'ils n'ont l'industrie de bastir des maisons, à l'exemple de ceux qui se tiennent en la planure. Au commencement du Cap et Promontoire de *Cingaporla,* est prinse la quatriesme partie des Indes, tendant jusques au grand fleuve de *Sian.* Ceux du païs appellent aussi cest riviere *Menan,* à cause de la grandeur et estendue d'icelle: veu que *Menan* en langue Indienne signifie autant que Mere des eaux. Mais allant à la Chine, vous laissez le chemin de Sian à gauche, et allez passer en pleine mer par les isles d'*Anibbe*, *Pulgor,* et *Palotigue*, qui sont du Royaume de Malaca: puis prenez la route des isles de *Pulocandor,* et *Pulosian:* l'une desquelles est faite tout ainsi que la figure d'un cœur, l'autre e figuree en triangle: lesquelles deux sont du Royaume de Cambaie, qui est une grande estandue de terre, commençant au destroit de *Sian,* jusques au Royaume de *Iangome,* vers le Septentrion, et qui confine aux terres de *Campaa,* tirant au *Catai* de l'Orient. Le long de ce Royaume court le grand fleuve de *Mecon,*[176] qui descend des terres de *Catai,* et depuis les montaignes de *Cambalu,* ayant son cours de plus de mille ou douze cens lieuës: dans lequel entrent tant de rivieres, que lors que le *Mecon* (dit *Mesollam* par les Indiens naturels, qui n'a autre signification en langue Syriaque, que Chose parfaite et paisible) veult entrer en mer, il fait un Lac, qui s'estend en longueur plus de soixante lieuës, et large plus de quinze, et a ses emboucheures si grandes et admirables, que pas un des fleuves susnommez n'est digne de luy estre egalé. Mais d'autant que la mer est mal navigable en ce costé, e que non sans grand peril lon approche l'entree de ce Lac, à cause que la coste e chargee des seches et battures, à peine de quatre navires s'en peult sauver un. Cambaie est assise sur ledit fleuve de Mecon, lequelle passe par le milieu de la ville, et tout aussitost fait le grand Lac, qui porte le nom de la Province. Elle est posee à quinze degrez de l'Equateur, ayant pareille elevation que le Pegu, estant grande et riche, non pour le trafic de la marine, mais plustost par ce qui est porté là du Catai, et goulfe de Bengala.

English Translation

Book XI, chapter 24, "Of the Island of *Cingaporla,* Near Malaca, and a Few Islands in the Direction of China."[177]

To describe the location of *Cingaporla,*[178] and how it is separated from Melaka, and what distance there is between the two, let us look at how Sicily is distant from the country of Calabria, what points and promontories there are, and then we see that the space and distance between Sicily and Calabria is quite comparable to the one between Melaka and Cingaporla. If we then look at the tip of Sicily that faces the island of Malta, we recognise that this is like the tip of Cingaporla facing the island of Borneo, from which it is some 60 *lieues* away.[179] If we believe the ancients who say that Sicily was formerly connected to Calabria and that it became separated through an earthquake, then we could make a similar statement also for this island and the kingdom of Melaka, seeing that the two are separated from each other by a small maritime channel that is only two or three *lieues* wide. But I strongly advise you not to enter this channel: and those who leave the port of Cingaporla called Muare (Muar), a city built on the shore, should enter the open sea, leaving the canal to their right,[180] taking the Melaka route, which makes the voyage somewhat longer, just like the Strait of Calais is avoided in our sea for fear of the tempests and thunderstorms, and it is preferable to go on the high sea in order to reach a harbour in England. This island is large, over 30 *lieues* long,[181] beautiful and rich, except near the centre where it is hilly: for which reason the valleys are an abundant source of water for the emerging brooks and small streams. In bygone days, before the city of Melaka was built, and while the king of Sian (Siam) by the name of Chamos, named after a former idol of the Moabite people,[182] was the ruler, the richest [people] of the country lived on this island and from there conducted their business with those of Sumatra, Borneo and the Maluku Islands, unlike at present because only those of the adjacent land now come to barter for whatever they need. During that time they had a governor who was like a little king of the land, by the name of Perchoa (King Phrachai),[183] which means lord over all because this island and the neighbouring land where Bumatta (Burma) is now located,[184] were subservient to him. This Perchoa (King Phrachai) was followed by another by the name of Aiam Campetit (Oya Kampenget),[185] who was a viceroy in the upper regions towards Pegu. The governor of Cingaporla had not only the king of Sian (Siam) as his overlord, but also a Paraà (Phra-Klang),[186] that is, a secretary, and a Concussaà (Klang) who was the treasurer,[187] levying imposts and tolls for the king as well as his lord. The island abounds with pepper; you should be aware that the island is very hot and exposed to the heat of the sun.

Around this island of Cingaporla there are monstrous fish for which the designation monster is more appropriate than fish: among other [names] there is one that they call *tiburon*,[188] which is more than 12 feet long, and thick in proportion to its length, with a very large head and long snout, with teeth in two rows like land-based animals, ferocious beyond measure, and there is nothing in the sea that it will not devour. On the shore that it visits it is of great danger to the livestock that grazes there or to any person that stays there because this marine beast kills and devours them. It is sometimes caught with a baited hook three fingers long, attached to a thick rope, after which they kill it. It is the best meat for eating known anywhere. This fish meat, after it has been salted, is used as provision on the ships of this land. The carcass as such is not without virtue, as the liver and heart are of great benefit to those who suffer from hot fever as they alleviate the ardour of the ailment and prevent a relapse. In its head it has a bone, said to be of stone, which is good and useful to those who are tormented by urinary gravel or calculi, as has been shown by experience. After this bone has been crushed and pulverised, a filbert shell full of this powder is taken in the morning fasting, together with palm wine which is their [local] brew, or in a bouillon, and a patient who has taken it for two or three mornings will find himself feeling well without fail. The Indians carry these bones suspended around their neck on account of some superstition which they have of which I cannot tell you the origin, but I have seen the same practice in certain regions of Africa. There are other hideous fish in this ocean. There is one that uses its tail to break the tiller of a bark whenever it is able to reach it, and very often turns it over into the sea, so that several paroz (prahus),[189] which means "vessel" in the language of the Indians, were overturned by the force of these beasts. This fish is not suitable for eating. The Indians going to war use the fat, mixed with another venomous drug, to grease their lances, spears and arrows, so that anyone touched by it will have great difficulty in escaping.

The blood is carefully collected as it is suitable against women's ailments. Those who see themselves afflicted by it drink the blood of said *tiburon* on six mornings; and they know that its natural power is as effective as that of elephant blood. These people live fairly long, but I believe that it is their sobriety and low food consumption that keeps them alive this long. Those who live near the mountains dwell in grottos and caverns either to escape the heat or because they are not industrious enough to build houses like those who live in the plains. The area from the tip of the Cape and Promontory of Cingaporla up to the great river of Sian (Siam) is referred to as the "fourth part of the Indies". The natives also call this river Menam (Chao Phraya)[190] because of its magnitude and length, for Menam in the Indian language signifies as much as mother of the waters.

But if you go to China you leave the Sian (Siam) route to your left and sail on the open sea towards the islands of Anibbe (Anambas), Pulgor (Pulau Aor) and Pulotigue (Pulau Tiga),[191] which belong to the Kingdom of Melaka.[192] You then take the route to the islands of Pulocandor (Pulau Condor, Côn Đao)[193] and Pulosian (Ku Lao Tu, Phú Quý),[194] one of which has the shape of a heart and the other the shape of a triangle. These two belong to the Kingdom of Cambai (Cambodia),[195] which is a vast land, beginning at the Strait of Sian (Siam), up to the Kingdom of Iangome (Lanna-Thai)[196] toward the north, and which borders on the country of Campaa (Champa),[197] situated in the direction of Catai (Cathay,

China) of the East. The entire length of this kingdom is traversed by the river Mecon (Mekong), which flows down from the region of Catai and from the mountains of Cambalu,[198] having a length of more than 1,000 or 1,200 *lieues*. It has many tributary streams so that the Mecon (the native Indians call it Messolam, which in Syriac has no meaning other than something perfect and pleasant) upon approaching the sea forms a lake that is more than 60 *lieues* long and more than 15 wide,[199] and its estuary is so great and wonderful that it is unrivalled by any of the aforementioned rivers. But the sea along this coast is difficult to navigate and the entry to this lake cannot be approached without danger because the coast is so full of shoals and outcroppings that out of four vessels only one can make it safely. Cambaie (Cambodia) is situated on the aforementioned Mecon River, which passes through the middle of the city and quite often forms a great lake that carries the name of the province. It is situated 15 degrees [north] of the equator,[200] having the same latitude as Pegu, and is large and rich, not because of the marine traffic but because goods are transported there from Catai and the Gulf of Bengal.

APPENDIX 5

> [The Biblioteca Nacional in Madrid owns a bundle of manuscripts whose authorship is traced Jaques de Coutre, a gem merchant who spent many years of the late 16th and early 17th centuries travelling through Southeast Asia. One text is reproduced here in the original Spanish (with a distinct Portuguese influence)[201] as well as the modern English translation. It assumes the form of a memorial (called *Emformación* by de Coutre) written in the 1620s in which he advises the construction of three forts around the Singapore and Melaka Straits: one on present-day Sentosa at the site of Fort Siloso, one along the east coast of Singapore island (near Changi) and one at the Muar River estuary in the present-day state of Johor. The construction of the forts was part of a broader plan devised by de Coutre to reverse the declining fortunes of the *Estado da Índia,* plug weak spots in Portuguese networks of trade, rein in Dutch freebooting in the Singapore and Melaka Straits, and to consolidate Johor within Iberian geo-strategic and mercantile interests. The letter is of central interest to the discussion of forts and security arrangements for the Singapore and Melaka Straits discussed in Chapter 3.[202]]

Madrid, Biblioteca Nacional de España, Ms. 2780, Jaques de Coutre, "Emformación para se hazer algunos castillos o fortaleças en el Estrecho de Sincapura y otras partes del sur, etc.", fols. 270 recto–274 recto.[203]

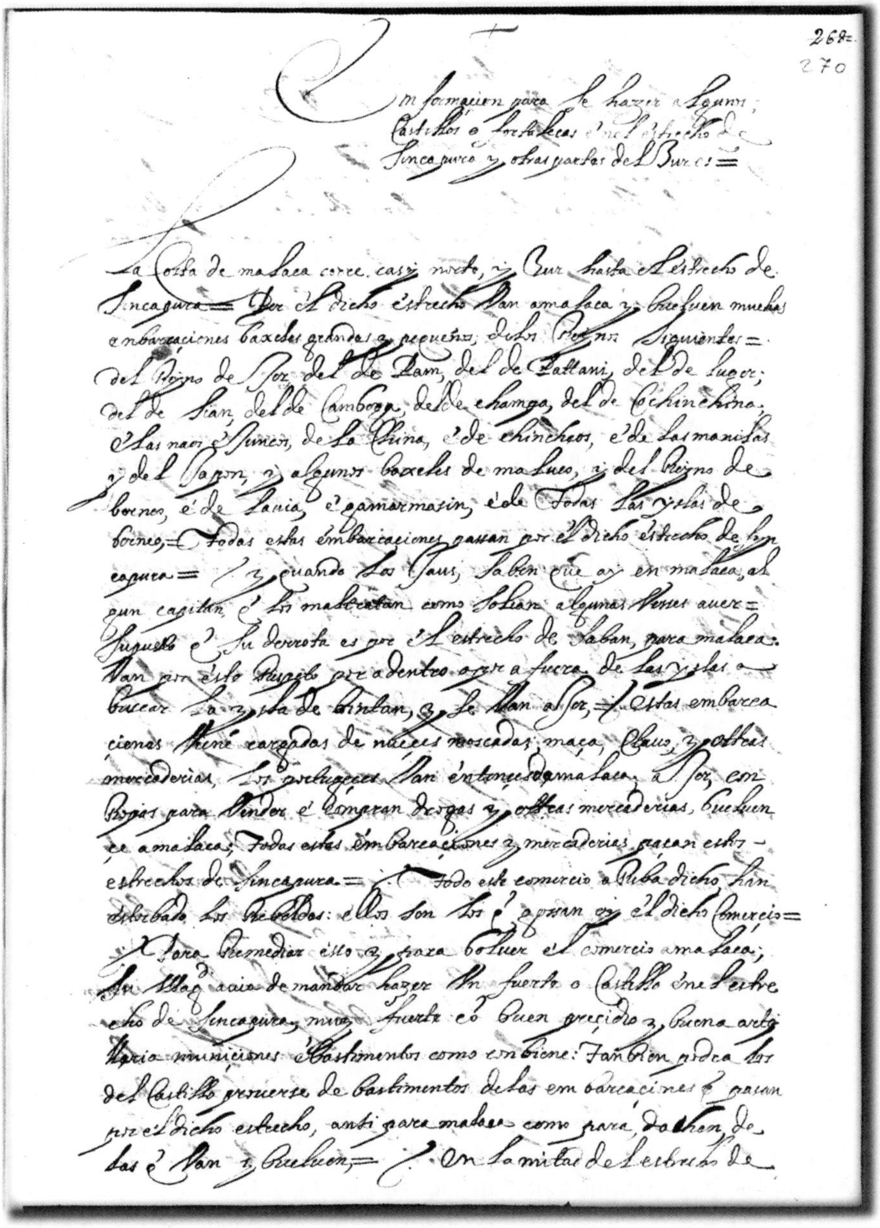

270

Informacion para se hazer algunos Castillos e fortalezas en el estrecho de Sincapura y otras partes del Sur

First page of the memorial in which Jaques de Coutre advises the King of Spain and Portugal to construct fortresses on present-day Sentosa, along the east coast of Singapore around Changi, and at the Muar River estuary. (Biblioteca Nacional de España, Madrid, ms. 2780, fol. 270 recto)

La costa de Malaca corre casy norte y sur hasta el Estrecho de Sincapura. Por el dicho Estrecho van a Malaca y buelven muchas embarcaciones, baxeles grandes y pequeños de los reynos siguientes: del reyno de Jor, del de Pam, del de Pattani, del de Lugor, del de Sian, del de Camboya, del de Champa, del de Cochinchina, e las naos e juncos de la China, e de Chincheos, e de las Manilas, y del Japón, y algunos baxeles de Maluco, y del reyno de Borneo, e de Lavio, e Gamarmasin, e de todas las yslas de Borneo. Todas estas embarcaciones passan por el dicho Estrecho de Syncapura.

Y quando los Jaus saben que ay en Malaca algún capitán que los maltratan, como solían algunas vesses aver, supuesto que su derrota es por el Estrecho de Saban para Malaca, van por este respeto por adentro o por afuera las yslas a buscar la Ysla de Bintan, y se van a Jor. Estas embarcaciones vienen cargadas de nueces moscadas, maça, clavo, y otras mercaderías. Los Portugeçes van entonces de Malaca a Jor, con ropas para vender, e compran drogas y otras mercaderías; buélvençe a Malaca. Todas estas embarcaciones y mercaderías paçan estos Estrechos de Sincapura.

Todo este comercio ariba dicho han estorbado los rebeldes. Ellos son los que gossan oy el dicho comercio. Y para remediar esso y para bolver el comercio a Malaca, Su Magestad avía de mandar hazer un fuerte o castillo en el Estrecho de Sincapura muy fuerte, con buen precidio y buena artillaría, municiones e bastimentos como conbiene. También podrá los del castillo proverse de bastimentos de las embarcaciones que pasan por el dicho Estrecho, ansí para Malaca como para d'Achén, de las que van y buelven.

Y en la mitad del Estrecho de /[204] Sincapura ay una ysla, que será de tres leguas poco más o menos. La dicha ysla corre de una parte el Estrecho Viejo, de la otra parte el Estrecho Nuevo. Viene esta ysla a hazer en medio del Estrecho una punta de pietra a modo de un fuerte de naturaleça. Esta punta se llama Surgidera; haze un lado el Estrecho Viejo, y del otro lado el Nuevo. En esta punta avía de mandar Su Magestad hazer un castillo muy fuerte: todas las embarcaciones que passan por estos Estrechos, ansí por el Viejo como por el Nuevo, se paran y echan áncora en la dicha punta poco más adelante o menos. Es forçado porque paçan estos Estrechos en dos mareas, ansí entrando por un lado como por otro.

Y el Estrecho Viejo es tan angosto que se puede serrar con una cadena; el Estrecho Nuevo es más ancho, pero no podrá paçar ninguna embarcación por ningunos destos Estrechos que los del castillo con la artillería no los metan a fondo. En esta punta ay catorce braças de fondo, yendo de Malaca passando por la punta de Tangonburi, entrando por el dicho Estrecho de Sincapura entre la Ysla de las Cobras y otra de muchos arboledos que llaman salgeros, entrando por el medio son ocho braças; pasando pegado la punta dies y dosse braças, y catorce en la dicha punta arriba dicha. Y de aý por el Estrecho Viejo son ocho y siette y seis hasta salir fuera; y desta punta por el Estrecho Nuevo son doce y dies y ocho braças hasta salir afuera.

En todo este Estrecho se puede hechar áncora por ser estos canales muy seguros de tormientas, como si estuvieran en un río, supuesto que tiene corrientes de agua. Pueden passer por ellos naves de a tres y quatro cubiertas, como las carracas de Portugal. Sobre esta punta de la dicha ysla pueden estar los baxeles tan serca de la tierra que se puede desenbarcar en una plancha si quisieran. La ysla es muy fresca de frondossos árboles y tiene muy buena agua. Y por esso Su Magestad avía de mandar que se haga un fuerte o castillo en esta ysla, como está arriba dicho. Esta ysla es algo alcantilada de piedra, no se puede desenbarcar tan facilmente, ny por esso es peor. A par de esta punta están unos salgeros. /[205]

Del lado del Estrecho Nuevo, allí se podía hazer una desenbarcadera para los bateles y galeras, naves, y para todo el servicio del dicho castillo. La ysla es playna y tiene algunos penhascos. Quando vienen o van nuestras naves para la China e Manilas e otras partes, podrán recojer — y los demás baxeles amigos — debaxo del castillo, quando tubieren noticia de enemigos. En este Estrecho ay muchos pescadores que llaman Salettes; viven desso. Es gente de la tierra, son Malayos. Como les hizieren buena compañía servirán bien. Estos hombres corren todas las yslas destos Estrechos, y adonde estubieren enemigos vendrán a avisar a trueco de un paño de quarto reales que den, y para ellos estaren a nuestra sombra.

Para efeto del dicho comercio es neseçario que Su Magestad tenga en el dicho estrecho sinco o seis galeras de Manilas bien armadas, sugetas al castillo, para franquear el Estrecho. Son las dichas galeras de Manilas ligeras para poder entrar y salir quando les estar bien. El enemigo no podrá hazer tantas presas como suele, ny podrán estar con una nao en una boca del Estrecho y con otra en otra boca, como suele hazer agora y toman todos las baxeles que paçan por los dichos Estrechos, por respeto de las galeras. No podrá el enemigo apartar sus naves unas de otra por las calmarías y poco viento que ay en estas partes. De este modo podrán franquear estos Estrechos y podrán venir las embarcaciones susodichas a este fuerte y a Malaca, las quales no pueden venir agora porque los enemigos los empiden. La dichas galeras podrán yr al Estrecho de Saban;

de allí no ay mais que dies leguas de estancia uno del otro y ay muchos canales para las galeras passar el dicho Estrecho de Saban. Luego en pocos días sabrán todos los passos por los pescadores que llaman Saletes. Estos Saletes viven en unas embarcaciones muy pequeñas; allí duermen y viven y nacen en las dichas enbarcaciones. Al fin es su cassa.

Quando llegare nuestra armada a este puesto para hazer el dicho castillo, avrá menesterse luego yntrincherarse en la propria punta que arriba diximos con sestones de tierra, y meter la artillería en medio con el modo y traça del fuerte que á-de quedar. No falta allí madera para se entrincherarse mientras se apareja materiales para se labrar el castillo. Allí no falta mucha piedra y muchas piedras blancas de la mar que llaman caran, que es como cal o yesso; ny tanpoco mucha leña para quemar después /[206] de aver hecho provizión de los materiales. Podrán entonces començar los muros y los baluartes y lo que conviniere. En acabando un baluarte enpeçar otro, de manera que siempre queden yntrincherados por lo que pudiere suseder. Para este y otros efettos Su Magestad avía de mandar yngenieros que entienda de fortificaciones.

Conviene que estos castillos sean muy fuertes, entonces los rebeldes no podrán passer por allí, ny este Achén con sus armadas para saquear a Jor ny al reyno de Pam. Les será fuerça passar por el Estrecho de Saban y rodear las yslas, o entre ellas; costaríanles mucho. Teniendo los nuestros allí galeras podrán franquear el dicho Estrecho de Saban, puesto que es ancho y tiene muchos baxos. Algunas vesses están las naos sette y ocho días sin poder passer por tener el viento contrario, aunque tienen la marea por sy. Es estrecho emfodasso, por este respecto son buenas las galeras para poder coger las naves surtas. De este modo harán gran daño al enemigo.

Vienen los rebeldes con sus naves, hechan áncora, y surgen en el dicho Estrecho de Saban afuera del río de Andregiri e Janbi, por ser poco hondo, para cargar pimienta. Dende la punta susodicha hasta este río no ay más que veinte y sinco leguas poco más o menos por los boquerones. Entretanto nuestras galeras podrán dar de noche o de día sobre ellos, y no podrán los enemigos cargar pimienta, que es el principal del comercio que ellos tienen. Como es serca de nuestra fortaleça, podrán los nuestros comerciar y tartar. En este río no entran syno enbarcaciones pequeños. Ny los rebeldes podrán estar seguros in Polinban, que es un reyno que siempre mostró ser nuestro amigo. De modo que con estas galeras y el castillo se podrá hazer gran daño al enemigo en su comercio, e franquear estos estrechos. Como estos estrechos estuvieren francos y libres vendrán de unas y otras partes todas las embarcaciones a este fuerte y a Malaca sussodichas, porque los Yndios se huelgan de vender sus mercaderías antes a nós que a los rebeldes, porque los dichos rebeldes hacen todas sus mercaderías estancos, ansí lo que compran como lo que benden. Y quieren notablemente mal a los dichos rebeldes, porque no venden ny compran como solían hazer los Portuguesses.

Es neçeçario hazer otra fortaleça o castillo en la barra de Jor, en la punta de la Ysla de la Sabandaría Vieja. Esta ysla haze la barra del río de Jor confina con el /[207] Estrecho Viejo y Salet Boru. Esta fortaleça quedará de ystancia de tres leguas poco más o menos del castillo del Estrecho. La dicha Ysla de Sabandería es de siette leguas poco más o menos. El castillo de esta boca del río de Jor y el del Estrecho podrán socorrer uno al otro por mar y tierra. Entre una ysla y otra queda el Estrecho Viejo; es como un río que se puede serrar con una cadena. Sobre la punta susodicha Su Magestad á-de mandar hazer un castillo como el otro que está dicho. Quedará señor de este puerto que es uno de los mejores que sirve la Yndia. Podrán hazer allí una ciudad y quedar señor de este reyno. Haziéndose este castillo allí no podrán entrar las naves enemigas que no metan en el fondo, supuesto que el río de Jor es ancho y la punta de Jor Viejo hecha una restinga mucho a la mar.

Y quando vienen las embarcaciones grandes, se arriman a la punta andonde se á-de hazer la fortaleça, y enfrente a tiro de piesa queda la restringa susodicha. En la dicha restinga podrán hazer un fuerte pequeño para franquear todo el río y enpedir que no entren baxeles pequeños ny grandes. Los enemigos rebeldes adereçan y dan carena a sus naves dentro de este río. El dicho río es muy ancho y hermoso; pueden entrar las naves cargadas y salir sin peligro hasta dies y dosse leguas por el río adentro. Y no falta en estas partes maderas para se entrincherarse luego en lleguando, ny falta materiales para labrar el castillo, ny falta piedras para hazer cal o yeso. Los Portugueses tomaron en este puerto junto a la punta susodicha — tomó Don Pablo de Lima — Jor Viejo, y no quisieron sustentar.

El rey de la dicha ciudad de Jor Viejo huyó y se fue a vivir en la ysla de Bintan, y después bolvió e hizo otra ciudad, que está el río adentro catorce leguas, que se llama Batusavar y los Portugueses llaman Jor Nuevo. Este puerto tomó el rey Achén y lo tiene ocupado, mas con mil y quinientos hombres se pueden desocupar, y tanbién la ciudad de Pam, que tienen el dicho rey de Achén ocupada. Y para este efetto fuera bueno llamar el dicho rey de Jor, que son quatro hermanos, y poner uno de ellos de posse. Como tuviéramos hecho los dichos castillos estaríamos seguros de gente de la tierra, y Su Magestad tendría un rey basallo como solía ser el de Ormús. Hasta que el tiempo /[208] diere más lugar y tendrán mantenimiento para sus castillos y lo que fuere necesario, ayuda y socorre para qualquier efetto, y el dicho rey de Achén no tendrá tan gran poder. Como los naturales vieren su rey y favor nuestro, en la ysla de Samatra: Çiaca, y Campar, e Bincales, y las terras de d'Arú todos se levantarán contra el Achén, que son Malayos.

Esta tierra era del rey de Jor, y la ysla de Samatra es un reyno que gobernava el raxo Siaca, que era hermano del dicho rey de Jor. Siaca queda a la entrada del Estrecho de Saban, era señor de más de sesenta leguas de costa; todo tiene agora ocupado el rey de Achén. En este río de Jor Su Magestad pudiera tener galeras y galeones. Pueden entrar y salir con marea e viento, e si Su Magestad tuviere en este puerto seys o siete galeones de Dunquerque, en ninguna parte del sur estarían los rebeldes seguros. Porque los dichos rebeldes hechan áncora y surgen en todos y más puertos del sur más de legua y media a la mar. Podíanse llegar a ellos, porque están apartados unos de los otros — en un puerto están una nao, en otro dos — y por la vía de los pescadores, como está dicho, podrá nuestras naves tener avisso adonde quedan los dichos rebeldes e hir sobre ellos. Como son de una nación muchas vezes se engañarán los nuestros a los rebeldes, ansí de noche como de día. De este modo se podrá quitar el comercio a los rebeldes y desruirlos.

Y para efetto de se hazer estos fuertes avrá menester que Su Magestad enbíe veinte galeones de Españoles castellanos, entre ellos algunos seis o siette galeones de Dunquerque, que haga quantía de veinte galeones bien guarnecidos de artillería y bastimentos con dosientos y sincoenta hombres en cada uno, y algunos yngenieros con petrechos que conviene para las fortificaciones. Y en llagando al Estrecho de Sincapura podrán enbiar avisso a Manila para si allá ubiere alguna armada que se venga a juntar con esta, prencipalmente las galeras que allá uviere. Y Su Magestad avía de embiar oficiales que sepa hazer galeras en el río de Jor. No falta sityo ny madera para labrallos, no falta árboles para mástil de las galeras, ny liames, ny curbas, ny remos, pez, aseyte para sifallas.

Quanto a la chusma para las galeras, /[209] pueden mandar a Goa buscar Cafres, que son negros fuertes como los de Angola. Se compran en Goa a veinte reales de a ocho cada cabessa. De Manila van a Goa a conprar para sus galeras, y cargan embarcaciones de essa gente. Tanbién podrán nuestros naos hir a la Costa de Cheramandel a cargar ropas y llevar drogas como hazen los Olandeses. Su Magestad tiene dos puertos en la Costa de Cheramandel, que se llama el uno Negapatán y el otro San Thomé, adonde se podrán descargar, y los Portuguesses se holgarán mucho con este comercio. De Jor o del Estrecho podrán embiar naves cargadas de drogas a España como hazen los Portuguesses, y de este modo se enchirá Espanha, Castilla y Portugal de drogas, y renderán las aduanas de Su Magestad mucho más. Y de aquí podrán los mercaderes enbiar a Francia y Alemania.

De esta manera no podrán los Olandesses hazer tanto provecho; de este modo se diminuirán ellos y su trato. Como es companhía de marcaderes, en no aviendo provecho cada uno se retirará de la dicha companhía, viendo el poco provecho. Manila y estos dos castillos a fortaleças, y Malaca e Macao podrán socorrer unos a otros, por ser serca. Los dos castillos, uno del Estrecho y el otro de la boca del río de Jor, á menester que se haga entranbos en un ynstante, los quales se podrá socorrer y ayudar unos a otros por la mar y por la tierra, como arriba está dicho. Y será neseçario entrincherarce luego: no faltará recaudo ni avrá quien los empida. Antes que vaya a noticia de los rebeldes ya estarán entrincherados. Podrán dexar dies galeones en el Estrecho debaxo del fuerte y otros dies en la boca del río de Jor, hasta asegurar los dichos castillos. Y después de aver hecho los dichos dos castillos podrán hazer otro en la punta del río de Muar; no podrá entonces el rey de Achén socorrer a Jor de ningún modo ny por mar ny por tierra.

Este río es muy hermoso y mucho mejor que el de Malaca. Pueden entrar en el dicho río de Muar con los juncos, balas, lanchares — que son embarcaciones de la gente de la tierra — y galeotas cargadas. E las naves no podrán entrar, mas podrán hechar /[210] hierro y surgir a tiro de piesa como en Malaca. Tiene buen sitio para tener galeras y fustas, tanbién no falta recaudo para hazerlas. Podrán hazer este fuerte sin enpidimiento de la gente de la tierra. Allí serca está un pueblo muy pequeño, cossa de muy poco momento — se llama Muar — mas tiene un playa de dos leguas muy hermosa. Al lado de la dicha playa ay unas caserías, cossa de poco momento; son de pescadores. Luego esta gente nos obedecerán y vendrán a vivir debaxo de nuestro fuerte, y la gente de Jor por consiguiente. En la dicha ciudad de Jor ay mucha gente que no viven sino de mercaderías y navegación de una parte y de otra.

Este es el mejor modo para destruir y deminuir los rebeldes que yo entiendo en my conciencia. Sy Su Magestad embiare quarenta galeones, sería de más efetto para acabar, y destruir, y espulción de los Olandesses que están en la Yndia Oriental.

Jaques de Couttre hizo aquella planta del sitio de los Estrechos de Sincapura y de Saban. Para remediar las dichas partes da a Vuestra Excelencia esta emformación comforme lo que se parece y trató con Vuestra Excelencia los días passados sobre el particular de quitar a los Olandesses el comercio que ellos tienen en la Yndia Oriental, etc.

Jaques de Coutre /[211]

Emformación que Jaques de Couttre da a Vuestra Excelencia para se hazer los fuertes en el Estrecho de Sincapura y en la punta del río de Jor en el sur, etc.

English Translation

"Information about Building Some Castles and Fortresses in the Straits of Singapore and Other Regions of the South, etc.", folios 270 recto–274 recto.[212]

The coast of Melaka extends north and south nearly as far as the Straits of Singapore. Many ships go to Melaka and return through these Straits, large and small *baxeles*[213] from the following kingdoms: from the Kingdoms of Johor, Pahang, Patani, Ligor, Siam, Cambodia, Champa, Cochinchina, and ships and junks from China, and Zhangzhou,[214] and from Manila, and Japan, and some *baxeles* from the Malukus, and from the Kingdom of Borneo, and Ryukyu, and Banjarmasin, and from all the islands of Borneo. All these vessels pass through the said Straits of Singapore.

When the Javanese know that in Melaka there is some captain who treats them badly, as sometimes was the case, though their course is through the Strait of Kundur to Melaka, they go from inside or around the islands in search of the island of Bintan, and they go to Johor. These vessels come laden with nutmeg, mace, cloves and other merchandise. The Portuguese then go from Melaka to Johor, with cloth to sell, and buy spices[215] and other commodities; and return to Melaka. All these vessels and wares pass through these Straits of Singapore.

All this commerce described above has been disturbed by the [Dutch] rebels.[216] They are the ones who today benefit from the said trade. To remedy this [situation] and to bring back [this] trade to Melaka, Your Majesty must order that a very strong fortress or citadel be built in the Straits of Singapore, with a good dungeon[217] and good artillery, munitions and supplies as is advisable.[218] The residents of the citadel could also acquire supplies from the vessels that pass through the said Straits, both from those that sail towards Melaka as well as those that are going to Aceh, from the ships that go and return.

In the middle of the Singapore Straits/[219] there is an island, which measures more or less three *leguas*.[220] The Old Strait is [situated] on one side of the said island, the New Strait on the other side. This island forms a stone peak [which is located] between the [two] Straits [and] that resembles a fortress created by nature.[221] This peak is called Surgídera;[222] the Old Strait lies on one side [of it], and the New Straits on the other. Your Majesty should order that a very strong citadel be built on this peak; all the vessels that pass through these Straits, through the Old Strait as well as the New Strait, stop and drop anchor around the said peak. It is necessary because two [daily] tides pass through these Straits, entering from one side as well as from the other.

The Old Strait is so narrow that it can be closed off with a chain;[223] the New Strait is wider, but no vessel can pass through either of these straits without being within reach of the citadel, which can sink them with artillery.[224] At [Surgídera] point[225] [the water] is 14 *brazas* deep. As one comes from Melaka [one passes] the tip of Tanjong Bulus, and enters the said Strait of Singapore between the Ilha das Cobras[226] and another island that is densely forested with trees that they call *salgeros*.[227] Entering by the middle [the water measures] eight *brazas* deep; when approaching the aforementioned [Surgídera] point ten and 12 brazas, and 14 next to it.[228] [Passing] through the Old Strait from this point [the water measures] eight, seven and six [*brazas*] up to the exit; [passing through] the New Strait from [Surgídera] point the water measures 12 and 10 and 8 *brazas* until one exits.

One can drop anchor anywhere in these Straits since these channels are safely sheltered from storms, as though one were in a river, although there are currents of water. Ships with three and four decks can pass through these Straits, such as the carracks from Portugal. At the tip of the said island the *baxeles* can come so close to shore that it is possible to disembark on a plank if necessary. The island is very lush with trees with [thick] foliage, and it [also] has very good [fresh] water.[229] This is why Your Majesty should order a fort or citadel to be built on this island, as mentioned above. This island has a number of stone cliffs, [where] it is not easy to disembark, but it is none the worse for this. There are some willows beside this point. /[230]

On the side of the New Strait, here one could build a quay for skiffs and galleys, [and] ships, and to service the said citadel. The island has places that are flat,[231] and others with cliffs. When our ships come and go to China, Manila and other parts, they — and other friendly *baxeles* — can take shelter below the citadel when they hear news of enemies.[232] There are many fishermen called *saletes* [*orang laut*][233] in these Straits. They are local people, Malays. If one accompanies and pays them, they will serve well. These *orang laut* visit all the islands around these Straits, and where there are enemies, they come to warn [us] in exchange for [a piece of] cloth worth four reales, which they are given, and for them to remain under our protection.

For the purposes of [maintaining] the said commerce, Your Majesty must maintain in the said Straits five or six well-armed Manila galleys, [that be] placed under [the command of] the citadel to patrol the Straits.[234] These Manila galleys are sufficiently light that they can enter and leave whenever necessary. The enemy will [then] not be in a position to capture as many [vessels] as they habitually do now, nor given the presence of the galleys will they be able to keep one ship at one entrance of the Straits and another at the opposite entrance, as they habitually do now, and capture all the junks that pass through these Straits. The enemy will no longer be able to separate their ships one from the other because of the lulls and the absence of wind that prevails in this region. In this manner the [galleys] can patrol the Straits, and the aforementioned vessels would be able to call at this fort and [also] at Melaka, which is presently not possible because the enemy impedes them from doing so. The galleys can proceed to the Strait of Kundur; from there one [Strait] is no more than ten *leguas* away from the other and there are many channels for the galleys to pass through the said Strait of Kundur. Thus, in a few days they will know all the passages thanks to the fishermen who are known as *orang laut*. These *orang laut* live aboard very small vessels; they sleep there and live and are born on their boats. In short, these vessels are their home.

When our armada will reach this place to build the said citadel, it will then be necessary to entrench oneself on the aforementioned peak [Surgídera] with sacks of earth, and place the artillery in the middle according to the manner and design of the citadel to be built. There is no lack of wood there to entrench oneself while one prepares materials to build the fortification. There is no lack of stone here and [there are] lots of white stones from the sea that they call [*batu*] *karang*,[235] which is like limestone or gypsum; there is also a lot of firewood to burn after /[236]

having made provisions for materials. They will then be able to begin the walls and the bulwarks and whatever else is advisable. When they finish a bulwark they can begin to build another, so that they are always entrenched [and prepared] for whatever might happen. For this and other purposes Your Majesty must dispatch engineers who are well versed in [building] fortifications.

It is advisable that these [proposed] citadels be very strong, [for] then the rebels will not be able to pass through here, nor the [king of] Aceh with his armadas to sack Johor or the Kingdom of Pahang. They would be forced to pass through the Strait of Kundur and bypass the islands, or sail between them; [in any case] it would be very difficult for them. When we have galleys stationed there, they can patrol the Strait of Kundur, although it is broad and features a lot of shoals. Sometimes carracks remain here seven or eight days without being able to sail through because of contrary winds, even when the tide is in their favour. It is a challenging Strait, and the galleys are thus ideally suited for capturing ships lying at anchor. In this way the [galleys] will inflict a great deal of damage on the enemy.

The rebels come with their ships to load pepper, drop anchor and moor around the said Strait of Kundur outside the Indragiri and Jambi Rivers, where [the water] is not very deep. No more than about 25 *leguas* separate the aforementioned point from these river estuaries. Meanwhile, our galleys can be on [their heels] night or day, and our enemies will not be able to load pepper, which is the mainstay of their commerce [in these regions]. Since it [would be] close to our [proposed] fortress, our men would be able to trade and negotiate. Only small vessels enter these rivers. Nor would the rebels find refuge in Palembang, which is a kingdom that has always been a friendly power. So with these galleys and the citadel one could inflict a great [deal of] damage to the enemy and his trade, and [also] patrol the Straits. When these Straits are patrolled and free [of enemy craft], all the vessels will come from all around to call at the fort and [also] Melaka. The Malays[237] are happy to sell their wares to us rather than to the [Dutch] rebels, because the rebels charge levies on all their merchandise, both what they buy as well as what they sell. They visibly do not like the [Dutch] rebels, because they do not sell nor buy like the Portuguese used to do.

It is necessary to build a second fortress or citadel in the Johor River estuary at the promontory of the Isla de la Sabandaria Vieja. This island is situated in the Johor River estuary and is bordered by the /[238] Old Strait and Tebrau Strait. This [second] fortress should be located about three *leguas* from the [first located] at the [Singapore] Straits. The said Isla de la Sabandaria Vieja measures about seven *leguas* across. The [second] citadel situated at the Johor River estuary and the [first one] at the Singapore Straits can lend each other assistance either by sea or by land. The Old Strait is situated between one island and the other;[239] it resembles a river that can be sealed off with a chain.[240] At this [second] location Your Majesty must order a citadel to be built like the first one that has been mentioned [above]. [Your Majesty] should become the lord of this port, which is one of the best that serves the [East] Indies. [Your Majesty] can build a city there and become the lord of this kingdom. By constructing this citadel there, no enemy ships would be able to enter without being sunk, even though the Johor River is wide and at the promontory of Old Johor is a shoal that is surrounded by sea.[241]

When large ships arrive, they move closer to the point where the fortress should be built, and across, [just] a stone's throw away, is the shoal. A small fort could be built on the said sandbank to patrol the entire [Johor] River and to prevent both large and small junks from entering. The enemy rebels repair and careen their ships in this river estuary. The [Johor] River is very wide and beautiful; ships laden with wares can enter and exit without any danger up to ten or even 12 *leguas* upstream. There is no lack of wood in these parts to entrench oneself after arriving, nor is there a lack of materials [with which] to build the citadel, nor a dearth of stones with which to make lime and plaster. In this port, near the aforesaid promontory, the Portuguese captured — [or should one better say] Dom Paulo de Lima captured — Johor Lama, but they did not wish to keep it.[242]

The king of the city of Johor Lama fled and went to live on the island of Bintan, and later returned and built another city, [located] 14 *leguas* upstream, which is called Batu Sawar, [but which] the Portuguese call New Johor. The king of Aceh captured this port and has kept it occupied, but it could be taken with 1,500 men, as could the city of Pahang, which the said king of Aceh has [also] occupied. For this purpose it would be good to call on the aforementioned king of Johor, since there are four brothers, and put one of them in power. Once we have constructed the citadels, we will be safe from the local people,[243] and Your Majesty would have a vassal king [just] like the king of Hormuz used to be. Over time there will be more space, and there will be more provisions for citadels and whatever is necessary, help and assistance for any purpose, and the said king of Aceh will no longer be so powerful. When the locals will see their king and our protection, on the island of Sumatra, Siak, Kampar,

Bengkalis and the lands of Aru, all of them will rise up against the [king of] Aceh, for they are Malays.

This land used to belong to the king of Johor, and the island of Sumatra features a kingdom that was governed by the raja of Siak, who was a brother of the said king of Johor. Siak is situated at the entrance of the Kundur Strait, [and the raja] controlled more than 60 *leguas* of coastline. The king of Aceh has now occupied all of it. Your Majesty could maintain galleys and galleons in this Johor River. They can enter and exit with the tide and wind. If Your Majesty had six or seven Dunkirk galleons[244] in this port, the rebels would not be safe anywhere in the South[ern Seas], because the [Dutch] rebels drop anchor and moor more than a *legua* and a half [from the shore][245] in each and every port of the South[ern Seas]. It is possible to get close to them, because they are separated from one another — there is one ship in one port, two in another. As has been said, with the help of the *orang laut*, our ships can garner information on the whereabouts of the [Dutch] rebels and attack them. As they belong to a single people, our men are very often mistaken for the [Dutch] rebels, both by night and by day.[246] In this way one can deprive the rebels of commerce and destroy them.

In order to construct these fortifications, it will be necessary that Your Majesty dispatch 20 galleons with Castilian Spaniards, among them [should be] about six or seven Dunkirk galleons, which make a total of 20 galleons. [They need to be] well-equipped with artillery and supplies, with 250 men on each one, and some engineers with the appropriate tools [to build] the fortifications. On arriving in the Straits of Singapore they can inform Manila, should there be an armada [stationed] there that could come and join them. [In Manila there are] principally the galleys. Your Majesty must dispatch skilled craftsmen who know how to construct galleys in the Johor River. There is no lack of [construction] sites or wood to construct them, there is [also] no lack of trees to make masts for the galleys, nor [a lack of] cordage, nor ribs,[247] nor oars, pitch, [or] oil with which to seal the hull.

As for the crews for the galleys, /[248] kaffirs can be brought from Goa. They are strong, dark-skinned people like those from Angola. They can be bought in Goa for 20 ryals-of-eight per head. From Manila the Spanish[249] go to Goa to buy for their galleys, and they load ships [full] of these people. Our ships could also proceed to the Coromandel Coast and load textiles and take on spices like the Dutch do. Your Majesty has two ports on the Coromandel Coast, one of which is called Nagapatnam and the other

São Tomé, where one could dispose of the cargoes. The Portuguese profit greatly from this commerce. From Johor or from the Straits one can send ships laden with spices to Spain like the Portuguese do, and in this way one will fill Spain, Castile and Portugal with spices, and Your Majesty's customs houses will yield much more. From there merchants can send [these wares] to France and Germany.

In this way, the Dutch will not be able to make such profits. In this way they and their trade will diminish. As [the VOC][250] is a company of merchants [and] if there are no profits, each one will withdraw from this company, seeing low profits. Manila and these two citadels or fortresses, [together with] Melaka and Macao, can assist one another, because they[251] are nearby. [As for] the two citadels, one in the Straits and the other at the mouth of the Johor River, it is necessary that they both be built in a trice. This will enable them to assist and help one another by sea and by land, as has been mentioned above. It will be necessary to entrench oneself quickly: there is no absence of safe locations, nor will there be anyone [there] to [stop] them. Before the [Dutch] rebels learn about [the arrival of our men],[252] they will already have established themselves. [Your Majesty] can leave ten galleons in the Straits by the fortress and another ten at the mouth of the Johor River, until the said citadels have been secured. After constructing the two citadels, [Your Majesty] can build [a third][253] at the tip of the Muar River; then the king of Aceh will not be able to assist Johor in any way, neither by sea nor by land.

The Muar River[254] is very beautiful and much better than the Melaka River.[255] One can enter the Muar River with junks, *balas*,[256] *lancharas* — which are vessels of the local people — or [also] laden galliots. [Large] ships cannot enter [the river], but they can cast /[257] anchor and moor close by as they do in Melaka.[258] It has a good site to harbour galleys and foists, and there is also no lack of secure places to construct them. [Your Majesty] can construct this fortress without hindrance from the local people.[259] There is a very small village nearby. It is not very noteworthy — it is called Muar — but it has a very beautiful beach that is two *leguas* long. Next to this beach there are some huts of minor significance; they belong to fishermen. Afterwards, these people will obey us and will come to live around[260] our fort, and consequently also the people of Johor. In the aforementioned city of Johor[261] there are many people who make a living only from merchandise and [from] sailing from one land to another.

This is the best way to destroy and diminish the [Dutch] rebels as per my understanding in good faith. If Your Majesty were to send 40 galleons, it would be more effective to put an end to, destroy, and expel the Dutch who are in the East Indies.

Jaques de Coutre devised this plan of the site of the Straits of Singapore and Kundur.[262] To remedy the said parts he gives to Your Excellency[263] this information according to what [the situation] appears [to be] and [as] discussed with Your Excellency recently, especially about depriving the Dutch of the commerce that they have in the East Indies.

Jaques de Coutre /[264]

Information that Jaques de Coutre sends to Your Highness to construct forts in the Straits of Singapore and in the Johor River estuary[265] in the South[ern Seas], etc.

APPENDIX 6

[The present excerpt from a letter by Afonso de Albuquerque to King Manuel I of Portugal, dated 1 May 1512, explains how the Portuguese, at a relatively early stage of their expansion into the maritime waters of Southeast Asia gained knowledge about the geography of the Malay Peninsula and the Indonesian Archipelago from a Javanese pilot. This recorded knowledge was vastly superior to anything the Portuguese possessed at the time, but the original sank with Albuquerque's flagship *Frol de la Mar* off the coast of Sumatra. The letter is of significance to the evolution of the 16th century cartography of the Malay Peninsula and the Indonesian Archipelago discussed in chapter 1 where the modern English translation of this Portuguese original is reproduced.]

Affonso de Albuquerque, *Cartas de Afonso de Albuquerque*, vol. 1 (Lisbon: Academia das Ciências Morais, Políticas e Belas-Artes 1884), letter from Affonso de Albuquerque to King Manuel I of Portugal, dated 1 May 1512, pp. 64–5.

… [Q]ue se tirou d ũa gramde carta d um piloto de jaoa, a quall tinha ho cabo de bõoa esperamça, portugall e a terra do brasyll, ho mar rroxo e ho mar da Persia, as ilhas do cravo, a navegaçam dos chins e gores, com suas lynhas e caminhos dereytos por omde as naos hiam, e ho sertam quaees reynos comfynavam huns cos outros: parece me, senhor, que foy a milhor cousa que eu nunca vy, e voss alteza ouuera de folgar muyto de ha ver; tinha os nomes por letra jaoa, e eu trazia jao que sabia ler e esprever; mamdo esse pedaço a voss alteza, que francisco rrodriguez empramtou sobre a outra, domde voss alteza poderá ver verdadeiramente os chins domde vem e os gores, e as vossas naos ho caminho que am de fazer pera as ilhas do cravo, e as minas do ouro omde sam, e a ilha de jaoa e de bamdam, de noz nozcada e maças, e a terra delrrey de syam, e asy ho cabo da terra da navegaçam dos chins, e asy pera omde volve, e como daly a diamte nam navegam: a carta primcipall se perdeo em froll de la mar: co piloto e com pero dalpoem pratiquey ho symtir desta carta, pera lá saberem dar Rezam a voss alteza; temde este pedaço de padram por cousa muyto certa e muyto sabida, porque he a mesma navegaçam por omde eles vam e vem: mimgualhe o arcepelago das ilhas que se chamam celate, que jazem amtre jaoa e malaca.

APPENDIX 7

[The log of one of the earliest Dutch captains to the East Indies, Joris van Spilbergen, provides a little known summary of the cargo found on the carrack *Sta. Catarina* that was taken by Jakob van Heemskerk off the east coast of Singapore on 25 February 1603. Spilbergen met Heemskerk in Banten in 1603 before the latter set sail on his homeward journey to Europe. The excerpt is taken from Spilbergen's log entry of 20 August 1603. This description of the rich cargo from China is relevant for discussing the so-called "Sta. Catarina incident" in Chapter 2 where a modern English translation of the original Dutch text is reproduced.]

F. C. Wieder, ed., *De reis van Joris van Spilbergen naar Ceylon, Atjeh en Bantam, 1601–04* (The Hague: Martinus Nijhoff, 1933), pp. 82–3.

Den 20. ditto is op de Reede voor Bantam ghecomen den Admirael Sr. Jacob Heemskerck met zijn schip ghenaemt den Witten Leeuw, ende Jan Pauwelssz sijnen Vice-Admirael het schip ghenaemt Alcmaer, met hun brenghende een groote nieuwe Crake, comende van Macau, wt China, wilde naer Malacca, de selfde hebben sy ghewacht ontrent Iorre, naer langhe wachtens heeftse God in haren handen ghegheven, hoe wel de Portugisen haer een tijt lanck dapper gheweert hadden, moesten haer met schip, goedt, ende persoonen overgheven. Dese voorsz. Cracke heeft voor ballast Coper, Pyaster, Alluyn, menichte Lignom oliom, Radisina. Voorder zijde ghewrocht ende onghewrocht, een partije onghemunt Goudt ende veel ander costelickheydt, alzo dat sy boven de plunderinghe wort gheextimeert over de tseventich hondert duysend Gulden.

APPENDIX 8

[Pedro de Teixeira is one of the early 17th century Iberian travelers to the East Indies. The following excerpt has been taken from his rare Spanish-language *Relaciones* printed in 1610 and provides a little-known description of the maritime passage along the west coast of Singapore (Pasir Panjang) and the route through the Old Strait of Singapore between present-day Sentosa and Telok Blangah. The description is of importance to Chapter 1 where a modern English translation is also reproduced.]

Leiden University Library, 1365.H.17. Pedro Teixeira, *Relaciones ... d'el origen descendencia y successión de los Reyes de Persia, y de Harmuz* (Amberes: En casa de Hieronymo Verdussen, 1610), bound together with *Relación del camino que hize dende la India hasta Italia*, p. 48.

… [E]ncostandonos àl cóntinente passando por Muar y Polé Rios en el de nombre, llegamos al estrecho de Sincá purá, que entre el y las islas que hazen el otro de Sabam se contiene: el qual haziendo la figura de una 5. es por espacio de media legua tan estrecho; que las naves que de la India van a la China, o por el contrario, no pudiendo (si a caso les fuesse forçoso) dar en medio del una buelta en redondo, por su mucha angostura; suelen en llegando a el, por qualquiera de las bocas echar ancla, aguardando occasion de marea, para con ella llevando el batel por delante para susten ella y hazerle cabeça, passar el estrecho: y acaesce algunas vezes aguardar por esta coniuncion tres, y quatro, y cinco dias, que tantos y mas y menos sin orden cierta succede correr la marea hazia una parte, que cierta succede correr la marea hazia una parte, que cierto es cosa digna de admiracion.

APPENDIX 9

[The *Dag-Register Batavia* is a diary recorded and kept at the fortress of Batavia during the lifespan of the Dutch East India Company (VOC). Transcription and publication began in the late 19th century, but the project was never fully completed. The published volumes broadly cover the period between the 1620s and the 1680s. The *Dagh-Register* features a broad palette of information brought in by captains, mariners and merchants from around Asia and the east coast of Africa. Scholars and students of history have long recognized the *Dagh-Register* to be a treasure trove of information for 17th century politics, trade and society in Asia and beyond. The following exceprt provides an account of how the Dutch chased down a Portuguese merchant in 1633 who sought to evade VOC squadrons patrolling the Straits of Singapore by sailing between the islands of the Riau Archipelago. The excerpt in the original Dutch reproduced below is important in the context of Chapter 5 where it is also featured in a modern English translation.]

Dagh-Register Batavia, 1631–4, pp. 162–3.

Item, dat d'onse vuijt zeecker Mallaijer van Bintang vernomen hadden, dat vier cloucke Portugeesche navetten comende van Maccauw vuijt vreese van onse cruijssende jachten te rescontreren, haere passagie door de eijlanden ende drooghten van Bintam genomen hadden, ende dat d'onse daer over te raede geworden waeren, deselve door de voorseijde eijlanden ende drooghten, met de gantsche vloote te vervolgen, ende tot een guide te gebruijcken den voornoemden Malleijer die van dito eijlanden ende drooghten niet alleenlijk goede kennisse hadde, maer ook met zijnen vader (wien de Portugeesen tot haeren leijtsman gebruijkten) versproocken was, de Portugeesen tot de aencompste onser scheepen inde voorseijde eijlanden ende drooghten dralende te zullen houden. Welken volgende d'onse de voorseijde Portugeesche navetten ... nagejaecht ende den weg (die deselve nootwendich mosten passeeren) affgesneden hebben, naerder ende naerder aprocherende, t' welcke de Portugeesen vermerckende, ende haer tegen onse macht te swack vindende, hebben deselve navetten alvooren met alderhande brandende materie ende vierwerken behangen sijnde, in brandt gesteecken, zonder dat zij vuijt deselve iets zonderlings als het gerede gout hebben connen salveeren, alsoo soo schierlijcken in den brandt geraeckten, dat die noch door ons noch door de inwoonders van de voorseijde eijlanden (die in groote menichte de selve geplundert ende grooten buijt becomen hebben) geblust conden werden.

Notes

Introduction

1 For a useful synopsis of the structure, inner workings and problems of the Portuguese *Estado da Índia* in and around the Southeast Asian region at large, see the very useful article by John Villiers, "The Estado da Índia in Southeast Asia", in Kratoska, gen. ed., *South East Asia*, I, "Imperialism before 1800", ed. Peter Borschberg, pp. 151–78. This can be supplemented by Scammell, "Indigenous Assistance in the Establishment of Portuguese Power in Asia in the Sixteenth Century", in Kratoska, gen. ed., *South East Asia*, I, pp. 141–50.

2 Miksic, *Archeological Research on the "Forbidden Hill" in Singapore*, p. 34.

3 Derek Heng Thiam Soon, "Reconstructing Banzu", *JMBRAS* 75, 1 (2002): 69–90. See also Miksic, "Geography and Traditional Warfare", in *Between Two Oceans*, ed. Murfett, Miksic, Farrell and Shun.

4 Wolters, *Early Indonesian Commerce.*

5 Ptak, "Reconsidering Melaka", in *Iberians*, ed. Borschberg, pp. 1–22; Ptak, *China, the Portuguese.*

6 Geoff Wade, ed., *Southeast Asia-China Interactions.*

7 Ptak, *Die Maritime Seidenstrasse.*

8 For a comprehensive critique of this model, see also Sutherland, "Southeast Asian History", *JSEAS* 34, 1 (2003): 1–20.

9 See, for example, Thomaz, *De Ceuta*; *Early Portuguese Malacca*; *Nina Chatu*; "The Malay Sultanate", in *Southeast Asia*, ed. Anthony Reid, pp. 69–90;

"Malaka et ses communautés marchandes au tournant du 16ᵉ siècle", in Lombard and Aubin, *Marchands et hommes d'affaires asiatiques*, pp. 31–48.

10 See, for example, Alves, *O domínio*; Pinto, *Portugueses e malaios*; Lobato, *Política e comércio*; Guedes, *Interferência e integração.*

11 Meilink-Roelofsz, *Asian Trade*; Reid, *Southeast Asia.* See also Borschberg, "Malacca as a Sea-Borne Empire", in *Water and State*, ed. Borschberg and Krieger, pp. 35–74; Dunn, *Kampf um Malakka*; Muhammad Yusof Hashim, *The Malay Sultanate*; Milner, McKinnon and Luckman Sinar, "Aru and Kota Cina", *Indonesia* 26 (1978): 1–42; Subrahmanyam, *Improvising Empire*; Teixeira, *The Portuguese Missions*; Wake, "Melaka in the Fifteenth Century", in *Melaka: The Transformation*, ed. Singh Sandhu and Wheatley, I, pp. 128–61.

12 Andaya, "Melaka under the Dutch", in *Melaka: The Transformation*, I, ed. Singh Sandhu and Wheatley, pp. 195–241; Barnard, *Multiple Centres*; Fernando, *Murder Most Foul*; Hussin, *Trade and Society*; Lewis, *Jan Compagnie*; Meyer Timmerman Thijssen, *Twee Gouverneurs*; Vos, *Gentle Janus*. See also Fernando, "Metamorphosis", in *Iberians*, ed. Borschberg, pp. 161–84.

13 Netscher, *De Nederlanders* (NJS); Winstedt, "A History of Johore", *JMBRAS* 10, 3 (1932): 1–167. This classic exposé has appeared as a separate book in several *JMBRAS* reprints. For a synopsis of the criticisms brought against Winstedt, see especially Kwa, "Records and Notices of Early Singapore", in Miksic, *Archeological Research on the "Forbidden Hill" in Singapore*, p. 107 note 5.

14 Leonard Andaya, *The Kingdom of Johor*. See also the criticism brought forward by Miksic, *Archeological Research*, p. 34, "The period of Singapore's history between the Portuguese attack of 1613 and the British arrival in 1819 is nearly completely blank. Dr. Andaya's analysis of the Melaka sultanate's successors between 1641 and 1728 has nothing to say on the subject...."

15 Das Gupta, "Acheh in Indonesian Trade and Politics, 1600–1641".

16 Lombard, *Le Sultanat d'Atjéh*; van Ittersum, *Profit and Principle*; van Veen, *Decay or Defeat.* See also Alves and Manguin, *O Roteiro*; Manguin, *Les Portugais sur les côtes du Viêt-Nam*; Manguin, "The Merchant and the King: Political Myths of Southeast Asian Polities", *Indonesia* 52 (1991): 41–54; Manguin, "Palembang and Sriwijaya: An Early Malay Harbour-City Rediscovered", *JMBRAS* 66, 1 (1993): 23–46; Manguin, "The archaeology of early maritime polities", in Glover and Bellwood, *Southeast Asia*, pp. 282–313; van Ittersum, "Hugo Grotius in Context", *Asian Journal of Social Sciences* 31, 3 (2003): 511–48; Pinto, "Melaka, Johor and Aceh", in *Nouvelles Orientations*, pp. 111–33.

17 Lombard, *Le Sultanat d'Atjéh.* See also Lombard, "Le sultanat malais comme modèle socio-économique", in Lombard and Aubin, *Marchands et hommes d'affaires asiatiques*, pp. 117–24.

18 Manguin, P.-Y., *Les Portugais sur les côtes du Viêt-Nam*; "The Merchant and the King: Political Myths of Southeast Asian Polities", *Indonesia* 52 (1991):

41–54; "Palembang and Sriwijaya", *JMBRAS* 66, 1 (1993): 23–46; Alves and Manguin, *O Roteiro*.

19 Ruangsilp, *Dutch East India*.

20 See also van Ittersum's introduction in Grotius, *De Jure Praedae Commentarius*; Borschberg, "Hugo Grotius, East India Trade", *JSEAS* 33, 2 (1999): 225–48, "De Societate Publica", *Zeitschrift der Savigny-Stiftung für Rechtsgeschichte*, Romanistische Abteilung 115 (1998): 355–93; Borschberg, *Hugo Grotius' Theory*, pp. 10–2.

21 See also Borschberg, "Luso-Johor-Dutch Relations", in *Rivalry and Conflict*, ed. van Veen and Blussé, pp. 188–218.

22 See classically the contribution of "The Estado da Índia in Southeast Asia", in Kratoska, gen. ed., *South East Asia*, I, pp. 151–78.

23 Hill, ed. and tr., "Hikayat Raja-Raja Pasai", *JMBRAS* 33, 2 (1960): 1–215.

24 See Teeuw and Wyatt, eds., *Hikayat Patani.*

25 Concering the dating of Nuruddin al-Raniri's *Bustan-as-Salatin* to 1638 or thereabouts, see Winstedt, *A History of Classical Malay Literature*, p. 162; Winstedt, "Bustan as-Salatin", *JSBRAS* 82 (1920): 151–2.

26 For a useful synopsis of extant Chinese and Malay source materials touching on pre-modern Singapore and the Straits, see the useful synopsis by Kwa, "Records and Notices of Early Singapore", in Miksic, *Archeological Research*, pp. 101–17, 129–30 together with the sources mentioned in the main text and the footnotes, as well as the sailing directions translated from Chinese into English on pp. 124–6.

27 Tibbets, *Arab Navigation*; Tibbets, "The Malay Peninsula", *Malayan Journal of Tropical Geography* 9 (1956): 21–57. See also Kwa, "Records and Notices of Early Singapore", in Miksic, *Archeological Research*, pp. 126–7.

28 Ferrand, *Relations de voyages*; Ferrand, ed., *Voyage du Marchand*; Bittner and Tomaschek, *Die Topographischen Capitel*; see also Tibbets, "The Malay Peninsula", pp. 44–6; Pijnappel, "Over de kennis", *BKI* 7 (1873): 135–58.

29 Tibbetts, "The Malay Peninsula", pp. 43–4.

30 See for example *John Leyden's Malay Annals*, introduction by V.M. Hooker and M. Barry Hooker, MBRAS Reprints, pp. 45, 46, 47 where "Singapura" refers to a kingdom and possibly a city; p. 48, where the name refers to a city or a location, and pp. 49–65, as a city or a *negeri* (polity, kingdom).

Chapter 1

1 Colenbrander, ed., *Gedenkschriften*, pp. 560–1.

2 As the author has not found a single reference to "Temasek" (or any orthographical variant) on any map of European origin dating from the late medieval or early modern period, this name shall not be employed in the present book. In any case, doubts have been raised as to whether ancient

Temasek was really located on the present-day island of Singapore. The eclipsed trading city is mentioned by Barros, *Décadas da Ásia*, déc. III, book V, ch. IV, where one finds the reference to ancient Singapura "que ali esteve antigamente" [which was there in ancient times]. See also Roland Braddell, "Lung-Ya-Men and Tan-Ma-Hsi", *JMBRAS* 42, 1 (1969): 10–24, especially p. 11, "The *Sejarah Melayu* tells us that a settlement was made on the island of Temasek, which Dr. Blagden says is pronounced by Malays as Temasak ..., and that the name of Singapura (or Singhapura) was given to this settlement. This custom of giving honorific names to places was obtained from the Hindus and persists among Malays to the present time. Singapura was a Hindu-Malay rajadom. Dr. Linehan's latest dating gives Singapura an existence from 1299 to 1391 A.D. and places its sack, so graphically recorded in the *Sejarah Melayu*, as having occurred in 1376 A.D."

3 Anonymous, *Held-dadige Scheeps-togt*, pp. 202–3. Barros, *Décadas da Ásia*, déc. II, liv. VI, cap. I, déc. III, liv. V, cap. V.

4 *Held-dadige Scheeps-togt*, pp. 207–9. See also Josselin de Jong and van Wijk, "The Malacca Sultanate (An Account from a hitherto untranslated Portuguese source)", *JSEAH* 1 (1960): 22.

5 This etymological deconstruction of the name is not far removed from Paul Wheatley's understanding of "singgah pura", that is, the "city where one breaks one's journey". See Wheatley, *Impressions*, p. 103. By contrast, some modern scholars have sought to establish connections with Buddhist religious groups, Siam, Sunda, or related toponyms see for example the account in Miksic, *Archeological Research on the "Forbidden Hill" in Singapore*, pp. 26–30. An additional account on the founding of Singapore encountered in Portuguese sources can be found in the *Commentarios* of Albuquerque first published in 1576. For a modern English translation of Albuquerque's account of the founding of Singapore, see Kwa, "Records and Notices of Early Singapore", in Miksic, *Archeological Research*, pp. 118–9. For a translation of Barros, see Kwa, "Records and Notices", pp. 120–1.

6 As is the case with any early modern source, be it of European or even Asian origin, the exhortation of Wolters should be borne in mind: "Nowhere are errors more likely than in the spelling of ancient place-names, of the meaning of which the copyist was almost certainly ignorant." Wolters, *The Fall of Srivijaya*, p. 95.

7 For an English language example of this, see the text of "The Estates, Empires and principalities of the World" dating from 1615 and republished by Caldecott in 1920: "The towne of Sincapure lies in the remotest Southerne part of this countrie upon a cape, which some take for the great Promontorie wheras Ptolemee sets the town of Zabe. ..." See Caldecott, "The Malay Peninsula in the XVIIth and XVIIIth Centuries", *JSBRAS* 82 (1920): 131.

8 See, for example, Mercator (1541), Gastaldi (1561, 1564), Ortelius (1567, 1570), Claesz, and Langren (the latter having been added to the published edition of van Linschoten's *Itinerario*). Koeman, Schilder, van Egmond and van der Krogt, "Commercial Cartography and Map Production in the Low Countries, 1500–ca. 1672", in Woodward, *History of Cartography*, III, pp. 1309, 1310; Schilder and van Egmond, "Maritime Cartography in the Low Countries during the Renaissance", in Woodward, *History of Cartography*, III, pp. 1410–1. A copy of the printed map of Asia included in Linschoten's *Itinerario* is found in the University Library, Amsterdam, sign. O.K. 139.

9 See Reinel (1518, 1519), Salviati (1525), Castiglioni (1525), Ribero (1529) and Gutierrez (1551). There are a few instances dating from the 16th and the first half of the 17th centuries known to the author where the name Singapura refers to the port, namely, in the letters of the Florentine nobleman Giovanni da Empoli, the chronicles of Fernão Lopes de Castanheda as well as the biography and memorials of the Flemish diamond merchant de Coutre. The 16th-century Portuguese chronicler Barros mentions Cingapura as a (single) strait on a number of occasions as do John of Lisbon and later Bocarro. See Barros, *Décadas da Ásia*, déc. II, liv. IX, cap. II and III; déc. III, liv. II, cap. VIII; déc. III, liv. V, cap. IV, déc. III, liv. VIII, cap. VII; déc. III, liv. X, cap. VI; Rebello, ed., *Livro de Marinharia*, pp. 268–70, "Rota pera Çimquapura, Borneeo e Maluquo". On p. 269, John of Lisbon mentions the strait (*estreito*) of *Çimquapure*, which he claims measures only a gunshot wide. On the same page he also speaks of Singapore as a settlement (*povoçã*). Bocarro, *Década XIII*, pp. 96, 416, 427, 428, 625, 742 (continuous pagination across both volumes). António Galvão understands Singapura strictly in terms of a strait, while Pigafetta's account of the Magellan expedition refers to Singapura as a town or city. See *Tratado dos Descobrimentos*, pp. 84, 166, and Pigafetta, *Magellan's Voyage*, pp. 152, 205.

10 Barros, *Décadas da Ásia*, déc. II, liv. VI, cap. I; déc. III, liv. V, cap. IV; déc. III, liv. V, cap. VII. Note especially the wording in déc. III, liv. V, cap. IV, "que ali esteve antigamente", which is freely translated as (a city that) "used to be there" or "was there in ancient times".

11 The charts penned by the VOC hydrographer Gerritsz in 1620 and 1621 are the oldest three maps known to the author on which the equator is shown in its correct location, namely, running through the island of Lingga rather than farther to the north through the island of Bintan. The manuscripts concerned can be found in the Staatsbibliothek Berlin, sign. Kart. T 7557, T 7567 and T 7165. The author would like to thank the curators in Berlin for arranging reproductions of these singularly important charts. On the charts of Gerritsz generally, see Schilder and van Egmond, "Maritime Cartography in the Low Countries during the Renaissance", in Woodward, *History of Cartography*, III, pp. 1426–8.

[12] Miró, Algàs and Cantón, ed., *Atlas Miller*. See also Thomaz, "The Image", in Kratoska, gen. ed., *South East Asia*, I, pp. 42–62 and the 22 map plates belonging thereunto. One must bear in mind what a map intended to achieve. See for example Fernández-Armesto, "Maps and Explorations in the Sixteenth and Seventeenth Century, in Woodward, *History of Cartography*, III, p. 751, "Except where indigenous prototypes were available, the earliest surviving efforts at mapping by explorers seem feeble and amateurish. Once dubious or authentic material is excluded, no map or anything that might be called a map has survived from any exploring venture until near the end of the second decade of the 16th century. The sketch of the Caribbean (c. 1520) — known, from the name of the expeditions patron, as the Pineda map — was obviously intended not to be of any practical help to a navigator in the Gulf of Mexico, but merely to convey to lay eyes on a general impression of an immense, roughly circular gulf with the Yucatán Peninsula intruding form one side and an etiolated shape, intended to represent Cuba, from the other."

[13] Leiden University Library, Collectie Bodel Nijenhuis, 006-15-021, "De Straat van Sincapura, leggende aan den hoek bij Malaka en 't eiland Bintang". The map is catalogued and described in Vries, *Uit de Kaartenwinkel*, p. 54, no. 61.

[14] Jacques N. Bellin, *Carte Réduite des Détroits de Malaca, Sincapour et du Governeur*, 1755. Also Gibson-Hill, "Singapore Old Strait", p. 58.

[15] See, for example, Costa, ed., *Livro de Marinharia*, p. 97, section 3, "Declaração da monção de Malaca para a China e as agues onde correm". Barros, *Décadas da Ásia*, déc. IV, liv. IX, cap. XIII. According to Tibbets, however, there appear to be a number of features that are known to the Portuguese as the *Varela* and represent a corruption of the Arabic term *berhala* known, amongst other sources, from the rutter of Ibn Majid. See Tibbets, *Arab Navigation*, p. 496.

[16] This interpretation has been cast into doubt in more recent times by Lin Wo-lin who contends that the "dragon teeth gate" or "longya-men" is found in the Riau Strait (between Batam and Bintan) or the towering twin peaks of Lingga Island. The findings of his research certainly merit further investigation. See Lin, *A Re-examination of the Place Name 'Long-ya Men'* (in Chinese). For an older debate on the subject, see also Miksic, *Archeological Research*, pp. 14–7; Kwa, "Records and Notices of Early Singapore", in Miksic, *Archeological Research*, pp. 105–6; Braddell, "Lung-Ya-Men and Tan-Ma-Hsi", *JMBRAS* 42, 1 (1969): 10–24, esp. pp. 15–7.

[17] Gibson-Hill, "Singapore: Note", *JMBRAS* 27, 1 (1954): 163–214; Gibson-Hill, "Singapore Old Strait"; Horsburgh, *Zeemans-Gids*, p. 870. See esp. Barnes, "Singapore Old Straits", *JSBRAS* 60 (1911): 25, "It has long been a tradition that the old straits of Singapore were the Sĕlat Tĕbrau between the Island and the Johore mainland and a new tradition is now springing up that the passage through the New or Keppel Harbour was discovered by the late

Admiral Keppel. The object of this paper is to show that both these traditions are without foundation of fact and that the old Straits of Singapore are none other than the present Keppel Harbour."

18 Erédia, "Descripsão chorographica dos estreitos de Singapura e Sabbam Ano 1604", in his *Declaraçam de Malaca*, fol. 60 (see p. 29).

19 Van Linschoten, *Naer Oost Ofte Portugaels Indiën*, IV, chapter XX, "Die Navigatie ende rechte Coursen van Malacca af nae Macau in China …", pp. 101–2.

20 The course plied here is not dissimilar to what Chinese and Arab sources record. See Wheatley, *Impressions*, pp. 124ff.

21 Van Linschoten, *Naer Oost Ofte Portugaels Indiën*, IV, pp. 94–5, 109–10. In recent years, doubts have been cast upon whether these two stone formations were really identical. See especially the excellent study (in Chinese) by Lin *A Re-examination*.

22 Horsburgh confused the Governor's Strait with the New Strait of Singapore. See Horsburgh, *Zeemans-Gids*, p. 862.

23 In some older Portuguese sources, Johor is often referred to as Viontana, Ugentana and other variant spellings.

24 It should be emphasised that terms such as "discovery" (and especially the Portuguese equivalent, *descobrimento*) are not always synonymous with modern usage. *Descobrimento* was widely used in this period of the European Reconnaissance to designate technical advancement or accomplishment, as much as the opening up to a European audience of knowledge pertaining to geographic features and spaces.

25 Barros and do Couto, *Da Ásia*, XXI, pp. 210–1; English text adopted from Gibson-Hill, "Singapore Old Strait" (1956), p. 52. See also pp. 53–6 passim. An additional reprint of this passage appears in Kwa, "Records and Notices of Early Singapore", in Miksic, *Archeological Research*, p. 127.

26 See also Barros, *Décadas da Ásia*, déc. IV, liv. I, cap. XVI, where similar observations are made. The Strait is a gunshot wide in many parts and measures less than 6 *braças* deep: "D. Jorge de Malaca com pilotos mouros … entrou pelo Estreito de Singapura, que é de largura de um tiro de berço, e tam baxo, que em muitas partes não tem de fundo seis braças …". According to de Coutre, the strong currents in the Old Strait eventually cleared all the debris and rendering the Strait viable for maritime traffic again. See Borschberg, "Jacques de Coutre as a Source", *JMBRAS* 81, 2 (2008): 84, 86.

27 Translated into English by the author. For the original Dutch text, see appendix 3, as well as Rouffaer, "Was Malaka emporium vóór 1400 A.D.", *BKI* 77 (1921): 389–95, for the Dutch text with critical commentary. The early modern English "rendition" of the text is reprinted in Gibson-Hill, "Singapore old Straits and New Harbour", *JMBRAS* 27, 1 (1954): 168; Kwa, "Records and Notices of Early Singapore", in Miksic, *Archeological Research*, pp. 127–8.

28 In the Netherlands, a *vadem* (fathom) could range anywhere from 1.7 to 1.9 metres, depending on the region or town in the Netherlands. For purposes of the present calculation into metres, the *vadem* mentioned here in the text are assumed to be the Amsterdam *vadem*, measuring approximately 1.7 metres.

29 A 16th-century weapon that shoots lead balls.

30 A cast (in contrast to forged) bronze cannon that normally loads shots of 12 pounds.

31 The English translation is taken from Sinclair ed., *The Travels of Pedro Teixeira*, pp. 2–3. For the original Spanish text, see appendix 8.

32 Etymologically, this appears to represent a corruption of the Malay word *pulau* (island), but from the context it might very well be a reference to the present-day Batu Pahat River. It is unlikely, however, that this name Polé bears any reference to the name Pulau Polle, which appears on some 18th-century maps such as Joachim Ottens (Royaume de Siam, 1710) and François Valentijn (Sumatra, 1724) in the vicinity of Singapore, or indeed as a name for Singapore island proper.

33 Judging from early modern cartographical evidence, including Erédia, reference is made here to the Karimun islands.

34 In Portuguese it is generally Sabão or Sabam. For its location and course, see the map of Erédia's "Descripsão chorographico dos estreitos de Singapura e Sabbam Ano 1604", in his *Declaraçam de Malaca*, fol. 61 (see p. 29). A general description can be found in Galvão, *Tratado dos Descobrimentos*, p. 168. Specific navigational instructions for the Strait of Sabam are also provided by van Linschoten, *Naer Oost Ofte Portugaels Indiën*, IV, pp. 135–7. Its commercial significance is also described by Barros, *Décadas da Ásia*, déc. III, liv. V, cap. IV, in the following words: "Per o canal chamado de Sabão navegam toda las que vão e vem pera a Jaua, Banda, Maluco e a todas aquelas ilhas a elas adjacentes, que jazem da Linha Equinocial pera o Sul" (Through the channel known as Sabam navigate all those who come and go to Java, Banda, the Malukus and those islands nearby which are situated south of the equator). Translated from Portuguese by the author. Victor Obdeijn confuses the Strait of Sabam with the Strait of Bangka, see Obdeijn, "De oude zeehandelsweg", p. 754.

35 A similar observation concerning the strong currents running through the Old Strait is found in AA, pp. 107, 400. See also generally Borschberg, "Jacques de Coutre as a Source", *JMBRAS* 81, 2 (2008): 83.

36 Gibson-Hill, "Singapore Old Strait" (1956), p. 59.

37 Maxwell, "Barreto de Resende's Account", *JSBRAS* 60 (1911): 10: "[The Straits of Singapore] has many channels so narrow that in places the branches of the trees on shore touch the ships; and the currents are very strong."

38 Carletti, *My Voyage*, p. 187. Carletti's comments are virtually identical to comments made by Giovanni Botero in his *Relatione Universale* of 1595 as well as by the Portuguese historian Bocarro in his *Década XIII*. See

Obdeijn, "De oude zeehandelsweg", *Koninklijk Nederlandsch Aardrijkskundig Genootschap*, tweede serie, 59 (1942): 745. *AA* explains that the islands between the Karimuns and around the Straits of Singapore were heavily populated with large, sprawling trees, and that ships passing through the Straits, especially the *estreito velho* (*estrecho viejo*), had to be particularly careful. See *AA*, p. 95.

39 Maxwell, "Barreto de Resende", p. 10.

40 Carletti, *My Voyage*, p. 187.

41 De Coutre, *Como Remediar*, intr. by Teensma, p. vii. See also generally Borschberg, "Jacques de Coutre as a Source", *JMBRAS* 81, 2 (2008): 71–97.

42 De Coutre, *Como Remediar*, p. 16, *AA*, p. 396.

43 De Coutre, *Como Remediar*, p. 16; *AA*, p. 396; Borschberg, "Jacques de Coutre as a Source", *JMBRAS* 81, 2 (2008): 83. According to an entry in the Madrid manuscript, the original once contained a map of the Straits of Singapore and Sabam, but this is now missing. See de Coutre, *Como Remediar*, introduction by Teensma, p. x.

44 See also Horsburgh, *Zeemans-Gids*, p. 862.

45 Gibson-Hill, "Singapore Old Strait", pp. 175, 176, note 29.

46 Horsburgh's navigational instructions for the Governor's Strait (Phillip's Channel) begin similarly. See Horsburgh, *Zeemans-Gids*, p. 862, where in the Dutch translation of the text the name is given as Boom Eiland.

47 Leiden University Library, Collectie Bodel Nijenhuis, 006-14-015. According to the text legend, this chart in turn claims to be substantially based on an earlier (French) map by Jean-Baptiste Nicholas Denis d'Après de Mannevillette dating from around 1787. Seventeenth- and 18th-century English and French maps evidently also give prominence to this navigational landmark, variously referred to as Sec des arbres or Banc aux Arbres, or in English, Tree Bank, Trees Island or Boom Keys. See Gibson-Hill, "Singapore Old Strait and New Harbour", between pp. 66 and 67, plate 2 (map of J. Lindsey, 1798), p. 68 (map of l'Oiseau, 1687), p. 70 (map of Thomas Jeffreys, 1794), p. 74 (map of James Horsburgh, 1806). Van Braam van Houckgeest is the brother of Pieter van Braam, the Dutch admiral who defeated Johor and its allies in battle in 1784. Van Braam van Houckgeest lived in Melaka and served in various capacities in China and later as a Dutch diplomat in Philadelphia. On his activities in Melaka, see Meyer Timmerman Thijssen, *Twee gouverneurs*, p. 57.

48 This is sometimes featured on naval charts of Portuguese origin as the Derrota de Romania (see, for example, PMC, V, plate 578, chart 15C). Technically, ships could choose one of two routes between Romania Point and Tioman. One brought them around the western side of Romania shoals, the other around the east. The two routes (including, importantly, water depths) are marked on

several charts, including significantly the van Braam van Houckgeest chart of 1795 preserved in the Collectie Bodel Nijenhuis in Leiden University Library (see p. 37).

49 Van Linschoten, *Naer Oost Ofte Portugaels Indiën*, IV, chap. XX, pp. 101–2: "Van dese Eylandekens 2 mylen z.z.o aen, is gelegen die Pedra Branqua, (dat is, witte steen geseyt) welke is een Eylandeken van witte steen-rootsen ofte Clippen, hebbende daer dicht by noch etlicke andere Rudtsen ende Clippen, ghelegen aende zuydtzyde daer van af, van welcke zyde inghelijcks ghelegen 't Eylandt van Binton … Men heeft rontsom de Pedra branqua, en daer dicht by 6 vadem diepten, suyver gront; sult u altoos wachten vande Clippen ende Rudtsen daer by gelegen. … [S]o sult ghy houden na de Pedra brancqua ofte witte steen toe … [E]n sout de Riffen niet voor by moghen comen, waer door gedwongen soudt wesen te loopen door 't Canael (dat tusschen Pedra branqua ende d'Eylanden loopt) …" Translated from Dutch by the author.

50 This is presumably a reference to outcroppings that would include Middle Rocks and the low-tide protrusion South Ledge.

51 Gerini, *Researches on Ptolemy's Geography*, p. 534.

52 Horsburgh, *Zeemans-Gids*, p. 870; Barnes, "Singapore Old Straits", *JSBRAS* 60 (1911): 25–34; see also Rouffaer, "De Sĕlat Singapoera", *BKI* 77 (1921): 383ff.

53 The present author wishes to underscore the value of Gibson-Hill's two contributions to the history of the Singapore Straits which, most unfortunately, remains obscure even in Singapore academic circles and therefore remains largely unappreciated in present times.

54 See particularly de Coutre, *Como Remediar*, intr. by Teensma, p. xi, and p. 16, note 1. The present author has personally discussed cartographical and topographical questions with Benjamin Teensma on at least two occasions in Leiden.

55 Doubts have been voiced as to whether the Tebrau Straits were even used by Chinese vessels during the Ming period. See Braddell, "Lung-Ya-Men and Tan-Ma-Hsi", *JMBRAS* 42, 1 (1969): 17, where the Tebrau Strait is said to have been treated by many Chinese sailors as an "inland sea". Also: "At all events, sailing past Singapore, there is no particular reason to realize that it is an island, the western and eastern entrances of the Selat Tebrau (Johore Strait) looking like river mouths; and there is no reason to think that the Chinese in Cheng Ho's time made Johore a place of call or entered the Selat Tebrau at all."

56 Van Linschoten describes the Tebrau Strait as a "river estuary" that leads to the port of "Iantana" or Johor Lama. He appears to ascribe its accidental "discovery" by the Portuguese to one Antonio de Mello. See van Linschoten, *Naer Oost Ofte Portugaels Indiën*, IV, p. 95, "Ontrent een mijl van dese punt [that is *Tanjamburo* or present-day Tanjong Bulus] af leyt een Revier, ende een cleijn mijl voorder aen, heeftmen een ander Revier, met eenen grooten mont,

alwaer een Eylandeken leyt, ghenaemt oudt Sincapura, hebbende diepe ende suyvere gront. Dese Revier comt inde haven van Iantana weder uyt, alwaer eens onverhoets in gheloopen is Antonio de Mello met een Schip van acht honderd Bharen groot … ende quamen inde Revier van Iantana weder uyt." (About one [nautical] mile from this point [Tanjong Bulus] there is a river and a small mile further ahead there is another river featuring a large estuary, where there is situated a small island named old Sincapura. Here there is deep and clean ground. This river leads back out to the port of Iantana [Johor Lama]. Antonio de Mello accidentally sailed into [this waterway] with a ship of eight hundred bahar … and he came out again in the Johor River.)

57 Rouffaer, "De Sĕlat Singapoera", *BKI* 77 (1921): 398: He later adds, p. 399: "Eerst toen omstreeks 1600 de macht van Djohor sterk was gedaald, en de Hollanders als Djohor's helpers tegen de Portugeezen na 1603 begonnen op te treden, gin de groote zeevard al meer en meer gebruik maken van de Sĕlat Tĕbĕrau …" (Only when around 1600 the power of Johor had weakened significantly, and when the Dutch began to play a role as allies of Johor against the Portuguese after 1603, did large maritime navigation begin to make increased use of the Tebrau Strait.) Translated from Dutch by the author.

58 According to extant sources, this was particularly the case during the years 1603–4, 1606–7 and 1609–10. After the last, economically crippling blockade, the Johor monarch signed a peace treaty with the Portuguese, which was subsequently rejected by the viceroy in Goa.

59 Van Opstall, ed., *De reis*, II, "Journaal van de Griffioen", p. 337.

60 See the Portuguese armada's composition described in "Historische Verhael", *BV*, II, p. 37; according to the testimony of one David Lochum, who witnessed the naval confrontation between the Dutch and Portuguese in the Johor River estuary and off the coast of northern Bintan, the Portuguese armada consisted of "two gallions or large ships, six galley and twenty-four bantins or foists". See Coolhaas, "Een bron", p. 506.

61 This may have possibly been influenced by texts such as van Linschoten. See van Linschoten, *Naer Oost Ofte Portugaels Indiën*, IV, p. 95, where the Tebrau Strait is described as a "river" that, when taken from west to east, leads to the "river and port of Iantana" (Johor River and Johor Lama).

62 This Malay name, which was sometimes also translated into Dutch and other European languages, survived well into the 19th century. The names Pulau Panjang and 't Lange Eylant were occasionally also applied to present-day Sentosa, as is the case, for example, on the anonymous late 17th-century map in the Leiden University Library, Bodel Nijenhuis Collection, 006-15-021.

63 See Chapter 5.

64 Judging from what de Coutre experienced, they also acted as "flying merchants" around the Straits of Malacca and Singapore, approaching European vessels to sell "refreshments: [fresh] water, fruit, chicken, fish and other things", see

AA, p. 143, and Borschberg, "Jacques de Coutre as a Source", *JMBRAS* 81, 2 (2008): 85.

65 Obdeijn, "De oude zeehandelsweg", pp. 751ff. Importantly, see also Kwa, "Records and Notices of Early Singapore", in Miksic, *Archeological Research*, p. 132, "Obdeijn, followed by R.W. Bemmelen speculated that Marco Polo did not mention Singapura when he sailed through the region in 1292 because there was no navigable passage past Singapura, as the peninsula formed a promontory as far as Bangka and Belitung. The speculation is that the final post-Pleistocene submergence of the Sunda peneplain continued well into historic times." See Obdeijn, "De oude zeehandelsweg", pp. 768–70. For the reception of Obdeijn's thesis and the reference to van Bemmelen, see Kwa, "Records and Notices", p. 132 note 1.

66 A copy of de Haan's *Ligtende Zeefakkel* can be found in the Nationaal Archief van Nederland in The Hague.

67 De Coutre, *Como Remediar*, intr. by Teensma, p. xi. The map in question (Gerrit de Haan's) is reprinted as plate H, located between pages 19 and 20.

68 Van Opstall, ed., *De reis*, entry of 6 February 1609, p. 256.

69 Attention is drawn in this context to the entries on Bellin's 1755 map that read, "Il y a ici un grand nombre de petites isles don't la situation n'est pas connue" (Here is a large number of small islands of which the situation is not known), and "Toutes les îles paroissent faire une grande terre" (All these islands appear to form a large landmass).

70 Miksic, "Archaeology and Paleography", in *Economic Exchange*, Hutterer, ed., pp. 161, 168–74; also Wolters, "Landfall on the Palembang Coast", *Indonesia* 20 (1975): 1–58.

71 For further background reading on the development and usage of cartography in Europe, see the excellent chapter by Fernández-Armesto, "Maps and Exploration in the Sixteenth and Seventeenth Centuries", in Woodward, *History of Cartography*, III, pp. 738–59.

72 The copy of Thevet's two-volume *Cosmographie Universelle* consulted belongs to the University of Leiden. The curators and the board of governors kindly consented to a microfilm reproduction of this rare print. On the biographical data on Thevet, see, for example, Jöcher, *Allgemeines Gelehrten-Lexicon*, IV, cols. 1130–1; Lestringant, *Le Brésil d'André Thevet*, pp. 13–20.

73 Thevet, *Cosmographie Universelle*, II, fol. 414 verso.

74 Already Tomé Pires had pointed out that Muar was the second largest settlement on the western shores of the Malay Peninsula, counting about 2,000 men and governed by a *bendahara*. SO, p. 489.

75 Van Linschoten, *Naer Oost Ofte Portugaels Indiën* (Amsterdam: Cornelis Claesz, 1596).

76 As a result of this policy of secrecy, one should distinguish in cartographic terms between intentional omissions on the one hand and uncharted or

unknown territory on the other. In practice, however, such a distinction can prove tricky and speculative. For a short exposé of different types of silences on maps, see Harley's article "Silences and Secrecy", in *The New Nature of Maps*, pp. 83–107.

77 Albuquerque, *Cartas*, I, pp. 64–5.

78 Translation of the text according to *PMC*, I, p. 80. The original Portuguese text is reproduced in appendix 6.

79 See the "Guores" in *SO*, pp. 128ff, where they are described as the inhabitants of Formosa and the Ryukyu or "Loochoo" Archipelago. The name appears to be a corruption of the Arabic name *al-Ghūr*; see Tibbets, *Arab Navigation*, p. 500.

80 This is almost certainly a reference to the same Francisco Rodrigues whose *Livro* is bound together with Tomé Pires' *Suma Oriental* and forms part of the Hakluyt Society edition of 1944 edited by Cortesão. According to Brotton, *Trading Territories*, p. 82: "Rodrigues had sailed to Malacca with d'Albuquerque in 1511 and went under the grand title of 'Pilot-major of the first armada that discovered Banda and the Malukus'. He was reputed to be a Javan seconded by d'Albuquerque whilst on his travels, and in 1513 he produced a manuscript book of *roteiros* (rutters), or maritime charts, supplemented with written navigational descriptions of coasts."

81 The *Frol de la Mar* sank in a storm in December 1511. On board were Affonso d'Albuquerque and the rich treasure of the Melaka Sultanate captured by the Portuguese earlier that year. Giovanni da Empoli provides an eyewitness account of this historic event in Bausani, *Lettera*, p. 141.

82 In Malay, *selat* actually means "strait", not "archipelago".

83 This is probably a reference to the Riau Archipelago, but probably not Bangka and Belitung which at that time were well known among Javanese, Chinese, Arab and other merchants.

84 The idea of the "Lion City", popularised by John Leyden and also Raffles, marks only one interpretation of the etymological deconstruction of Singapura. Barros, as has been mentioned above, says that the name translates into Portuguese as *falsa demora* or "a place where you land but subsequently discover that it is not what you were looking it". There are of course more such etymological deconstructions that would merit a scholarly discourse in their own right.

85 The name "Cingaporla" is specifically attributed by Ramusio (*Delle viaggi e navigazioni*, I, p. 369B) to Antonio Pigafetta, the chronicler of the Magellan expedition (1519–21). Thevet had access to this volume, and certainly used it, not least because the French cosmographer also mentions the sea monsters named *tiburon* that are also encountered in Pigafetta's account. There are important differences, however. Pigafetta mentions Cinghapola within a list of cities that are all "subject to the King of Siam". Thevet, by contrast, treats Cinghapola chiefly as an island or a polity. See Pigafetta, *Magellan's Voyage*,

p. 152 for the reference to Cinghapola and p. 34 for the reference to the sea monsters (actually sharks) called *tiburoni*. See also note 190 below.

86 Thevet, *Cosmographie Universelle*, II, chap. 24, fols. 413 recto and following. This and all subsequent sections from Thevet translated from the original French by Peter Borschberg Sr.

87 Thevet, *Cosmographie Universelle*, II, fol. 414 verso. For the original French text, see appendix 4.

88 Thevet, *Cosmographie Universelle*, II, fol. 414 verso.

89 Thevet, *Cosmographie Universelle*, II, fol. 413 verso.

90 Thevet, *Cosmographie Universelle*, II, fol. 414 recto. Thevet also speaks of the "Cap et Promontoir de Cingaporla" (Cape and promontory of Cingaporla).

91 Thevet, *Cosmographie Universelle*, II, fol. 414 recto/verso.

92 If Thevet is referring to the route from Melaka to China, it would be on the left.

93 This map is found at the beginning of the discussion on Asia in Thevet, *Cosmographie Universelle*, I, no foliation.

94 On the general scientific context and background of the 1541 Mercator globe, see Brotton, *Trading Territories*, pp. 160–1.

95 Ramusio, *Delle navigationi*, the *Terza tavola*, which immediately precedes p. 1.

96 Ortelius, *Theatrum Orbis Terrarum*. There are two different versions of the *Asia Nova Descriptio*; one depicts, among other features, the maritime channel, while the other does not. For a comparison of the two maps, and the respective editions where the maritime channel appears, see van den Broecke, *Ortelius Atlas Maps*, pp. 46–7. For a general background to Ortelius' *Theatrum Orbis Terrarum* of 1570 (Atlas), see the useful discussion by Brotton, *Trading Territories*, pp. 170–9 and Koeman, Schilder, van Egmond and van der Krogt, "Commercial Cartography and Map Production in the Low Countries, 1500–ca. 1672", in Woodward, *History of Cartography*, III, pp. 1318–21. Depending on the format, the price of Ortelius' Atlas ranged between 5 guilders and 10 stuiver to 16 guilders. See van den Broecke, *Ortelius*, p. 17 — The painted wall map of 1573 in the Guardaroba Nova at the Palazzo Vecchio in Florence depicting parts of mainland and insular Southeast Asia shows a strong influence of Ortelius and clearly depicts the cross-Peninsular Pahang-Muar riverine channel. See Francesca Fiorani, "Cycles of Painted Maps in the Renaissance", in Woodward, *History of Cartography*, III, p. 819, fig. 32.6.

97 The colouring was done individually by hand. On the globe specimen preserved in the Herzog-August-Bibliothek in Wolfenbüttel, Germany, the ink stops at the shoreline.

98 The only known copy of the Asia wall map is located at the Universitätsbibliothek Basel.

99 Compare these observations with the account in Fell, *Early Maps of Southeast Asia*, p. 65, which provides a poorly researched and garbled account of the early mapping of Singapore island and its immediate surroundings.

100 The map of Giovanni Vespucci forms part of the Harvard Map Collection, Sign. 51-2573 PF; the Ghisolfi map is found in the Huntington Library, Sign. HM 28 f. 13; and the Homem map is in the Herzog-August-Bibliothek, Wolfenbüttel, Sign. 102. Aug. fol. (ex 94. Aug. Fol).

101 Barros, *Décadas*, déc. I, liv. IX, cap. I, déc. III, liv. V, cap. IV, and déc. III, liv. V, cap. VII, "Cabo de Cingapura"; déc. II, liv. 6, cap. I: "Antiguamente a mais célebre povoação que havia naquela terra de Malaca era ũa chamada Cingapura, que em sua língua quere dizer falsa demora, a qual estava situada em ũa ponta daquela terra, que é a mais austral da Ásia, situada em altura de meio grau da parte do Norte, segundo nossa graduação" (Since ancient times, the most famous settlement that exists in the said lands of Melaka is one called Cingapura, which in its language means to say "*falsa demora*" [a place where you land but subsequently discover that it is not what you were looking for]. It is situated at the tip of that land, which [also] marks the southernmost point of Asia). Barros then drew connections between the promontory and Ptolemy's Zaba, before telling the story of Parameswara and the founding of Melaka. Portuguese text freely translated by the author.

102 Van Linschoten additionally speaks of an island which he calls "old Singapura" which he describes as a small island near the western exit of the Tebrau Strait. See van Linschoten, *Naer Oost Ofte Portugaels Indiën*, IV, p. 95, "Ontrent een mijl van dese punt [that is *Tanjamburo* or present-day Tanjong Bulus] af leyt een Revier, ende een cleijn mijl voorder aen, heeftmen een ander Revier, met eenen grooten mont, alwaer een Eylandeken leyt, ghenaemt oudt Sincapura …" (About one [nautical] mile from this point [Tanjong Bulus] there is a river, and a small mile further ahead there is another river featuring a large estuary, where there is situated a small island).

103 This island should not be confused with a second island named Pulau Panjang, which is located off the coast of Banten in the Sunda Strait. This second island is where VOC ships loaded and unloaded their cargos. Many references to this latter island can be found in *DRB* as well as *GM*.

104 See, for example, the hydrographic chart belonging to the Leiden University Library, Collectie Bodel Nijenhuis, no. 006-15-021, "De Straat van Sincapura …" It is catalogued and described by Vries, *Uit de Kaartenwinkel*, p. 54, no. 61.

105 A copy of the Milner map can be found in the British Library, London, Sign. C.12.f.1.(30).

106 Leiden University Library, Collectie Bodel Nijenhuis, no. 006-14-015.

107 De Vries, *Uit de Kaartenwinkel*, p. 54, no. 62.

108 Hill, ed. and tr., "Hikayat Raja-Raja Pasai", *JMBRAS* 33, 2 (1960): 160. Other variants of this name include "Jantana velha" on a chart of the VOC

hydrographer Hessel Gerritsz (c. 1620) and "Iantan velha" in Valentijn's *Oud en Nieuw Oost-Indiën.*

109 For a short biography and summary of his accomplishments, see Maria Fernanda Alegria, Suzanne Daveau, João Carlos García and Francesc Relaño, "Portuguese Cartography in the Renaissance", in Woodward, *History of Cartography*, III, pp. 1022–3.

110 Erédia, "Informação" in Caminha, *Ordenações*, pp. 65–151; and Erédia, *Declaraçam de Malaca.*

111 Erédia, "Informação", pp. 65–6, 76, where on the latter page he employs the term "Promontorio de Sincapura". See also Erédia, *Declaraçam de Malaca*, fols. 24 recto, 25 verso, 26 recto, 28 recto, 45 recto, 60 verso and 61 recto, where, in contrast to the earlier *Informação*, the Peninsula is called "Viontana" and its southern extremity the "Promontorio de Ujontana". For the text, see the Portuguese transcript in Erédia, *Declaraçam de Malaca*, 22 verso–23 verso, 26 recto–27 verso and 33 recto–35 recto. On the name Maleucolone, see Gerini, *Researches on Ptolemy's Geography*, p. 104, and the possible Tamil origin of that name, which means "Mountain of the west"; see also Gerini, *Researches*, pp. 730–1, 759. The name "Maleucolon Promont" (Promontory of Maleucolone) can be found on Ptolemy's Tab. XI *Asiae.* The presence of this name invariably implies that the name was already well established by the second century.

112 *SO*, p. 490 (Portuguese text). Note, however, the terminology employed here "... canall de sijmgapura ...". Pires sees the "channel" of Singapura located *beyond* the Rio Fermoso, which means from the point of view of Melaka, to the south of the Batu Pahat River. On the reliability, transmission and problems surrounding the *Suma Oriental* of Pires — and indeed many other 16th-century sources; see appendix 1. See also Miksic, *Archeological Research*, p. 33.

113 Erédia, *Declaraçam de Malaca*, fols. 45 recto, 60 verso and 61 recto.

114 The call numbers for the maps are as follows: Erédia's maps are found in the 1882 facsimile edition of his *Declaraçam de Malaca*, the original manuscript of which is owned by the Bibliothèque Royale in Brussels; maps and charts that do not form part of the Brussels manuscript can be found in *PMC*, IV, pp. 47 and following, and esp. plates 417B (Colecção Dr. C. M. C. Machado Figueira, Lisbon). There are two charts of Pereira dos Reis that are very similar but not identical. Only the manuscript in the Maritiem Museum Prins Hendrik in Rotterdam, W. A. Engelbrecht Collection, sign. WAE 900-10, features the name Singapura on the island, but it is admittedly insufficiently clear whether the name refers to a settlement on the island, or to the island itself; the Bowrey map is found in the British Library, sign. Additional MS. 5222.10; the Eberard Dupré map is found in the British Library, sign. Additional MS. 15,738.29; the Gerard van Keulen map is owned by the Angelica in Rome, and repeated requests for reproduction have gone unanswered. However, a

basic colour reproduction can be found in Guiso and Muratore, *Ad Usum Navigantium*, p. 55. The van Braam van Houckgeest chart forms part of the Bodel Nijenhuis Collection in the Leiden University Library and has been previously mentioned (see p. 37).

115 Other names include the "Isla de la Sabandaria Vieja" mentioned by the Flemish diamond merchant de Coutre, both in his autobiography as well as in his memorials addressed to the king of Spain. See Borschberg, "Jacques de Coutre as a Source", *JMBRAS* 81, 2 (2008): 82.

116 It has been suggested in conversations with leading academics in Singapore and Australia that the name Singapura may be historically linked to an honorific or title bestowed on an officer or member of the Johor nobility. Wherever this officer or nobleman lived, the settlement would thus carry the name Singapura. The author places this here for information within the realm of possibilities.

117 Borschberg, "Jacques de Coutre as a Source", *JMBRAS* 81, 2 (2008): 71–97, esp. p. 86, "Finally, we passed through the Old Strait, which the King of Johor had blockaded when Dom Paulo de Lima, the captain of Malacca, took the city of Johor [Lama]. Meanwhile the [Old] Strait has become [a] viable [passage] again thanks to the [strong] currents [which have cleared away the logs and debris]. We dropped anchor at a place inhabited by Malays which they call *Sabandaría.* These [Malays] are subjects of the aforementioned King of Johor to whom the *orang laut*, who come to the straits here, [also] pay tribute".

118 Valentijn, *Oud en Nieuw Oost-Indiën*, VII, part 5.

119 This episode is discussed in greater detail in Chapter 2.

120 "Historische Verhael", *BV*, II, p. 38. Renditions of this important work into French and English are as follows: Renneville, *Recueil des voiages*; and anon., *A Collection of Voyages*. On the limitations of these two "renditions" (they do not merit the title of translation), see Boxer, "Isaac Commelin's Begin ende Voortgang", in *Opera Minora*, ed. Ramada Curto, II, pp. 127–47, see specifically p. 133.

121 Codices Urbinus Graecus 82 and Vaticanus Latinus 5698, both in the Vatican Library; Codex Napoli ms. 1466, British Library ms. 7182, and Codex Parisiensis Latinus no. 4801. On the role of the Codex Urbinas 82 in the revival of Ptolemy's *Geography of Europe* of the 15th century, see Fischer, *Claudii Ptolomaei*, I, "De Cl. Ptolomaei vita operibus geographia praesertim eiusque fatis pars prior commentatio"; J. Keuning, *De Tweede Schipvaart*, V, "Overzicht van de ontwikkeling van de kartographie van den Indischen Archipel tot het Jaar 1598", pp. 231–3.

122 Several reports from the period of Portuguese colonial rule on the Malay Peninsula attest to gold panning activities in the upstream regions, especially between Melaka, Muar and Pahang. Erédia was particularly keen on highlighting the availability of gold, sometimes exaggerating river panning activities to the

scale of vast mining operations. See especially his "Informação", pp. 67, 75, 81 (*grandes minas de oro*), 82 (mentioning the *minas auriferas* of Pahang), p. 83 (describing Pahang as "terra de oro"), his *Declaraçam de Malaca*, fols. 39 verso–40 recto (*minas de oro de Pam*), as well as Erédia's "Lista das principaes Minas auriferas" in Caminha, *Ordenações*, Supplemento, p. 81. See also AA, p. 98.

123 See also AA, p. 98. In his Spanish-language *Vida*, de Coutre explains that the Portuguese were well aware of the overland route to Pahang. But the trans-peninsular route was not favoured among the Melaka traders it because the overland trail through jungle and across the fens was simply too cumbersome and taxing. In normal times at least, they clearly preferred the sea route through the Singapore Strait. See Borschberg, "Jacques de Coutre as a Source", *JMBRAS* 81, 2 (2008): 94.

124 Erédia, "Descripsão chorographico do Sertão de Malaca. Anno 1602", in *Declaraçam de Malaca*, fol. 11 verso and 60 recto. Here, interestingly, the *panarícan* appears to be located in the *Districto de Ior*. The southern "border" or "sphere of influence" of Portuguese Melaka reaches to the left bank of the Muar River. The *panarícan* is also depicted on the two unfoliated maps of Portuguese Melaka found on fols. 11 verso, 12 verso and 13 recto. Other anonymous maps depicting the *panarícan* that are not contained in the manuscript of the *Declaraçam de Malaca* and have been ascribed to Eredía can be found in *PMC*, IV, plate 411B (Biblioteca Nacional do Brazil, Rio de Janeiro, see also p. 55) and plates 417A and 417C (Colecção Dr. C.M.C. Machado Figueira, Lisbon). On the expedition of Erédia to the interior of the Malay Peninsula, see Parmentier, Davids and Everaert, *Peper, Plancius en Porcelein*, pp. 76–7. Several authors mention the significance of the *penarícan* for the 16th century, either during the period of the Melaka Sultanate or after its fall to the Portuguese. See, for example, Sandhu and Singh, *Early Malaysia*, I, p. 50.

125 These VOC activities will be discussed in the following chapters.

126 In fact, Arabic sources of the 9th and 11th centuries translated by Ferrand already mention Tioman as a place to bring on fresh water. See Ferrand, *Voyage du marchand Arabe*, pp. 19, 42.

127 PMC, IV, p. 41, where it is reported that Erédia accompanied Furtado de Mendonça in 1604 "when he took Johor [Lama]".

128 According to Jorge Faro, the fortress in Muar was founded by Erédia by order of Portuguese Viceroy Aires de Saldanha and Furtado de Mendonça on 2 February 1604. See Faro, *Godinho de Erédia*, fol. 6 recto. See also the map of the Muar River estuary featured in Erédia, *Declaraçam de Malaca*, fol. 61 verso. De Coutre's testimony is found in both the original text and in English translation in appendix 5.

129 See especially Erédia, *Declaraçam de Malaca*, the two maps of Portuguese Melaka found between pp. 11 and 13, where the "border" or "sphere of influence" (marked *Districto de Malaca*) had already been extended across the left bank of the Muar River. But his chart of Melaka dated 1602 and bearing the manuscript foliation 60 recto has the Muar River estuary outside of Portuguese Melaka's influence (see p. 56). See also the additional maps by or ascribed to Erédia in *PMC*, IV, plates 411B (Biblioteca Nacional do Brazil, Rio de Janeiro; the border extends only to the right bank of the Muar River estuary) and 417C (Colecção Dr. C. M. C. Machado Figueira, Lisbon; Melaka's "border" extends to beyond the left bank of the Muar River estuary and indicates Portuguese control of the port and town). Tomé Pires and Paul Wheatley hold that in the early 16th century Melaka extended southwards up to about the Muar River but not beyond it. See Wheatley, *The Golden Khersonese*, p. 317. An account of 1615 reproduced in Caldecott, "The Malay Peninsula in the XVIIth and XVIIIth Centuries", *JSBRAS* 82 (1920): 130, claims that Portuguese Melaka ran 270 "miles in length", but quickly adds that the territory "is nothing but a desert, if you except that which is neere unto the towne". The extension of Portuguese influence outside the confines of the settlement and down the coast to Muar is denied by some contemporary historians such as for example Hussin, "A Tale of Two Colonial Port-Towns in the Straits of Melaka: Dutch Melaka and English Penang", *JMBRAS* 75, 2 (2002): 79, "During the Malay sultanate period in the 1500s, Melaka controlled an empire which covered part of eastern Sumatra and the western Malay Peninsula. During the Portuguese occupation of Melaka, however, the Portuguese controlled and occupied only a small area, including the fort of Melaka and the town and its suburbs."

130 See, for example, *PMC*, IV, plate 464 (J. Teixeira, 1630) and plate 532B (A. Sanches, 1641).

131 Nieuhof, *Zee en Lant-Reize*, p. 60: "In de riviere van Pahan, hoewel zy vry wijt is, kan men gene galeyen gebruiken, dan met hoogh water" (In the Pahang River one cannot use any galleys unless there is high water, even though the river is quite wide).

132 As late as the third quarter of the 17th century, the Dutch diplomat and traveller Johan Nieuhof explained in his *Zee en Lant-Reize*, p. 58: "Sinkapura is situated at the southern tip or cape of all Asia, about one half a degree north of the equator, and 20 miles (*mijl*) from Malacca./The Strait of Sinkapura is named after this [cape] Sinkapura./Sinkapura was once ruled by a separate (*bysonderen*) king, and before the founding of Melaka it was the most important centre of trade and settlement along the coast. Traders from China and Cambodia and other regions called here." Translated from Dutch by the author.

133 *John Leiden's Malay Annals*, p. 45.

Chapter 2

1 Concerning the arrival and activities of the Danish in the waters of Southeast Asia, see Stephan Diller, *Die Dänen in Indien.*

2 Markham, ed., *The Voyage of Sir James Lancaster*, p. 93; Subrahmanyam, *Improvising Empire*, p. 42.

3 Wieder, ed., *De Reis van Joris van Spilbergen*, pp. 66–71 and 81–2; *DJP*, p. 482, where Grotius explains that the booty from the seizure of the Portuguese carrack was shared by the English and the Dutch. See also Subrahmanyam, *Improvising Empire*, p. 42, and "The Coromandel Malacca Trade in the Sixteenth Century: A Study of Its Evolving", in Prakash, *European Commercial Expansion*, p. 57.

4 *DJP*, introduction by van Ittersum, p. XIII.

5 Boxer, *The Portuguese Seaborne Empire*, p. 107, "The massive Dutch attack on the Portuguese colonial empire was ostensibly motivated by the union of the Spanish and Portuguese crowns in the person of Philip II of Spain, against whose rule in the Netherlands the Dutch had rebelled in 1568." The Union of the Two Crowns comprising Portugal, Spain and their respective empires was symbolically expressed by the person of Philip II of Spain and his heirs. The period of six decades spanning 1580 to 1640 is considered by some historians as the "dark age" of Portugal's overseas empire. Although merged in the person of the monarch, the two colonial empires continued to be run separately, with Spain clearly having the upper hand in decision and policy making. As Boxer explains, this period of the union has been treated as something of a "Babylonian captivity" among the nationalist historians in Portugal.

6 Borschberg, "Hugo Grotius, East India Trade", *JSEAS* 30, 2 (1999): 228–9, 243–5.

7 Das Gupta, "Acheh in Indonesian Trade and Politics", pp. 154, 200; Davies, *A Primer of Dutch Seventeenth Century Overseas Trade*, p. 52; for the bigger picture see Stapel, "The 'Ambon Massacre' (9 March 1623)", in *Dutch Authors on Asian History*, ed. Meilink-Roelofsz, van Opstall and Schutte, pp. 184–95.

8 Das Gupta, "Acheh in Indonesian Trade and Politics", pp. 98–178, 182, 195, 198 (all pages with a focus on Anglo-Dutch commercial rivalry in Aceh).

9 For a useful synopsis of the corporate foundations of the VOC and also of Anglo-Dutch relations in the East Indies in the first decades of the 17th century, see Somers and Roelofsen, "*Mare Liberum* and the Dutch East India Company", *Grotiana*, New Series, 24-5 (2003–4): 68–72.

10 For a more detailed account of the Luso-Dutch conflict in the 16th and 17th centuries, see the synopsis in Boxer, *The Portuguese Seaborne Empire*, pp. 106–27, and the very useful contribution by Peter Kirsch, "VOC — Trade Without Ethics?" in Sprengard and Ptak, *Maritime Asia*, pp. 189–202. The latter also touches on Dutch relations with Asian allies. For the conflict in Asia,

see the miscellaneous contributions by Boxer, van Ittersum, Meilink-Roelofsz, and Pinto; for the Atlantic world, see Israel, *Conflicts of Empires*; and *Dutch Primacy in World Trade*, and *The Dutch Republic and the Hispanic World*; Postma and Enthoven, ed., *Riches from Atlantic Commerce.*

11 A hitherto unknown letter from Dom Paulo Lima de Pereira to King Philip II of Spain, dated 28 November 1587, is transcribed and translated in appendix 2. It provides a personal account of the events leading to the destruction of Johor Lama, and the destruction itself, earlier that year. See also the classic exposé which is based chiefly on Diogo do Couto by MacGregor, "Johore Lama", *JMBRAS* 28, 2 (1955): 48–125.

12 Parmentier, Davids and Everaert, *Peper, Plancius en Porselein*, p. 60.

13 On the merger of the six *voorcompagniën* or regional trading firms into the VOC, see the authoritative overview in Bruijn and Gaastra, *Roemrucht verleden*, pp. 14–21, and the more detailed account in Gaastra, *Geschiedenis van de VOC*, pp. 16–25. For a useful synopsis, see also Somers and Roelofsen, "Mare Liberum and the Dutch East India Company", *Grotiana*, New Series, 24-5 (2003–4): 68–70.

14 The best-known defence of the Portuguese Empire was undertaken by Seraphim de Freitas in his *De Justo Imperio Asiatico*, written in the second decade of the 17th century but published at Valladolid, Spain in 1625. There are no extant English translations of this important work at hand, but translations into German, French and Portuguese are available. On the significance of Freitas in general, see Borschberg, "Grotius' Theory of Trans-Oceanic Trade Regulation", *Institute for International Law and Justice Working Paper*, History and Theory of International Law Series, no. 14 (2006): 28, 39ff.

15 Translations of both of these epoch-making treaties can be found in *The Philippine Islands, 1493–1898*, ed. Emma H. Blair and James A. Robertson, I, pp. 115ff and 222ff.

16 Clark and Eysinga, "The Colonial Conferences", Part I, *Bibliotheca Visseriana* 15 (1940): 118.

17 Elias, *Schetsen*, p. 76.

18 Steensgaard, *The Asian Trade*, p. 132.

19 Matelieff de Jonge's attack on Melaka in 1606 is discussed at the beginning of Chapter 5.

20 The position of Elias, Steensgaard and Enthoven contradicts the claims of Meilink-Roelofsz, who underscored the essentially peaceful trading activity of the early Dutch voyages. See Meilink-Roelofsz, "Aspects of Dutch Colonial Development", in *Britain and the Netherlands*, ed. Bromley and Kossmann, pp. 60–1.

21 Enthoven, *Zeeland en de opkomst*, pp. 210–1.

22 See also Borschberg, "Hugo Grotius, East India", *JSEAS* 30, 2 (1999): 246, 247.

23 Many of these treaties have been reproduced in Heeres, *Corpus Diplomaticum Neërlando-Indicum*. It should be stressed that the Dutch were not alone in forging these legally secured alliances and relations of trade. Portugal, too, secured its rights by treaty. Many of these agreements after 1600 contain "anti-Dutch" clauses, provisions that specifically mention the Dutch for exclusion from trade and formal diplomatic relations.

24 Clark and Eysinga, *The Colonial Conferences*, part I, p. 191; Clark and Eysinga, *The Colonial Conferences*, part II , p. 105.

25 Borschberg, "Hugo Grotius, East India", p. 243.

26 Borschberg, "Hugo Grotius, East India", pp. 230ff.

27 Botelho e Sousa, *Subsídios para a história*, I, p. 548; Teixeira, *The Portuguese Missions*, I, pp. 224–5. See also the letter of King Philip III/II to Dom Martim Afonso de Castro, viceroy of India, dated Valladolid, 5 March 1605, document 15, in Pinto, *Portugueses e malaios*, p. 291, where the king recommends dispatching an armada against the king of Johor to punish him for assisting the rebels (the Dutch) in taking the carrack from China (probably the *Santa Catarina*). See also the letter from the king of Portugal to his viceroy of India, dated Valladolid, 27 December 1604, document 14, Pinto, *Portugueses e malaios*, pp. 287–9.

28 See the discussion on the choice of this proposed rendezvous location in Chapter 5.

29 The merits of these arguments were debated and re-debated in Spain and its dominions in the 16th century. Several well-known and historically influential discussions on the problems and legality of early colonial expansion were written by the learned authors of the "School of Salamanca", but the best-known and historically most influential of these discussions remain Francisco de Vitoria's *Two Relections on the Indies*. Modern translations of these can be found in Francisco de Vitoria, *Political Writings*, ed. Pagden and Lawrence.

30 See also Borschberg, "Grotius' Theory of Trans-Oceanic Trade Regulation", *Institute for International Law and Justice Working Paper*, History and Theory of International Law Series, no. 14 (2006): 47–51.

31 See the anonymous pamphlet *Corte ende sekere Beschryvinghe*. One of this very rare copies of this pamphlet can be found in Amsterdam University Library.

32 Borschberg, "The Seizure of the Sta. Catarina Revisited", *JSEAS* 33 (2002): 35.

33 See, for example, Cruysse, *Louis XIV*, pp. 57–60.

34 On the role of the *Santa Catarina* incident in the formulation of a "freebooting strategy" within the early VOC, see particularly the account in Veen, *Decay or Defeat*, pp. 190–1.

35 For a broader picture, see Chapter 3, "Naval Security and Forts for the Straits"; see also Meilink-Roelofsz, *Asian Trade*, pp. 60–170.

36 See the *Consulta* of 7 February 1607 in Mendes da Luz, *O Conselho da Índia*, p. 462; also Lobato, *Política e Comércio*, p. 200. On the taking of Johor Lama, see the extensive account provided by Diogo de Couto in his *Vida D. Paulo*, pp. 123ff.

37 See generally Borschberg, "Hugo Grotius, East India Trade", *JSEAS* 30, 2 (1999): 225–48; "De Societate Publica cum Infidelibus", *Zeitschrift der Savigny-Stiftung für Rechtsgeschichte*, Romanistische Abteilung, 115 (1998): 355–93; "Grotius' Theory of Trans-Oceanic Trade Regulation", *Institute for International Law and Justice Working Paper*, History and Theory of International Law Series, no. 14 (August 2006).

38 Van Ittersum, *Profit and Principle*, see pp. 1–20, 30–43; van Ittersum, "Hugo Grotius in Context", *Asian Journal of Social Sciences* 31, 3 (2003): 511–48.

39 *DJP*, appendix II, document 2, "Jacob van Heemskerck to the Directors of the United Amsterdam Company, 13 July, 1602" and appendix II, document 3, "Jacob van Heemskerck and His Council of Naval Officers Resolve to Attack Portuguese Shipping Indiscriminately, 4 December, 1602", pp. 531–2. Van Heemskerk originally sailed to Asia as a venture of the United Amsterdam Company, one of the *voorcompagniën* amalgamated into the VOC in 1602. He was at the time not aware of the creation of the VOC and continued to address all correspondence to the United Amsterdam Company.

40 For further background on this, see Tiele, "De Europeërs in den Maleischen Archipel", part VI, *BKI* 30 (1882): 192–6.

41 *DJP*, appendix II, document 4, "Jacob van Heemskerck to the Directors of the United Amsterdam Company, 27 August, 1603", p. 533. For the biography and distinguished career of Jakob van Neck, see de Bruijn, *The Dutch Navy*, pp. 35–6. The story of Admiral van Neck and van Heemskerk at Patani is mirrored by de Coutre in AA, pp. 154–69.

42 *DJP*, appendix II, document 4, pp. 533, 534.

43 *DJP*, appendix II, document 4, p. 534; Tiele, "De Europeërs in den Maleischen Archipel", part VI, *BKI* 30 (1882): 196.

44 Van Ittersum, *Profit and Principle*, p. 35; van Ittersum, "Hugo Grotius in Context", p. 518.

45 Van Ittersum, "Hugo Grotius in Context", p. 520.

46 *DJP*, appendix II, document 4, p. 535.

47 *DJP*, appendix II, document 4, pp. 535–6.

48 There are several references to the identity of the Prince of Siak as a "brother of the king" (Ala'ud'din Ri'ayat Shah III), and implicitly also of Raja Bongsu. See *DJP*, appendix II, document 4, p. 534, esp. also van Ittersum's comment in note 9; Bassett, "Changes in the Pattern of Malay Politics", *JSEAH* 10, 3 (1969): 431. Netscher thinks him to be an illegitimate brother of the Johor monarch (*NJS*, p. 29) while the Standish-Croft Journal, sees him as the king's

"brother-in-law". *The Voyage of Thomas Best to the East Indies, 1612–14*, ed. William Foster, p. 169.

49 *DJP*, appendix II, document 4, p. 536.

50 *DJP*, appendix II, document 4, p. 538; Tiele, "De Europeërs in den Maleischen Archipel", part VI, *BKI* 30 (1882): 196.

51 *DJP*, appendix II, document 4, p. 538, "… here were many people aboard the carrack, including one hundred women, who, for decency's sake, could not be searched too closely. About seven hundred and fifty souls went aboard the two yachts [that ferried all survivors of the *Santa Catarina* to land]."

52 Van Ittersum, *Profit and Principle*, pp. 35–6.

53 Van Meteren, *Commentariën ofte Memoriën*, II, fol. 148 recto.

54 De Bry, *Indiae Orientalis Pars Octava*, p. 86; Hervey, "François Valentyn's Account of Malacca", p. 128; Borschberg, "Hugo Grotius, East India Trade", *JSEAS* 30, 2 (1999): 231, 234.

55 *DJP*, appendix II, document 4, p. 538, "According to the carrack's captain, there were seventy casualties among the passengers and crew. If half the shots that we fired at the mainsails had been aimed any lower, there would have been many more casualties, for the large number of passengers and crew made them an easy target."

56 Tiele, "De Europeërs in den Maleischen Archipel", part VI, *BKI* 30 (1882): 196.

57 *DJP*, appendix I, document 5, "The Council of Malacca to the Four Representatives of the Dutch ships who Accompanied the Portuguese Prisoners to an Island near Malacca, 9 March, 1603", p. 523.

58 *DJP*, appendix I, document 5, p. 523.

59 *DJP*, appendix I, document 6, "The Governor of Malacca to Admiral Jacob van Heemskerck, 9 March, 1603", pp. 524–5.

60 *DJP*, appendix I, document 6, pp. 524.

61 *DJP*, appendix I, document 6, pp. 524–5, "What happened to the Hollanders in China grieves me not a little, and it troubles me that such a heavy punishment was imposed with so little cause. Be assured, however, that the public prosecutor of Macao, the perpetrator of this misdeed, already languishes in jail, and will have to pay for it with his life. I nullified the charges against the Hollanders who arrived here from China and the Moluccas and showed myself a good friend to them."

62 *DJP*, appendix I, document 6, p. 525.

63 *DJP*, appendix I, document 7, p. 526.

64 *DJP*, appendix I, document 7, p. 526, "In the knowledge that Your Honor cares deeply for the fate of all captives and oppressed Christians, I entreat Your Honor to do me the favor of negotiating with the King of Johor and his brother. I want him to release the Portuguese and Christians whom he keeps prisoner under the pretext of peace. I do not speak of, or wish to reclaim, the

cargo of the junk, which has undoubtedly been divided among the soldiers of his navy. I only desire the release of the Portuguese and Christian prisoners, who are of little importance to the Malayans. I therefore send you Philippe Lobo and Pero Mascarenhas, whom I entreat Your Honor to take into your protection, so that they may safely return with the Portuguese prisoners and not lack your favor and goodwill." — The individual by the name of "Filipe Lobo" is probably identical to the one mentioned by de Coutre in *AA*, p. 159.

65 *DJP*, appendix I, document 8, "Captain of the *Santa Catarina* to Admiral Jacob van Heemskerck, 24 March, 1603", pp. 526–7.

66 *DJP*, appendix I, document 8, p. 526.

67 *DJP*, appendix I, document 8, pp. 526–7.

68 For the Dutch text, see appendix 7.

69 Alum, aloeswood and *radix Chinae* were widely used in early modern medicine, and aloeswood was one of the highest-priced commodities of its day. According to Johannes Schröder, one of the most republished and widely used pharmacopoeiae of the 17th century, alum is a salt-like substance obtained from rocks, soil or ashes that was used to cure tooth, gum and throat disorders. It was also used to cure high fever and dysentery and, infamously, to restore virginity in women. *Radix Chinae*, a knotty rhizome introduced into European medicine around the middle of the 16th century, found use chiefly in the treatment of skin disorders and advanced stages of syphilis. See Schröder, *Medicin-Chymische Apotheke*, pp. 704–6; Borschberg, "The Euro-Asian Trade", *Revista de Cultura*, international edition, no. 20 (2006): 102–15; Flückiger and Hanbury, *Pharmacographia*, pp. 648–9.

70 That is, the carrack *Santa Catarina*.

71 A more detailed cargo list found in van Heemskerk's letter to the directors of the United Amsterdam Company of 27 August 1603, can be found in *DJP*, appendix 2, document 4, pp. 540–1.

72 Boxer, *Fidalgos in the Far East*, p. 50.

73 The Dutch were clearly aware of such objectives. See the resolution of van Heemskerk and his naval council dated 4 December, 1602, *DJP*, appendix II, document 3, pp. 531–2.

74 On the location of this former capital of Johor, see Rouffaer, "Was Malaka Emporium vóór 1400?", *BKI* 77 (1921): 482ff. From the letter of Van Heemskerk to the Directors of the United Amsterdam Company dated 27 August 1603, it transpires that Buys was left behind in Batu Sawar at the same time that the king of Johor expressed his desire to despatch an embassy to the Dutch Republic. Van Heemskerk's thoughts and deliberations are found in *DJP*, appendix II, document 4, p. 539, "In addition, he [the King of Johor] insisted that cape merchant Jacob Buys remain at Johore instead of Pieter Opmeer [van Heemskerk's choice as agent for Johor], which put me [van Heemskerk] in a difficult position. I figured that Buys was wanted at Cambay in order to

establish a factory there, which is essential for our trade with Southeast Asia. Since our commodities were already ashore and since I had consented to a Johorese embassy, I decided to humor the King in this point as well, also because of the kingdom's geographic location and commercial potential. It is clearly the most suitable place in all of the East Indies to load pepper and sell textiles from Cambay and San Thomé. Yet I had to use all my persuasive powers in order to convince Jacob Buys, who preferred to go home and share in the booty of the *Santa Catarina.*"

75 According to extant Portuguese sources, the Johor fortress, Kota Batu, was rebuilt with thick wooden palisades within an astonishingly short period of time. It may very well represent a rhetorical pose on the part of Dom Henrique when he claims that the new fortress was even better than the one destroyed in the previous year by Dom Paulo Lima de Pereira (see appendix 2). The swift reconstruction of the fortress is mentioned in a letter by Dom Henriques dated 16 December 1588, which is featured as document appendix 5 in Pinto, *Portugueses e malaios*, pp. 271–2.

76 Ioannes Theodoricus and Ioannes Israel de Bry, *Icones seu Gennuinae et Expressae Delineationes.*

77 For a fuller bibliographic description of this work, see Landwehr, *VOC: A Bibliography*, ed. Peter van der Krogt, entry no. 192: de Bry's "Small Voyages" Latin, VIII, 1607, pp. 69–70. No mention is made here of plate XII. For biographical details of Arthus, see Liliencron, *Allgeimeine Deutsche Biographie*, I, p. 613.

78 Commelin, *Begin ende Voortgang.*

79 Renneville, *Recueil des voiages*; Bernard, *A Collection of Voyages*. The latter English text is incomplete and represents a "translation" of volume 1 of Commelin's original compilation.

80 Jakob Pietersz van Enkhuysen is erroneously attributed the name "Cornelis" by *JO*, III, p. 17. Several authors have copied this error, including Tiele, Mac Leod and Terpstra, all of whom are cited in the present chapter. See also Coolhaas, "Een bron van het historische gedeelte", *Bijdragen en Mededelingen van het Historisch Genootschap* 79 (1965): 505, note 4. The vice-admiral's name is rendered correctly in Wieder ed., *De reis van Joris van Spilbergen*, p. 76, Spilbergen's log entry of 8 March 1603. The Portuguese naval officer is sometimes referred to as "Teixeira de Made" or "Teixeira de Macedo". See, for example, Teixeira, *The Portuguese Missions*, I, p. 223, note 3; Boxer and Vasconcelos, *André Furtado*, appendix V, p. 127, note 1; de Bry, *Indiae Orientalis Pars Octava*, p. 85, refers to the Portuguese naval officer as "Estenao Teixeira de Made". According to Bocarro, an officer by the name of Estevão Teixeira de Macedo later acted as an ambassador of the Portuguese to the Great Moghul. He was murdered aboard his galleon off the coast of Melaka in 1615 or early 1616. On the embassy, see Bocarro,

Década XIII, pp. 391–8, esp. pp. 391–2; on his assassination at Melaka, see pp. 514, 630. The episode is also mentioned by MacGregor, "The Portuguese in Malaya", *JMBRAS* 28, 2 (1955): 35, note 127.

81 Tiele, "De Europeërs in den Maleischen Archipel", part VI, *BKI* 30 (1882): 217–8.

82 Jacobs, "The Portuguese Town", *Segundo Seminário internacional*, ed. Albuquerque and Guerreiro, p. 604; Lobato, *Política e comércio*, p. 357. The fort surrendered to the Dutch in 1605; see Jacobs, "The Portuguese Town", p. 606.

83 Tiele, "De Europeërs in den Maleischen Archipel", part VI, *BKI* 30 (1882): 220; Coolhaas, "Een bron van het historische gedeelte", *Bijdragen en Mededelingen van het Historisch Genootschap* 79 (1965): 506.

84 Pinto, *Portugueses e malaios*, document 13, dated 6 April 1603, p. 286.

85 Vice-Admiral de Weert "founded" the VOC factory at Aceh in early 1603. A factory of one of the Zeeland-based *voorcompagniën* was already established at Aceh in 1600.

86 The incident is described at length in de Bry, *Indiae Orientalis Pars Octava*, pp. 51ff.

87 De Bry, *Indiae Orientalis Pars Octava*, pp. 53–4.

88 The Hague, Nationaal Archief, *Recueil concernent les voyages des Hollandais aux Indes Orientales, la Compagnie des Indies, etc. 1600–1616*; (personal and working papers on East India affairs deriving from the possession of Hugo Grotius) call number 1.10.35.02, "Discours ende Advertentie van de navolgende scheepen", fols. 458 recto and following; "Historische Verhael", *BV*, II, p. 23; de Bry, *Indiae Orientalis Pars Octava*, p. 65; van Meteren, *Commentariën ofte Memoriën*, II, fols. 148 verso–149 recto; Coolhaas, "Een bron van het historische gedeelte", *Bijdragen en Mededelingen van het Historisch Genootschap* 79 (1965): 505; *DJP*, pp. 474–5; Mac Leod, *De Oost-Indische Compagnie*, I, pp. 13–4.

89 Latinised as *Iacobus Petri Enchusanus*.

90 De Bry, *Indiae Orientalis Pars Octava*, p. 67; Mac Leod, *De Oost-Indische Compagnie*, p. 14.

91 Terpstra, "De factorij der Oostindische Compagnie te Patani", *Verhandelingen van het Koninklijk Instituut voor de Taal-, Land- en Volkenkunde van Nederlandsch-Indië*, I, p. 18; Mac Leod, *De Oost-Indische Compagnie*, p. 14.

92 De Bry, *Indiae Orientalis Pars Octava*, pp. 78ff; "Historische Verhael", *BV*, II, pp. 34–6.

93 "Historische Verhael", *BV*, II, p. 36.

94 The depth of water was traditionally measured in fathoms (Dutch *vadem*, Latin *orgya*). The Amsterdam *vadem* measures about 1.7 metres. See also *BOC*, I.1, p. 741.

95 The term *scapha* is used in the Latin text of 1607.

96 "Historische Verhael", *BV*, II, pp. 36–7.

97 Described in the Latin text of 1607 as *Æthiopes* (dark-skinned people, or *swaerten* as they were sometimes referred to in the vernacular Dutch).

98 De Bry, *Indiae Orientalis Pars Octava*, pp. 83–4; "Historische Verhael", *BV*, II, p. 37.

99 "Historische Verhael", *BV*, II, p. 37. Grotius briefly touches upon this incident in his *De Jure Praedae Commentarius* (Commentary on the Law of Prize and Booty). In chapter 15 of this work he claims that the Portuguese had "two galleons" and more than 25 "brigantines and other ships of war", see *DJP*, p. 482. According to the testimony of David Lochum, printed in Coolhaas, "Een bron van het historische gedeelte van Hugo de Groots De Jure Praedae", *Bijdragen en Mededelingen van het Historisch Genootschap* 79 (1965): 506, the Portuguese armada consisted of "two gallions or large ships, six galley and twenty-four bantins or foists".

100 De Bry, *Indiae Orientalis Pars Octava*, p. 84.

101 "Historische Verhael", *BV*, II, p. 38; Botelho e Sousa, *Subsídios*, I, p. 554.

102 "Historische Verhael", *BV*, II, p. 38; Tiele, "De Europeërs in den Maleischen Archipel", part VI, *BKI* 30 (1882): 217, 218; Botelho e Sousa, *Subsídios*, I, p. 553.

103 Name latinised as *Buis[s]ius*; see de Bry, *Indiae Orientalis Pars Octava*, p. 85; Mac Leod, *De Oost-Indische Compagnie*, p. 14; *NJS*, p. 8.

104 Tiele, "De Europeërs in den Maleischen Archipel", part VI, *BKI* 30 (1882): 217.

105 "Historische Verhael", *BV*, II, p. 37.

106 Rouffaer, "Was Malaka Emporium vóór 1400?", *BKI* 77 (1921): 386–7.

107 "Historische Verhael", *BV*, II, pp. 37, 40; similar descriptions are found in other sources, see especially Gibson-Hill, "Singapore: Note on the History of the Old Straits", *JMBRAS* 27, 1 (1954): 163–214.

108 "Historische Verhael", *BV*, II, pp. 37–8; "Was Malaka Emporium vóór 1400?", *BKI* 77 (1921): 388, 401.

109 "Historische Verhael", *BV*, II, p. 38; Rouffaer, "Was Malaka Emporium vóór 1400?", *BKI* 77 (1921): 401.

110 De Bry, *Indiae Orientalis Pars Octava*, p. 85; "Historische Verhael", *BV*, II, p. 38.

111 Rouffaer, "Was Malaka Emporium vóór 1400?", *BKI* 77 (1921): 433, 438; Dennys, *Descriptive Dictionary*, p. 273.

112 De Bry, *Indiae Orientalis Pars Octava*, p. 85; "Historische Verhael", *BV*, II, p. 38.

113 Hervey, "François Valentyn's Account of Malacca", p. 128; Teixeira, *The Portuguese Missions*, I, p. 223.

114 De Bry, *Indiae Orientalis Pars Octava*, p. 86: "Codsa ab Delsab". This is almost certainly a corrupted name.

115 De Bry, *Indiae Orientalis Pars Octava*, p. 86; "Historische Verhael", *BV*, II, p. 39.

116 Tiele, "De Europeërs in den Maleischen Archipel", part VI, *BKI* 30 (1882): 218; De Bry, *Indiae Orientalis Pars Octava*, p. 87.

117 Hervey, "François Valentyn's Account of Malacca", p. 129.

118 Latinised as *Rahu Bongso*.

119 De Bry, *Indiae Orientalis Pars Octava*, p. 87: "... Araka et fructus offerentes ..." (Offering arak and fruit); "Historische Verhael", *BV*, II, p. 40. In this context, it is also useful to see what Erédia has to say about abiding by Islamic dietary restrictions at this period in time. See his *Declaraçam de Malaca*, fols. 38 verso–39 recto.

120 De Bry, *Indiae Orientalis Pars Octava*, p. 87; Tiele, "De Europeërs in den Maleischen Archipel", part VI, *BKI* 30 (1882): 218; Mac Leod, *De Oost-Indische Compagnie*, p. 14.

121 De Bry, *Indiae Orientalis Pars Octava*, p. 88; Hervey, "François Valentyn's Account of Malacca", p. 129.

122 De Bry, *Indiae Orientalis Pars Octava*, p. 88, referred to in the Latin text by its commonly used Portuguese name, Pedra Branca (White Rock). This navigational landmark, however, is depicted on de Bry's map as *Pedro Blanco*, a literal translation into Spanish of the Portuguese name.

123 De Bry, *Indiae Orientalis Pars Octava*, p. 88; "Historische Verhael", *BV*, II, p. 41.

124 Coolhaas, "Een bron van het historische gedeelte", *Bijdragen en Mededelingen van het Historisch Genootschap* 79 (1965): 506.

125 "Historische Verhael", *BV*, II, p. 40.

126 De Bry, *Indiae Orientalis Pars Octava*, p. 88.

127 De Bry, *Indiae Orientalis Pars Octava*, p. 89; "Historische Verhael", *BV*, II, p. 42; Tiele, "De Europeërs in den Maleischen Archipel", part VI, *BKI* 30 (1882): 218.

128 De Bry, *Indiae Orientalis Pars Octava*, p. 89.

129 Terms based on the Dutch text printed in Commelin. The Latin description reads slightly differently. See De Bry, *Indiae Orientalis Pars Octava*, p. 89.

130 De Bry, *Indiae Orientalis Pars Octava*, p. 89; "Historische Verhael", *BV*, II, p. 42; Teixeira, *The Portuguese Missions*, I, p. 223.

131 *DJP*, pp. 482–3; Terpstra, "De factorij", pp. 18–9. On the cargo loaded at Patani and the subsequent fate of the vessels, see also Terpstra, "De factorij", pp. 19–20.

132 De Bry, *Indiae Orientalis Pars Octava*, p. 89; "Historische Verhael", *BV*, II, p. 42; Terpstra, "De factorij", p. 18; Mac Leod, *De Oost-Indische Compagnie*, p. 14.

133 *DJP*, p. 482. Grotius' assertion that the "whole [Portuguese] fleet" was vanquished is a grossly exaggerated claim made in the heat of enthusiasm.

134 Teixeira, *The Portuguese Missions*, I, pp. 224–5.

135 Tiele, "De Europeërs in den Maleischen Archipel", part VI, *BKI* 30 (1882): 238.

136 *NJS*, letter by the king of Johor dated 6 February 1609, pp. 17ff, see pp. 19–20, where the origin of the dynastic quarrel (approximately 1602–3) is explained

by the monarch in some detail. See also Linehan, *History of Pahang*, pp. 31–2. See also Winstedt, "The Early Rulers of Perak, Pahang and Acheh", *JMBRAS* 10, 1 (1932): 36–7.

137 Pelliot, "Les Relations du Siam et de la Hollande en 1608", *T'Oung Pao* 32 (1936): pp. 223–9; Duyvendak, "The First Siamese Embassy", *T'Oung Pao* 32 (1936): 285–92; Rodao, *Españoles en Siam*, p. 41. See also Ruangsilp, Dutch East, pp. 18, 30–1.

138 *LM*, I, document 60, letter from King of Portugal, Philip III/II, to his viceroy of India, Dom Alfonso de Castro, dated Lisbon, 4 January 1608, p. 174; see also *LM*, I, p. 177.

139 *LM*, IV, doc. 933, letter from the king to his viceroy of India dated 17 January 1618, pp. 260–1.

140 Valentijn, *Oud en Nieuw Oost-Indiën*, VII, p. 329.

141 Van Meteren, *Commentariën ofte Memoriën*, II, fol. 518 recto.

142 Van Meteren, *Commentariën ofte Memoriën*, II, fol. 516ff; Jacobs, "The Portuguese Town", pp. 604, 606; Lobato, *Política e comércio*, p. 357. The fort was surrendered to the Dutch in 1605.

143 "Historische Verhael", *BV*, II, p. 82; Valentijn, *Oud en Nieuw Oost-Indiën*, VII, p. 329.

144 "Chinese camphor" or "Japanese laurel camphor" refers to camphor synthetically produced in China. It should not be confused with tropical camphor from Sumatra (specifically Barus) and Borneo. Tropical camphor, also known as "edible camphor", was widely used in the treatment of intestinal parasites. Chinese camphor is used in the treatment of skin disorders and lesions but is otherwise toxic to the human body. During the early modern period, the price of tropical camphor was approximately ten times greater than its synthetic counterpart.

145 *DUP*, II, p. 255; "Historische Verhael", *BV*, II, pp. 79, 82–3; Hervey, "François Valentyn's Account of Malacca", p. 130; Tiele, "De Europeërs in den Maleischen Archipel", part VI, *BKI* 30 (1882): 238.

146 *DUP*, I, p. 255; "Historische Verhael", *BV*, II, p. 83; Valentijn, *Oud en Nieuw Oost-Indiën*, vol. VII, p. 329; Hervey, "François Valentyn's Account of Malacca", pp. 130–1.

147 "Historische Verhael", *BV*, II, p. 81.

148 Pinto, *Portugueses e malaios*, pp. 120–1.

149 Botelho e Sousa, *Subsídios*, I, p. 554.

150 This was the common form of fortification in the Malay world. See, for example, the diary of Roelof Roelofsz published in *De Vierde Schipvaart*, ed. Foreest and de Booy, I, p. 259 (description of Patani).

151 Boxer and Vasconcelos, *André Furtado*, pp. 55–6; Lobato, *Política e comércio*, p. 353.

152 Boxer, *The Great Ship*, p. 68.

153 Boxer and Vasconcelos, *André Furtado*, p. 56; *DUP*, I, p. 255; Lobato, *Política e comércio*, p. 353.

154 Mendes da Luz, *O Conselho da Índia*, document XXIX, "Relação", p. 430; Terpstra, "De factorij der Oostindische Compagnie te Patani", p. 24; Teixeira, *The Portuguese Missions*, I, p. 225.

155 Mendes da Luz, *O Conselho da Índia*, document XXIX, "Relação", p. 430; Terpstra, "De factorij der Oostindische Compagnie te Patani", p. 24.

156 Teixeira, *The Portuguese Missions*, I, p. 225.

157 Mendes da Luz, *O Conselho da Índia*, document XXIX, "Relação", p. 430; Ijzermann, "Hollandsche Prenten", *Gedenkschrift*, p. 84.

158 See also van Meteren, *Commentariën ofte Memoriën*, II, fol. 550 verso.

159 Mendes da Luz, *O Conselho da Índia*, p. 266, simply states that the carrack was "ricamente caregada" (richly laden).

160 *DUP*, I, p. 254; Boxer and Vasconcelos, *André Furtado*, p. 55.

161 Mendes da Luz, *O Conselho da Índia*, p. 266, states that the ship was taken in the "bay" (*na baía*) of Patani.

162 Van Meteren, *Commentariën ofte Memoriën*, II, fol. 518 recto.

163 Van Meteren, *Commentariën ofte Memoriën*, II, fol. 518 recto, claims that the Portuguese mates abandoned ship.

164 *JO*, III, p. 25; Enthoven, *Zeeland*, p. 201. Terpstra, following Valentijn, claims that the *Santo António* was taken by Vice-admiral Sebastiaanse.

165 "Historische Verhael", *BV*, II, pp. 82–3.

166 Valentijn, *Oud en Nieuw Oost-Indiën*, VII, p. 329.

167 On the Euro-Asian musk trade in general, see Borschberg, "O comércio europeu de almíscar", *Oriente* 5 (2003): 90–9.

168 Vermilion is a sulphur-mercury compound that is found naturally, or was already synthetically produced in China during the early modern period.

169 Taffettas and damask are forms of woven silk.

170 This cargo list, in fact, represents what could be deemed a standard or conventional load for its day. Compare it with the list of marketable goods listed by Morga in his discussion on Manila's trade with the Chinese merchants. *PI*, 15: 305–6.

171 "Historische Verhael", *BV*, II, p. 82; van Meteren, *Commentariën ofte Memoriën*, II, fol. 518 recto. Additional purchases of Chinese silks were also made in Banten.

172 *AA*, pp. 160–1.

173 Terpstra, "De factorij der Oostindische Compagnie te Patani", p. 25.

174 Mendes da Luz, *O Conselho da Índia*, document XXIX, "Relação", p. 431.

175 "Historische Verhael", *BV*, II, p. 82.

176 Van Meteren, *Commentariën ofte Memoriën*, II, fol. 518 recto: "... begonden dat Schip [the *Santo António*] wat lagher te timmeren ..." (They began to

reduce the height of that ship ...), Terpstra, "De factorij der Oostindische Compagnie te Patani", p. 25.

177 Tiele, "De Europeërs in den Maleischen Archipel", part VI, *BKI* 30 (1882): 239.

178 Pinto, *Portugueses e malaios*, p. 197.

179 Tiele, "De Europeërs in den Maleischen Archipel", part VI, *BKI* 30 (1882): 229, note 2.

180 As is known the English were indeed active in the Strait of Melaka, as James Lancaster's seizure in October 1602 of an in-bound carrack from São Thomé doubtlessly testifies. Still, a confusion with the Dutch should not be dismissed.

181 This information from Dutch sources is not confirmed by statistical material published by de Matos. According figures published by the Portuguese academic, the *Estado da Índia* continued to reap considerable surpluses from Melaka for the year 1607. See de Matos, *Na Rota*, p. 77, "Quadro III. Receita e Despesa do Estado da Índia em 1607". In the statistics compiled in this work, Melaka only began to record deficits after 1620, resulting from both from declining (trade) receipts and considerably higher expenses. See de Matos, *Na Rota*, pp. 79–80.

182 Valentijn, *Oud en Nieuw Oost-Indiën*, VII, p. 329.

183 Valentijn, *Oud en Nieuw Oost-Indiën*, VII, pp. 329–30; Terpstra, "De factorij der Oostindische Compagnie te Patani", p. 26; Tiele, "De Europeërs in den Maleischen Archipel", part VI, *BKI* 30 (1882): 240.

184 "Historische Verhael", *BV*, II, p. 84; Valentijn, *Oud en Nieuw Oost-Indiën*, VII, p. 330.

185 *JO*, III, pp. 245–6.

186 This ship is evidently the same *Mauritius* that belonged to the fleet of Matelieff de Jonge and was at the time carrying on board the ambassadors of King Ekathotsarot of Siam to the Netherlands. See also Borschberg, "The Seizure of the Sta. Catarina Revisited", *JSEAS* 33, 1 (2002): 60, note 132. It appears, however, that the Siamese ambassadors were transferred to another vessel at Banten or perhaps even thereafter, as there are no reports of their shipwreck.

187 Bruijn, Gaastra and Schöffer, ed., *Dutch-Asiatic Shipping*, III, pp. 12–3, entry 0098.

188 Present-day Cape Lopez on the coast of Gabon. It is located near Port Gentil.

189 Veenendaal, ed., *Johan van Oldenbarnevelt*, II, no. 248, "De Bewindhebbers van de Oostindische Compagie te Amsterdam aan Oldenbarnevelt", 6 August 1609, p. 338.

190 Veenendaal, ed., *Johan van Oldenbarnevelt*, II, no. 248, "De Bewindhebbers van de Oostindische Compagie te Amsterdam aan Oldenbarnevelt", 11 September 1609, pp. 343–4.

191 "Historische Verhael", *BV*, II. p. 86.

192 *Dutch-Asiatic Shipping*, III, pp. 12–3, entries 0068, 0082 and 0093.
193 Enthoven, *Zeeland*, p. 209.
194 Enthoven, *Zeeland*, p. 209, note 238.
195 Enthoven, *Zeeland*, p. 208.
196 Enthoven, *Zeeland*, p. 209.
197 *BOC*, I.1, p. 499.
198 See note 160.
199 Van Meteren, *Commentariën ofte Memoriën*, II, fol. 450 recto.
200 The capture of the *São Jorge*, known in some early modern sources as the *St. Jago*, is featured prominently in several secondary works on early Dutch freebooting activities. Among the ill-fated ship's passengers was the Florentine merchant Carletti, whose accumulated fortune was seized by the Dutch. After lengthy court proceedings, Carletti eventually had a part of his wealth returned to him. See van Ittersum, *Profit and Principle*, pp. 123–30; Roelofsen, "Het trieste slot", *Mededelingen van de Nederlandse Vereniging voor Zeegeschiedenis* 20 (1970): 13–30.
201 *BOC*, I.1, pp. 499, 517.
202 Borschberg, "Hugo Grotius, East India Trade", *JSEAS* 30, 2 (1999): 243–4.
203 Matelieff de Jonge claims to have seen a copy of the provisional agreement with his own eyes. See *NJS*, p. 24; Rietbergen, *De Eerste Landvoogd*, II, p. 207. The "Historische Verhael Vande treffelijcke Reyse, gedaen naer de Oost-Indien ende China, met elf Schepen door den Manhaften Admirael Cornelis Matelief de Ionge", *BV*, III, p. 131, also alludes to a peace treaty made after the Portuguese had attacked and burnt Batu Sawar around 1607, forcing Raja Bongsu to flee to Lingga.
204 See, for example, *CB*, VII-A, letter by Pieter van den Broeck *et al.* dated 30 September 1615, p. 45.
205 *NJS*, p. 25.
206 *JO*, III, letter by Obelaer, 25 November 1610, p. 304; *NJS*, pp. 27–9 passim; see also Teixeira, *The Portuguese Missions*, I, p. 242, which contains a seriously garbled account of this episode.
207 Teixeira, *The Portuguese Missions*.
208 Teixeira, *The Portuguese Missions*, I, p. 242. See also *TB*, I, letter from Steven van der Hagen to the Heren XVII, dated 10 March 1616, p. 129.
209 Biker, *Collecção de tratados e concertos de pazes*.
210 Saldanha, *Iustum Imperium*, p. 371, note 10.
211 *TB*, I, "Cort verhael", dated 10 November 1614, p. 76; *CB*, I, report of 12 November 1618, p. 414.
212 *CB*, I, report of 6 September 1622, p. 793.
213 *JO*, III, letter by Obelaer, 25 November 1610, p. 306.
214 *NJS*, letter by Raja Bongsu, dated 6 February 1609 and passed to Admiral van Caerden, p. 18.

215 *NJS*, letter by Raja Bongsu, 8 December 1609, p. 27: "Verder wordt in 't schrijven van onzen broeder verzocht ons voorgaande verbond vermerderen of vernieuwen. Waarom dan toch telkens veranderd of vernieuwd? 'T ware derhalve wel onze begeerte, dat onze broeder gelieve eens een persoon van aanzien met volle magt en autoriteit herwaarts te willen zenden, opdat men dien een onverbrekelijk accord mag gemaakt worden, 'twelk moge duren tot den dag des oordeels toe. Al kwamen er dan twintig of dertig admirals …; wantnu, zoo komt een admiraal, met welken wij een goed accord hebben gemaakat, komt daarna een ander en verandert 'tzelve. Zoo doende zal 't geen eind hebben accoorden te maken. …" Translated from Dutch by the author.

216 The truce signed between the Dutch Republic and Spain for a period of Twelve Years (the so-called Twelve Years Truce) was later amended. It foresaw peace between the Dutch Republic and all Spanish dependencies in Europe, but a continuation of the war in the extra-European theatre, such as importantly in the Americas and Asia. Just as the Dutch Republic "inherited" its war against Portugal through the Union of the Two Crowns (where the King of Spain also ruled as the King of Portugal), the 1609 Truce had immediate implications for VOC hostility against Portugal in the East Indies.

217 *NJS*, letter by Raja Bongsu, 8 December 1609, p. 26.

218 Tiele, "De Europeërs in den Maleischen Archipel", part VI, *BKI* 30 (1882): 229, note 2. Matelieff de Jonge suggested that routine attacks and seizure of Portuguese vessels inbound from China would inflict the most damage on the Lusitanian traders. Whether or not the company actually heeded this counsel shall be left aside here. However, it is beyond dispute that the southern tip of the Johor mainland and the Straits of Singapore became one of the preferred sites for Dutch freebooting operations. Most of the ships taken by the Dutch were seized around the eastern entrance of the Singapore Strait (around Pedra Branca and the Hook of Berbukit) or, less frequently, near the approach to the western entrance of the Straits (near Pulau Pisang, the Sembilan Islands, and the western coast of Singapore). See also Rietbergen, *De Eerste Landvoogd*, II, p. 208; *GM*, I, p. 468 (incident of 22 June 1634).

219 See especially Linehan, *History of Pahang*, p. 35.

220 *NJS*, p. 30; Ralph Standige and "Crofte, purser", "A Journal of the Tenth East Indea Vaige, maid by … Thomas Best … Anno Domine 1611 [1612]" (hereafter Standish-Croft *Journal*), contained in *The Voyage of Thomas Best*, pp. 93ff, entry for 28 June 1613, p. 169: "His army [that is, the naval force of the Acehnese monarch] was 100 small frigotts and gallies, some haveing ordinance, some none; the number of souldiers 20,000." For another account of the strength of the Acehnese navy at that time, see Münster, *Cosmographia*, p. 1598.

221 Rietbergen, *De Eerste Landvoogd*, II, p. 357.

[222] Gibson-Hill holds that the settlement of Singapura went up in flames in 1613, which the present author does not contest. See Gibson-Hill, "Singapore Old Strait and New Harbour", *Memoirs of the Raffles Museum*, no. 3 (1956): 20. Questions however remain as to the identity of these agents of Singapura's destruction. The archeologist Miksic has identified the Portuguese as the culprits, a view that the present author does not find conclusive. See especially Miksic, *Archeological Research*, pp. 33, 34.

[223] According to the Standish-Croft *Journal* entry for 28 June 1613, p. 170, the fire was set deliberately: "But the Capttain of the Flemings and his merchants ashoare burned ther housse and fleed. …"

[224] See the letter from Pieter Both to the Heren XVII dated 1 November 1614, in Rietbergen, *De Eerste Landvoogd*, II, p. 295. This action was also reported by the English in Aceh. See Standish-Croft *Journal* entry for 28 June 1613, p. 169: "A Flemish shipp att this tyme hapened to be att [the] ille of Joar, tradinge there; which did, in the King of Joars behalf, resist and shott at the army of this Kinge of Achen and Sumatra."

[225] *TB*, I, report of Jan Pieterszoon Coen to the Heren XVII, dated 10 November 1614, p. 67; *CB*, I, report of 1 January 1614, pp. 27–8, and report of 27 December 1614, p. 100; *De Eerste Landvoogd Pieter Both*, II, p. 295; Bocarro, *Década XIII*, II, p. 165, pp. 417ff; *The Voyage of Thomas Best*, pp. 58–9; Standish-Croft *Journal* entry for 28 June 1613, pp. 169–70: "… for … his [that is, the king of Aceh's] army was returned from Joar, and had brought the King prisoner … Butt the younge King of Joar yielded, and they weere taken and brought hither to Achen prisoners, mariners and merchants, to the number of 20"; letter from Thomas Best at Aceh to Thomas Aldsworth at Surat, dated 12 July 1613, in *The Voyage of Thomas Best*, p. 257: "… the Kings armada of frigatts came from Joor, bringinge the kinge thereof, with his brother, many of their people, and 22 Dutch prisoners (most of them of the factorie there, the rest a Dutch shippe then there ridinge)". Bocarro, *Década XIII*, pp. 165, 417–22. See also Lombard, *Le Sultanat d'Atjéh*, p. 92.

[226] Foster, ed., *The Voyage of Thomas Best*, pp. 170, 257; Standish-Croft *Journal* entry for June 1613, p. 169.

[227] See also *NJS*, p. 31, undated letter by Admiral Steven van der Hagen (assumed to have been written about 1616); Gibson-Hill, "The Alleged Death", *JMBRAS* 29 (1956): 124–45; Rouffaer, "Was Malaka Emporium vóór 1400?", *BKI* 77 (1921): 596.

[228] Coolhaas, ed., *Pieter van den Broecke in Azië*, journal entry of 10 August 1618, p. 175; *CB*, VII-A, letter by Pieter van den Broeck and others, dated 30 September 1615, p. 42. Another letter written by Governor-General Pieter Both to the Heren XVII, dated 1 January 1614, reports that Iskandar Muda of Aceh wed his son to a daughter of the Johor king. See Rietbergen, *De Eerste Landvoogd*, II, p. 295. Evidently marriage was used to seal the new

alliance "in perpetuity", and both marriages may very well have served the same purpose.

229 See also *NJS*, p. 30.

230 *CB*, I, report of 3 March 1615, p. 110.

231 *TB*, I, letter by Coen to the Heren XVII, dated Banten, 1 January 1614, p. 60; Teixeira, *The Portuguese*, I, p. 245; *CB*, I, 1 November 1614, pp. 90–1; 27 December 1614, p. 101; see also 22 October 1615, pp. 130, 140; 31 March 1616, p. 180.

232 *CB*, I, pp. 134–5.

233 *TB*, I, report (*Cort verhael*), dated 10 November 1614, p. 70.

234 *TB*, I, p. 68; *CB*, I, report of 10 November 1614, pp. 62, 90.

235 Rietbergen, *De Eerste Landvoogd*, II, p. 207.

Chapter 3

1 For a full transcript and translation of Dom Paulo Lima de Pereira's letter of 28 November 1587, see appendix 2.

2 Barros and Couto, *Da Ásia*, década 10, pt. X, lib. 10, cap. XIV.

3 Lobato, *Política e comércio*, pp. 67–8.

4 Alves and Manguin, *O Roteiro*, pp. 98ff.

5 Alves and Manguin, *O Roteiro*, p. 99.

6 Alves and Manguin, *O Roteiro*, pp. 99–100.

7 Pinto, *Portugueses e malaios*, p. 287.

8 The classic testimony to this effect is the letter by Bishop Dom Ribeiro Gaio and addressed to Philip III/II of Spain and Portugal, dated 30 April 1600, published in *DJP*, appendix I, document 4, pp. 517–22.

9 Pinto, *Portugueses e malaios*, p. 112.

10 Gibson-Hill, "Singapore: Note on the History of the Old Straits", *JMBRAS* 27, 1 (1954): 156.

11 Gibson-Hill, "Singapore: Note", p. 157.

12 See also Pinto, *Portugueses e malaios*, p. 122.

13 *LM*, I, p. 131. See also an earlier letter, dated Lisbon, 12 January 1607 in *LM*, I, p. 60.

14 *LM*, IV, reply of Viceroy João Coutinho, dated Goa, 7 February 1619, pp. 279–80.

15 De Coutre, *Como Remediar o Estado da Índia?*, pp. 16–21; *AA*, pp. 395–405. On the authorship of this and other memorials, see Winius and Chorba, "Literary invasions in La Vida de Jaques de Coutre: Do They Prejudice Its Value as an Historical Source?" in *A Carreira da Índia*, ed. de Matos and Thomaz, p. 712: "… [A]t least, Jaques de Coutre's other writings, his memorials to the crown, or *arbítrios*, are surely from his own hand." See also Winius and Chorba, "Literary invasions", p. 714: "[De Coutre's] *arbítrios*, his

memorials to the crown about conditions in and remedies to be applied to the *Estado da Índia* almost certainly were known at court."

16 See appendix 5 and de Coutre, *Como Remediar*, p. 30; *AA*, pp. 107, 422.

17 See appendix 5.

18 This probably refers to the present-day island of Lingga rather than Bintan, as it is known and depicted by Erédia in his *Declaraçam de Malaca*, fol. 34 verso.

19 See appendix 5.

20 See appendix 5. Lombard, *Le Sultanat d'Atjéh*, p. 92, where the first Acehnese assault on Pahang is dated 1617; see also Winstedt, "The Early Rulers of Perak, Pahang and Acheh", *JMBRAS* 19,1 (1932): 36–9; Linehan, *A History of Pahang*, pp. 33ff, esp. p. 35.

21 De Coutre, *Como Remediar*, p. 41.

22 De Coutre, *Como Remediar*, pp. 16–21; *AA*, pp. 395–405.

23 De Coutre, *Como Remediar*, p. 31; *AA*, p. 423.

24 On the Portuguese and Spanish understanding of the native *Chincheo*, see *South China in the Sixteenth Century*, ed. Boxer, appendix I, pp. 313–26.

25 Coolhaas, "Een bron van het historische gedeelte van Hugo de Groots De Jure Praedae", *Bijdragen en Mededelingen van het Historisch Genootschap* 79 (1965): p. 528; J. Kathirithamby-Wells, "Regional and State Integration in the Western Archipelago, c. 1500–1700", *JSEAS* 18 (1987): 36.

26 Borschberg, "Hugo Grotius, East India Trade", *JSEAS* 30, 2 (1999): 234.

27 Andaya, *The Kingdom of Johor*, p. 35, note 44; *NJS*, pp. 7–8, 18; Pinto, *Portugueses e malaios*, pp. 112, 119; van Ittersum, *Profit and Principle*, pp. 40–1.

28 See also *BOC*, I.2, p. 309; Rouffaer, "Was Malaka Emporium vóór 1400?", p. 451; Winstedt, "A History of Johore", *JMBRAS* 10, 3 (1932): 30.

29 See the letter by the king of Johor, Ala'ud'din Ri'ayat Shah, dated 6 February 1609, passed on to Admiral Paul van Caerden, printed in *NJS*, pp. 17ff.

30 Van der Chijs, *Nederlandsch-Indisch Plakaatboek*, I, p. 8; *NJS*, p. 28.

31 *JO*, IV, letter by Peter Seeger to the Heren XVII, 5 December 1612, p. 7. A study of the resolutions of the Heren XVII indicates that the choice of a location for this rendezvous was a matter of protracted deliberation; see, for example, The Hague, Nationaal Archief, VOC 100, resolution of 15–16 August 1612, pp. 183–4; resolution March 1614, p. 234, where under the heading "nopende de verkiesinge van een Rendesvous" (Concerning the choice of a rendezvous) Jacatra, Banten and the Sunda Strait are mentioned as preferred locations. Similar resolutions follow in the session of 9–20 September 1614, p. 264, session of 14 August 1617, p. 388, and session of 28 October–4 November 1617, pp. 413, 428, 437.

32 Van der Chijs, *Nederlandsch-Indisch Plakaatboek*, I, p. 15.

33 *JO*, III, p. 80.

34 See the letter by Ala'ud'din Ri'ayat Shah dated 6 February 1609, reproduced in *NJS*, pp. 17ff.

35 This document is dated 13 October 1607. See *JO*, III, pp. 72ff.

36 *JO*, III, *Instructie*, p. 72.

37 *JO*, III, *Instructie*, p. 72.

38 On Matelieff de Jonge's campaign against Melaka in 1606, see also Chapter 5.

39 *NJS*, p. 21; see also the Johor ruler's letter dated 6 February 1609, reproduced in that work on p. 19.

40 Van Opstall, ed., *De reis*, I, "Journael", p. 245, entry of 7 December 1608; The Hague, Nationaal Archief, VOC 543, "Lijst van de door Verhoeff buitgemaakte goederen uit het veroverde schip, *Nossa Senhora del Pare*, 12 December 1608" (List of the Goods Taken Booty by Verhoeff from the captured ship *Nossa Senhora del Pare*, 12 December 1608).

41 Van Opstall, ed., *De reis*, I, "Introduction", p. 83, and the entry of 18 December 1608, p. 248.

42 Valentijn, *Oud en Nieuw Oost-Indiën*, VII, part 5, p. 335.

43 Van Opstall, ed., *De reis*, I, "Introduction", pp. 81–2.

44 Van Opstall, ed., *De reis*, I, "Introduction", p. 83.

45 Van Opstall, ed., *De reis*, I, "Journael", entry of 28 December 1608, pp. 244−5.

46 Van Opstall, ed., *De reis*, I, "Introduction", p. 85; "Journael", entry of 17 January 1609, p. 251.

47 Van Opstall, ed., *De reis*, I, "Journael", pp. 251–2.

48 Van Opstall, ed., *De reis*, I, "Journael", p. 252.

49 *NJS*, p. 23.

50 Van Opstall, ed., *De reis*, I, "Journael", entry of 12 January 1609, p. 251; *NJS*, p. 24.

51 Hervey, "François Valentyn's Account of Malacca", *JSBRAS* 16, 1 (1885): 130–2.

52 Hervey, "Francois Valentyn's Account of Malacca", p. 131.

53 Hervey, "Francois Valentyn's Account of Malacca", pp. 293–4.

54 Van Opstall, ed., *De reis*, I, "Introduction", p. 81; Boxer, "The Affair", *Transactions and Proceedings of the Japan Society of London* 26 (1929): 40.

55 Van Opstall, ed., *De reis*, I, "Journael", entry of 23 January 1609, p. 253.

56 Van Opstall, ed., *De reis*, I, "Journael", entry of 26 January 1609, p. 254.

57 Van Opstall, ed., *De reis*, I, "Introduction", p. 86; "Journael", entry of 23 January 1609, p. 253. *Tintinago* is a metal alloy from China. See the explanation in the glossary.

58 Van Opstall, ed., *De reis*, I, "Journael", entry of 23 January 1609, p. 253; *NJS*, pp. 23–4.

59 *JO*, III, p. 307, "Memorie en instructie aangebragt in Indië met het jagt, de *Goede Hoop*, op den 4.den Mei, 1609." The original document brought by the crew of the cutter *Goede Hoop* is dated Amsterdam, 11 April 1608. For the

arrival of the *Goede Hoop*, see also van Opstall, ed., *De reis*, I, "Journael", entry of 6 February 1609, p. 255.

60 Van Opstall, ed., *De reis*, II, "Journaal van de Griffioen", p. 337.

61 *JO*, III, p. 308.

62 See also *NJS*, pp. 27–8.

63 Van Opstall, ed., *De reis*, II, "Journaal van de Griffioen", p. 337. This happened in the early days of April 1609.

64 *JO*, III, letter by Raja Bongsu to Prince Maurice of Orange, p. 306.

65 *JO*, III, letter by Jacques Obelaer to the Heren XVII, pp. 304–5.

66 *JO*, III, pp. 304–5.

67 *TB*, I, letter by Coen to the Heren XVII, 10 November 1614, pp. 67–8.

68 *TB*, I, report (*Cort verhael*) filed by Adriaen van der Dussen with his superior Pieter Both, governor-general of the East Indies, dated 10 November 1614, concerning his mission to the Johor court at Batu Sawar, p. 70.

69 *TB*, I, letter by Coen, 10 November 1614, pp. 67–8.

70 *TB*, I, p. 68.

71 *TB*, I, p. 68.

72 *TB*, I, pp. 70ff.

73 *TB*, I, letter by Coen, 10 November 1614, p. 69.

74 There appear to have been a series of on-going campaigns against Pahang by Johor between 1612 and 1614, interrupted notably by the Acehnese invasion of Johor and the destruction of Batu Sawar. See Linehan, *History of Pahang*, pp. 31–3.

75 *TB*, I, pp. 70–1 (van der Dussen: *Cort verhael*).

76 *TB*, I, p. 71.

77 *TB*, I, letter by Coen, 10 November 1614, p. 67; see also *TB*, I, p. 77 (van der Dussen: *Cort verhael*), where a more detailed list of the losses is featured.

78 *TB*, I, p. 68.

79 In other words, the Kingdom of Johor's principal trade route.

80 *TB*, I, pp. 72–3.

81 *TB*, I, p. 73.

82 *TB*, I, pp. 73–4.

83 *TB*, I, p. 75. See also Gibson-Hill, "Singapore: Note on the History of the Old Straits", *JMBRAS* 27, 1 (1954): 179.

84 *TB*, I, p. 75.

85 *TB*, I, p. 75.

86 *TB*, I, pp. 74–5.

87 The Hague, Nationaal Archief, VOC 1058, fols. 48–56.

88 VOC 1058, fol. 48 verso.

89 VOC 1058, fols. 51 verso–52 recto.

90 VOC 1058, fol. 55 verso.

91 VOC 1058, fol. 55 recto–verso.

92 *LM*, II, letter by King Philip III/II to Viceroy Dom Jerónimo de Azevedo, dated Lisbon, 7 January 1614, document no. 400, p. 473. A partial translation of this letter can be found in Gibson-Hill, "Singapore: Note on the History of the Old Straits", *JMBRAS* 27, 1 (1954): 179.

93 Dom Frey Christóvão previously served as bishop of Melaka, prior to his investiture as archbishop of Goa.

94 *LM*, III, letter by King Philip III/II to Viceroy Dom Jerónimo de Azevedo, dated Lisbon, 6 February 1616, doc. 635, p. 380.

95 *LM*, IV, letter by King Philip III/II to Viceroy Dom João Coutinho, dated Lisbon, 23 January 1618, doc. 942, pp. 277–8.

96 *LM*, IV, p. 278.

97 *JO*, IV, pp. 20ff.

98 This preference is also reflected in the resolutions of the Heren XVII at the time.

99 *JO*, IV, letter by Coen to the Heren XVII, 10 November 1614, p. 21.

100 *BOC*, I.2, p. 520.

101 Borschberg, "Hugo Grotius, East India Trade", *JSEAS* 33, 2 (1999): 228–9.

102 Bruijn, Gaastra and Schöffer, ed., *Dutch-Asiatic Shipping*.

103 Roderich Ptak, "An Outline of Macao's Economic Development, circa 1557–1640", in *Collected Papers*, ed. Grimm, Kuhfus and Wacker; Boyajian, *Portuguese Trade*, p. 153: "The reports of a few spectacular Portuguese losses, such as the capture of the *Santa Catarina* in 1603, and the abandonment of cessionary voyages from Melaka to Pegu, Bengal, Mergui (Tenasserim) and Banda during the first decade of the European competition also have led scholars to exaggerate the immediate impact of Dutch piracy on the Estado da Índia's trading regime."

104 Ptak, "An Outline", p. 171.

105 Boyajian, *Portuguese Trade*, p. 232.

Chapter 4

1 *LM*, II, letter by King Philip III/II to Viceroy Dom Jerónimo de Azevedo, 7 January 1614, p. 473; Gibson-Hill, "Singapore: Note on the History of the Old Straits, 1580–1850", *JMBRAS* 27, 1 (1954): 179.

2 Coolhaas, *Pieter van den Broecke in Asië*, journal entry of 10 August 1618, p. 175; see also *CB*, VII-A, letter by Pieter van den Broeck *et al.*, dated 30 September 1615, p. 42.

3 *TB*, I, "Cort verhael", 10 November 1614, p. 76; *CB*, I, letter by Coen, 3 March 1615, p. 110.

4 *JO*, II, p. 306, letter by Obelaer, 25 November 1610; *NJS*, pp. 29–30; Teixeira, *Portuguese Missions*, I, p. 242; Saldanha, *Iustum Imperium*, p. 371, note 10.

5 *NJS*, p. 30.

6 *CB*, I, p. 135.

7 *TB*, I, p. 129. On the peace, see also *TB*, I, pp. 118, 119.

8 Pinto, *Portugueses e malaios*, document 19, p. 301.

9 *TB*, I, pp. 118–9; Lombard, *Le Sultanat d'Atjéh*, p. 96. Basing his insights on the 17th century chronicle *Bustan us-Salatin* (The Garden of Kings), Lombard identifies another attack by Aceh on the Portuguese in 1615, which took place off Bintan. This location is not corroborated by the letter from van der Hagen. According to the text *Bustan us-Salatin*, Acehnese troops took a high-ranking Portuguese official prisoner, seized several ships, and killed or captured many Portuguese soldiers. See Lombard, *Le Sultanat d'Atjéh*, pp. 190, 197, 200.

10 Juan de Rivera and Valerio de Ledesma, "Portuguese and Spanish Expedition", *PI*, XVII, p. 252.

11 *LM*, III, royal letter, Madrid, 3 March 1615, p. 291, and royal letter, 5 March 1615, pp. 294, 295; Rivera and Ledesma, "Portuguese and Spanish Expedition", *PI*, XVII, p. 252.

12 *BOC*, II.2, p. 490. See also Israel, *The Dutch Republic*, p. 27.

13 *GM*, letter by Pieter Both, dated 26 July 1612, p. 9, and Both's report of 10 November 1614, pp. 29–30; Rivera and Ledesma, "Portuguese and Spanish Expedition", *PI*, XVII, p. 277; de la Costa, *The Jesuits in the Philippines*, pp. 329ff; van Veen, *Decay or Defeat*, p. 187.

14 Lauts, *Geschiedenis*, I, pp. 150, 157–8; de la Costa, *The Jesuits in the Philippines*, p. 344; Hernando de los Ríos Coronel, "Memorial and Relation, for His Majesty of the Procurator-General of the Philippines, of Which It Is Advisable to Reform, and the Wealth Contained in Them, and in the Islands of the Malucos; Madrid, 1621", in *PI*, XIX, p. 201.

15 De los Ríos Coronel, "Memorial and Relation", *PI*, XIX, p. 202.

16 De los Ríos Coronel, "Memorial and Relation", *PI*, XIX, p. 180.

17 Warnsinck, ed., *De reis*, vol. 1, p. 105.

18 De los Ríos Coronel, "Memorial and Relation", *PI*, XIX, p. 203; De la Costa, *The Jesuits in the Philippines*. According to the letter from Steven van der Hagen to the Heren XVII dated 10 March 1616, New Spain (Mexico) provided two ships without artillery with 500 to 600 men, plus 300,000 pesos (ryals-of-eight) in cash on behalf of the king of Spain and 1,500,000 pesos in equipment and provisions. See *TB*, I, letter by Steven van der Hagen, 10 March 1616, p. 124.

19 De los Ríos Coronel, "Memorial and Relation", *PI*, XIX, p. 205. On the problem of procuring and casting weapons in the Indies, see also Parker, *The Military Revolution*, p. 131.

20 Rivera and Ledesma, "Portuguese and Spanish Expedition", *PI*, XVII, p. 272.

21 Spilbergen's logbook entry of 8 March 1616 claims that de Silva's armada set out after "rijpe deliberatie vanden gantschen Raet" (ripe deliberation of the whole council). See Warnsinck, *De reis*, I, p. 105.

22 De los Ríos Coronel, "Memorial and Relation", *PI*, XIX, p. 211. The Dutch were clearly aware of this opposition voiced by the authorities in Manila; see *CB*, I, letter by Coen, 31 March 1616, p. 179.

23 De los Ríos Coronel, "Memorial and Relation", *PI*, XIX, p. 210.

24 Pinto, *Portugueses e malaios*, p. 131.

25 Francisco Paulo Mendes da Luz, *O Conselho da Índia*, p. 169.

26 De la Costa, *The Jesuits in the Philippines*, p. 332; C. Wessels, *De Katholieke Missie*, p. 56, see note 42.

27 De los Ríos Coronel, "Memorial and Relation", *PI*, XIX, p. 206.

28 Rivera and Ledesma, "Portuguese and Spanish Expedition", *PI*, XVII, p. 253; Pinto, *Portugueses e malaios*, p. 132; Mendes da Luz, *Conselho da Índia*, p. 345; De la Costa, *The Jesuits in the Philippines*, p. 332. Captain-General Francisco de Miranda Henriques is also mentioned in an anonymous letter dating from around 1615 and printed as appendix 19 in Pinto, *Portugueses e malaios*, p. 300.

29 Faria y Sousa, *Portugues Asia*, pp. 212–3; Rivera and Ledesma, "Portuguese and Spanish Expedition", *PI*, XVII, p. 253; *TB*, I, letter by Steven van der Hagen, 10 March 1616, p. 121; De la Costa, *The Jesuits in the Philippines*, p. 333; Lauts, *Geschiedenis*, I, p. 161, speaks of ten ships expected by de Silva; Veen, *Decay or Defeat*, p. 189, note 65; van der Hagen in his letter of 10 March 1616 reports of two galleons that had been destroyed by the English before Surat. See *TB*, I, p. 121. Another testimony holds that on his return to Manila in July 1615, Father Gomes spoke of four galleons being provisioned by the Portuguese for the joint offensive. See Wessels, *De Katholieke Missie*, p. 56.

30 Faria y Sousa, *Portugues Asia*, p. 213.

31 Rivera and Ledesma, "Portuguese and Spanish Expedition", *PI*, XVII, pp. 252–3, 273.

32 Rivera and Ledesma, "Portuguese and Spanish Expedition", *PI*, XVII, pp. 267–8; Faria y Sousa, *Portugues Asia*, p. 212; *CB*, VII-A, letter by van der Hagen, 25 December 1615, p. 68; De la Costa, *The Jesuits in the Philippines*, p. 333.

33 Pinto, *Portugueses e malaios*, appendix 19, p. 302.

34 Faria y Sousa, *Portugues Asia*, p. 218; Pinto, *Portugueses e malaios*, p. 132.

35 *CB*, VII-A, letter by Steven van der Hagen, 25 December 1615, p. 67.

36 *CB*, VII-A, p. 67; De la Costa, *The Jesuits in the Philippines*, p. 333; *TB*, I, letter by Steven van der Hagen, 10 March 1616, p. 121.

37 Faria y Sousa, *Portugues Asia*, pp. 213–4.

38 Rivera and Ledesma, "Portuguese and Spanish Expedition", *PI*, XVII, p. 268; De la Costa, *The Jesuits in the Philippines*, p. 333; *CB*, VII-A, letter by Steven van der Hagen, dated 25 December 1615, p. 63 places the figure at between 30,000 and 40,000 men. An anonymous letter written in Melaka toward the

end of 1615 estimates the strength of the Acehnese navy at 350 vessels each carrying more than 600 men and armed with artillery. The king's vessel carried 1,000 armed men and 25 pieces of artillery, among the cannon was also heavy artillery. The vessels of the Acehnese navy reportedly outsized the Portuguese carracks. See Pinto, *Portugueses e malaios*, document 19, p. 300. Faria y Sousa further inflates this estimate to 500 sailing vessels and 60,000 men; see his *Portugues Asia*, p. 213.

39 *CB*, I, letter by Coen, 14 January 1616, p. 171; *CB*, VII-A, letter by Steven van der Hagen, 25 December 1615, p. 64; letter by Abraham van den Broeck, 26 December 1615, p. 73.

40 *CB*, VII-A, pp. 70, 73; letter by Andries Soury, Jambi, 27 May 1616, p. 87; letter by Hans de Haze, Masulipatnam, 5 June 1616, p. 97.

41 *CB*, I, letter by Coen, 27 October 1615, p. 147; Faria y Sousa, *Portugues Asia*, pp. 213–6; Rivera and Ledesma, "Portuguese and Spanish Expedition", *PI*, XVII, p. 265; Sloos, *Nederlanders in de Filippijnse wateren*, pp. 31ff; Stapel, *Geschiedenis van Nederlandsch-Indië*, III, p. 98; van Veen, *Decay or Defeat*, p. 189, note 65.

42 *CB*, I, 1 November 1614, pp. 90–1; 27 December 1614, p. 101; 22 October 1615, pp. 130, 140; 31 March 1616, p. 180.

43 Faria y Sousa, *Portugues Asia*, p. 218; *CB*, I, letter by Coen, 14 January 1616, p. 171.

44 For a parallel account, see *CB*, VII-A, letter by Steven van der Hagen, 25 December 1615, p. 64, where the island concerned is positively identified as the Ilha das Naus on which Admiral Matelieff de Jonge, during his attack on Melaka in 1606, had placed a battery of artillery. The same letter (p. 66) speaks about the booty gained by the Dutch from this operation. See the parallel account in TB, I, letter by van der Hagen, 10 March 1616, p. 120. It appears that the Dutch overwhelmed the positions of de Miranda (Enriquez), who had been ordered there by the Melaka city council. It seems the Portuguese were able to hold their position on this island throughout the course of hostilities. Pinto, *Portugueses e malaios*, document 19, p. 301.

45 Pinto, *Portugueses e malaios*, document 19, pp. 301–2.

46 Pinto, *Portugueses e malaios*, document 19, p. 301.

47 Rivera and Ledesma, "Portuguese and Spanish Expedition", *PI*, XVII, p. 258.

48 *TB*, I, letter by Steven van der Hagen, 10 March 1616, p. 121, places the Portuguese casualties at well over 200, including the vice-admiral and unnamed captains. Similar estimates are found in Faria y Sousa, *Portugues Asia*, p. 218.

49 Pinto, *Portugueses e malaios*, document 19, p. 302.

50 *CB*, VII-A, letter by Steven van der Hagen, 25 December 1615, p. 67; *TB*, I, letter from Steven van der Hagen to the Heren XVII, 10 March 1616, p. 121.

51 Rivera and Ledesma, "Portuguese and Spanish Expedition", *PI*, XVII, pp. 259, 272. According to *CB*, VII-A, letter by Steven van der Hagen, 25 December 1615, p. 65, it was not feasible for the Dutch to board the Portuguese galleons.

52 Rivera and Ledesma, "Portuguese and Spanish Expedition", *PI*, XVII, p. 272.

53 Pinto, *Portugueses e malaios*, document 19, p. 302.

54 De los Ríos Coronel, "Memorial and Relation", *PI*, XIX, p. 208.

55 Rivera and Ledesma, "Portuguese and Spanish Expedition", *PI*, XVII, p. 275.

56 This is presumably a reference to Banten.

57 De los Ríos Coronel, "Memorial and Relation", *PI*, XIX, p. 207.

58 "Historisch Journael vande Voyagie ghedaen … door de Strate Magallanes near de Moluques … onder 't gebiedt vanden Heere Joris van Spilberghen … in den Jaere 1615, 1616, 1617", in *BV*, IV, p. 58; Lauts, *Geschiedenis van de Vestiging, Uitbreiding, Bloei en Verval*, I, pp. 160ff; De la Costa, *The Jesuits in the Philippines*, pp. 320, 334.

59 De la Costa, *The Jesuits in the Philippines*, p. 335.

60 Warnsinck, ed., *De reis*, vol. 1, p. 105; "Historisch Journael", *BV*, IV, p. 61; Lauts, *Geschiedenis*, I, p. 161.

61 *CB*, I, letter by Coen, 14 January 1616, p. 171; report of 31 March 1616, p. 179; *CB*, VII-A, letter by Steven van der Hagen, 25 December 1615, p. 68; *TB*, II, letter by Steven van der Hagen, 10 March 1616, p. 122.

62 Rivera and Ledesma, "Portuguese and Spanish Expedition", *PI*, XVII, p. 260; *CB*, VII-A, letter by Steven van der Hagen, 25 December 1615, p. 68, where the two ships are described as a "carrack" and a "galleon".

63 *CB*, I, letter by Coen, 31 March 1616, p. 179.

64 *CB*, I, 25 December 1615, p. 159, where it is evident that the VOC was well-aware of the Spanish armada's imminent departure from Manila, and also the impending arrival of Joris van Spilbergen from South America. See also *TB*, II, letter from Steven van der Hagen to the Heren XVII, 10 March 1616, p. 124. This report places the departure of de Silva from Manila slightly later, around mid-January 1616. An even later departure date is provided by Coen in his report to the Heren XVII dated 10 October 1616. He places the departure of de Silva's armada from Manila on 4 February 1616. See *CB*, I, p. 42. The identical departure date is provided in "Historisch Journael", *BV*, IV, p. 61, and the specific source of this information is identified as Manila's city council. Rivera and Ledesma, "Portuguese and Spanish Expedition", *PI*, XVII, p. 278, seem to erroneously indicate a departure date of 31 December 1615.

65 *CB*, I, letter by Coen, 31 March 1616, p. 179.

66 *CB*, I, letter by Coen, 14 January 1616, p. 171; *TB*, I, letter by Steven van der Hagen, 10 March 1616, p. 120, where the number of prisoners is indicated at 11 Portuguese and 4 *swaerten*, presumably Asians.

67 *CB*, I, letter by Coen, 31 March 1616, pp. 179, 182.

68 See also Warnsinck, ed., *De reis*, I, p. 104, "Historisch Journael", *BV*, IV, entry of 6 March 1616; Wessels, *De Katholieke Missie*, p. 57. An anonymous letter written in Melaka and dating from the end of 1615 speaks of ten galleons and ten galleys. See Pinto, *Portugueses e malaios*, document 19, p. 302.

69 Rivera and Ledesma, "Portuguese and Spanish Expedition", *PI*, XVII, pp. 261, 272, 274; see also de la Costa, *The Jesuits in the Philippines*, p. 333; *CB*, VII-A, letter by Andries Soury, Jambi, 27 May 1616, pp. 85, 91. Different figures are provided in the letter by van der Hagen, where the number of men on board the vessels of the Spanish armada is estimated at 1,500, in addition to an unspecified number of native Asian volunteers and Japanese mercenaries. Soury confirms the number of Japanese mercenaries at 500, but reveals that most of the Spanish soldiers on board were *casados* who had been taken along, evidently against their will. Coen's report to the Heren XVII, dated 31 March 1616, speaks of 1,500 Spanish soldiers, 400 Japanese, 200 Chinese "craftsmen", and Pampangos (mercenaries from Pampanga province, outside Manila) "in great number". See *CB*, VII-A, p. 179.

70 Rivera and Ledesma, "Portuguese and Spanish Expedition", *PI*, XVII, p. 278; *CB*, I, report of 31 March 1616, p. 179; *CB*, VII-A, letter by Andries Soury, Jambi, 15 June 1616, p. 119.

71 *CB*, I, report of 10 October 1616, p. 192; *CB*, VII-A, letter by Andries Soury, Jambi, 27 May 1616, p. 86.

72 *CB*, VII-A, letter by Hans de Haze, 5 June 1616, p. 97.

73 *TB*, II, letter by van der Hagen, 10 March 1616, p. 126.

74 *TB*, II, pp. 130–1, letter from Juan de Silva, anchored off Singapore, to Abdullah Hammayat Shah of Johor, dated 28 February 1616 (the letter is written and printed in Spanish). *CB*, I, report of 31 March 1616, p. 179. The king of Johor had fled to Bintan for fear of Acehnese reprisals and also on account of his peaceful relations with the Portuguese. See also *CB*, VII-A, letter by Hendrik Janszoon, Patani, 25 November 1615, pp. 58–9; *CB*, VII-A, letter by Steven van der Hagen, 25 December 1615, pp. 63, 68. Soury reports that the king of Johor was preparing for his impending departure for Pahang, where he evidently stayed for some months, certainly until July 1616; see *CB*, VII-A, letter by Andries Soury, 27 May 1616, pp. 82, 87; *CB*, VII-A, letter of 30 June 1616, p. 123; *CB*, VII-A, letter of 17 July 1616, pp. 151–2.

75 *CB*, I, letter by Coen, 10 October 1616, pp. 193–4.

76 *CB*, I, p. 194.

77 *CB*, report of 5 January 1616, p. 165; report of 14 January 1616, p. 171; report of 10 October 1616, p. 194.

78 *CB*, I, letter by Andries Soury, 27 May 1616, p. 91; also Rivera and Ledesma, "Portuguese and Spanish Expedition", *PI*, XVII, p. 260.

79 On the size of the two cities, see Johann Verken, "Molukkenreise", in *Reisebeschreibungen*, ed. L'Honoré Naber, II, p. 58. Similar observations are found in *Onzième volume*, p. 202.

80 *CB*, VII-A, letter by Andries Soury, 17 July 1616, p. 152.

81 *CB*, VII-A, letter by Soury, 15 June 1616, p. 104.

82 Gibson-Hill, "Singapore: Note on the History of the Old Straits, 1580–1850", *JMBRAS* 27, 1 (1954): 175, 176, note 29; De la Costa, *The Jesuits in the Philippines*, p. 333.

83 Rivera and Ledesma, "Portuguese and Spanish Expedition", *PI*, XVII, p. 279.

84 For de Silva's quotation, see De la Costa, *The Jesuits in the Philippines*, p. 332.

85 De los Ríos Coronel, "Memorial and Relation", *PI*, XIX, p. 208; Rivera and Ledesma, "Portuguese and Spanish Expedition", *PI*, XVII, p. 279; *CB*, VII-A, letter by Soury, 15 June 1616, p. 119; letter of 30 June 1616 by Soury, p. 123.

86 *CB*, VII-A, letter of Jacques Specx, Hirado, 1 October 1616, p. 203.

87 *CB*, VII-A, letter by Andries Soury, 15 June 1616, p. 119; *GM*, p. 29, note 6; Lauts, *Geschiedenis*, I, p. 161. In contrast, Sloos diagnoses de Silva's life-robbing illness as dysentery. Sloos, *Nederlanders in de Filippijnse wateren*, p. 33. Bocarro, *Década XIII*, p. 429 mentions an unspecified "fever" as the cause of death.

88 De los Ríos Coronel, "Memorial and Relation", *PI*, XIX, p. 182, the figure is placed at 700.

89 De los Ríos Coronel, "Memorial and Relation", *PI*, XIX, pp. 208–9.

90 De los Ríos Coronel, "Memorial and Relation", *PI*, XIX, p. 208; Stapel, *Geschiedenis van Nederlandsch-Indië*, III, p. 98.

91 De la Costa, *The Jesuits in the Philippines*, p. 334.

92 *CB*, VII-A, letter by Soury, 27 May 1616, p. 91.

93 *CB*, I, report of 10 October 1616, p. 192.

94 Rivera and Ledesma, "Portuguese and Spanish Expedition", *PI*, XVII, pp. 261, 280.

95 Rivera and Ledesma, "Portuguese and Spanish Expedition", *PI*, XVII, p. 261; *CB*, I, report of 10 October 1616, 192; *CB*, VII-A, letter of 15 June 1616, p. 119; letter of 30 June 1616, p. 123; letter of 31 October 1616, p. 221; letter by Jacques Specx, 1 October 1616, p. 203.

96 *CB*, I, letter by Coen, 10 October 1616, p. 192; *CB*, VII-A, letter by Andries Soury, 30 June 1616, p. 123; Veen, *Decay or Defeat*, p. 189, note 65.

97 *CB*, VII-A, letter by Soury, 15 June 1616, pp. 119ff; letter by Reael, p. 135.

98 De la Costa, *The Jesuits in the Philippines*, p. 321.

99 Wessels, *De Katholieke Missie*, p. 57.

100 De los Ríos Coronel, "Memorial and Relation", *PI*, XIX, p. 208.

[101] For the bigger picture of Luso-Spanish relations in Asia and beyond during the Union of the Two Crowns, see the useful article by Sanjay Subrahmanyam, "Holding the World", pp. 1359–85.

[102] *CB*, VII-A, letter by Reael, 11 July 1616, p. 134.

[103] Van Veen, *Decay or Defeat*, p. 190, note 66; Israel, *The Dutch Republic*, p. 68.

Chapter 5

[1] *NJS*, p. 9; *BV*, II, p. 6; *PI*, XV, pp. 312–3. In the account of Admiral Cornelis Matelieff de Jonge reproduced in *BV*, III, p. 7, Encik Kamar is described in Dutch as as "Ambassadeur Camar", that is "Ambassador Kamar" who was set ashore with a sloop before Melaka. He was instructed to notify his monarch about the arrival of the Dutch fleet and request the latter's armed assistance in the forthcoming siege of Portuguese Melaka. According to a letter of Gabriel Towerson, the chief English factor at Banten, dated 30 April 1607, the fleet of Matelieff arrived at Melaka on 6 April 1606, set on land "the Iore ambassadour wich they brought out of Holland", see Corney ed., *The voyage of Sir Henry Middleton to Bantam and the Maluco Islands*, pp. 36–7. For other accounts of Admiral Matelieff's siege of Melaka and diplomatic activities at the Johor court, see Jacques l'Hermite (de Jonge), *Breeder verhael ende klare beschrijvinghe*, as well as Hulsius, *Zehende Schiffart.*

[2] See "Historische Verhael Vande treffelijcke Reyse, gedaen naer de Oost-Indien ende China", *BV*, III, p. 10. This Dutch source identifies the shahbandar as the "Seri Raya Nugara". Also Borschberg, "The Seizure of the Sta. Catarina Revisited", *JSEAS* 33, 1 (2002): 59–60, esp. note 134, and Kwa, "Records and Notices of Early Singapore", in *Archeological Research*, ed. Miksic, p. 121, "… [I]n 1606, the Dutch Cornelis Materlief (sic!) reported meeting a representative of the Sultan of Johor to coordinate an attack on Portuguese Melaka. The representative styled himself the Sabander (Shahbandar) of Singapura, named Seri Raja Nugara, a title awarded, according to a later (Shellebaer) edition of the *Sejarah Melayu*, to the Datin of Singapura, an acknowledge *hulubalang* of the Sultan of Johor."

[3] Rouffaer, "Was Malaka Emporium voor 1400 A.D.", *BKI* 77 (1032): 402–3.

[4] The preliminary agreement is dated 17 May 1606 and can be found in the "Corpus Diplomaticum Neerlando-Indicum", ed. J. E. Heeres, eerste deel (1596–1650) *BKI* 57 (1907): 41–5, in the "Historische Verhael Vande treffelijcke Reyse", *BV*, III, pp. 13–4; Valentijn, *Oud en Nieuw Oost-Indiën*, V, p. 335, as well as in *NJS*, p. 2. English translations of the preliminary agreement are also found in Hervey, "François Valentyn's Account of Malacca", *JSBRAS* 16, 1 (1885): 136–7; and Winstedt, "A History of Johore", *JMBRAS* 10, 3 (1932): 31–3.

5 "Historische Verhael Vande treffelijcke Reyse, gedaen naer de Oost-Indien ende China", *BV*, III, pp. 9, 15 as well as the appendix to the "Historische Verhael" being the second letter by Jacques l'Hermite to his Father", pp. 152–3, 154. According to these testimonies the Portuguese set fire to dwellings all around Melaka. The fire in the suburb smoldered for many days.

6 Heeres, "Corpus Diplomaticum", *BKI* 57 (1907): 44.

7 The Dutch text of the extension is found in Heeres, "Corpus Diplomaticum", *BKI* 57 (1907): 47–8. See also *NJS*, p. 2. Grotius had evidently been briefed about the conclusion of this treaty, and he is also known to have drafted several agreements for the VOC for ratification with the "Emperor of Borneo" (Sultan of Brunei) and, of course, Johor. For a Portuguese account of the naval confrontations between the fleets of Viceroy Dom Martim Alfonso de Castro and Matelieff de Jonge, see the undated report published as appendix 16 in Pinto, *Portugueses e malaios*, pp. 293–7.

8 On the dispatch of the Portuguese armada to Melaka, see the letter by Philip III/II dated Valladolid, 27 December 1604, and printed as appendix 14 in Pinto, *Portugueses e malaios*, pp. 287–9. This document shows that the Iberian king was already planning to assemble a powerful *armada de remo* is evident accompanied by other warships to be dispatched from Goa to Melaka in April 1606. The ships were to assume control of crucial nodal positions in the Straits of Singapore, Sabam and Sunda under the command of Álvaro de Carvalho and Manuel Mascarenhas. Further details derive from the king's letter of 3 March 1605, printed as appendix 15 in Pinto, *Portugueses e malaios*, pp. 290–3. The armada was to divide into four parts and severely punish Southeast Asian princes such as the rulers of Sunda and Johor, for welcoming the Dutch and trading with them, and also for the seizure of the "ship from China", that is, the *Santa Catarina*.

9 "Historische Verhael Vande treffelijcke Reyse, gedaen naer de Oost-Indien ende China", *BV*, III, p. 35ff; *JO*, III, pp. 48ff.

10 "Historische Verhael Vande treffelijcke Reyse", *BV*, III, p. 128.

11 Subrahmanyam, *Improvising Empire*, p. 171. See also Bocarro, *Década XIII*, p. 525; Pinto, *Portugueses e malaios*, pp. 122–3.

12 Pontanus, *Rerum et Urbis Amstelodamensium Historia*.

13 Boxer, *Fidalgos*, p. 52, and generally Mills, "Two Dutch-Portuguese Sea-Fights", *JMBRAS* 16, 1 (1938): 145ff. Valentijn claims that in May 1606 Melaka was being defended by 400 Portuguese and African soldiers. See Hervey, "François Valentyn's Account of Malacca", p. 137. See also *PI*, XVII, p. 253, for another account of African soldiers brought to Melaka by the Portuguese to defend the fortress.

14 See Pinto, *Portugueses e malaios*, appendix 16, p. 294.

15 Rietbergen, *De Eerste Landvoogd*, I, p. 134, note 3, and II, pp. 196–211. There are two pieces of writing by Admiral Cornelis Matelieff de Jonge addressed

to Grotius. The first is dated 12 November 1608, and the second 16 January 1609. An English summary of one of these epistolary reports is found in *PI*, XV, pp. 314–22. Matelieff de Jonge is the author of four memoranda compiled between 1608 and 1609. For their significance within the context of VOC policy making in Europe, see also Gaastra, *Geschiedenis van de VOC*, p. 39.

16 Borschberg, "Grotius, East India Trade", pp. 226–7; Borschberg, "Grotius' Theory of Transoceanic Trade Regulation", pp. 7–8.

17 *DJP*, pp. 212–3, "When I think of this monarch, I sincerely feel as if we are gazing upon the supreme and true reward of our voyages to the East Indies. ..."

18 Rietbergen, *De Eerste Landvoogd*, I, p. 209.

19 Rietbergen, *De Eerste Landvoogd*, I, p. 197. See also Gaastra, *Geschiedenis van de VOC*, p. 40.

20 Rietbergen, *De Eerste Landvoogd*, I, p. 198, Matelieff's *Discours* of 1608: "The city of Melaka, apart from being difficult to wrest [from the Portuguese], is also not well situated [geographically], for it is not possible to reach it at all times at the year, or at least we can only reach it with difficulty, chiefly because we use large and heavy vessels, that as a result of the long voyage [from Europe] have become rotten and difficult to sail. We need a place where, arriving from the Cape of Good Hope, we can drop anchor and are not at the mercy of the monsoon [winds]." Translation from the original Dutch by the author.

21 Rietbergen, *De Eerste Landvoogd*, I, p. 198, Matelieff, *Discours*, "For this reason I should chose one of two places: [first] either the city of Jacatra, or the fresh [water] river located 3 or 4 [Dutch sea] miles to the west of Banten, or [second] the city of Palembang on Sumatra. Palembang is also reached with difficulty, as it is located against the monsoon winds when we exit the Strait of Sunda. This was recently evident in January of the year 1608 when Paul van Caerden attempted to sail from Banten to Johor...." Translated from Dutch by the author.

22 Rietbergen, *De Eerste Landvoogd*, I, p. 208.

23 According to Valentijn, *Oud en Nieuw Oost-Indiën*, V, p. 339B, the VOC directors, the Heren XVII, issued instructions to lay siege to Melaka, but no military campaign appears to have been launched in that year. See also *NJS*, p. 32; Lewis, *Jan Compagnie*, pp. 14–5.

24 See the report of Governor-General Pieter Both, dated 14 November 1611, §24, reprinted in *NJS*, p. 28; van der Chijs, *Nederlandsch-Indisch Plakaatboek*, I, p. 15. See also the letter by Coen to the Heren XVII, 5 January 1616, in *TB*, II, p. 38; *JO*, IV, letter by Peter Seeger to the directors in Amsterdam, 5 December 1612, p. 7; The Hague, Nationaal Archief, VOC 100, resolution of 15–16 August 1612, pp. 183–4; resolution of March 1614, p. 234, where under the comment "nopende de verkiesinge van een Rendesvous" (concerning the selection of a rendezvous) Jacatra (later Batavia), Banten and the Sunda Strait

are listed as preferred locations. Similar deliberations followed in the sessions of 9–20 September 1614, p. 264; 14 August 1617, p. 388; and 28 October–4 November 1617, pp. 413, 428, 437.

25 Coen weighed several possible locations, including Johor, but opined that a location near the Strait of Sunda was to be preferred. See *JO*, I, p. 21.

26 *NJS*, p. 33, concerning the blockade of June 1640 to 14 January 1641.

27 *GM*, I (1610–38), p. 403.

28 Also written as Coper or Koper, varying across documents.

29 A short biography of Cooper is found in the *GM*, I (1610–38), p. 394, note 2. According to *TB*, II, p. 263, Cooper made prize of 63 vessels between 16 September 1633 and November 1634.

30 *DRB* (1640–1), p. 39, entry of 28 September 1640.

31 *BOC*, I.2, p. 318, note 2, and p. 331.

32 Andaya, "Melaka under the Dutch", in *Melaka, the Transformation of a Malay Capital*, I, ed. Singh and Wheatley, pp. 195–241; Lewis, *Jan Compagnie in the Straits of Malacca*.

33 Ahmed, *Indo-Portuguese*, pp. 48–9; Ames, *Renascent Empire?*, pp. 12–3; Boyajian, *Portuguese Trade*, pp. 231–2; van Veen, *Decay or Defeat?*, pp. 199–202.

34 Leupe, "The Siege and Capture of Malacca", *JMBRAS* 14, 1 (1936): 1–178; Bassett, "Changes in the Pattern of Malay Politics", *JSEAH* 10, 3 (1969): 429–52.

35 Barendse, "Blockade: Goa", in *Rivalry and Conflict*, ed. van Veen and Blussé, pp. 232–66.

36 Lombard, *Le Sultanat d'Atjéh au temps d'Iskandar Muda 1607–1636*.

37 Borschberg, "Remapping the Straits", in *Iberians in the Singapore-Melaka Area*, ed. Borschberg, pp. 106–7; Borschberg, "Luso-Johor-Dutch Relations", in *Rivalry and Conflict*, ed. van Veen and Blussé, p. 190.

38 Lombard, *Le Sultanat d'Atjéh*, p. 187; Das Gupta, "Acheh in Indonesian Trade and Politics", p. 201.

39 *GM*, I (1610–38), report by Governor-General Hendrik Brouwer *et al.* dated 15 December 1633, p. 395. According to Ruangsilp, *Dutch East India Company Merchants*, p. 20, the VOC rushed military assistance to Siam and were apparently rewarded with trading privileges in animal skins in 1634.

40 See, for example, *DRB* (1631–4), entry of 6 February 1634, p. 237, where it is reported that the king of Aceh had promised assistance and intended to dispatch an armada with the last eastern monsoon against Portuguese Melaka. But it is subsequently reported (*DRB*, 1631–4, p. 238) that he did not deliver on this promise. Despite repeated requests for help from the VOC, the king failed to muster assistance and excused himself on the grounds that he already had to deploy his armada against Perak, Aru and the west coast of Sumatra. The campaign in Perak alone required 1,100 men and 4 war elephants.

41 The Hague, Nationaal Archief, VOC 1132, fols. 483–9; VOC 1109, fols. 43–51, *Dagh-Register Siam*, 10 April 1633–6 November 1633; Pompejra, *Siamese Court Life*, pp. 195–6, 201–2, 226; Cruyssé, *Louis XIV et le Siam*, pp. 55, 61–4; Ruangsilp, *Dutch East India Company Merchants*, p. 27. Rodao in his book *Españoles in Siam* mentions the disturbances surrounding the accession of Prasat Thong (Rodao, *Españoles*, p. 57) but does not otherwise mention the "failed" military expedition to conquer Siam.

42 Ruangsilp, *Dutch East India Company Merchants*, p. 73. According to Bassett, Johor, Pahang and the Portuguese did not recognise Prasat Thong as a legitimate monarch, see Bassett, "Changes in the Pattern of Malay Politics", *JSEAH* 10, 3 (1969): 431.

43 *DRB* (1631–4), entry of 6 February 1634, p. 238. Entry of 10–14 April 1632, p. 69, reports that the Spanish had dispatched several vessels, 300 "white" soldiers and 1,500 Pampangos to the "river of Cambodia" (the Mekong) to destroy and plunder "the Empire of Siam". They also planned to seize Dutch ships destined for Patani, Siam, Cambodia and Taiwan. Some Portuguese prisoners were cross-examined on these schemes. According to a later entry (*DRB*, 1631–4, p. 70), it is clear that this Spanish operation had failed and that the ships had set sail for Manila.

44 Ruangsilp, *Dutch East India Company Merchants*, pp. 26–7. The Spanish and Portuguese prisoners taken by the Siamese during one incident committed against a Dutch trading vessel in 1624 were not released until 1636. See Ruangsilp, *Dutch East India Company Merchants*, p. 75.

45 Ruangsilp, *Dutch East India Company Merchants*, p. 75: "In early 1639, the Siamese King sent another envoy to Malacca, which was then unfortunately under Dutch siege. Even so, when his attempt became known to Macao, its Captain General Do[m] Sebstião Lobo da Silveira (1638–45) decided to send an embassy to Ayutthaya. Under these circumstances, in 1639 the visit of a Portuguese embassy from Macao turned the Siamese court into a virtual battlefield between the Dutch and the Portuguese."

46 At the time, the Javanese kingdom of Mataram was experiencing problematic relations with the VOC in Batavia. For additional background on these strained mutual relations, see Fruin-Mees, "Why Batavia and Mataram did not make Peace between 1629 and 1646", in *Dutch Authors on Asian History*, ed. Meilink-Roelofsz, van Opstall and Schutte, pp. 243–74.

47 The Hague, Nationaal Archief, VOC 1117, fols. 561–8; Lewis, *Jan Compagnie in the Straits of Malacca*, p. 15: "They [the VOC] believed the ruler of Mataram had aimed, by assisting Portuguese Malacca, to divert the VOC's attention from Java. Now Mataram was forced to look to Batavia instead of Malacca as the market for their most important export, rice"; *GM*, II (1639–55), report of Antonio van Diemen 18 December 1639, p. 68. See also Lombard, *Le Sultanat d'Atjéh*, p. 97. According to

Ruangsilp, the Siamese also dispatched a diplomatic mission to Melaka in 1639.

48 In 1636 the Dutch sought the consent of the Tokugawa Shogunate for imposing a naval blockade on Melaka and other ports of the *Estado da Índia*. Such a move doubtless affected Japan's reliance on Portuguese imports, especially textiles. The Dutch assured the Tokugawa shogun that his country would suffer no disruption of supplies. *GM*, I (1610–38), pp. 508, 514.

49 Mesquitela, *História de Macau*, III.1, p. 23.

50 On the discomfort experienced by Dutch merchants with acting as an arm of the war effort against Spain and Portugal, see also Bruijn and Gaastra, *Roemrucht verleden*, pp. 16–7.

51 Such targets were forts and ports, such as Goa, Melaka and the Malukus.

52 See Chapter 2.

53 The Hague, Nationaal Archief, VOC 1115, fols. 754–60, 791–2; VOC 1121, letters by Jakob Cooper (1636), fols. 1–67; VOC 1131, fols. 1283–8; VOC 1132, fols. 135–41.

54 The Hague, Nationaal Archief, VOC 1118, fols. 483–8, letters from the Jambi factory to the governor-general at Batavia, 1634; VOC 1119, fols. 1240–7, letters from Jambi to the governor-general at Batavia, 1 September 1636 and 3 October 1636.

55 Pissurlencar, ed., *Assentos do Conselho do Estado da Índia.*

56 See, for example, The Hague, Nationaal Archief, VOC 4818, fol. 561 recto et seq. The intercepted correspondence here covers the years 1633 to 1636. See also VOC 1136, fols. 963–5, where trade relations between Japan, China, Melaka and Goa are discussed together with the closure of the Japan market to the Portuguese.

57 For an overview of the *Livros das Monções*, see the very useful synopsis of da Silva Rego, "Monsoon Codices at the National Archives of the Torre do Tombo", in *Indo-Portuguese History*, ed. John Correia-Afonso, pp. 51–71.

58 Linhares, *Diário do 3.o Conde de Linhares.*

59 See, for example, *DRB* (1631–42), entry of 17 April 1632, pp. 122–3, where it is evident that the VOC has signed new treaties, or renewed existing ones, with the "kings" of Patani, Johor, Cambodia, Jambi, Indragiri and other surrounding places against all attacks by the Spanish and the Portuguese. Siam was not among the treaty partners because its king, Prasat Thong, was considered "an usurper".

60 On the background to this new diplomatic strategy that also included tighter relations with Mataram, see de Souza, *The Survival of Empire*, p. 97.

61 *PI*, XXIX, "Events, August 1639–August 1640", pp. 197–8, "... went from Malacca as an envoy to the king of Achen, regarding himself as quite safe; but that the king gave orders that his men should arrest the envoy as soon as he enter the palace. When they tried to carry out this command, this man and the

other Portuguese placed themselves on the defensive; all the men on the ship hastened to their aid with fireballs, and with these they killed many Acehnese, and the palace was set on fire, being entirely consumed. They estimate the losses of the king at five million [ryals-of-eight]. All the Portuguese were killed." The source, adduced and translated by Blair and Robertson, names the head of the Lusitanian embassy as "Caldeira", but Lombard positively identifies him as Francisco de Soza de Castro. The latter underscores that he is not aware of any other Portuguese mission dispatched to Aceh to strike a peace deal with Iskandar Thani. Lombard, *Le Sultanat d'Atjéh*, pp. 97–8, 233–4.

62 See Lombard, *Le Sultanat d'Atjéh*, letter by de Soza de Castro dated March 1643.

63 *TB*, II, pp. 355–6.

64 *TB*, II, p. 357.

65 *TB*, II, p. 356.

66 The Hague, Nationaal Archief, VOC 1108, fols. 619–20, List of Dutch Naval Power in the East Indies, dated 15 August 1633.

67 *DRB* (1631–34), p. 238, report of 6 February 1634; report of 18 February 1634, p. 246; report of 9–13 April 1634, p. 291, entry of 11 April; report of 10 December 1634, p. 453; *GM*, I (1610-38), report by Brouwer *et al.* dated 15 December 1633, p. 395.

68 *DRB* (1631–4), p. 452, report of 10 December 1634. *GM*, I (1610–38), report of Brouwer dated 15 December 1633, p. 395, where in the instructions to Commander Cooper the location is described as follows: "… bijoosten de Straet van Sincapura, tusschen het vaste lant van Yhoor en de eylanden van Bintangh" (… east of the Strait of Singapore between the mainland of Johor and the islands of Bintan).

69 *DRB* (1631–4), p. 294, report of 27 April 1634.

70 The Johor Strait is also known as the Tebrau Strait.

71 *DRB* (1631–4), p. 452, report of 10 December 1634.

72 The Hague, Nationaal Archief, Report of Adriaen van der Dussen, dated 19 May 1615, VOC 1061, fols. 76–83.

73 *DRB* (1631–4), p. 385.

74 *DRB* (1631–4), p. 386, entry of 28 July 1634. After the attack of Cornelis Matelieff de Jonge on Melaka, a fortification was supposedly built on the island with the evident intention of thwarting a second shelling of the city by Dutch artillery. See *PMC*, V, plate 590/60 I (*Demonstração da Ilha das Naos*), and *PMC*, V, 59B (*Demonstração da Fortaleza de Malaca*). Prior to the construction of these structures, warships patrolled the waters around the islets and outside Melaka harbour.

75 *DRB* (1631–4), p. 384, entry of 9 September 1634; incident of 13 July 1634, p. 387. Leupe, "The Siege and Capture of Malacca", *JMBRAS* 14, 1 (1936): 156 (Instructions to Antonisz). See also note 69 above.

76 *DRB* (1631–4), p. 387, entry of 20 June 1634; entry of 9 September 1634, p. 387.
77 *DRB* (1631–4), p. 389.
78 *BOC*, II.1, p. 821.
79 Dijk, *Seventeenth-century Burma*, pp. 17, 88.
80 *GM*, I (1610–38), pp. 467–9.
81 See, for example, *DRB* (1631–4), p. 388.
82 In Portuguese documents it is also spelt Timão, Timaon and Tymão.
83 The port city is also variously spelt as Pam, Paan or Pahão in Portuguese sources. See also *DRB* (1631–4), p. 386, report of 28 July 1634. Three defectors report that four vessels inbound from Macao had been rerouted to Pahang, where they lay at anchor. They were expected to arrive in Melaka soon. A classic account of the "Tioman agent" (albeit from an earlier period) can be found in the *journaal* of Hendrick Janszoon Craen, chief merchant (*opperkoopman*) aboard the Dutch merchantman *Gelderland*, entry of 17 March 1609. According to this testimony, an "envoy" (*ambassedoor*) from Pahang showed the Dutch a message written in Portuguese warning a "captain of a gallion coming from Macao" that when he arrived in Tioman, he should not under any circumstances sail beyond the navigational landmark Pedra Branca near the eastern entrance of the Singapore Straits, but that he should unload his cargo and ship it "overland" to Melaka. See de Booy, ed., *De derde reis van de VOC naar Oost-Indië*, II, p. 78.
84 *DRB* (1631–4), p. 388, report of 28 July 1634, where it is reported that the two cutters (*jachten*) *Salm* and *Daman* captured about seven vessels around "Pulo Piçan". It is located off the western coast of Peninsular Johor, between Pontian and Tanjong Bulus, probably present-day Pulau Pisang.
85 *DRB* (1631–4), pp. 411–2, entry of 16–20 October 1634.
86 *DRB* (1636), pp. 165–6.
87 *GM*, I (1610–38), p. 376.
88 The Hague, Nationaal Archief, VOC 1108, List of Dutch Naval power in the East Indies, 15 August 1633, fol. 619 recto, where it is explained that the cutters *Dieman* and *Daman* as well as two unnamed sloops were stationed "before Melaka". The words "voor Malacca" were subsequently deleted and replaced in a different hand with the two words "omtrent Lingen" (around Lingga).
89 *DRB* (1634), p. 388, report of 20 June 1634.
90 The Hague, Nationaal Archief, VOC 4818, Intercepted Portuguese Correspondence (1634), fols. 565 verso–566 recto, under heading number 8. This section reports the existence of several passages to the south of Pedra Branca across the archipelago that are little-known except to the Malay and the *saletes* (or *celates*, *orang laut*) who frequent them with smaller craft. Pedro Bertollo is reported to be cognisant of such uncharted passages.
91 *PMC*, V, plate 578, chart 15C.

92 *PMC*, V, plate 543, chart B.

93 *DRB* (1631–4), pp. 162–3. The original Dutch text can be found in appendix 9. Translation into English by the author.

94 *DRB* (1631–4), p. 412.

95 *TB*, II, p. 263. Also *GM*, II (1639–55), report of Antonio van Diemen, 18 December 1639, p. 68.

96 Boxer, "A Glimpse of the Goa Archives", *Opera Minora*, I, p. 251, reference to vol. IV of the Livro de Assentos do Conselho de Estado (1635–45).

97 *GM*, I (1610–38), p. 387.

98 *TB*, II, pp. 298ff, see p. 305. Similar observations are also made in Valentijn, *Oud en Nieuw Oost-Indiën*, V, p. 340A, where the dearth of food is seen as critical in the fall of Portuguese Melaka. But Valentijn later admits on p. 314A that the Dutch never succeeded in completely severing supplies to the city, a point that is also made by special commissioner Schouten published by Leupe. See also Faria y Sousa, *The Portugues Asia*, III, part IV, chapter 13, p. 411.

99 *TB*, II, report of Antonio van Diemen to the Heren XVII, 22 December 1638, p. 358.

100 Faria y Sousa, *The Portugues Asia*, III, part IV, chapter 13, p. 411.

101 *TB*, II, report of van Diemen to the Heren XVII, 22 December 1638, p. 359.

102 *DRB* (1640–1), p. 39; *NJS*, p. 33; Cooper's important role is also briefly mentioned by Valentijn, *Oud en Nieuw Oost-Indiën*, V, p. 340A, where he is named Koper.

103 Leupe, "The Siege and Capture of Malacca", *JMBRAS* 14, 1 (1936): 110, where Schouten reports that half the Dutch forces of 3,000 men perished.

104 *BOC*, I.2, p. 318, note 2, and p. 331; Leupe, "The Siege and Capture of Malacca", *JMBRAS* 14, 1 (1936): 109 (Schouten's report); Valentijn, *Oud en Nieuw Oost-Indiën*, V, p. 314A.

105 Valentijn, *Oud en Nieuw Oost-Indiën*, V, p. 341B; Leupe, "The Siege and Capture of Malacca", *JMBRAS* 14, 1 (1936): 109 (Schouten's report).

106 Valentijn, *Oud en Nieuw Oost-Indiën*, V, p. 341B, says nothing about the expulsion of women and children from the city, but mentions only those who defected to the Dutch side because they were starving.

107 *TB*, II, report of van Diemen to the Heren XVII, 22 December 1638, p. 358.

108 Valentijn, *Oud en Nieuw Oost-Indiën*, V, p. 341B. One *gantang* in Melaka (800 *gantang* being equivalent to 1 *koyang* or 4,800 Amsterdam pounds) was equivalent to about 6 pounds. See Anon., *Verhandeling der Munten*, p. 488.

109 *DRB* (1640–1), p. 58.

110 On the dispatch of rice to Melaka from the Philippines at the end of the blockade, see *PI*, XXIX, "Events in the Philippines August 1639–August 1640", p. 197. It is not known whether this consignment arrived.

111 *DRB* (1631–4), p. 452.
112 *DRB* (1631–4), p. 387.
113 *DRB* (1631–4), p. 389.
114 *DRB* (1631–4), p. 386.
115 According to Bassett, Johor and Patani were allies between 1629-45, see Bassett, "Changes in the Pattern of Malay Politics", *JSEAH* 10, 3 (1969): 431.
116 *TB*, II, p. 390.
117 See, for example, *TB*, II, report of van Diemen and Council to the Heren XVII, 12 January 1639, p. 365.
118 Borschberg, "Luso-Johor-Dutch Relations", in *Rivalry and Conflict*, ed. van Veen and Blussé, pp. 189ff.
119 *TB*, II, p. 390.
120 In response thereto, Portuguese Melaka sought to negotiate a peace deal with Aceh.
121 *TB*, II, p. 390.
122 Valentijn, *Oud en Nieuw Oost-Indiën*, V, p. 340; *NJS*, p. 33.
123 Andaya, "Melaka under the Dutch", in *Melaka, the Transformation of a Malay Capital*, ed. Singh and Wheatley, I, p. 197. Concerning the assistance lent to the Dutch by the Johorean *laksamana*, see Leupe, "The Siege and Capture of Malacca", *JMBRAS* 14, 1 (1936): 122–3 (Schouten's report).
124 *GM*, II (1639–55), report of van Diemen, 18 December 1639, p. 55.
125 *TB*, II, p. 390, van Diemen to the Heren XVII, 12 December 1639.
126 See also *GM*, II (1639–55), report of van Diemen, 18 December 1639, p. 13, where it is reported that maritime traffic between Goa, Macao and Manila was re-routed through the Sunda Strait. See also van Veen, *Decay or Defeat*, p. 200, see note 121.
127 *GM*, I (1610–38), p. 403.
128 *GM*, II (1639–55), p. 68, report of 18 December 1639.
129 Boyajian, *Portuguese Trade*, p. 231; Lewis, *Jan Compagnie*, pp. 135–6.
130 Lewis, *Jan Compagnie*, p. 12.
131 Andaya, B., "Melaka under the Dutch" in *Melaka, the Transformation of a Malay Capital*, ed. Singh and Wheatley, I, p. 197; Lewis, *Jan Compagnie in the Straits of Malacca*, pp. 16, 17.
132 Leupe, "The Siege and Capture of Malacca", *JMBRAS* 14, 1 (1936): 162–3 (Instruction to Antonisz) where it is reported that Goa could not muster a crew to man vessels for Melaka, as no sailor wanted to go.

Conclusion

1 See also Holden Furber, *Rival Empires of Trade*, II, pp. 310–1.
2 See Borschberg, "Grotius, East India Trade", *JSEAS* 30, 2 (1999): 239.

3 See Grotius, *The Free Sea*, ed. Armitage; Borschberg, "Hugo Grotius' Theory of Trans-Oceanic Trade Regulation", *IILJ Working Paper* (August 2006), pp. 1–23; van Ittersum, *Profit and Principle*, esp. pp. 356–8, 485–6.

4 Borschberg, "Hugo Grotius' Theory", *IILJ Working Paper* (August 2006), esp. pp. 8–9, 34–46.

5 Borschberg, "Grotius, East India Trade", *JSEAS* 30, 2 (1999): 243–4.

6 Pearson, *Before Colonialism*, p. 52.

7 See also Furber, *Rival Empires of Trade*, II, p. 311.

8 Steensgaard, "Violence and the Rise of Capitalism", *Review* 5, 2 (1981): 261.

9 Furber, *Rival Empires of Trade*, II, p. 310.

10 In practice the VOC was eager to convert to Calvinism those souls whom the Portuguese had brought into the Roman Catholic fold. Certainly, the Dutch company was not spared of religious hubris, as is evidenced by Ricklefs' *War, Culture and Economy in Java*, p. 129.

11 Letter from VOC Governor-General Pieter de Carpentier to the Heren XVII, 29 January 1624, *CB*, 7b, p. 1092.

12 Andaya, *The Kingdom of Johor*, p. 26.

13 See Furber, *Rival Empires of Trade*, II, p. 312 on the absence of unequal and irrevocable treaties until the middle of the 18th century.

14 Furber, *Rival Empires of Trade*, II, pp. 312, 313.

15 Van Ittersum, *Profit and Principle*, p. lii.

16 For a recent historiographical survey on developments in the history of European trade in Southeast Asia, and especially also van Leur, see the account by van Ittersum, *Profit and Principle*, pp. xliv–liii.

17 Kling and Pearson, *The Age of Partnership*.

Appendices

1 Tomé Pires, *A Suma Oriental*, ed. Cortesão (1978), p. 3; Cortesão, *A propósito do ilustre boticário*, pp. 4, 8, 9; Correia da Silva, *Um boticário na história da expansão*, p. 21. For a modern biography of Pires, see Cortesão, *Primeira Embaixada Europeia à China*.

2 Some of the most noteworthy publications in this respect include Armando Cortesão's new edition with foreword of the *Suma Oriental*, Tomé Pires, *A Suma Oriental* (1978), Cortesão, *A propósito*, pp. 1–15. Cortesão, *Primeira Embaixada*, Loureiro, "O Sudeste Asiático na Suma Oriental de Tomé Pires", *Revista de Cultura* 4 (2003): 107–23; Smith, *A Projected Portuguese Voyage to China in 1512*; Correia da Silva, *Um boticário na história da expansão*. Da Costa Torres, *Breve Noticia de Tomé Pires*; Da Costa Torres, "Tomé Pires na Intimidade", *Journal dos Farmacêuticos* (1943): 5–31. See also the edition of the Lisbon manuscript featured in note 3 below. Tomé Pires, along with an account of his activities as an apothecary and diplomat, is encountered in

several period sources of Portuguese origin, including significantly Galvão, *Tratado dos Descobrimentos*, pp. 182–3 and Barros. Concerning the latter, see his *Décadas* déc. III, liv. II, cap. VIII; déc. III, liv. V, cap. X; déc. III, liv. VI, cap. II; déc. III, liv. VI, cap. II; déc. III, liv. VIII, cap. V; déc. IV, liv. I, cap. VI.

3 To the present author's knowledge, the best textcritical analysis of the *Suma Oriental* can be found in Wolters' chapter "The Founder of Malacca", in *The Fall of Srivijaya*, pp. 108–27, where the insights of Pires are juxtaposed and critically analysed against the backdrop of Asian sources, such as notably the *Sejarah Melayu*. An in-depth textcritical analysis focusing on the internal consistencies and differences among the manuscripts of the *Suma Oriental*, however, is still missing. See also note 5.

4 Milner, "Who Created Malaysia's Plural Society?" *JMBRAS* 76, 2 (2004): 1–24. Pires' letters of 7 November 1512 and 10 January 1513, as well as his *rol de drogarias* of 1516 preserved in Lisbon, can be found in da Costa Torres, "Tomé Pires na Intimidade", pp. 9–14, 24–9.

5 Cortesão takes the variant readings of the Paris and Lisbon manuscripts of the *Suma Oriental* into consideration in both his 1944 and 1978 editions of the text, but otherwise has little to say about the implications of these alternate readings. Some basic differences between the two manuscripts are mentioned in Cortesão, *A propósito*, pp. 8–9. See also Cortesão, *Primeira Embaixada*, pp. 30–1. The Lisbon manuscript was published as a self-standing text by Loureiro, *O Manuscrito de Lisboa da 'Suma Oriental' de Tomé Pires*.

6 According to Cortesão, the Paris manuscript came into the possession of Bishop D. Jerónimo de Osório around, but in any case before, 1580. See Pires, *A Suma Oriental*, pp. 5, 7.

7 For Cortesão's verdict on the Lisbon manuscript, see *SO*, I, pp. 65–7. The shorter text of the Lisbon manuscript is explained away (p. 66) as being a "preliminary draft which Pires sent off [to the Viceroy] not long after his arrival in Melaka". He reckons that manuscript (p. 66) is a "copy of a some original now lost". Both hypotheses remain unproven. Also Correia da Silva, *Um boticário*, p. 21.

8 For Cortesão's statement, see *SO*, I, p. xvi: "The present copy of Pires' *Suma* is not the original he himself wrote, and the copyist has left only too many instances of his own carelessness. Pires' style is far from clear, and this, added to the transcriber's mistakes and the most anarchic punctuation, or absolute lack of it, makes the interpretation of the text often extremely difficult; sometimes the translation has to be very free, perhaps even more of a guess than anything else." Cortesão also describes the original Portuguese text of the Paris manuscript as "very difficult and etymologically very interesting".

9 *The Book of Duarte Barbosa*, ed. Dames. For the most recent Portuguese-language edition, see *O Libro de Duarte Barbosa*, introduction and notes by

Neves Aguas. The relevant passages on Melaka cover Barbosa, *O Libro*, pp. 164–8.

10 Erédia, "Informação", in Caminha, *Ordenações da Índia*, p. 76. For a short biography on Erédia, see Faro, *Godinho de Erédia, cosmógrafo*, and the introduction in Erédia, *Suma de Árvores e Plantas da Índia Intra Ganges*, ed. Everaert, Mendes Ferrão and Cândida Liberato, pp. 28ff.

11 Erédia, *Declaraçam de Malaca*; a precursor of this work appeared significantly earlier as Erédia, "Informação", in Caminha, *Ordenações da Índia*, pp. 95ff.

12 See classicly Basset's criticism of Meilink-Roelofsz in Bassett, "European Influence in Southeast Asia, c.1500–1630", *JSEAH* 4, 2 (1963): 135–6, "Meilink-Roelofsz may have accepted Pires' descriptions of Malay-Indonesian society, trade and government with fewer reservations than a historian trained in more politically-documented fields would approve. Even a historian of South-East Asia, I suggest, would prefer to apply more stringent tests to the internal evidence of the *Suma Oriental* than Dr. Meilink-Roelofsz has done."

13 *Portuguese Documents on Malacca*, I, 1509–11, collected, translated and annotated by Pintado, esp. pp. 210ff.

14 Concerning the "historicity" of the *Sejarah Melayu*, see especially the deliberations of Wolters, *The Fall of Srivijaya*, pp. 84–5.

15 Winstedt, "The Malay Annals or Sejarah Melayu", *JMBRAS* 16, 3 (1938): 34, "One thing is certain: The bulk of the 'Malay Annals' was written at least eighty years before 1612"; Winstedt, *A History of Classical Malay Literature*, p. 158; Sweeney, "The Hikayat Raja-Raja Pasai and the Sejarah Melayu", *JMBRAS* 40, 2 (1967): 104. Miksic, *Archeological Research*, p. 23.

16 Winstedt, *A History of Classical Malay Literature*, pp. 158–9; and Roolvink's objections in his introduction to *Sĕjarah Mĕlayu or Malay Annals*, pp. xxiv–xxv.

17 Khalid-Taib, *Sastera Sejarah in the Malay World*, p. 126: "It has now been generally agreed among the Malay studies scholars that the *Sejarah Melayu*'s prototype was a kinglist. This kinglist was a very sketchy compilation which emphasized the genealogical relationships of the Malacca royal dynasty." See also Walls, *The Legacy of the Fathers*, pp. 15, 17–8, 22, 27, 40–7, 91, 95, 117–20; Wolters, *The Fall of Srivijaya*, pp. 84, 91.

18 De Josselin de Jong, "Malayan and Sumatran Place-Names", p. 61.

19 *Undang-undang Melaka: A Critical Edition*, ed. Liaw Yock Fang, Proefschrift University of Leiden; Winstedt and de Josselin de Jong, "The Maritime Laws of Malacca. Edited, with an outline translation", *JMBRAS* 29, 3 (1956): 22–59. On the question as to whether the *Undang-undang Melaka* and *Undang-undang Laut* represent actual legal codes or digests (compilations), see Liaw Yock Fang, "The Undang-undang Melaka", in *Melaka*, ed. Singh and Wheatley, I, pp. 170, 181, 183.

[20] See also Lombard, "Le sultanat malais comme modèle socio-économique", in Lombard and Aubin, *Marchands et hommes d'affaires asiatiques*; Winstedt, *A History of Classical Malay Literature*, p. 167.

[21] Influence is also traced to Indian or Hindu laws; see Alexandrowicz, *An Introduction*, p. 63, note 12; Winstedt, *A History of Classical Malay Literature*, p. 168.

[22] Kathirithamby-Wells, "Ethics and Enterpreneurship in Southeast Asia, c. 1400–1800", in Sprengard and Ptak, *Maritime Asia. Profit Maximisation, Ethics and Trade Structure*, pp. 178–9.

[23] *Undang-undang Melaka*, p. 38; Liaw, "The Undang-undang Melaka", ed. Singh and Wheatley, *Melaka*, I, pp. 182, 185; Winstedt, *A History of Classical Malay Literature*, p. 167.

[24] Parameswara and his band of thieves and hoodlums are described as having been previously very active around Singapura (where he lived for six years and later murdered his host) and then Muar, with 2,000 men; see Anonymous, *Held-dadige Scheeps-togt*, pp. 202–3. The anonymous text is attributed by the curators of Leiden University Library to the Portuguese chronicler and historian João de Barros. See also *SO*, II, p. 232: "[Parameswara] remained there [Muar] for six years, and there he planted things to live on; and they [Parameswara and his men] used to fish and sometimes robbed and plundered sampans ...". See also *SO*, II, p. 233. Van Stein Callenfels, "The Founder of Malacca", *JMBRAS* 42, 1 (1969): 63–4. Similar sources were evidently used in Teixeira, *Portuguese Missions*, I, p. 17; Wolters, *The Fall of Srivijaya*, pp. 108–10, 117–8; Wolters, *Early Indonesian Commerce*, pp. 222–3; Winstedt, "The Malay Founder of Medieval Malacca", *Bulletin of the School of Oriental and African Studies*, University of London, 12.3-4 (1948): 726–7; and Kwa, "Records and Notices of Early Singapore", in *Archeological Research*, ed. Miksic, pp. 122–3 for accounts by Pires and Barros on the relation between Parameswara and the *orang laut*.

[25] See also the Chinese testimonies of Fei-Hsin (1436) and Ma-Huan (1451) reproduced in translation by Wheatley in his *Golden Khersonese*, pp. 321–5, where it is reported that Melaka (evidently even after the chief was elevated to the position of king by the Chinese emperor) paid an annual tribute to Siam of "40 taels" in gold (Wheatley, *Golden Khersonese*, pp. 321, 324). On the origin of this tribute, see also *Held-dadige Scheeps-togt*, p. 206. Unlike for the case of Siam (... *el rey de Sião ser senhor de muyta terra* ...), Castanheda does not claim that Melaka itself represented a great territorial empire, but only that the king of Melaka no longer obeyed Siam by 1509. The 16th-century Portuguese chronicler opens his chapter on Melaka (book II, chapter CXII) with the following words: "Esta cidade de Malaca esta na costa de hum grande reyno chamado Sião situada na boca de hum pequeno rio. ..." (This city of Melaka is situated along the coast of a great empire named Siam, and

situated at the mouth of a small river). See Castanheda, *História da Índia*, II, pp. 458, 459; Barbosa, *The Book*, II, p. 178; Hageman, "Geschiedenis der Verovering van Malakka en der Oorlogen Tusschen de Portugezen en Maleijers", *Verhandelingen van het Bataviaasch Genootschap van Kunsten en Wetenschappen* 24 (1852): 11.

26 On the origins of Melaka, see also Wheatley, *Impressions*, pp. 119–76; Wilkinson, "The Malacca Sultanate", *JSBRAS* 61 (1912): 67–8.

27 See *The Itinerary of Ludovico de Varthema*, trans. John Winter Jones from the original Italian edition of 1510 and ed. Norman Mosely Penzer; Bausani, *Lettera*; Spallanzani, *Giovanni da Empoli*. In Portuguese sources, including the *Décadas da Ásia* of Barros, Empoli is referred to as "Joanes Impole". See, for example, Barros, *Décadas*, déc. II, liv. X, cap. VIII; déc. III, liv. I, cap. I; déc. III, liv. II, cap. VI and VIII.

28 Wheatley, *Impressions*, pp. 132–3. Also *Held-dadige Scheeps-togt*, p. 203.

29 *Held-dadige Scheeps-togt*, p. 204, where for Melaka a form of *convivencia* (peaceful living together) is described between the *orang laut* (celates) and the Malays.

30 Barbosa underscores that food was brought into Melaka from "outside", but that the city "abounds in fruit and good water". See Barbosa, *The Book of Duarte Barbosa*, II, p. 178. Still, given the city's dependence on outside supplies the cost of living remained high, see MacGregor, "The Portuguese in Malaya", *JMBRAS* 28, 2 (1955): 7–8 and esp. also his extensive source references in notes 17 and 18.

31 See also Wheatley, *Impressions*, pp. 140–2.

32 Ferrand, *Relations de voyages*.

33 For Conti's influence on Fra Mauro, see Bouchon and Ménard, *Le Voyage aux Indes de Nicolò de Conti*, p. 86, and generally the definitive study by Falchetta, *Fra Mauro*'s pp. 59–69, 232, 233.

34 As is known from published research on Ottoman maritime policies and endeavours, the "age of exploration" is not a phenomenon limited to the European or even Iberian powers, but part of a much broader development that spanned Europe, Asia and the coastal regions of the African continent. On the Ottoman-Turkish developments coinciding with the European age of exploration of the 15th and 16th centuries, see especially Brotton, "Disorienting the East: the Geography of the Ottoman Empire", in *Trading Territories*, pp. 87–118; Hess, "The Evolution of the Ottoman Seaborne Empire", *The American Historical Review* 75, 7 (1970): 1892–1919.

35 Bittner and Tomaschek, *Die Topographischen Capitel*. For a general background on the development of Ottoman cartographical science and its use of knowledge gained by European maritime powers such as the Portuguese and the Catalans in general terms, see Brotton, *Trading Territories*, pp. 87–118.

36 Rouffaer, "Was Malaka Emporium vóór A. D. 1400?" pp. 168–9, 383ff; Obdeijn, "De oude zeehandelsweg", pp. 751ff; Wheatley, *The Golden Khersonese*, pp. 306–25; Wheatley, *Impressions*, see pp. 119–76.

[37] Wolters, *The Fall of Srivijaya*, p. 160; Muhammad Yusof Hashim, *The Malay Sultanate*, p. 185. Winstedt contended that Iskandar Shah and the legendary founder of Melaka, Parameswara, are one and the same individual, explaining that Parameswara had taken on a new name on his conversion to Islam. See Winstedt, "The Malay Founder", p. 727. On this claim, and the problems surrounding the Melaka ruler Xarquem Darxa mentioned by Pires in the *Suma Oriental*, see the excellent forensic exposé by Wolters, *The Fall of Srivijaya*, pp. 108–27.

[38] Pintado, *Documents*, para. 96, p. 233: "Malacca is the most populous town in the Indies …"; para. 185, p. 255: "This is the principal town in these parts, rich in trade …"; also Pintado, *Documents*, para. 304, p. 281: "[Melaka is] the greatest trading centre in the world". Similar statements can be gleaned from other early Portuguese sources. See Barbosa, *The Book of Duarte Barbosa*, II, p. 175.

[39] Pintado, *Documents*, para. 216, p. 261. See also Hageman, "Geschiedenis der Verovering van Malakka", p. 4.

[40] *SO*, II, p. 279.

[41] Pintado, *Portuguese Documents on Malacca*, p. 117, parag. 14 (De Goes); p. 131, parag. 2 (De Araújo).

[42] Bausani, *Lettera di Giovanni da Empoli*, p. 132.

[43] Petrzilka, *Die Karten*. On the historical background to the de Vries map, see Johnson, *Carta Marina: World Geography in Strassburg, 1525*.

[44] *AA*, pp. 426–7.

[45] Thomaz, *Early Portuguese Malacca*, pp. 51ff. See also Hageman, "Geschiedenis der Verovering", pp. 4, 9.

[46] On this point see also Ptak, "Reconsidering Melaka and Central Guangdong", in *Iberians in the Singapore Melaka Area*, ed. Borschberg, p. 3.

[47] Varthema, *Itinarary*, p. 84.

[48] *SO*, I, pp. 145–7. On the *Bajau* in Melaka, see Thomaz, *Early Portuguese Malacca*, p. 3.

[49] On this practice in the Malay world, see especially Heng, "Reconstructing Banzu", *JMBRAS* 75, 1 (2002): 71, 84–5. Note especially his claim on p. 84 that "Malacca, for example, was not recorded for having a [chain] boom".

[50] Transcript of source M (Madrid) with major or interesting spelling variations indicated in the footnotes for source L (London). As in many early modern manuscripts, the letters "i" and "e" are often difficult to distinguish. A period above the vowel was taken to indicate the letter "i". Due to the nature of the hand and the writing instrument used, words are often written together, or alternatively, if the author lifted his hand, the cursive is interrupted and as a result letters become severed from the full word. Where this is the case, modern Portuguese spelling rules were followed as far as possible. Nasalisation of vowels that are no longer used in modern Portuguese, such as "hũa", have been transliterated as "huma". Minor spelling differences such as a single

"s" rather than "ss" or in the use of diacritical characters have not been highlighted. The Latin ligand "&" has been transliterated as "e". Abbreviated words have been written out in full. Capitalisation and punctuation follows manuscript M. A double bar similar to the symbol "=" is understood to indicate a period or the end of a sentence.

51 A second but shorter account touching on the destruction of Johor Lama dated 21 March 1588 and written in Spanish (Castilian) can be found in the Biblioteca Nacional de España, Madrid, Ms. 1750, fols. 181 recto–182 verso, incip. *De las victorias que don Paulo de Lima Pereyra tuvo en la India en las partes del Sur* ... (Of the victories that Dom Paulo Lima Pereira scored in the sourthern parts of India …). Similar accounts of Dom Paulo's attack on Johor Lama are also found in dos Santos, *Etiópia Oriental*, ed. Lobato and Guerreiro Vieira, pp. 547–52; and Barros and do Couto, *Décadas da Ásia*, XXI, pp. 466–504. See also do Couto, *Vida Dom Lima de Pereira*, pp. 77–144.

52 L: "Dachem".

53 L: "absent".

54 L: "Li".

55 L: "Cochim".

56 M: fol. 233 verso.

57 L: Adds "e os mais".

58 M: Adds a second "de".

59 L: "Pedir".

60 L: "Pajem".

61 L: fol. 10 verso.

62 L: "d'Abreu".

63 L: "Pulobutam".

64 L: "adeberem".

65 M: fol. 234 recto.

66 L: "atinarão".

67 Fol. 11 recto.

68 Dom António served as the captain-major of Melaka.

69 M: fol. 234 verso.

70 L: fol. 11 verso.

71 M: fol. 235 recto.

72 L: fol. 12 recto.

73 M: Deleted "las".

74 M: fol. 235 verso.

75 L: fol. 12 verso.

76 M: fol. 236 recto.

77 L: fol. 13 recto.

78 L: Repeats "combatendo elles".

79 M: fol. 236 verso.

80 L: fol. 13 verso.

81 M: fol. 237 recto.
82 L: "num".
83 L: fol. 14 recto.
84 M: fol. 237 verso.
85 L: Erroneously adds a second "a".
86 L: fol. 14 verso.
87 L: "tinhe".
88 M: fol. 238 recto.
89 L: Omits text marked between brackets.
90 L: fol. 15 recto.
91 M: fol. 238 verso.
92 L: "Fucal"; M: Deletes reading "El rey de"; do Couto, *Vida*, p. 110, reads "Tugual".
93 Do Couto, *Vida*, p. 110, reads "Dandragir".
94 L: "Bintau".
95 L: "Ray".
96 L: "Serina".
97 L: "Serima".
98 L: "Serinda".
99 L: Omits the entire line.
100 L: Omits the entire line. Do Couto, *Vida*, p. 134, provides the following testimony and list of names as prisoners or casualties: "As pessoas conhecidas e capitães principaes da sua parte que morrerarem e captivarem, são as seguintes: Serinará, Serimadaraja, Serpidra, Jalella, Gaiailate, Siribridaja, Chegalá Nimalate, Simirambanca, Ariodraja, capitão de Sábão, e Basiderá, que morreu depois no mato, todas capitães d'aquelles Reis, afóra outros muitos a que não sabemos os nomes".
101 L: "com Dachem".
102 L: fol. 15 verso.
103 L: "Joar".
104 M: fol. 239 recto.
105 M: fol. 239 verso.
106 L: fol. 16 recto.
107 Translated from the original 16th-century Portuguese text by Roopanjali Roy (Lisbon) and the author. Given the occasionally long sentences featured in the original letter, it was deemed that the English translation could not — and should not — be too literal or closely shackled to prevailing grammar or sentence structures. In order to render the text more reader-friendly, sentences have been restructured or broken up. The translators agree that the underlying message has been preserved. Words in the text within square brackets have been added by the editors/translators to help clarify the text. For the historical background to this campaign in 1587, see the now classic article by MacGregor,

"Johore Lama in the Sixteenth Century", *JMBRAS* 28, 2: 48–125, see pp. 94–101, for the immediate prelude to Paulo Lima de Pereira's attack on Johor Lama.

108 Compare with MacGregor, "Johore Lama", p. 101, and his references in notes 217–8.

109 Monte Delly, or Monte Deli as it is referred to on occasion, is spelt in the present manuscript as "Monte de Ly". It is situated up the coast, to the northwest of Calicut and Cannanore. This important navigational landmark finds mention in several early modern travel accounts, including significantly the letters of Giovanni da Empoli. Their modern editor, Marco Spallanzani, describes the feature as an "alta montagna sulla costa del Malabar" (high mountain along the Malabar coast). See Spallanzani, *Lettera*, p. 168, note 32. Other references are found there on pp. 38, 142, 144, 168. Bausani claims the name derives from the Malayalam *eli mala* (high mountain). See Bausani, *Lettera di Giovanni da Empoli*, p. 117, note 33.

110 L and M both clearly read "Cobar". This is evidently a transcription error committed by a scribe not sufficiently familiar with geography. The name should read "Cotiar". The former is an island situated within Roe Bay on the eastern coast of present-day Sri Lanka and is located to the south of Trincomalee.

111 Compare with MacGregor, "Johore Lama", p. 101, and his references in notes 217–8.

112 The Portuguese text reads "or"; the context appears to indicate that they took on fresh water in Sumatra as well as on the island of Polvoreira. Thus the term "or" is translated as "and".

113 The island of Polvoreira (sometimes also spelt Apolvoreira) is featured on many 16th- and 17th-century maps of both Portuguese and Dutch origin. In the Portuguese chronicles of Barros and do Couto, the island is specifically identified by the (corrupted) Malay names Barala and Barelá. See Barros and do Couto, *Décadas da Ásia*, vol. 4, p. 11, where a connection between the Ilha Polvoreira and Pulau Barala is established. Barros then adds the following important explanation: "… junto de uma ilha a que os nossos chamam a Polvoreira e os da terra Barala, que quere dizer 'Casa de Deus', por razão de um antigo templo que ali esteve" (… next to an island which our people call Polvoreira, and those of the land call Barala, which is to say, "House of God", on account of an ancient temple which used to be there). The explanation seems plausible, as the modern Malay term *berhala* means "idol" or "image", which may be a reference to a Buddhist, Chinese or Hindu temple. The phonetically similar terms *bihara* or *biara* are employed in modern Malay to designate ancient Hindu ruins, specifically in the context of Sumatra. The island is also described as a navigational landmark in Galvão, *Tratado dos Descobrimentos*, p. 161. On Dutch charts of the late

17th and early 18th centuries, "Polvoreira" is further corrupted into "Pulo Vera" or "Pulo Verera" and is depicted in the Strait of Melaka roughly at the height of Dili (Medan) on Sumatra and Perak on the Malay Peninsula. According to Mark Dion, the island of Polvoreira is located about 40 *legoas*, or 160 miles, from Melaka, between the islands Belawan and Lumut. See Dion, "Sumatra through Portuguese Eyes", *Indonesia* 9 (April 1970): 138, note 14.

114 On d'Abreu de Mello, see MacGregor, "Johore Lama", p. 102, note 220.

115 The original Portuguese text does not specify who could not go further. This is a free translation.

116 This island finds mention in several early modern sources, including the *Muhit*, where it is called "fulo Butang". It is situated off the western coast of the Peninsula, between present-day Phuket (formerly Junçalão or Junk Ceylon) and the coast of Kedah. On the maps of the Malay Peninsula it is often featured prominently with the name "Pulo Botum". The hydrographic chart of Gerritsz depicting Sumatra, the Melaka Strait and the Peninsula preserved in Berlin places the name "P. Butum" off the coast of Kedah.

117 On this maritime route plied by the Portuguese expedition from Goa, see especially MacGregor, "Johore Lama", p. 102, note 219.

118 "Their" refers to the Portuguese inflicting damage.

119 This weapon is a precursor of the musket.

120 Leitão, *Dictionário*, p. 79, describes the *bâlos* as an oriental type of ship. See also Erédia, *Description of Malaca*, p. 36: "the bâlos, used for cargo, are propelled by means of breast oars: they also have sails which are almost the same shape as the sails of the *alfragattas*".

121 Leitão, *Dictionário*, p. 488, describes the *sôma* as a vessel similar to a junk, used either as a naval or as a commercial vessel. Possibly similar to a *prahu*. See also Erédia, *Description of Malaca*, p. 37, where the *sôma* is described as a "tall boat like freight-bearing carracks, with 2 rudders and masts and with sails made of woven palm-leaves and matting, traversed by bamboos at definitive intervals …".

122 Compare with MacGregor, "Johore Lama", p. 102.

123 The *navette* is a type of sea-going cargo ship. See the glossary for further details.

124 The *bantin* is a type of Malay vessel used in naval warfare.

125 Compare with MacGregor, "Johore Lama", p. 103, and his references in note 222, and p. 97, note 201.

126 Reference is made here to the settlement situated on the site of present-day Kampung Johor Lama.

127 The actual word employed in the text is "natives".

128 Compare with MacGregor, "Johore Lama", p. 104, see note 225.

129 The "fortress of timber" called "Corritão" by do Couto in his *Vida* is also mentioned by MacGregor, "Johore Lama", p. 105, note 225. Malay fortifi-

cations of the period tended to consist of earthen ramparts and thick wooden palisades. On this point, see Everaert, "Erédia, Humaniste ou Aventurier?" p. 55, note 91; and MacGregor, "Johore Lama", p. 106.

130 This early modern weapon is later identified in this present source as a piece of "light artillery".

131 Compare with MacGregor, "Johore Lama", p. 104, note 225. The information in this letter corresponds to the "17 pieces of artillery" mentioned by dos Santos but differs more substantially from the 30 mentioned by do Couto.

132 Compare with MacGregor, "Johore Lama", p. 104, note 226, where Dom António is identified as António d'Ándria, "the commander of the bantins and himself a Malacca man".

133 Reference here is to the Portuguese generically; it does not include Paulo Lima de Pereira himself.

134 Compare with MacGregor, "Johore Lama", p. 105.

135 Reference here is to the blockade of the Old Strait of Singapore, between present-day Telok Blangah and Sentosa. According to Barros, this was achieved in 1584 by submerging large logs in the Strait and sinking old junks so as to impede ships from passing through the waters. On this tactic, see Barros and do Couto, *Décadas da Ásia*, vol. 21, p. 210.

136 That is, the Portuguese in general.

137 This is a statement of some historical interest. Kota Batu and Johor Lama are not, in fact, situated in the southern hemisphere, but at more than one degree northern latitude. At the time Lima de Pereira was writing his letter from Melaka in 1587, the early 16th-century dispute as to whether the equator ran through the Malay Peninsula had been long settled. The question at the time was whether the equator ran through Bintan (see, for example, Erédia's charts of 1604–13 that are very evidently inspired by Abraham Ortelius' *Theatrum Orbis Terrarum* of the 1570s) or whether it ran slightly farther south still through the island of Lingga. The latter has proven to be the case, and the first charts to depict the equator correctly cutting across Lingga were penned by the VOC hydrographer Hessel Gerritsz in the 1620s. Evidently Lima de Pereira did not consult any charts for his voyage and campaign, and if he did, they were based on already outdated cartographical knowledge.

138 MacGregor, "Johore Lama", p. 106: "On the seaward side of this fort there was another [fort], which they called Cotabato, which means earth fort, for it was made of very thick walls of beaten earth and roofed with great beams, thus forming a storehouse below …". Of course the Malay word "batu" means "stone", and Kota Batu probably refers to the high point with gun emplacements built of stone.

139 Reference here is to the "enemy" in Johor.

140 The *lancha* or *lanchara* is a type of Malay vessel used for transporting cargo. See Erédia, *Description of Malaca*, p. 36, including the illustration titled "Lanchara de Malayos", and the glossary.

[141] The author Lima de Pereira is probably referring here to Javanese of the Muslim religion. In the period, expressions such as as "Turk", "Moor" or "Saracen" are generically used in European sources to designate Muslims.

[142] Dom Nunalverez in the present document is almost certainly "Dom Neno Álvares" identified by MacGregor, "Johore Lama", p. 104.

[143] That is, the street or road that leads to the royal palace.

[144] A *palmo* is literally the "palm" of the hand; a "span", about 225 millimetres.

[145] Leitão, *Dictionário*, p. 130, describes the *camelo* as a piece of artillery with a short trajectory.

[146] According to Leitão, *Dictionário*, p. 130, a camelete is a small *camelo* that fires ordinance of stone.

[147] Leitão, *Dictionário*, p. 134, describes a *cão* as a small piece of artillery of minor calibre. Similar to the *espera.*

[148] According to Leitão, *Dictionário*, p. 244, the *espera* is a piece of artillery with a short trajectory. The *meia espera* or half-cradle is a smaller version of the *espera.*

[149] Reference here is to a range of artillery common in 16th century warfare comprising pieces of the cannon and culverin classes, and in all appearance featured here in descending order of calibre. For example, a basilisk generally features approximately a 250 millimetre calibre and is capable of firing a 7,000 gramme shot (but there are reports of far larger artillery); a falcon features a 650 millimetre calibre and is capable of firing a 1,000 gramme shot; a falconet features a 100 millimetre calibre and is capable of firing a 500 gramme shot; a serpentine features a 150 millimetre calibre and is capable of firing a 250 gramme shot. On the English names of these artillery pieces, see the translation in MacGregor, "Johore Lama", p. 106; p. 108, note 235; pp. 111–2. According to Boxer, the Portuguese at Diu in the 16th century "captured a gigantic bronze basilisco ("basilisk") firing a shot of 110 lbs." See Boxer, "Asian Potentates and European Artillery", *JMBRAS* 38, 2 (1965): 158–9.

[150] The actual term employed by Lima de Pereira is "estreito" or "strait". This is probably a reference to the Johor River, which he may have thought to be a "strait", as the area around Johor Lama features salt water and is affected by tidal changes.

[151] According to Erédia, *Description of Malaca*, p. 36, the *balões* are swift-moving, hand-paddled vessels that are chiefly used for fishing in rivers. See also the glossary.

[152] The term *kling* or *keeling* generically refers to merchants of South Indian origin, usually ethnic Tamils. Technically, the sale of firearms and munitions to "enemies", especially enemies of the Christian faith, was prohibited by law, but as argued by Boxer, this rule was pretty much a dead letter in Asia. See Boxer, "Asian Potentates and European Artillery", *JMBRAS* 38, 2 (1965): 161.

[153] The present English translation includes the reading from M *os que assi mas* [acima] *digo* which is completely absent in L. The expression translates roughly as "those mentioned above" and has been liberally translated in the present context with "as mentioned previously".

[154] The reading of the original Portuguese text is insufficiently clear. The text appears to read *a fuga dos*, that means "taking flight from", but the reading *afogados*, that is "drowned" fits better both grammatically and also contextually.

[155] This title is also employed for Raja Ali Jalla by de Coutre, see *AA*, p. 105. See also the list of nobles featured in Pinto, *Portugueses e malaios*, p. 166.

[156] M and L both read "Fucal", which is evidently an error made by an earlier copyist. MacGregor, "Johore Lama", p. 108, note 236, identifies the ruler of "Tugual" as the ruler of Tringal in Terengganu.

[157] Pinto, *Portugueses e malaios*, p. 166, identifies the King of Bintan as the Raja Dampol.

[158] This is almost certainly "Giailate". See below, note 165.

[159] See MacGregor, "Johore Lama", p. 110.

[160] Compare this name with "Jadella" in note 165. Pinto, *Portugueses e malaios*, p. 166, "Rajalela".

[161] Compare this name with "Serimadaraja" mentioned in note 165. MacGregor, "Johore Lama", p. 112, identifies him as the Sri Nara'diraja.

[162] This may represent a corruption of "Silindra", that is Sri Indra. Compare with the list of names and titles in Pinto, *Portugueses e malaios*, p. 166.

[163] Compare this name with "Chengala" in note 165.

[164] This name is very evidently corrupted and almost certainly corresponds to the name "Mimalate". The Portuguese text resorts to the masculine to describe the gender of the individual concerned. The name probably represents a phonetic corruption of "Menggalane" or a similar male name or title.

[165] Compare this list of names to the one found in Couto and Barros, *Da Ásia*, vol. 21, pp. 506–7, "Sirinará, Serimadaraja, Seriandra, Serimara, Jadella, Giailate, Seribidraja, Chengala, Mimalate, Serimambaca, Aria Draja, Capitão de Sabão, Bozedra." The name Seribidraja is identified by MacGregor, "Johore Lama", p. 112 as the Sri Bija'diraja.

[166] Being Kota Batu.

[167] See MacGregor, "Johore Lama", p. 113, "Yet Dom Paulo's success was not conclusive. As early as 15 October, he had to send out his younger brother, Dom Pedro de Lima, in charge of a squadron to protect shipping against Ali Jalla's fleet".

[168] According to information passed to the author by Miksic, the location in question here is probably up the Sungei Riau in the vicinity of Kota Piring, where archeological remains of settlement and trading activity have been discovered.

[169] The actual term employed is "natives".

[170] This sentence evidently represents a later textual insert, but it is featured as part of the main text in M and L. In the present location at the end of this epistolary report, it is certainly taken out of its proper context.

[171] Partial transcription of the original 16th century French text. The letters "v" and "u" as well as "i" and "j" were used interchangeably, especially when capitalised. The present transcript has adapted all of these to modern spelling conventions. The Latin ligand "&" is rendered as "et". Nasalisation symbols such as "ā" and "ō" have been transcribed as "an" or "am", and "on" or "om" respectively, in full conformity to modern French spelling conventions. Correspondingly, the symbol "ē" is rendered as "en" or "em". The early modern "ſ" and the ligand "ß" are transcribed as "s" and "ss" respectively. Accents, capitalisation and punctuation featured in the late 16th-century print text have been retained.

[172] Fol. 413 verso.

[173] Marginalia reads: "Destroit qui fait le chemin long".

[174] Fol. 414 recto.

[175] Marginalia: "Sang propre aux femes".

[176] Marginalia: "Mecon rivier fort grande".

[177] Translation from the original 16th-century French by Peter Borschberg Sr. Revision of the translation, notes and comments by the author.

[178] It would appear that Thevet probably derived this particular corruption of Singapura from Pigafetta, where the name applies to a city. See Pigafetta, *Magellan's Voyage*, p. 152, "And to the east of this cape [of Melaka], along the coast, there are many towns and cities, the names of some of which are: Cinghapola, which is at the cape, Pahan, Calantan, Patani, Braadlun, Benan, Lagon, Chereggiegharan, Tumbon, Pihan, Cui, Brabri, Bangha, Iudia (and this is the city where dwells the king of Siam, named Siri), then Zacabedra, Jundibun, Langonpipha, and Lauu."

[179] One French nautical league is approximately 4.45 kilometres. Thevet's estimate is incorrect and probably based on Gastaldi's or Ramusio's maps, where the distance between Borneo and the Malay Peninsula appears smaller than it really is.

[180] Thevet is evidently confused here. The text should read "left", not "right".

[181] Thirty leagues approximates 133 kilometres.

[182] According to 1 King 11:7 and Judg. 11:12, Chemosh was the god of the Moabites and Ammonites. This connection made by Thevet is pure conjecture, but not unusual in a day where scholars sought to find — or in this instance seek to forcefully establish — connections with Biblical history.

[183] This is a corruption of King Phrachai of Siam. The immediate source of this spelling, "Perchoa", appears to be taken from Ramusio's *Viaggi* (Tomé Pires), *Sommario di tutti li regni*, chap. 79; SO, p. 109, reads "Prechayoa".

184 "Bumatta" may be a corruption of "Burma". Ramusio (Tomé Pires), *Sommario*, p. 79, and SO, pp. 109–11, read "Brema" and "Bremao".

185 This is a reference to Governor Oya Kampengpet. The corrupted spelling appears to derive directly from Ramusio (Tomé Pires), *Sommario*, 79; SO, p. 109, reads "Aja Capētit".

186 This spelling and the information on this officer has been adopted from Ramusio, (Tomé Pires) *Sommario*, chap. 79; the officer is not mentioned in SO.

187 This information is found in Ramusio (Tomé Pires), *Sommario*, chap. 79; SO, p. 110.

188 Reference is here possibly to a shark, as it is used in Pigafetta, *Magellan's Voyage*, p. 34. It is also not sufficiently clear whether Thevet actually has a shark in mind. The animal he describes could also be a crocodile, or he had difficulty keeping the two apart. Further, it is questionable whether this "giant fish" described by Thevet has a connection with the "swordfish" legend of the *Sejarah Melayu*. If there be any connection, it would almost certainly imply that Thevet had access to sources of Malay literature, possibly through Portuguese channels. Such access is unlikely, but within the current state of research should not be entirely dismissed. On the "swordfish" episode, see Kwa, "Records and Notices of Early Singapore", in *Archeological Research*, ed. Miksic, pp. 114.

189 This is almost certainly a phonetic corruption of the Malay term *prahu*, or *prao*. This information may be taken from Ramusio (Tomé Pires), *Sommario*, chap. 80, where the term reads *haraos*; and SO, p. 111, *paraos*.

190 The "River of Siam", or the present-day Chao Phraya River, was known in early modern times to trace its source to a location in the Kingdom of Ava. It is said to flow through the Kingdoms of Pegu and Siam until finding its estuary in the Gulf of Siam. According to the 18th-century German Zedler's *Universallexicon*, vol. 20, column 609, the term *Menan* translates as "Mother of the Rivers".

191 These names represent corruptions of the Anambas Islands, Pulau Aor and Pulau Tiga, all of which are located off the southeastern coast of the Malay Peninsula. It appears that Thevet adopted the corrupted nomenclature from Gastaldi's *Planisphere* (1561), *Terza Parte dell' Asia*, and not from the map of Southeast Asia reproduced in the first volume of Ramusio's *Viaggi* (1554). Ramusio and Gastaldi are known to have collaborated in their map productions and as a result feature similar topography and almost identical toponyms.

192 Thevet may have in mind here the Melaka Sultanate, which fell to the Portuguese, or more probably its successor, Johor.

193 This appears to represent a corruption of the name Pulau Condor, a group of islands known for centuries to mariners as a watering and provisioning station. The islands are situated off the southern coast of Vietnam and are known today as Côn Đao. It is almost certain that Thevet adopted this corrupted

nomenclature of Pulau Condor from the map of Southeast Asia added in the first volume of Ramusio's *Viaggi* (1554), which he is known to have consulted, or perhaps alternatively from Gastaldi's *Planisphere* of 1561, *Terza Parte dell' Asia*.

194 This island is not featured in the first volume of Ramusio's *Viaggi*, but it is featured in the form described by Thevet in Gastaldi's *Planisphere* (1561), *Terza Parte dell' Asia*.

195 It is not certain whether Thevet is confusing two similar sounding names, Cambay and Cambaia or Camboia. Cambay is a port in Gujarat (India), while Cambaia is Cambodia.

196 *Iangome* appears to be a phonetic corruption of "Chiang Mai". According to the map of Asia found in Thevet's *Cosmographie Universelle*, the Kingdom of Iangome spans across present-day north and northeast Thailand and Laos. See also SO, pp. 109, 111. Cortesão's editorial note, SO, p. 109, notes: "The town and state of Siamese Laos, called by the Burmese *Zimmé*, by the Siamese *Xieng-mai* or *Kiang-mai*, etc.".

197 This particular spelling conforms to Gastaldi's *Planisphere* (1561), *Terza Parte dell' Asia*.

198 This is probably a reference to the Himalayas, but in early modern sources the name Cambalu refers to present-day Beijing.

199 This is a reference to the Tonle Sap, a large but shallow lake in Cambodia.

200 This measurement appears to conform to the cartographic materials of Abraham Ortelius, published around 1570.

201 De Coutre's son Esteban, a Portuguese-speaking Goan, is known to have edited the text in its present form. Esteban may have also translated an original Portuguese draft into Spanish. See Winius and Chorba, "Literary Invasions in La Vida de Jaques de Coutre: do they prejudice its value as an historical source", in *A Carreira da Índia e as Rotas dos Estreitos*, ed. de Mota and Thomaz, p. 718.

202 For further information concerning the authorial intention and historical context of de Coutre's writings as well as the value of his manuscripts for the history of the region, see Borschberg, "Jacques de Coutre as a Source", *JMBRAS* 81, 2 (2008): 71–97.

203 Transcript according to the Spanish text edited by Benjamin N. Teensma, *Como Remediar o Estado da Índia?*, Intercontinenta, no. 10, Leiden, 1989, pp. 16–21. The Latin ligand "&" is rendered as "et". Nasalisation symbols such as "ā" and "ō" have been transcribed as "an" or "am", and "on" or "om" respectively, in full conformity to modern Spanish spelling conventions. Correspondingly, the symbol "ē" is rendered as "en" or "em". Accents, capitalisation and punctuation prevailing in the late 16th-century print text have been retained.

204 Fol. 270 verso.

205 Fol. 271 recto.

206 Fol. 271 verso.

207 Fol. 272 recto.

208 Fol. 272 verso.

209 Fol. 273 recto.

210 Fol. 273 verso.

211 Fol. 274 recto.

212 Translated from the original by Roopanjali Roy (Lisbon) and the author. Sentences have been broken up or restructured to smoothen comprehension for the modern reader. Words placed within square brackets have been added by the editors to clarify the text.

213 According to Leitão, *Dicionário*, p. 75, the Portuguese expression *baixel* refers to a ship or barque. The Malay craft in question is probably a *prahu* or more likely a junk. In another document penned by de Coutre entitled *Emformacíon para Su Magestad remediar el estado en la India Oriental* that is "Information for His Majesty to remedy the State in the East Indies", which one also finds transcribed in *Como Remediar o Estado da Índia?*, p. 23, it is claimed that the *baxeles* are also known as junks (… baxeles que llaman juncos).

214 The Spanish term *Chincheo* refers to Chinese merchants and sailors from along the Fujian coast (Amoy). The term, which the Spanish sometimes also use to speak of the Chinese generically, represents a terminological corruption of the town and port of Zhangzhou.

215 The Spanish and Portuguese term *drogas* was broadly employed in the early modern body of literature and can be translated as "spices and medicinal substances". In practice, the two meanings overlap considerably, as many spices were — and are still — believed to possess certain medicinal properties.

216 De Coutre, who was Flemish, from Bruges in the Spanish Netherlands, speaks here of the Dutch from the Dutch Republic as "rebels", as they had technically deposed the king of Spain as their legitimate ruler and seceded as a separate state, a move that was not formally recognised by Spain until the ratification of the Peace of Westphalia in 1648.

217 The term *presídio* is used variously to designate a permanent military garrison. In the present context, however, the *presídio* should be understood as a prison or a dungeon.

218 A similar proposal for the fortress on present-day Sentosa is also found in a second memorial of de Coutre, *Como Remediar*, p. 30; *AA*, p. 422.

219 Fol. 270 verso.

220 It is insufficiently clear which "legua" de Coutre has in mind here, the Spanish *legua* or the Portuguese *legoa.* According to Teensma, the former measures approximately 5,500 metres while the latter is larger at just over 6,100 metres. Given the context of Portuguese India, the present author believes the *legua* in question here is the Portuguese sea-mile and not the Spanish mile. This view, however, is not shared by Teensma. See *Como Remediar*, introduction,

p. xi — a similar observation on the location of the island is repeated in the *Vida de Jaques de Coutre*, AA, p. 107, and a second memorial of de Coutre titled "Information for His Majesty to Remedy the State in the East Indies", in *Como Remediar*, p. 30, and AA, p. 422.

221 The statement about the "fortress by nature" is repeated in a second memorial of de Coutre titled "Information for His Majesty to Remedy the State in the East Indies", in *Como Remediar*, p. 30, and AA, p. 422.

222 The precise etymological origin of this name is uncertain. It might derive from the Portuguese term *surgidoiro*, meaning "roadstead" or "anchorage". It could also be derived from *surgir*, which means "to rise up" or "emerge". From the present context and de Coutre's further explanations that follow, either interpretation makes perfect sense. The location described here is in any case the northwestern tip of present-day Sentosa, which is also home to Fort Siloso. Part of the original hill was levelled to make room for the British fort. Teensma understands Surgídera to be a place of anchorage, see *Como Remediar*, p. 69.

223 De Coutre repeats this statement below, see note 240.

224 This point is repeated in a second memorial of de Coutre titled "Information for His Majesty to Remedy the State in the East Indies", in *Como Remediar*, p. 30, and AA, p. 422.

225 Reference here is to the northwestern tip of present-day Sentosa, where Fort Siloso is currently situated. De Coutre refers to the location as Surgídera. He repeats the depth of water at this location a few lines below.

226 Situated at the western entrance of the Tebrau or Johor Strait. The islet is featured on British colonial maps as "Snake Island".

227 For a similar description, see AA, p. 95. Salgeros are willow trees, but one surmises that de Coutre is referring here to banyan trees. The location of this "island" is not exactly certain. According to navigational instructions surviving from the late 16th and early 17th centuries, including Linschoten's *Reysgeschrift* and *Itinerario*, ships passed between present-day Jurong island (formerly Pulau Sembilan) and Singapore island, skirted the coastline at Pasir Panjang, and then entered one of the two Singapore Straits that ran either along the north or south side of present-day Sentosa.

228 See note 218.

229 These points are repeated in a second memorial of de Coutre titled "Information for His Majesty to Remedy the State in the East Indies", in *Como Remediar*, p. 30, and AA, p. 422. Fresh water on the island is also mentioned in the *Vida de Jaques de Coutre*, AA, p. 107.

230 Fol. 271 recto.

231 The Spanish text reads literally that the island is flat. This would not fit into the present context and also contradict what de Coutre claims about Surgídera. The present English translation is thus a free one.

[232] A similar claim is repeated in a second memorial of de Coutre titled "Information for His Majesty to Remedy the State in the East Indies", in *Como Remediar*, p. 30, and AA, p. 422.

[233] Saletes, celates, *orang laut* or sea gypsies. The name is etymologically linked to the Malay word *selat*, meaning "the sea, strait". See also AA, pp. 95, 96.

[234] See also *Como Remediar*, p. 30; AA, pp. 422–3.

[235] *Karang*, or *batu karang*, is the Malay term for coral.

[236] Fol. 271 verso.

[237] The actual word employed is *Indios*, or "Indians". In this context, the word refers to the local or native population.

[238] Fol. 272 recto.

[239] That is to say, the Old Strait of Singapore is located between the main island of Singapore (Isla de la Sabandaria Vieja, or "Island of the Old Shabandar's Compound") and Sentosa (Isla de Arena).

[240] De Coutre mentions this possibility a second time; see note 223.

[241] Reference here is almost certainly to the so-called Johor Shoal, which is featured prominently on many early modern maps and charts, including de Bry's sketch of 1607. It was located approximately where Tanah Merah and the present-day Changi International Airport are situated.

[242] Concerning the capture of Johor Lama and Kota Batu, see appendix 2 in this volume.

[243] The actual word employed by de Coutre is *naturales*, or "natural people of the land".

[244] De Coutre, *Como Remediar*, introduction, p. viii, "… [S]hips of this fleet should be manned by Spanish Dunkirkers who in the twenties of the 17th century were extremely popular in Spain for their successful privateering against the Dutch 'rebels'."

[245] The text reads literally "one and a half leguas at sea", which means they are one and a half leguas from the shoreline.

[246] What de Coutre is saying here is that all these European peoples derive from a single ethnic group, and to the Asians all Europeans tend look alike. He recommends that the Spaniards use this confusion of nationalities to their advantage.

[247] According to Leitão, *Dicionário*, p. 193, a *curba* or *curva* refers to pieces of wood or iron that are used in the construction of boats or ships.

[248] Fol. 273 recto.

[249] The text reads "they can go". From the context, it is evident that reference is to the Spanish from Manila.

[250] From the context, it is clear that reference here is to the Dutch East India Company, the VOC.

[251] From the narrow wording of the text, it is not certain whom "they" actually refers to. One presumes that de Coutre is talking here only about the "two

citadels" around Singapore, and not in Melaka, Manila and Macao. Those would certainly not be "nearby". The subsequent sentence reinforces the view that "they" refers only to the two proposed Singapore citadels.

252 This interpretation is based on the context.

253 The text reads literally "another".

254 The text reads "this river".

255 The text reads "than that of Melaka".

256 The term *balas* is probably a corruption of the Portuguese *bâlos*. This is an Asian type vessel that is propelled by brest oars and can also be sailed. See also the glossary.

257 Fol. 273 verso.

258 The text literally reads "a stone's throw away like in Melaka".

259 De Coutre's testimony here would appear to deny the earlier claim of Manoel Godinho de Erédia that a fortress had been founded and constructed at Muar in or around 1604. The triangular-shaped fortification featured in the original manuscript of the *Declaraçam de Malaca* was not a depiction of an actual fortification, but what in modern terminology would be called an "artist's impression".

260 Literally, "below".

261 Reference here is to Batu Sawar.

262 Unfortunately, this plan is no longer extant.

263 This final paragraph does not belong to the main text of the memorial and is evidently a note addressed to a third party.

264 Fol. 274 recto.

265 Literally, at the "tip of the Johor River".

Glossary

Naval Jargon

armada — Portuguese and Spanish term for navy, fleet, often assembled for a specific mission.

armada de remo — Portuguese and Spanish term for a fleet of navy vessels comprising chiefly galleys that are propelled by oars.

banteen — (also *bantin*, *bantijn* and other variant spellings) According to JV Mills' notes to chapter 13 of Manoel Godinho de Eredia's *Declaraçam de Malaca*, a "bantis" was a Malay craft used in the 16th and 17th centuries in naval warfare. It was "propelled by breast oars" and featured "two rudders and two masts".

braça — A unit for measuring the depth of water. The *braça* (Portuguese), *braza* (Castilian, Spanish) or *brasse* (French) literally means "arm". In the marine world it represents a unit to measure the depth of water and evidently traces its origins to the span of two human arms. The Portuguese *braça* generally measures about 1.65 metres and the Spanish *braza* about 1.67. See also the entry for "*vadem*".

caravel The term, which is probably of Turkish origin, is the proper name for a type of sailing vessel built in Europe mainly by the Portuguese and later also by the Spanish. Caravels were deployed chiefly as trading vessels and were thus lightly armed. They feature a roundish hull design and use both square and lateen sails. Caravels were preferred by merchants and captains for their speed as well as easy handling in all wind conditions.

carrack (also *nao*, plural *naus*) Lightly armed Portuguese trading ship used mainly in the 16th and early 17th centuries. The design characteristically features a forecastle and an elevated poop deck. For the *Carreira da Índia* or India Fleet, the Portuguese built progressively larger vessels that were capable of transporting more men, military personnel and cargo, but these ships also became the victims of their enhanced size. The great carracks built in the second half of the 16th century could carry well over 1,000 people, but they also became difficult to manoeuvre, rendering them relatively easy targets for pirates and freebooters. Although admired as "floating cities" in some period writings, the carracks eventually made way for the smaller, but far better designed galleon.

cutter (Dutch: *jacht*) A sailing vessel favoured by the VOC in the early 17th century that as a rule features a single mast with lateen sails and more than one lateen headsail. It is usually equipped with oars. Similar in design to a sloop.

foist (also *fusta*) A category of vessels that as a rule features a single row of oars and a single mast. Foists were lightly armed and often deployed for patrolling the coast.

galleon (also *galeón*, *gallion* and other variant spellings) A type of ocean-going sailing ship of the late 16th to 18th century that was deployed either as a vessel of burden or in naval wars. Galleons feature an elongated hull, multiple decks (especially if designed to house artillery) and three to five masts. Galleons supplanted the carracks as commercial ships not least because they could sail faster and were easier to handle under various wind and sea conditions.

galley — (also *galés*, *galea*, *galeia* and other variant spellings) A type of rowed vessel that traces its origins to ancient Greece and Rome. In later centuries, galleys were widely deployed in the Mediterranean and also around parts of West Asia, such as the Red Sea and the Persian Gulf. Galleys served chiefly as warships and feature several rows of oars on each side of the vessel together with one or two masts.

galliot — (also *galeota*, *galiota* and other variant spellings) A type of rowed vessel featuring a single row of oars. A smaller type of galley (see the entry above).

jacht — See the entry for "cutter".

lanchara — (also *lancharan, lancharã*) Portuguese name for a small commercial sailing craft used in the Malay world and across much of the South China Sea during the early modern period. The expression is thought to be of Malay etymology, deriving from the word *lancar*, meaning "fluent", "quick" or "swift".

lateen sail — A triangular-shaped sail.

legoa — Portuguese sea mile, comprising 3 *milhas* (miles); amounting to 6,174 metres.

legua — A Spanish mile, measures approximately 5,500 metres.

lieue — The French geographic mile (*leuca gallica*) measures 2,223 metres. The French nautical mile measures about 4,450 metres.

mijl — (also *Duitsche mijl*) A Dutch sea mile, equivalent to 7,407 metres.

navette — A type of small sailing craft, usually deployed as a vessel of burden.

patache — A type of small commercial sailing craft common in Spain, Portugal and France. A *patache* usually features two masts.

prahu (also *prau, prao*, *parao*, *praw*, *prow* and other variant spellings) A type of small craft that can be either sailed or rowed. Prahus were — and still are — common in the Malay world and the Indian subcontinent. They were used as vessels of burden or in naval combat.

rutter A handbook giving more or less detailed instructions for sailing from port to port, and describing main navigational landmarks. Rutters often also provide details about conditions of trade, taxes and dues to be paid, or describe the commodities that are best bought and sold in a given port.

sampan (also *sampão*, *champan*) A small vessel common in the Malay world that is similar to a skiff or dinghy. Sampans were, and remain, a favourite craft among fishermen and petty traders around Southeast Asia. Sampans were commonly rowed with a paddle and often feature a short mast and a single lateen sail.

sloop (also *sloep*) A sailing vessel that features a single mast together with one lateen main sail and a single head sail. Similar in design to a cutter or *jacht*. (See also the entry for "cutter" above.)

vadem (English: *fathom*) A Dutch unit for measuring the depth of water. The Dutch *vadem* equals about 1.88 metres, while the English fathom is equivalent to 6 feet or 1.82 metres.

Institutions, Titles and Officeholders

bendahara Commonly identified in many sources as the "minister of interior" and later also the "chief of police". Importantly, the *bendahara* also served as master of ceremonies who legitimised royal activity through ritual.

breede raad (Literally: broad council) An expression used in the Dutch navy and the VOC to refer to the naval council of an admiral, vice-admiral, etc., comprising the commanding officers of each ship within his fleet or convoy.

cabildo	Spanish term for designating the equivalent of a municipal council.
capitão-mór	Portuguese term for captain-major. The Portuguese official acting as de facto governor of Melaka and dependent territories held the title of captain-major.
casado	Portuguese term meaning "housed" or "resident". This refers to a Portuguese citizen who married and settled in a given colony. Often the Portuguese *casados* were soldiers-turned-traders.
Estado da Índia	Literally translated as the "State of India". Collectively this refers to the patchwork of Portuguese colonial possessions around the Indian Ocean rim and the Western Pacific that were administered from Goa. The expression is often used interchangeably with Portuguese India and its colonial bureaucracy.
kling	(also *kaling*, *k'ling*, *kĕling* and other variant spellings) A term used in the Malay world to refer to the (Hindu) peoples of the Indian subcontinent. In most Portuguese and Dutch documents of the 16th and 17th centuries, the term should be translated loosely as a Hindu person, usually a merchant, from southern India. The *klings* were mostly of Tamil origin.
laksamana	(also *laquesamana*, *laxamana* and other variant spellings) A Malay official often identified in historical sources as the commander of naval forces, an "admiral". The Portuguese chronicler João de Barros called this Malay official the "captain-major of the sea" (*capitão-mór do mar).*
orang kaya	A Malay term that literally translates as "wealthy man or individual". The *orang kaya* often engaged in trade and commerce. More liberally, the term can be understood or translated as "man of good standing or recognition".
orang laut	(also referred to in early modern sources as *saletes*, *celates* and other variant spellings) In English, the term "sea gypsy" was used in the past but is now considered a pejorative. *Orang laut* translates from the

	Malay language as "people of the sea". In pre-colonial times the *orang laut* were loyal to the Melaka sultan, but later they paid allegiance to the ruler of Johor. They often acted as the sultan's navy, patrolled the Straits and served as paid pilots to passing European, Chinese and Arab vessels.
raja	(also *raya*, *raia* and other variant spellings) A term of Sanskrit origin meaning "king". Historically the term was deployed in a very elastic manner, spanning from the title of a great king in India (maharaja) to a petty prince in Southeast Asia. The title of raja was commonly used on the Indian subcontinent as well as in the Indianised regions of insular and peninsular Southeast Asia, and remained in use well after the advent of Islam in the region. Dutch and Portuguese sources of the 16th and 17th centuries commonly refer to the Malay sultans as "rajas" or translate the title into their own language, as for example *raya*, *rayale* or *koninck.*
Real Audiencia	(also Audiencia Real) A body in Spain, the Spanish Americas and the Philippines tasked with the administration of justice in chiefly civil and criminal matters. The administration of justice in military and ecclesiastical affairs was regulated by other judicial bodies.
shahbandar	A term commonly used in the Indonesian Archipelago, in Malaya, along the coastal areas of the Indian subcontinent and around the western Indian Ocean as an equivalent of "port master" or "harbour master". In the Malay world, the term denotes a high-ranking official of state, such as in the case of the Melaka Sultanate. For this reason, the title is also applied to the port master of towns situated along major rivers.
soldado	Portuguese and Spanish term for "soldier".

Commodities and Substances

aloeswood	(also eaglewood, *pau d'aquila*) A wood drenched in a natural resin that when burned releases a sweet and

	pleasant odour. Aloeswood was, and remains, much sought after in the Arab world as well as in Japan and Greater China, where it is used in aromatherapy or burned as an offering in temples. See also the entry for "kalambak".
ambergris	A natural baleen excrement that when seasoned and oxidised exudes a sweet and pleasant odour. Ambergris was widely used in perfumery and medicine, in Asia as well as in Europe. It ranks among the most expensive commodities of the early modern trading world. Because of its price, ambergris was also commonly forged.
arak	An alcoholic beverage.
benzoin	(also *benjuin* and other variant spellings) An odoriferous resin of the *styrax benzoïn*. The substance was widely used in medicine of the early modern period, and also in the production of incense.
eaglewood	Literal English translation of the Portuguese pao d'aquila. See the entry for "aloeswood".
gummalacca	(also *gommelack*, *gomlak* or *schellak*) A red-coloured gum used as a varnish; red lacquer.
kalambak	(also *calambac* and other variant spellings) Highest-grade aloeswood, widely used in early modern medicine (both in Europe and in Asia) as well as in the production of incense.
kris	A Malay ceremonial dagger.
musk	(also *bisem*, *muscus*, *almíscar* and other variant spellings) Today, the word "musk" is used to designate many types of odoriferous substances, including those of animal and plant origin. In the early modern period, however, the word is used almost exclusively for the natural excrement of the Asian musk deer, which inhabits China, Siberia and the Himalayan range. In the early modern period, musk was widely used in perfumery as well as medicine and sometimes also as a flavouring in cooking, baked goods and confectionary.

radix Chinae — Also known as "China root", this is a knotty rhizome of the Sarsaparilla family. *Radix Chinae* was widely procured by both Dutch and Portuguese traders in China as it found widespread application in the treatment of gout, skin disorders and, infamously, symptoms of syphilis. In the Arab and Persian world, *radix Chinae* was used in herbal cooking. It is said to impart a "rosy complexion" to those who consume it.

tintinago — (also *tootnague*) A copper-zinc alloy used in a wide variety of industries, including the casting of cannonballs, musket shots and bells. Commercial vessels outbound from China often carried *tintinago* on board as part of the ship's ballast that could later be disposed of at a profit.

Units of Measurement

arróba — A unit of measurement widely used in the Iberian world to express the weight of bulk goods. The *arróba* weighs just short of 12.5 kilogrammes.

bahar — (also *baar*, *bhaer*, *baer*, *baru*, *baruay* and other variant spellings) A unit of measurement used across China, the Malay world, the Indian subcontinent and Arabia to denote the weight or mass of certain bulk goods. One *bahar* is generally divided into three *picul* of 100 *katí* (see also the entries on *picul* and *katí*). But according to the anonymous VOC pamphlet *Uytreckening* of 1691, the *bahar* in Timor and Solor was subdivided into five *picol* of 100 *katí*. In Indragiri, there are four *picul* to the *bahar*. Also, the actual weight or mass of the *bahar* differed widely from port to port. As a rule of thumb, the *bahar* weighed 181–85 kilogrammes, but in Goa it was equivalent to 225 and in Surat 408.

fardel — From the Italian *fardella*, meaning "pack" or "bundle". A common unit used for marketing or packaging silks, cottons and other piece cloths.

gantang — A measure of mass or weight used widely across the Malay world. The *gantang* varied from port to port.

According to the anonymous VOC pamphlet *Uytrekening* of 1691, a *gantang* in Batavia amounted to 1/230 of a *last*, or approximately 5.45 kilogrammes. In Melaka the *last* was equivalent to 500 *gantang*, but in Jambi it was equivalent to 800 *gantang* and in Ambon as much as 3,000 *gantang*. In Aceh, one *last* of rice amounted to about 600 *gantang*.

katí — (also *catte*, *cattee* and other variant spellings) A unit of weight or mass widely used across the Malay world and also in China. High-priced commodities such as spices, musk, ambergris and cardamom were often sold by the *katí*. It represents 1/100 of a *picul*, 1/300 of a *bahar* or, as a rule of thumb, 600 grammes.

koyang — (also *coyang* and other variant spellings) A unit of weight or mass used in the Malay world and beyond to measure certain bulk commodities. As a rule, a *koyang* comprised 30 *picul*. In the bulk trade, uncooked rice was usually sold, traded or transported in *koyang*. According to the anonymous VOC pamphlet *Uytreckening* of 1691, there were 300 *gantang* to the *koyang* in Bima, but 500 *gantang* in Cambodia. In Semarang, on the island of Java, one *koyang* of rice was equivalent to 28 *picul*.

last — A Dutch unit for measuring weight and often also cargo capacity of ships. As a rule of thumb, one *last* was equivalent to about 3,000 *pond* or, on average, about 1,250 kilogrammes.

picul — (also *pico*, *picol* and other variant spellings) A unit of weight widely used across the Malay world and also in China. Certain bulk commodities within the medium price range, such as sugar or pepper, were normally traded in *picul*.

Currencies and Coinage

Early modern currencies and coinage can prove utterly confusing even to the most seasoned historian. The following provides a rough guide to currencies and their parities. Where reliable information is available, approximate silver or gold contents are provided together with parities derived from actual period tables of exchange.

One of the most difficult concepts to grasp relates to the different parities between gold, silver and copper that were applied in Europe and Asia. The VOC distinguished between "heavy" and "light" parities, with "heavy" applying to the parity in Europe and "light" expressing the parity in Batavia and across East Asia at large. For example, the Spanish-American ryal-of-eight (see below) exchanged for 60 stuivers in "light" money in Batavia or 48 stuivers in "heavy" in Europe.

cruzado — Portuguese silver currency. In the period under review, the cruzado of 400 reis was worth about 10 per cent more than the Spanish-American ryal-of-eight (see below), but in practice the two were often used interchangeably on a one-for-one parity.

Flemish pound — In the early 17th century, the Flemish pound was worth about 6 Holland guilders, 2.4 ryals-of-eight or 2.2 Portuguese cruzados.

guilder — Currency of the Dutch province of Holland and accounting currency of the VOC. The guilder, equivalent to 10.61 grammes of silver, comprised 20 stuiver "heavy" or 25 stuiver "light".

pardao — Portuguese silver coin minted in Goa. Often used in historical sources as a synonym for a Spanish-American ryal-of-eight.

pataca(o) — (also *patação*, *patecoon* and other variant spellings) Silver coin struck in Portuguese Goa, weighing approximately 17.25 grammes of silver. This is also the name given by the Portuguese to the Spanish-American ryal-of-eight. See the following entry.

ryal-of-eight — Spanish colonial coin of eight reales face value minted in present-day Mexico, Peru and Bolivia. This coin was ranked among the first globally traded and recognised "currencies" and was widely used not only in the Americas but also in East and Southeast Asia. Period documents refer to the ryal-of-eight by a host of other names, including "piece of eight" and later also "Spanish

	dollar". In the early years of the VOC's activities in Asia, prices and inventory were often expressed in ryals-of-eight or equivalent value. For the period under review, the Spanish-American ryal-of-eight was equivalent to about 2.5 Holland guilders. The silver content of this coin remained stable at about 27.07 grammes. In the early years of its corporate lifespan, the VOC and even its predecessors, such as the United Zeeland Company, struck coins with a face value of 8 reales, thus issuing their own variant of the ryal-of-eight.
rijksdaalder	(also *arendsrijksdaalder*) Dutch equivalent of the Imperial German reichsthaler, being 50 stuiver in "light" money or 2.5 guilders. In Asia, the rijksdaalder amounted to 60 stuiver "heavy".
Spanish ducat	During the period under review, the Spanish ducat was equivalent to approximately 1.1 Portuguese cruzados, 1.2 Spanish-American ryals-of-eight or 3 guilders.
stuiver	Usually minted as a coin in units of 2, 6, 14, 20, 24 and 25 stuiver. The Holland guilder comprised 20 stuivers in "heavy" money, the ducaton comprised 40, the lion daalder 48, the rijksdaalder 50, and the double daalder 60.
tael	A unit of weight or mass, amounting as a rule of thumb to about 30 grammes. There were 20 *tael* to the *katí*. In Guangdong (Canton), a *tael* of silver was equivalent to 37.8 grammes of silver. This translates into 1.4 ryals-of-eight, 1.25 Portuguese cruzados or 3.5 Holland guilders.
xerafim	Silver or gold coin minted in Portuguese Goa. The silver xerafim weighed about 11 grammes, while the gold xerafim weighed about 0.6–0.7 grammes. Such tiny "coins" proved highly impractical, and it was thus far more common to find gold coins struck with a face value of 5 xerafims weighing 3.5–3.6 grammes.

Historical Names and Their Modern Equivalents

Aceh	(also Acheh, Atjin, Acheen and other variant spellings) Port city and kingdom on the northern tip of the great

	island of Sumatra. During the early 17th century, Acehese influence also extended to the Malay Peninsula, the Riau Islands and possibly as far as the southwest corner of Borneo.
Banten	Formerly Bantam, early capital of the Sultanate of Sunda in West Java.
Batu Sawar	Royal residence of Johor, situated in the upper reaches of the Johor River near present-day Kota Tinggi, in the state of Johor, Malaysia.
Berbukit	(also Barbukit) Present-day Johor Hill. The Hook of Barbukit or Berbukit is located near the estuary of the Johor River. For much of the early modern period, the Hook of Berbukit served European vessels as a place of safe anchorage.
Bulan	(also Bulão) Island to the west of present-day Batam. According to Portuguese sources, Bulan had a noteworthy port.
Governor's Strait	(also the Strait of John de Silva, later Phillip Channel) Approximates the main fairway used by international shipping through the present-day Strait of Singapore. It is named after Juan de Silva, the Spanish governor of the Philippines who is first recorded to have sailed through the channel in 1616.
Gresik	(also Grissée) Sultanate in coastal north-central Java.
Isla das Naus	"Island of the Carracks", or present-day Pulau Jawa. One of the islets off the coast of Melaka where larger commercial vessels would drop anchor and unload their cargo with the assistance of smaller vessels. VOC Admiral Cornelis Matelieff de Jonge set up a battery on the island when he besieged the Portuguese capital in 1606, enabling him to control all shipping calling at the port. According to some Portuguese charts, maps and documents, a basic fortification structure was built on the islet, mainly in response to the successes scored by Dutch Admiral Matelieff de Jonge. The Isla das Naus was out of artillery range from the town of Melaka.

Isla de Arena	(also Ysla de Arenas) Name attributed to present-day Sentosa by the early 17th century Flemish merchant and jeweler Jaques de Coutre.
Isla de la Sabandaria Vieja	(also Ysla de la Sabandaria Vieja or "Island of the Old Shahbandar's Compound") Name attributed to the main island of Singapore by Jaques de Coutre.
Johor Lama	(also Oudt Ior, including Kota Batu) Fortified royal residence of Johor, situated on the left bank of the Johor River. The fort and town were destroyed in 1587 in a campaign led by Portuguese Admiral Dom Paulo Lima de Pereira. According to the diary of the VOC servant Johann Verken, Johor Lama was rebuilt and burnt down by the Portuguese in a second wave of violence at the open of the 17th century.
Karimun	The Carimons, two islands of the Riau Archipelago comprising Carimon Maior and Carimon Minor, or Karimun Besar and Karimun Kecil today.
Kota Batu	Fortress at Johor Lama or Old Johor. See also the entry for "Johor Lama".
Maluku	(also Moluccas) The name refers chiefly to the islands of Tidor, Ternate, Ambon, Halmahera and Gilolo. This region is the original home of the clove tree. The Bandas are home to nutmeg and its by-product mace. The Bandas are located to the south of Ambon in the Java Sea. Historically, the Malukus and the Bandas are collectively referred to as the "Spice Islands".
Melaka	(also Malacca, Malaca, Melacha and other variant spellings) This is the name attributed to the town of Melaka, the surrounding territory or the whole of the Malay Peninsula. In 16th century cartography, Punta de Melaca is the southernmost tip of the Malay Peninsula.
New Spain	Administrative unit of Spanish colonial America, the capital city of which was Mexico City. In the present book, the term New Spain is used synonymously with Mexico.

Pahang	(also Paam, Pahão, Pão and other variant spellings) The present-day city and port of Pekan. The name was historically attributed to the port settlement, the river and the upstream region that feeds into the Pahang River.
Pedra Branca	Literally the "White Rock", named on account of the bird droppings that used to coat this uninhabited outcropping. Pedra Branca marks the eastern entrance to the Singapore Straits and is home today to the Horsburgh Lighthouse. It is not to be confused with an outcropping with the identical name located off the coast of southern China in the vicinity of Hong Kong and Macao.
penarikan	(also *panarícan* and other variant spellings) A stretch of land located around the present-day town of Jompol that separates the tributaries of the Pahang and Muar Rivers. Derived from the Malay word *tarik* (to pull), the *penarikan* was a portage place where cargo was either briefly carried by beasts of burden or probably also rolled along a series of logs from one river tributary to the other. The *penarikan* is featured, for example, on some late 16th and early 17th century maps of Manoel Godinho de Erédia.
Pulau Condor	Present-day Côn Đao, located off the coast of southern Vietnam. It was a watering hole and provisioning station in the long-distance intra-Asian trade. See also the entry for "Tioman".
Pulau Panjang	One of the names attributed to the main island of Singapore on European maps before c. 1800. It is not to be confused with an island by the same name used as a point of anchorage by the VOC in the Sunda Strait.
Punta de Romania	("Romania Point" in English) Southeastern tip of the Malay Peninsula. Adjacent to Romania Point are the Romania Shoals.
Strait of Bengkalis	Formerly the Brouwer Strait (sometimes also Brewer's Strait), named after the 17th century Dutch Governor-General Hendrik Brouwer.

Strait of Sabam (also Sabão, Sahá and other variant spellings) North-south maritime passage situated between the eastern coast of Sumatra and the islands of Karimun Besar and Kundur in the modern Indonesian province of Kepuluan Riau. The Strait of Sabam was important for seaborne traffic destined from ports of northern Sumatra and Melaka to ports in Java, Makassar, Timor and the Malukus.

Singapura (also Cincapura, Sincapura, Cingatola, Cingaporla and many other variant spellings) Name applied to one of the four maritime passages linking the Strait of Melaka with the South China Sea, sometimes the island of Singapore, the town of Singapura, the southernmost point of the Asian continent (Cabo de Cincapura), and in the 16th and early 17th centuries the whole of the Malay Peninsula located south of the Pahang and Muar Rivers.

Tioman (also Tymão, Tiomão, Timã and other variant spellings) An island located off the southeasthern coast of the Malay Peninsula. From the pre-colonial period into the 18th century, Tioman was a well-known and well-charted island where ships would call to bring on fresh water and provisions before heading northeastwards across the Gulf of Siam to Pulau Condor. In rare instances Tioman was confused with the island of Timor, as is evidenced by some Arabic documents translated by Gabriel Ferrand.

xabandaría (also *shahbandaria*) The shahbandar's compound.

Bibliography

Manuscripts and Charts

Amsterdam, University Library
O. K. 139
Berlin, Staatsbibliothek-Preussischer Kulturbesitz
Kart. T 7557, T 7567, T 7165
Brussels, Bibliothèque Royale
Ms. 7264
Cambridge, MA: Harvard Map Collection
51-2573 PF
Florence, Biblioteca Riccardiana
Ricc. 1813.c. 8r.
The Hague, Nationaal Archief
VOC 100, 1058, 1061, 1108, 1109, 1115, 1117, 1118, 1121, 1131, 1132, 1136, 4818, 1.10.35.02 (Verzameling Papieren afkomstig van Hugo de Groot)
Leiden University Library
Collectie Bodel Nijenhuis
006-15-021; 006-14-015
London, British Library
C.12.f.1.(30), Add. Ms. 15, 738.29; Add. Ms. 24065; Add. Ms. 5222.10, Add. Ms. 5415 A 17v-18, ms. Add 28461, 10–16
Madrid, Biblioteca Nacional de España
Ms. 1750/181 and 1750/233; Ms. 2780

Paris, Bibliothèque Nationale
Codex Parisienis Latinus, no. 4801
Rotterdam, Maritiem Museum Prins Hendrik, Collectie Dr. W. A. Engelbrecht
WAE 900-10
San Marino, Huntington Library
HM 28 f. 13; HM 41 fol. 12; HM 44 f. 9
Seville, Archivo General de Indias
Filipinas, 37, N, 46
Filipinas, 37, N, 37
Filipinas, 340, L.3, F71V-72R
Wolfenbüttel, Herzog-August-Bibliothek
102 Aug. Fol. (ex Aug. Fol.)
Vatican City, Biblioteca Apostolica Vaticana
Cod. Urbanus Gracus 82; Vaticanus Latinus 5698

Pre-1800 Printed Works

Anon., *Corte ende sekere Beschryvinghe vant veroveren der rijcke ende gheweldighe krake, comende uytet gheweste van China, door den Admirael Jacobus Heemskerke liggende met twee schepen voor de Straet of Fretum de Malacca, vanden Coninc van Ior een vyant der Portugesen opghehouden ende ghebeden sy gheweest, hy soude met zijn scgepen op een rijke ende wel geladene Portugaloise krake die dry jaran tot Makauw en int gheweste van China om syne Waren inne te nemen gelegen hadde, wachten.* Ghedruckt na de copy van Middelborch by Richard Schilders, 1604.

Anon., *Utyrekening Van de Goude en Silvere Munts Waardye, Inhout der Maten en Swaarte der Gewigten in de Respective Gewesten van Indiën* (Middelburg: Johannes Meertens, Drucker van de E. Geoctroyeerde Oost-Indische Compagnie, Anno 1691).

[Barros, João de], *Held-dadige Scheeps-togt van Alfonso de Albuquerque na de Roode-Zee In het Jaar 1506, en ervolgens gedaan: behelsende de geleegendheyd, opkomst en voortgang van de Koningrijken Ormuz, Goa, Malacca, etc.* (Leiden: Pieter van der Aa, 1706).

Anon., *Verhandeling der Munten, Maaten en Gewigten van Neerlandsch India* (Batavia: no publisher, c. 1785).

Barros, J. de, and D. do Couto, *Da Ásia, Dos feitos que os Portuguezes fizeram no conquista, e descubrimento das terras e mares do oriente* (Lisbon: Na Regia Officina Typographia, 1778).

Bernard, J. F., *A Collection of Voyages Undertaken by the Dutch East-India Company, for the Improvement of Trade and Navigation, Containing an Account of Several Attempts to Find Out the North-East Passage, and Other Discoveries in the East-Indies and the South Sea*, 1 vol. (London: no publisher, 1703).

Blaeu, J., *Onzième volume de la Geographie Blauiane contenant l'Asie qui est la IV partie de la terre* (Amsterdam: J. Blaeu, 1663).

Bry, J.T. de, J.I. de Bry and G. Arthus, *Indiae Orientalis Pars Octava: Navigationes Quinque. Primam a Iacobo Neccio ab anno 1600 usque ad Annum 1603, Secundam a Iohanne Hermanno de Bree ab anno 1602 usq. ad Annum 1604; Tertiam a Cornelio Nicolai Annis quatuor; Quartam a Cornelio de Vena, duobus Annis; Quintam, sub Staphano de Hagen tribus Annis in Indiam Orientalem susceptas & peractas continens* ... (Frankfurt/Main: Ex Officina Typographica Wolfgangi Richteri, 1607).

Bry, J.T. de, J.I. de Bry, *Icones seu Gennuinae et Espressae Delineationes Omnium Memorabilium, quae in hac Octava Indiae Orientalis Parte annotata sunt, varias simul populorum in Ternate, Patane, Cande et aliis locis habitantium ceremonias, mores, habitusque ob oculos ponentes* (Frankfurt/Main: In Officina typographica Wolfgangi Richteri, 1607).

Commelin, I., *Begin ende Voortgang Vande Vereenigde Neerlandsche Geoctroyeerde Oost-Indische Compagnie*, 4 vols. (Amsterdam: no publisher, 1646).

Faria y Sousa, M. de, *The Portugues Asia* or, *The History of the Discovery and Conquest of India by the Portuguese, etc.*, 3 vols. (London: Printed for C. Brome, 1694–95).

Genius, I. and L. Hulsius, *Neundte Shiffart, das ist: gründliche Erklärung, was sich mit den HoII- und Seeländern in Ost-Indien Anno 1604 und 1605 under dem Admiral Steffan von der Hagen zugetragen: und wie sie endlich in jüngst abgeloffenem Aprili mit zwey Schiffen in Hollandt ankommen* (Frankfurt am Main: bei Erasmus Kempffern in Verlegung Levini Huisius seligen Wittiben, 1612).

Hulsius, L., *Achte Shiffart. Kurtze Beschreibung was sich mit den Holländern und Seeländern, in den Ost Indien, die nechts verlauffene vier oder fünff Jahre, als 1599, 1600, 1601, 1602 und 1603 zugetragen* ... (Franckfurt am Mayn: no publisher, 1605).

———, *Zehende Schiffart oder Reyse der Holländer und Seeländer, beschehen unter dem Admiral Cornelis Matelief dem Jungen, so mit eylff grossen Schiffen Anno 1605 den 12 Maij auss Hollandt abgeloffen und im Mertzen diese 1608 wider mit zwei Schiffen wol ist angekommen. Zusammengebracht und beschrieben auss Niderländischer Verzeichnuss durch einen Liebhaber der Schiffahrten* (Frankfurt/M.: bey Erasmo Kempffern, 1613).

l'Hermite, J. (de Jonge), *Breeder verhael ende klare beschrijvinghe van tghene den Admiral Cornelis Matelief de Jonge inde Oost-Indien voor de stadt Malacca, ende int belegh der zelver wedervaren is: als ooc den vreesselijcke strijdt ter zee, tusschen den admirael voorsz. ende de Portugijsen, ende andere geschiedenissen meer. Overgeschreven bij eenen der commisen inde vlote* (Rotterdam: Jan Janssz., 1608).

Jöcher, C.G., *Allgemeines Gelehrten-Lexicon* (Leipzig: Johann Friedrich Gleditschen's Buchhandlung, 1751).

Linschoten, J.H. van, *Itinerario ofte schipvaert van Jan Huygen van Linschoten near Oost of Portugaels Indien inhoudende en corte beschryvinghe der selver landen ende zeecusten* ... (Amsterdam: Cornelis Claesz, 1596).

Meteren, E. van, *Commentariën ofte Memoriën van den Nederlantsen Staet, Handel, Oorloghen ende Gheschiedenissen van onsen tyden, etc.*, 2 vols. (Gedruckt op Schotlant buyten Danswijck by Hermes van Loven: no date [c. 1646]).

Nieuhof, J., *Zee en Lant-Reize, door verscheide Gewesten van Oostindien, Behelzende veele zeltzaame en wonderlijke voorvallen en geschiedenissen* (Amsterdam: Voor de Weduwe van Jacob van Meurs, 1682).

Pontanus, J.I., *Rerum et Urbis Amstelodamensium Historia, in qua Hollandiae primum atque inde Amstelandiae, oppidique, natales, exordia, progressus, privilegia, statuta eventaque mirabilia cum novis urbis incrementis commerciisque ac navigationibus longinquis, aliaque ad politiam spectantia* ... (Amsterdam: excudit Judocus Hondius, 1611).

Ramusio, G.B., *Delle navigationi et viaggi in molti luoghi corretta, et ampliata nelle quale si contengono da descrittione dell'Africa, & del paese del Prete Ianni, con varij viaggi, dalla Città di Lisbona, et dal Mar Rosso à Calicut, & infin'all'isole Molucche, dove nascono le Spetierie, Et la Navigatione attorno il Mondo* (Venice: Stamperia de Giunti, 1554).

Renneville, R.A.C. de, *Recueil des voiages qui ont servi à l'établissement & aux progrès de la Compagnie des Indes Orientales, formée dans les Provinces-Unies des Païs-Bas*, 7 vols. (Amsterdam: J.F. Bernard, 1725).

Schröder, J., *Medicin-Chymische Apotheke, Oder Höchstkostbarer Arznei-Schatz*, 2 vols. (Nürnberg: Johann Hoffman Buch- und Kunsthändler, 1685).

Teixeira, P., *Relaciones ... d'el origen descendencia y succesión de los Reyes de Persia, y de Harmuz* (Amberes: En casa de Hieronymo Verdussen, 1610).

Thevet, A., *La cosmographie universelle, ... illustree de diverses figures des choses plus remarquables veuës par l'Auteur, et incogneuës de noz Anciens et Modernes*, 2 vols. (Paris: Pierre l'Huilier, 1575).

Valentijn, F., *Oud en Nieuw Oost-Indiën, Vervattende Een Naauwkeurige en Uitvoerige Verhandelinge van Nederlands Mogentheyd in de Gewesten, etc.*, 5 parts in 8 vols. (Dordrecht and Amsterdam: Johannes van Braam and Gerard Onder de Linden, 1724–26).

Zedler, Johann Heinrich, *Universal-Lexicon* (Leipzig and Halle: Verlag Heinrich Zedler, 1743).

Post-1800 Printed Works

Documentação Ultramarina Portuguesa, 2 vols. (Lisbon: Centro de Estudos Históricos Ultramarinos, 1960–2).

Nouvelles Orientations de la Recherche sur l'histoire de l'Asie Portugaise, Actes du Colloque), Paris, 3–4 Juin 1994 (Paris: Fondation Calouste-Gulbenkian, 1997).

Albuquerque, A. de, *Cartas de Afonso de Albuquerque*, 7 vols. (Lisbon: Academia das Ciências Morais, Políticas e Belas-Artes, 1884–1935).

Albuquerque, L. de, and I. Guerreiro, ed., *Segundo Seminário internacional de história indo-portugesa. Actas* (Lisbon: Instituto de Investigação Científica Tropical and Centro de Estudos de História e Cartografia Antiga, 1985).

Alexandrowicz, C.H., *An Introduction to the History of the Law of Nations in the East Indies* (Oxford: Oxford University Press, 1967).

Alves, Jorge M. dos Santos, and Pierre-Yves Manguin, *O Roteiro das Cousas do Achem de D. João Ribeiro Gaio: Um olhar português sobre o norte de Samatra em finais do século XVI* (Lisbon: Comissão Nacional para as Comemorações dos Descobrimentos Portugueses, 1997).

Ames, G.J., *Renascent Empire? The House of Braganza and the Quest for Stability in Portuguese Monsoon Asia, ca. 1640–1683* (Amsterdam: Amsterdam University Press, 2000).

Andaya, L., *The Kingdom of Johor 1641–1728: Economic and Political Developments* (Kuala Lumpur: Oxford University Press, 1975).

Arasaratnam, S., *Maritime Trade, Society and European Influence in Southern Asia, 1600–1800* (Aldershot: Ashgate, 1995).

Barbosa, D., *The Book of Duarte Barbosa, An Account of the Countries Bordering on the Indian Ocean and Their Inhabitants ... Completed about the Year 1518*, trans. Mansel Longworth Dames, 2 vols. (London: Hakluyt Society, 1918–21).

———, *O Livro de Duarte Barbosa*, ed. N. Águas (Lisbon: Publicações Europa-América, n.d.).

Bausani, A., *Lettera di Giovanni da Empoli* (Rome — Jakarta: Istituto Italiano per il Medio ed Estremo Oriente — Centro Italiao di Cultura, 1970).

Biker, J.F. Judice, *Collecção de tratados e concertos de pazes que o Estado da Índia Portugeza fez com os reis e senhores com quem teve relações nas partes da Ásia e Africa Oriente, desde o princípio da conquista até ao fin do século XVIII*, 10 vols. (Lisbon: Imprensa Nacional, 1881–7).

Bittner M. and W. Tomaschek, ed. and tr., *Die Topographischen Capitel des Indischen Seespiegels Mohit. Festschrift zur Erinnerung an die Eröffnung des Seeweges durch Vasco da Gama, 1497* (Wien: Verlag der K.K. Geographishen Gesellschaft, 1897).

Blair, E.H., and J.A. Robertson, ed., *The Philippine Islands, 1493–1898*, 55 vols. (Cleveland: A. H. Clark Co., 1903–9).

Bocarro, A., *Década XIII da História da Índia*, ed. Rodrigo José de Lima Felner, 2 vols. (Lisbon: Typographia da Academia Real das Sciencias, 1876).

Booy, A. de, ed., *De derde reis van de VOC naar Oost-Indië onder het beleid van Admiraal Paulus van Caerden uitgezield in 1606*, 2 vols. (The Hague: Martinus Nijhoff, 1970).

Borschberg, P., and M. Krieger, ed., *Water and State in Europe and Asia* (Delhi: Manohar Publishers, 2007).

Borschberg, P., ed., *Iberians in the Singapore-Melaka Area and Adjacent Regions (16th to 18th Century)* (Wiesbaden and Lisbon: Harrassowitz — Fundação Oriente, 2004).

Botelho e Sousa, A., *Subsídios para a historia militar-marítima da Índia* (Lisbon: Impr. da Armada, 1930).

Bouchon, G., and D. Ménard, *Le Voyage aux Indes de Nicolò de Conti (1414–1439)* (Paris: Chandeigne, 2004).

Boxer, C.R., *Fidalgos in the Far East, 1550–1770: Fact and Fancy in the History of Macao* (The Hague: Martinus Nijhoff, 1948).

———, ed., *South China in the Sixteenth Century, Being the Narratives of Galeote Pereira, Fr. Gaspar da Cruz, Fr. Martín de Rada* (London: Hakluyt Society, 1953).

———, *The Portuguese Seaborne Empire, 1415–1825,* reprint (London: Hutchinson & Co., 1977).

———, *Opera Minora,* ed. Diogo Ramada Curto, 3 vols. (Lisbon: Fundação Oriente, 2002).

Boxer, C.R., and A. Frazão de Vasconcelos, *André Furtado de Mendonça, 1558–1610* (Macau: Fundação Oriente and Centro de Estudios Marítimos de Macau, 1989).

Boyajian, J.C., *Portuguese Trade in Asia under the Habsburgs, 1580–1640* (Baltimore and London: Johns Hopkins University Press, 1993).

Brenner, R., *Merchants and Revolution. Commercial Change, Political Conflict, and London's Overseas Traders, 1550–1653* (London and New York: Verso, 2003).

Broecke, M.P.R. van den, *Ortelius Atlas Maps: An Illustrated Guide* (Utrecht: H&S Publishers, 1996).

Bromely, J.S., and E.H. Kossman, ed., *Britain and the Netherlands in Europe and Asia: Papers Delivered to the Third Anglo-Dutch History Conference* (London: Macmillan, 1968).

Brotton, Jerry, *Trading Territories: Mapping the Early Modern World* (London: Reaktion Books, 1997).

Brown, C.C. and Roolvink R., trans. and ed., *Sĕjarah Mĕlayu or Malay Annals* (Kuala Lumpur and Singapore: Oxford University Press, 1970).

Bruijn, J.R., *The Dutch Navy of the Seventeenth and Eighteenth Centuries* (Columbia: University of South Carolina Press, 1990).

———, *Roemrucht Verleden. De Staten-Generaal en de VOC* (The Hague: Tweede Kamer der Staten-Generaal, 2002).

Bruijn, J.R., and F.S. Gaastra, ed., *Ships, Sailors and Spices: East India Companies and Their Shipping in the 16th, 17th and 18th Centuries* (Amsterdam: NEHA, 1993).

Bruijn, J.R., F.S. Gaastra and I. Schöffer, *Dutch-Asiatic Shipping in the 17th and 18th Centuries* (The Hague: Martinus Nijhoff, 1979–87).

Bulhão Pato, R.A. de, and A. da Silva Rego, ed., *Documentos Remettidos da Índia ou Livros das Monções*, 10 vols. (Lisbon: Typographia da Academia Real das Sciencias and Imprensa Nacional — Casa de Moeda, 1880–1982).

Caminha, A. L., *Ordenações da Índia do Senhor Rei D. Manoel, etc.* (Lisbon: Na Impressão Regia, 1807).

Carletti, F., *My Voyage around the World*, trans. H. Weinstock (New York: Pantheon Books, 1964).

Castanheda, F. Lopes de, *História do Descobrimento e Conquista da Índia Pelos Portugueses*, ed. P. M. Laranjo Coelho, 4 vols. (Coimbra: Imprensa da Universidade, 1924–33).

Chijs, J. A. van der, ed., *Nederlandsch-Indisch Plakaatboek, 1602–1811*, 17 vols. (Batavia: Landsdrukkerij; and The Hague: Martinus Nijhoff, 1885–1900).

———, ed. H.T. Colenbrander, *Dagh-Register gehouden int Casteel Batavia vant passerende daer ter plates als over geheel Nederlandts-India* (The Hague: Martinus Nijhoff, 1896–1931).

Colenbrander, H.T., ed., *Gedenkschriften van Anton Reinhard Falck* (The Hague: Martinus Nijhoff, 1913).

Colenbrander, H.T. and W. Ph. Coolhaas, ed., *Jan Pieterszoon Coen: Bescheiden Omtrent Zijn Bedrijf in Indië*, 9 vols. (The Hague: Martinus Nijhoff, 1919–53).

Coolhaas, W. Ph., ed., *Generale Missiven van Gouverneurs'Generaal en Raden aan Heren XVII der Verenigde Oostindische Compagnie*, part I, 1610–38 (The Hague: Martinus Nijhoff, 1960).

———, ed., *Pieter van den Broecke in Azië* (The Hague: Martinus Nijhoff, 1962).

———, ed., *Generale Missiven van Gouverneurs-Generaal en Raden aan Heren XVII der Verenigde Oostindische Compagnie*, part II, 1639–55 (The Hague: Martinus Nijhoff, 1964).

Corney, B. ed., *The voyage of Sir Henry Middleton to Bantam and the Maluco Islands, being the second voyage set forth by the Governor and Company of the Merchants of London Trading into the East Indies, from the Edition of 1606* (London: Hakluyt Society, 1855).

Corrêa (also Correia), G., *Lendas da Índia*, ed. R. J. de Lima Felner, 7 vols. (Lisbon: Academia Real das Sciencies, 1858–66).

Correia-Afonso, J., ed., *Indo-Portuguese History. Sources and Problems* (Bombay: Oxford University Press, 1981).

Cortesão, A., *Primeira Embaixada Europeia à China: O boticário e embaixador Tomé Pires e sua 'Suma Oriental'* (Macao: Instituto Cultural de Macau, 1990).

Cortesão, A., and A. Teixeira da Mota, *Portugaliae Monumenta Cartographica*, 6 vols. (Lisbon: no publisher, 1960).

Costa, H. de la, *The Jesuits in the Philippines, 1581–1768* (Cambridge, MA: Harvard University Press, 1967).

Costa, A. Fontoura da, ed., *Livro de Marinharia de Bernardo Fernandes (cêrca de 1548)* (Lisbon: Divisão de Publicações e Biblioteca Agéncia Geral das Colónias, 1940).

Couto, D. do, *Vida D. Paulo de Lima Pereira* (Lisbon: Escriptorio, 1903).

Coutre, J. de, *Aziatische Omzwervingen. Het levensverhaal van Jaques de Coutre, een Brugs diamantenhandelaar, 1591–1626*, trans. J. Verbeckmoes and E. Stols (Berchem: EPO, 1988).

———, *Como Remediar o Estado da Índia? Being the Appendices of the Vida de Jaques de Coutre* (Madrid: Biblioteca Nacional, ms. 2780), ed. Benjamin N. Teesma (Leiden: Centre for the History of European Expansion, 1989).

———, *Andanzas asiáticas*, ed. E. Stols, B. Teensma and J. Werbeckmoes (Madrid: História 16, 1991).

Cruysse, D. van der, *Louis XIV et le Siam* (Paris: Fayard, 1991).

Dam, P. van, *Beschryvinge van de Oostindische Compagnie*, ed. F.W. Stapel, 8 vols. (The Hague: Martinus Nijhoff, 1931).

Das Gupta, A., *The World of the Indian Ocean Merchant, 1500–1800. Collected Essays of Ashin Das Gupta,* comp. Uma Das Gupta and intro. S. Subrahmanyam (New Delhi: Oxford University Press, 2001).

Davies, D.W., *A Primer of Dutch Seventeenth Century Overseas Trade* (The Hague: Martinus Nijhoff, 1961).

Dennys, N.B., *Descriptive Dictionary of British Malaya* (London: London and China Telegraph Office, 1894).

Dijk, W.O., *Seventeenth-Century Burma and the Dutch East India Company, 1634–1680* (Singapore: Singapore University Press, 2006).

Diller, S., *Die Dänen in Indien, Südostasien und China (1620–1845)* (Wiesbaden: Harrassowitz Verlag, 1999).

Disney, A.R., *Twilight of the Pepper Empire: Portuguese Trade in Southwest India in the Seventeenth Century* (Cambridge: Harvard University Press, 1978).

Doursther, H., *Dictionnaire universel des poids et mesures anciens et modernes, contenant des tables des monnaies de tous les pays* (Amsterdam: Meridian Publishing Co., 1965).

Dunn, M., *Kampf um Malakka. Eine wirtschaftsgeschichtliche Studie über den portugiesischen und niederländischen Kolonialismus in Südostasien* (Wiesbaden: Franz Steiner Verlag, 1984).

Elias, J.E., *Schetsen uit de Geschiedenis van ons Zeewezen*, eerste gedeelte, 1568–1652 (The Hague: Martinus Nijhoff, 1916).

Empoli, G. da, *Lettera*, ed. A. Bausani (Rome — Djakarta: Instituto Italiano per il Medio ed Estremo Oriente — Centro Italiano di Cultura, 1970).

Enthoven, V., *Zeeland en de opkomst van de Republiek. Handel en strijd in de Scheldedelta, c. 1550–1621* (Leiden, Proefschrift, 1996).

Erédia, M. Godinho de, *Malaca L'Inde Méridionale e le Cathay: Manuscrit original autographe de Godinho de Eredia appartenant à la Bibliothèque Royale de Bruxelles*, trans. M. Léon Janssen (Bruxelles: Librairie Européenne C. Muquardt, 1882).

———, *Suma de Árvores e Plantas da Índia Intra Ganges*, ed. J.G. Everaert, J.E. Mendes Ferrão and M. Cândida Liberato (Lisbon: Commissão Nacional para as Comemorações dos Descobrimentos Portugueses, 2001).

Falchetta, P., *Fra Mauro's World Map* (Turnhout: Prepols Publishers, 2006).

Faro, J., *Godinho de Erédia, cosmógrafo* (Lisbon: Bolseiro do Instituto de Alta Cultura, 1955).

Felix, A. Jr., *The Chinese in the Philippines*, 2 vols. (Manila: Solidaridad Publishing House, 1966).

Fell, R.T., *Early Maps of Southeast Asia*, 2nd ed. (Singapore: Oxford University Press, 1991).

Ferguson, D., *Letters from Portuguese Captives in Canton* (Bombay: Education Society's Steam Press, 1902).

Ferrand, G., *Relations de voyages et texts geographiques Arabes, Persans et Turks, relatifs à l'Extrême-Orient du VIIIe au XVIIIe siècles*, 2 vols. (Paris: Ernest Leroux, 1913–14).

———, *Voyage du Marchand Arabe Sulaymân en Inde et en Chine, redigé en 851 suivi de remarques par Abû Zayd Hasan (vers 916)* (Paris: Éditions Bossard, 1922).

Fischer, J., ed., *Claudii Ptolomaei geographiae codex Urbinas graecus* 82, *phototypice depictus consilio et opera curatorum Bibliothecae Vaticonae* 4 vols. (Leiden: E.J. Brill and Leipzig: Otto Harrassowitz, 1932).

Flores, M. de C., *Portugal e o Sião no Seculo XVI* (Lisbon: Imprensa Nacional — Casa de Moeda, 1991).

Floris, P., *His Voyage to the East Indies in the Globe, 1611–1615*, ed. W. H. Moreland (London, 1934).

Flückiger, F.A., and D. Hanbury, *Pharmacographia: A History of the Principal Drugs of Vegetable Origin Met With in Great Britain and British India* (London: Macmillan and Co., 1874).

Foreest, H.A. van, and A. de Booy, ed., *De Vierde Schipvaart der Nederlanders naar Oost-Indië onder Jacob Wilkens en Jacob van Neck, 1599–1604,* 2 vols. (The Hague: Martinus Nijhoff, 1980).

Foster, W., ed., *The Voyage of Thomas Best to the East Indies 1612–1614* (London: Hakluyt Society, 1934).

Gaastra, F.S., *De Geschiedenis van de VOC*, 4th ed. (Zutphen: Walburg Pers, 2002).

———, ed., *The Organization of Interoceanic Trade in European Expansion, 1450–1800*, An Expanding World. The European Impact on World History, 1450–1800 (Aldershot: Ashgate, 1996).

Galvão, A., *Tratado dos Descobrimentos* (Porto: Livraria Civilização Editoria, 1944).

Gerini, G.E., *Researches on Ptolemy's Geography of Eastern Asia* (London: Royal Geographic Society, 1909).

Gibson-Hill, C.A., "Singapore Old Strait and New Harbour, 1300–1870", *Memoirs of the Raffles Museum*, no. 3 (Singapore: Government Printing Office, 1956).

Glete, J., *Warfare at Sea, 1500–1650: Maritime Conflicts and the Transformation of Europe* (London: Routledge, 2000).

Glover, I. and P. Bellwood, *Southeast Asia: From Prehistory to History* (London: Routledge, 2006).

Grimm, T., P.M. Kuhfus and G. Wacker, *Collected Papers of the XXIXth Congress of Chinese Studies* (Tübingen: Attempto Verlag, 1988).

Groslier, B.-P., *Angkor and Cambodia in the Sixteenth Century According to Portuguese and Spanish Sources*, tr. M. Smithies (Bangkok: Orchid Press, 2006).

Grotius, H., *De Iure Praedae Commentarius*, ed. H.G. Hamaker (The Hague: Martinus Nijhoff, 1868).

———, *De Jure Praedae Commentarius: Commentary on the Law of Prize and Booty. A Translation of the Original Manuscript of 1604*, trans. G.L. Williams and W.H. Zeydel (New York: Oceana Publishing, 1964).

———, *Briefwisseling van Hugo Grotius, zeventiende deel, supplement, 1583–1645,* edited by Henk Nellen and indices compiled by Cornelia M. Ridderikhoff (The Hague: Instituut voor Nederlandse Geschiedenis, 2001).

———, *De Jure Praedae Commentarius: Commentary on the Law of Prize and Booty*, ed. Martine J. van Ittersum (Indianapolis: Liberty Fund, 2006).

Guedes, M.A. Marques, *Interferência e integração dos Portugueses na Birmânia, ca. 1580–1630* (Lisbon: Fundação Oriente, 1994).

Guiso, M.A. and N. Muratore, *Ad usum navigantium: carte nautiche manoscritte di Gerard van Keulen, 1709–1713* (Rome: Istituto Poligrafico e Zecca dello Stato, 1992).

Hashim, M.Y., *The Malay Sultanate of Malacca: A Study of Various Aspects of Malacca in the 15th and 16th Centuries in Malaysian History* (Kuala Lumpur: Dewan Bahasa dan Pustaka, Ministry of Education, 1992).

Hattendorf, J.B., *Encyclopaedia of Maritime History*, vol. 4 (Oxford and New York: Oxford University Press, 2007).

Harley, J.B., *The New Nature of Maps: Essays in the History of Cartography*, ed. Paul Laxton (Baltimore and London: Johns Hopkins University Press, 2001).

Horsburgh, J., *Zeemans-Gids, naar, in en uit Oost-Indië, China, Japan Australië, de Kaap de Goede Hoop, Brazilië en tusschenliggende havens, volgens de laatste engelsche uitgave* (Horsburgh's Directory), translated into Dutch and annotated by G. Kuijper and D. Boens Lutjens (Amsterdam: C.F. Stemler, 1853).

Israel, J.I., *The Dutch Republic and the Hispanic World, 1606–1661* (Oxford: Clarendon Press, 1982).

———, *Dutch Primacy in World Trade, 1585–1740* (Oxford: Clarendon Press, 1989).

———, *Empires and Entrepots: The Dutch, the Spanish Monarchy and the Jews* (London: Hambledon Press, 1990).

———, *Conflicts of Empires: Spain, the Low Countries and the Struggle for World Supremacy, 1585–1713* (London: Hambledon Press, 1997).

Ittersum, M.J. van, *Profit and Principle: Hugo Grotius, Natural Rights Theories and the Rise of Dutch Power in the East Indies, 1595–1615* (Leiden: E.J. Brill, 2006).

Johnson, H.B., *Carta Marina: World Geography in Strassburg, 1525* (Minneapolis: University of Minnesota Press, 1963).

Jonge, J.K.J. de, *Opkomst van het Nederlandsch gezag in Oost-Indië: Verzameling van onuitgegeven stukken uit het oud-coloniaal archief*, eerste reeks (The Hague: Martinus Nijhoff, 1866–1925).

Keuning, J., ed., *De tweede schipvaart der Nederlanders naar Oost-Indië onder Jacob Cornelisz van Neck en Wybrant Warwijck*, 1598–1600: *journalen, documenten en ander bescheiden* 8 vols. (The Hague: Martinus Nijhoff, 1949).

Kley, E.J. van, and C.K. Pullapilly, ed., *Asia and the West: Encounters and Exchanges from the Age of Exploration* (Notre Dame: Cross Cultural Publications, 1986).

Kling, B.B. and M.N. Pearson, *The Age of Partnership. Europeans in Asia before Dominion* (Honolulu: University Press of Hawaii, 1979).

Knaap, G., and G. Teitler, ed., *De Verenigde Oost-Indische Compagnie tussen Oorlog en Diplomatie* (Leiden: KITLV, 2002).

Korte, J.P. de, *The Annual Accounting in the VOC* (Leiden: Martinus Nijhoff, 2000).

Kratoska, P. (gen. ed.), *South East Asia. Colonial History*, 6 vols. (London: Routledge, 2001).

Landwehr, J., *VOC: A Bibliography of Publications Relating to the Dutch East India Company, 1602–1800*, ed. Peter van der Krogt (Utrecht: H&S Publisher, 1991).

Lauts, G., *Geschiedenis van de Vestiging, Uitbreiding, Bloei en Verval van de Magt der Nederlanders in Indië* (Groningen: W. van Boekeren, 1852).

Leitão, H., and J.V. Lopes, *Dicionário da Linguagem de Marinha Antigua e Actual*, 2nd ed. (Lisbon: Centro de Estudos Históricos Ultramarinos da Junta de Investigações Científicas do Ultramar, 1974).

Lestringant, F., *Le Brésil d'André Thevet: Les Singularités de la France Antarctique (1557)* (Paris: Éditions Chandeigne, 1997).

Leur, J.C. van, *Indonesian Trade and Society: Essays in Asian Social and Economic History*, trans. J. S. Holmes and A. van Marle (The Hague: Van Hoeve, 1955).

Leyden, J., ed., *John Leyden's Malay Annals*, Introduction by V.M. Hooker and M. Barry Hooker (Kuala Lumpur: MBRAS Reprints, 2001).

Lewis, D., *Jan Compagnie in the Straits of Malacca, 1641–1795* (Athens: Ohio University, Center for International Studies, 1995).

Liaw Y.F., *Undang-undang Melaka: A Critical Edition*, ed. L. Yock Fang, Proefschrift Leiden University (The Hague: De Nederlandsche Boek- en Steendrukkerij/Smits, 1976).

Liliencron, R.W.T. Freiherr von, *Allgemeine Deutsche Biographie*, 56 vols. (Leipzig: Duncker & Humblot, 1875–1912).

Lin, W.L., *A Re-examination of the Place Name 'Long-ya Men'* (Singapore: The South Sea Society, 1999) (in Chinese).

Linehan, W., *A History of Pahang* (Kuala Lumpur: MBRAS, 1973).

Linhares, M. de, *Diário do 3.o Conde de Linhares, Vice-rey da Índia*, 2 vols. (Lisbon: Biblioteca Nacional, 1937).

Linschoten, J.H. van, *Naer Oost Ofte Portugaels Indiën, 1579–1592*, vierde deel, Reys-Gheschrift vande Navigatiën der Portugaloysers, ed. J.C.M. Warnsinck (The Hague: Martinus Nijhoff, 1939).

Lobato, M., *Política e Comércio dos Portugueses na Insulíndia: Malaca e as Molucas de 1575 a 1605* (Macau: Instituto Portugês do Oriente, 1999).

Lombard, D., *Le Sultanat d'Atjéh au temps d'Iskandar Muda 1607–1636* (Paris: École Française d'Extrême-Orient, 1967).

Lombard, D., and J. Aubin, ed., *Marchands et hommes d'affaires asiatiques dans l'Océan Indien et la Mer de Chine, 13e-20e siècles* (Paris: Éditions de l'École des Hautes Études en Sciences Sociales, 1988)

Loureiro, R.M., *O Manuscrito de Lisboa da 'Suma Oriental' de Tomé Pires (Contribuição para uma Edição Crítica)* (Macao: Instituto Português do Oriente, 1996).

Luz, F.P. Mendes da, *O Conselho da Índia* (Lisbon: Agência Geral do Ultramar, 1952).

Mac Leod, N., *De Oost-Indische Compagnie als Zeemogendheid in Azië*, 3 vols. (Rijswijk: Blankwaardt & Schoonhoven, 1927).

Manguin, P.-Y., *Les Portugais sur les côtes du Viêt-Nam et du Campa: Étude sur les routes maritimes et les relations commerciales, d'après les sources portugaises (XVIème, XVIIème, XVIIIème siècles)* (Paris: École Française d'Extrême-Orient, 1972).

Markham, C.R. ed., *The Voyages of Sir James Lancaster, Knight, to the East Indies with Abstracts of Journals of Voyages to the East Indies, during the Seventeenth Century, Preserved in the East India Office, and the Voyage of Captain John Knight (1600) to Seek the North-West Passage* (London: Hakluyt Society, 1877).

Massieu, A. de Béthencourt, ed., *IV Centenario del ataque de van der Does a Las Palmas de Gran Canaria* (Las Palmas: Cabildo Insular de Las Palmas, 2001).

Matos, A.T. de, and L.F.R. Thomaz, *A Carreira da Índia e as Rotas dos Estreitos: Actas do VIII Seminário Internacional de História Indo-Portuguesa, Angra do Heroísmo 7 a 11 de Junho de 1996* (Angra do Heroísmo: n. p., 1998).

Matos, A.T. de, *Na Rota da Índia. Estudos de História da Expansão Portuguesa* (Macao: Instituto Cultural de Macau, 1994).

Matos, L. de, *Um Livro de Marinharia Inédito* (Lisbon: Fundação Calouste Gulbenkian, 1969).

Meilink-Roelofsz, M.-A.P., *Eenige beschouwingen betreffende den ouden Aziatischen handel* (Middelburg: Den Boer, 1934).

———, *Asian Trade and European Influence in the Indonesian Archipelago between 1500 and about 1630* (The Hague: Martinus Nijhoff, 1962).

Meilink-Roelofsz, M.-A.P., M.E. van Opstall, and G.J. Schutte, *Dutch Authors on Asian History. A Selection of Dutch Historiography on the Verenigde Oostindische Compagnie* (Dordrecht: Foris Publications, 1988).

Mesquitela, G., *História de Macau*, vol. 3.1 (Macao: Instituto Cultural de Macau, 1998).

Miksic, J.N., *Archeological Research on the "Forbidden Hill" of Singapore: Excavations at Fort Canning, 1984* (Singapore: National Museum, 1985).

Miró, M., M. Algàs, and M.J. Canton, ed., *Atlas Miller* (Barcelona: Moleiro Editor, 2006).

Moree, P., ed., *Dodo's en galioenen: De reis van het schip Gelderland naar Oost-Indië, 1601–1603* (Zutphen: Walburg Pers, 2001).

Morga, A. de, *The Philippine Islands, Moluccas, Siam, Cambodia, Japan and China at the Close of the Sixteenth Century*, ed. L.V. de Torres and H.E.J. Stanley (London: Hakluyt Society, 1868).

Mota, A. Teixeira de, *Reflexos do Tratado de Tordesilhas na Cartografia Náutica do Século XVI* (Coimbra: Junta de Investigações do Ultramar, 1973).

Münster, S., *Cosmographia Oder Beschreibung der gantzen Welt etc.*, facsimile reproduction of the Basel edition of 1628 (Lindau: Antiqua Verlag, 1978).

Murfett, M.H., J.N. Miksic, B.P. Farrell and C.M. Shun, *Between Two Oceans: A Military History of Singapore from First Settlement to Final British Withdrawal* (Singapore: Oxford University Press, 1999).

Naber, S.P. l'Honoré, *Reisebeschreibungen von Deutschen Beamten und Kriegsleuten im Dienst der Niederländisch West- und Ost-Indischen Kompanien, 1602–1797*, 13 vols. (The Hague: Martinus Nijhoff, 1930–3).

Netscher, E., *De Nederlanders in Djohor en Siak* (Batavia: Bruining & Wijt, 1870).

Ollé, M., *La invención de China: Percepciones y estrategias filipinas respecto a China durante el siglo XVI* (Wiesbaden: Harrassowitz Verlag, 2000).

Opstall, M.E. van ed., *De reis van de vloot van Pieter Willemszoon Verhoeff naar Azië, 1607–1612*, 2 vols. (The Hague: Martinus Nijhoff, 1972).

Parker, G., *The Military Revolution, Military Innovation and the Rise of the West, 1500–1800* (Cambridge: Cambridge University Press, 1988).

Parmentier, J., K. Davids, and J. Everaert, *Peper, Plancius en Porselein, de reis van het schip 'Swarte Leeuw' naar Atjeh en Bantam, 1601–1603* (Zutphen: Walburg Pers, 2003).

Pearson, M.N., *Before Colonialism. Theories on Asian-European Relations, 1500–1700* (New Delhi: Oxford University Press, 1988).

Pedrosa, F. Gomes, ed., *Navíos, Marinheros e Arte de Navegar, 1139–1499* (Lisbon: Academia de Marinha, 1997).

Petrzilka, M., *Die Karten des Laurent Fries von 1530 und 1531 und ihre Vorlage, die 'Carta Marina' aus dem Jahre 1516 von Martin Waldseemüller* (Zürich: Buchdruckerei der Neuen Zürcher Zeitung, 1970).

Pigafetta, A., *Magellan's Voyage. A Narrative Account of the First Navigation.* Translated and edited by R. A. Skelton (London: The Folio Society, 1975).

Pintado, M.J. ed. and tr., *Portuguese Documents on Malacca*, vol. 1, 1509–11 (Kuala Lumpur: National Archives of Malaysia, 1993).

Pinto, P.J. de Sousa, *Portugueses e Malaios: Malaca e os Sultanatos de Johor e Achém, 1575–1619* (Lisbon: Comissão Nacional para as Comemorações dos Descobrimentos Portugueses, 1997).

Pires, T., *Suma Oriental*, trans. Armando Cortesão, 2 vols. (London: Hakluyt Society, 1944).

———, *A Suma Oriental de Tomé Pires e o Livro de Francisco Rodrigues*, ed. Armando Cortesão (Coimbra: Por Ordem da Universidade, 1978).

Pissurlencar, P.S.S., ed., *Regimentos das Fortalezas da Índia* (Bastorá-Goa: Cartório Geral do Estado da Índia, 1951).

———, ed., *Assentos do Conselho do Estado da Índia*, 5 vols. (Bastorá-Goa: Tip. Rangel, 1953–7).

Postma, J. and V. Enthoven, ed., *Riches from Atlantic Commerce. Dutch Trans-atlantic Trade and Shipping, 1585–1817* (Leiden: E. J. Brill, 2003).

Prakash, O., ed., *European Commecial Expansion in Early Modern Asia*, An Expanding World. The Euoropean Impact on World History, 1450–1800, vol. 10 (Aldershot: Ashgate, 1995).

Ramusio, G.B., *Navigazioni e Viaggi*, ed. Marica Milanesi, 6 vols. (Turin: Giulio Einaudi Editore, 1978–88).

Rebello, J.I. de Brito, ed., *Livro de Marinharia. Tratado da Agulha de Marear de João de Lisboa. Roteiros, sondas e outras conhecimentos relativos á navegação, Codice do seculo XVI que pertineceu á livraria do falecido Marquez de Castello Melhor em cujo catálogo de manuscriptos tinha o número 254, adquirido no respectivo leilão pelo Excel.mo Sr. Duque de Pamella e a expensas suas publicado* (Lisbon: Imprensa de Lipanio da Silva, 1903).

Reid, A.J.S., *Southeast Asia in the Age of Commerce, 1450–1680*, 2 vols. (New Haven: Yale University Press, 1988–93).

Ricklefs, M., *War, Culture and Economy in Java, 1677–1726. Asian and European Imperialism in the early Kartasura period* (Sydney: Allen & Unwin, 1993).

Rietbergen, P.J.A.N. van, *De Eerste Landvoogd Pieter Both (1568–1615): Gouverneur-Generaal van Nederlandsch-Indië*, 2 vols. (Zutphen: Walberg Pers, 1987).

Rodao, F., *Españoles en Siam (1540–1939): Una aportación al estudo de la presencia hispana en Ásia* (Madrid: Consejo Superior de las Investigaciones Científicas, 1997).

Ruangsilp, B., *Dutch East India Company Merchants at the Court of Ayutthaya: Dutch Perceptions of the Thai Kingdom c. 1604–1765* (Leiden: E.J. Brill, 2007).

Russell, A.J.R., *The Portuguese Empire, 1415–1808* (Baltimore and London: Johns Hopkins University Press, 1998).

Saldanha, A. Vasconcelos de, *Iustum Imperium, dos tratados como fundamento do império dos portugueses no Oriente: estudo de história do direito internacional e do direito português* (Lisbon: Fundação Oriente, 1997).

Santos, J. dos, *Etiópia Oriental e Vária História de cousas Notáveis do Oriente*, ed. M. Lobato and Maria do Carmo Guerreiro Vieira (Lisbon: Comissão Nacional para as Comemorações dos Descobrimentos Portugueses, 1999).

Sarkar, H.B., *Trade and Commercial Acivities of Southern india in the Malayo-Indonesian World (up to A.D. 1511)*, vol. I (Calcutta: Firma KLM, 1986).

Schurz, W.L., *The Manila Galleon*, reprint (New York: Dutton, 1959).

Silva, A.C. Correia da, *Um boticário na história da expansão portuguesa no mundo* (Porto: no publisher, 1960).

Sinclair, W.F. ed., *The Travels of Pedro Teixeira with His "Kings of Harmuz" and Extracts from His "Kings of Persia"* (London: Hakluyt Society, 1920).

Singh Sandhu, K., and P. Wheatley, *Melaka: The Transformation of a Malay Capital, c. 1400–1980*, 2 vols. (Kuala Lumpur: Oxford University Press, 1983).

Sloos, D.A., *Nederlanders in de Filippijnse wateren vóór 1626*, doctoral dissertation, University of Amsterdam (Amsterdam: De Wit, 1898).

Smith, R.B., *A Projected Portuguese Voyage to China in 1512 and New Notices Relative to Tome Pires in Canton* (Bethesda: Decatur Press, 1972).

Sopher, D.E., *The Sea Nomads, a Study Based on Literature of the Maritime Boat People of Southeast Asia* (Singapore: Lim Bian Han, 1965).

Sousa, A. Botelho e, *Subsídios para a historia militar-marítima da Índia*, 2 vols. (Lisbon: Imprimeria da Armada, 1930).

Souza, G.B., *The Survival of Empire. Portuguese Trade and Society in China and the South China Sea, 1630–1754* (Cambridge: Cambridge University Press, 1986).

Spallanzani, M., *Giovanni da Empoli: Un mercante fiorentino nell'Asia portoghese* (Florence: Studio per Edizioni Scelte, 1999).

Sprengard, K.A. and R. Ptak, ed., *Maritime Asia. Profit Maximisation, Ethics and Trade Structure*, South China and Maritime Asia, vol. 2 (Wiesbaden: Harrassowitz Verlag, 1994).

Subrahmanyam, S., *Improvising Empire. Portuguese Trade and Settlement in the Bay of Bengal, 1500–1700* (New Delhi: Oxford University Press, 1990).

———, *The Political Economy of Commerce in Southern India, 1500–1650* (Cambridge: Cambridge University Press, 1990).

———, *The Portuguese Empire in Asia, 1500–1700: A Political and Economic History* (London: Longman, 1993).

———, *Sinners and Saints. The Successors of Vasco da Gama* (New Delhi: Oxford University Press, 1995).

Steensgaard, N., *The Asian Trade Revolution of the Seventeenth Century: The East India Companies and the Decline of the Caravan Trade* (Chicago and London: University of Chicago Press, 1974).

Teeuw, A. and D.K. Wyatt, ed., *Hikayat Patani. The Story of Patani*, 2 vols. (The Hague: Martinus Nijhoff, 1970).

Teixeira, M., *The Portuguese Missions in Malacca and Singapore*, vol. 1, "Malacca" (Lisbon: Agência Geral do Ultramar, 1961).

Terpstra, H., *De factorij der Oostindische Compagnie te Patani*, Verhandelingen van het Koninklijk Instituut voor de Taal-, Land- en Volkenkunde van Nederlandsch-Indië, I (The Hague: Martinus Nijhoff, 1938).

Thomaz, F.L.R., *Nina Chatu and the Portuguese Trade in Malacca*, trans. M.J. Pintado (Melaka: Luso-Malaysian Books, 1991).

———, *De Ceuta a Timor* (Lisbon: Difel, 1994).

———, *Early Portuguese Malacca* (Macao: Commisão Territorial de Macau para as Comemorações dos Descobrimentos Potugueses — Instituto Politécnico de Macau, no date).

Tibbets, G.R., *Arab Navigation in the Indian Ocean before the Coming of the Portuguese, Being a Translation of Kitāb al-Fawā'id fī usūl al-bahr wa'l-qawā'id of Ahmad b. Mājid al-Najdī, Together with an Introduction on the History of Arab Navigation, Notes on Navigational Techniques and on the Topography of the Indian Ocean, and a Glossary of Navigational Terms* (London: The Royal Asiatic Society of Great Britain and Ireland, 1971).

Tiele, P.A., and J.E. Heeres, ed., *Bouwstoffen voor de Geschiedenis der Nederlanders in den Maleischen Archipel*, 3 vols. (The Hague: Martinus Nijhoff, 1886–95).

Torres, A. da Costa, *Breve Notícia de Tomé Pires (Botiário do principe D. Afonso, filho de D. João II e embaixador de Portugal na Côrte da China)* (Anadia: Tipogrâphia Comercial, 1939).

Varthema, L. de, *The Itinerary of Ludovico di Varthema of Bologna from 1502 to 1508*, trans. J. Winter Jones (London: Argonaut Press, 1928).

Veen, E. van, *Decay or Defeat: An Inquiry into the Portuguese Decline in Asia, 1580–1645* (Leiden: Research School of Asian, African and Amerindian Studies, 2000).

Veen, E. van, and L. Blussé, ed., *Rivalry and Conflict, European Traders and Asian Trading Networks, 16th and 17th Centuries* (Leiden: CNWS, 2005).

Veenendaal, A.J., ed., *Johan van Oldenbarnevelt: bescheiden betreffende zijn staatskundig beleid en zijn familie*, vol. II, 1602–13, Rijkgeschiedkundige Publicatiën, Grote Serie, vol. 108 (The Hague: Martinus Nijhoff 1962).

Vitoria, F. de, *Political Writings*, ed. A. Pagden and J. Lawrence (Cambridge: Cambridge University Press, 1991).

Vries, D. de, *Uit de Kaartenwinkel van de VOC: Cataloges van zeekarten van de Verenigde Oostindische Compagnie in the Collectie Bodel Nijenhuis* (Alphen aan den Rijn: Canaletto, 1996).

Wade, G., ed., *Southeast Asia — China Interactions. Reprint of Articles from the Journal of the Malaysian Branch of the Royal Asiatic Society* (Kuala Lumpur: MBRAS, 2007).

Wessels, C., *De Katholieke Missie in de Molukken, Noord-Celebes en de Sangihe Eilanden Gedurende de Spaansche Bestuurperiode, 1606–1677* (Tilburg: Drukkerij Bergmans & Cie., 1935).

Wieder, F.C., ed., *De Reis van Joris van Spilbergen naar Ceylon, Atjeh en Bantam, 1601–1604* (The Hague: Martinus Nijhoff, 1933).

Winius, G., *Studies in Portuguese Asia, 1495–1689* (Aldershot: Variorum, 2001).

Winstedt, R.O., *A History of Classical Malay Literature* (Kuala Lumpur and Singapore: Oxford University Press, 1969).

Wheatley, P., *The Golden Khersonese: Studies in the Historical Geography of the Malay Peninsula before A.D. 1500* (Kuala Lumpur: University of Malaya Press, 1961).

———, *Impressions of the Malay Peninsula in Ancient Times* (Singapore: Eastern Universities Press, 1964).

Wolters, O.W., *Early Indonesian Commerce: A Study of the Origins of Srivijaya* (Ithaca: Cornell University Press, 1967).

———, *The Fall of Srivijaya in Malay History* (Kuala Lumpur: Oxford University Press, 1970).

Woodward, D., ed., *The History of Cartography*, 4 vols. (Chicago and London: University of Chicago Press, 2007.)

Yule, H., and A.C. Burnell, *Hobson-Jobson: A Glossary of Colloquial Anglo-Indian Words and Phrases*, reprint (Sittingbourne: Linguasia, 1994).

Journal Articles

Anand, R.P., "Maritime Practice in Southeast Asia until 1600 A.D. and the Modern Law of the Sea", *The International and Comparative Law Quarterly* 30, 2 (1981): 440–54.

Andaya, L., "A History of Trade in the Sea of Melayu", *Itinerario* 24, 1 (2000): 87–110.

Barnes, W.D., "Singapore Old Straits and New Harbour", *JSBRAS* 60 (1911): 25–34.

Bassett, D.K., "European Influence in the Malay Peninsula, 1511–1786", *JMBRAS* 33, 3 (1960): 9–35.

———, "European Influence in Southeast Asia, c. 1500–1630", *JSEAH* 4, 2 (1963): 134–65.

———, "Changes in the Pattern of Malay Politics, 1629–1655", *JSEAH* 10, 3 (1969): 429–52.

Blagden, C. O., "Antiquity of Malacca", *JSBRAS* 57 (1910): 189–90.

Borschberg, P., "'De Societate Publica cum Infidelibus': Ein Frühwerk von Hugo Grotius", *Zeitschrift der Savigny-Stiftung für Rechtsgeschichte*, Romanistische Abteilung, 115 (1998): 355–93.

———, "Hugo Grotius, East India Trade and the King of Johor", *JSEAS* 30, 2 (1999): 225–48.

———, "The Seizure of the *Sta. Catarina* Revisited: The Portuguese Empire in Asia, VOC Politics and the Origins of the Dutch-Johor Alliance (c. 1602–1616)", *JSEAS* 33, 1 (2002): 31–62.

———, "O comércio europeu de almíscar com a Ásia no inicio da edad moderna" [The European Musk Trade with Asia in the Early Modern Period] (bilingual feature article, Portuguese-English), *Revista Oriente* 5 (2003): 90–9.

———, "O comércio de âmbar asiático no início da época moderna (séculos XV–XVIII)" [The Asiatic Ambergris Trade in the Early Modern Period (15th to 18th Century)] (bilingual feature article, Portuguese-English), *Revista Oriente* 8 (2004): 3–25.

———, "The Trade, Forgery and Medicinal Use of Porcupine Bezoars in the Early Modern Period (c. 1500–1750)" (bilingual article, Portuguese-English), *Revista Oriente* 14 (2006): 60–78.

———, "The Euro-Asian Trade and Medicinal Usage of Radix Chinae", in *European Travellers and the Asian Natural World*, part 1, ed. R.M. Loureiro, *Revista de Cultura*, International Edition, 20 (2006): 102–15.

———, "Grotius' Theory of Trans-Oceanic Trade Regulation: Revisiting Mare Liberum (1609)", *Institute for International Law and Justice Working Paper, History and Theory of International Law Series*, New York University Hauser School of Law, ed. Benedict Kingsbury and Mattii Koskenniemi, no. 14 (August 2006): 1–60.

———, "Grotius, Maritime Intra-Asian Trade and the Portuguese Estado da Índia: Problems, Perspectives and Insights from 'De Jure Praedae'", *Grotiana*, New Series, 26–8 (2008): 31–60.

———, "Jacques de Coutre as a Source for the Early 17th Century History of Singapore, the Johor River, and the Straits", *JMBRAS* 81, 2 (2008): 71–97.

Boxer, C.R., "The Affair of the Madre de Deus (A Chapter in the History of the Portuguese in Japan)", *Transactions and Proceedings of the Japan Society of London* 26 (1929): 4–90.

———, "Asian Potentates and European Artillery in the 16th –18th Centuries: A footnote to Gibson-Hill", *JMBRAS* 38, 2 (1965): 156–72.

———, "Portuguese and Spanish Projects for the Conquest of Southeast Asia", *JAH* 3 (1969): 118–36.

Braddell, R., "Lung-Ya-Men and Tan-Ma-Hsi", *JMBRAS* 42, 1 (1969): 10–24.

Branquinho, I., "O Tratado de Tordesilhas e a questão das Molucas", *Mare Liberum: Revista de História dos Mares* 8 (1994): 9–17.

Caldecott, A., "The Malay Peninsula in the XVIIth and XVIIIth Centuries", *JSBRAS* 82 (1920): 129–32.

Cheah Boon Kheng, comp. and ed., *Sejarah Melayu. The Malay Annals. Raffles ms. 18*, new Romanized edition (Kuala Lumpur: Malaysian Branch of the Royal Asiatic Society, 1998).

Clark, G.N., and W.J. M. van Eysinga, "The Colonial Conferences between England and the Netherlands in 1613 and 1615", Part I, *Bibliotheca Visseriana* 15 (1940): 1–270.

———, "The Colonial Conferences between England and the Netherlands", part II, *Bibliotheca Visseriana* 17 (1951): 1–155.

Colless, B.E., "The Ancient History of Singapore" *JSEAH* 10, 1 (1969): 1–11.

Coolhaas, W. Ph., "Een bron van het historische gedeelte van Hugo de Groots De Jure Praedae", *Bijdragen en Mededelingen van het Historisch Genootschap* 79 (1965): 415–537.

Cortesão, A., "A propósito do ilustre boticário quinhentista Tomé Pires", *Boletim da Escola de Farmácia* 23 (1964): 1–15.

Cowen, C.D., "Continuity and Change in the International History of Maritime South East Asia", *JSEAH* 9, 1 (1968): 1–11.

Daveau, S., "La géographie dans les 'roteiros' portugais des XVe et XVIe siècles", *Mare Liberum: Revista de História dos Mares* 3 (1991): 161–79.

Dion, M., "Sumatra through Portuguese Eyes: Excerpts from Joao de Barros' Decadas da Asia", *Indonesia* 9 (April 1970): 129–62.

Douglas, F.W., "Malay Place Names of Hindu Origin", *JMBRAS* 16, 1 (1938): 150–2.

Duyvendak, J.J.L.,"The First Siamese Embassy to Holland", *T'Oung Pao* 32 (1936): 285–92.

Gibson-Hill, C.-A., "Singapore: Note on the History of the Old Straits, 1580–1850", *JMBRAS* 27, 1 (1954): 165–214.

———, "Johore Lama and Other Ancient Sites on the Johore River", *JMBRAS* 28, 2 (1955): 126–99.

———, "The Alleged Death of Sultan 'Ala'udin of Johor at Acheh in 1613", *JMBRAS* 29, 1 (1956): 125–45.

Gomes, P.M., "L'Espagne et l'Orient au debut du XVIème siècle: Un autre droit que dans l'Amérique", *Mare Liberum: Revista de História dos Mares* 13 (1997): 83–93.

Heeres, J.E., ed., "Corpus Diplomaticum Neërlando-Indicum. Verzameling van politieke contracten en verdere verdragen door de Nederlanders in het Oosten gesloten, van privilegiebrieven, aan hen verleend, enz.", eerste deel (1596–1650), *BKI* 57 (1907): 1–586.

Hageman, J., "Geschiedenis der Verovering van Malakka en der Oorlogen Tusschen de Portugezen en Maleijers", *Verhandelingen van het Bataviaasch Genootschap van Kunsten en Wetenschappen* 24, 4 (1852): 1–52.

Heng, T.S.D., "Reconstructing Banzu, a Fourteenth Century Port Settlement in Singapore", *JMBRAS* 75, 1 (2002): 69–90.

Hervey, D.F.A., "François Valentyn's Account of Malacca", *JSBRAS* 16, 1 (1885): 289–301.

Hess, A.C., "The Evolution of the Ottoman Seaborne Empire in the Age of Oceanic Discoveries, 1453–1525", *The American Historical Review* 75, 7 (1970): 1892–1919.

Hill, A.H., "Hikayat Raja-Raja Pasai, a Revised Romanised Version of Raffles Ms. 67, together with an English Translation", *MBRAS* 33, 2 (1960): 1–215.

Hussin, N., "A Tale of Two Colonial Port-Towns in the Straits of Melaka: Dutch Melaka and English Penang", *JMBRAS* 75, 2 (2002): 65–98.

Ittersum, M. J. van, "Hugo Grotius in Context: Van Heemskerk's Capture of the *Santa Catarina* and Its Justification in De Jure Praedae (1604–1606)", *Asian Journal of Social Sciences* 31, 3 (2003): 511–48.

Josselin de Jong, P. E. de, "Malayan and Sumatran Place-Names in Classical Malay Literature", *Malayan Journal of Tropical Geography*, 9 (1956): 61–9.

Josselin de Jong, P.E. de, and Wijk, H.L.A. van, "The Malacca Sultanate (An Account from a Hitherto Untranslated Portuguese Source)", *JSEAH* 1, 1 (1960): 20–9.

Karthirithamby-Wells, J., "Regional and State Integration in the Western Archipelago, c. 1500–1700", *JSEAS* 18 (1987): 24–44.

Knefelkamp, U., "Martin Behaims Wissen über die portugiesischen Entdeckungen", *Mare Liberum: Revista de História dos Mares* 4 (1992): 87–95.

Leupe, P.G., "The Siege and Capture of Malacca from the Portuguese in 1640–1641. Extracts from the Archives of the Dutch East India Company", tr. Mac Hacobian, *JMBRAS* 14, 1 (1936): 1–178.

Linehan, W., "History of Pahang", *JMBRAS* 14, 2 (1936): 1–256.

Loureiro, R.M., "O Sudeste Asiático na Suma Oriental de Tomé Pires", *Revista de Cultura* 4 (2003): 106–23.

Lunde, P., "La llegada de los Portugueses al Oceano Índico según las fuentes Árabes", *Mare Liberum: Revista de História dos Mares* 10 (1995): 431–6.

Manguin, P.-Y., "The Merchant and the King: Political Myths of Southeast Asian Polities, *Indonesia* 52 (1991): 41–54.

———, "Palembang and Sriwijaya: An Early Malay Harbour–City Rediscovered, *JMBRAS* 66, 1 (1993): 23–46.

Matos, L.J.R. Semedo de, "As navegações Árabes e Portuguesas no Oceano Índico durante os séculos XV e XVI", *Mare Liberum: Revista de História dos Mares* 10 (1995): 565–80.

Maxwell, W.G., "Barreto de Resende's Account of Malacca", *JSBRAS* 60 (1911): 1–24.

MacGregor, I.A., "Notes on the Portuguese in Malaya", *JMBRAS* 28, 2 (1955): 5–47.

———, "Johore Lama in the Sixteenth Century", *JMBRAS* 28, 2 (1955): 48–125.

———, "A Portuguese Sea-Fight near Singapore in the 1570s", *JMBRAS* 29, 3 (1956): 5–21.

McRoberts, R.W., "The Examination of the Fall of Malacca in 1511", *JMBRAS* 57, 1 (1984): 26–39.

Mills, J.V., "Report on the Golden Chersonese", *JMBRAS* 8, 1 (1930): 228–55.

———, "Two Dutch-Portuguese Sea-Fights", *JMBRAS* 16, 1 (1938): 139–49.

Milner, A.C., "Who Created Malaysia's Plural Society?" *JMBRAS* 76, 2 (2004): 1–24.

Milner, A.C., E. Edwards McKinnon and Tengku Luckman Sinar, "Aru and Kota Cina", *Indonesia* 26 (1978): 1–42.

Obdeijn, V., "De oude zeehandelsweg door de Straat van Malaka in verband met de geomorfologie der Selat-Eilanden", *Koninklijk Nederlandsch Aardrijkskundig Genootschap*, tweede serie, 59 (1942): 742–70.

Pelliot, P., "Les Relations du Siam et de la Hollande en 1608", *T'Oung Pao* 32 (1936): 223–9.

Ptak, R., "The Northern Trade Route to the Spice Islands: South China Sea — Sulu Zone — North Moluccas (14th to Early 16th Century)", *Archipel* 42 (1992): 27–56.

Roelofsen, C.G., "Het trieste slot van een reis om de wereld in het begin van de zeventiende eeuw: de affaire Carletti", *Mededelingen van de Nederlandse Vereniging voor Zeegeschiedenis* 20 (1970): 13–30.

Rouffaer, G.P., "Was Malaka Emporium vóór 1400 A.D. genaamd Malajoer? En waar lag Woerawari, Ma-Hasin, Langka, Batoesawar?", *BKI* 77 (1921): 1–174 and 359–604.

Sar Desai, D.R., "The Portuguese Administration in Malacca, 1511–1641", *JSEAH* 10, 3 (1969): 501–12.

Scammell, G.V., "Seafaring in the Estado da Índia, c. 1500–1700", *Mare Liberum: Revista de História dos Mares* 9 (1995): 441–51.

Smail, J.R.W., "On the Possibility of an Autonomous History of Modern Southeast Asia", *JSEAH* 2 (1961): 72–102.

Somers, J.A. and C.G. Roelofsen, "*Mare Liberum* and the Dutch East India Company. The Freedom of the Seas and Feedom of Trade as the Legal Bases of the Dutch Colonial State in the Indonesian Archipelago", *Grotiana*, New Series, 24–5 (2004–5): 67–76.

Stein Callenfels, P.V. van, "The Founder of Malacca", *JMBRAS* 42, 1 (1969): 63–70.

Subrahmanyam, S., "Holding the World in Balance: The Connected Histories of the Iberian Overseas Empires, 1500–1640", *The American Historical Review* 112, 5 (2007): 1359–85.

Sutherland, H., "Southeast Asian History and the Mediterranean Analogy", *JSEAS* 34, 1 (2003): 1–20.

Sweeney, P.L.A., "The Connection between the Hikayat Raja-Raja Pasai and the Sejarah Melayu", *JMBRAS* 40, 2 (1967): 94–105.

Tibbets, G.R., "The Malay Peninsula as Known to the Arab Geographers", *Malayan Journal of Tropical Geography* 9 (1956): 21–57.

Tiele, P.A., "De Europeërs in den Maleischen Archipel", part VI, *BKI* 30 (1882): 141–242.

———, "De Europeërs in den Maleischen Archipel", part VII, *BKI* 32 (1884): 49–118.

Torres, A. da Costa, "Tomé Pires na Intimidade", *Journal dos Farmacêuticos* (1943): 5–31.
Wade, G., "The Zheng He Voyages: A Reassessment", *JMBRAS* 77, 1 (2005): 37–58.
Wheatley, P., "Chinese Sources for the Historical Geography of Malaya before AD 1500" *Malayan Journal of Tropical Geography* 9 (1956): 71–8.
Wilkinson, R.J., "The Malacca Sultanate", *JSBRAS* 61 (1912): 67–76.
———, "The Early Sultans of Pahang", *JMBRAS* 10, 1 (1932): 45–54.
Winstedt, R.O., "Bustan as-Salatin. It's Date and Author", *JSBRAS* 82 (1920): 151–2.
———, "The Early Rulers of Perak, Pahang and Acheh", *JMBRAS* 10, 1 (1932): 32–44.
———, "A History of Johore", *JMBRAS* 10, 3 (1932): 1–167.
———, "The Malay Annals or Sejarah Melayu", *JMBRAS* 16, 3 (1938): 1–226.
Winstedt, R.O., and P.E. de Josselin de Jong, "The Maritime Laws of Malacca: Edited, with an Outline Translation", *JMBRAS* 29, 3 (1956): 22–59.
Wolters, O.W., "Landfall on the Palembang Coast in Medieval Times", *Indonesia* 20 (1975): 1–58.

Unpublished Dissertations

Das Gupta, A.K., "Acheh in Indonesian Trade and Politics, 1600–1641", PhD thesis, Cornell University, Faculty of the Graduate School, 1962.
Khalid-Taib, Hj. M., "Sastera Sejarah in the Malay World: A Structural and Contextual Study of Folkloristic Elements in a Transitional Genre", PhD thesis, Indiana University, 1981.
Murteira Martins, A., "A Carreira da Índia e o Corso Neerlandês, 1595–1625", Mestrado thesis, Universidade Nova de Lisboa, 2006.
Noonan, L. A., "The Travels of John of Empoli: A Study of a Florentine Trader in the Service of Portugal, 1503–1517", PhD thesis, University of Western Australia, 1970.
Walls, C. B., "The Legacy of the Fathers: Testamentary Admonitions and the Thematic Structure of the Sejarah Melayu", PhD thesis, Yale University, 1974.

Index